Meeting the Needs of the Handicapped:

A Resource for Teachers and Librarians

Meeting the Needs of the Handicapped:

A Resource for Teachers and Librarians

Edited with a Preface and Introduction by
Carol H. Thomas and James L. Thomas

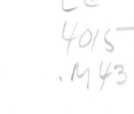

ORYX PRESS
1980

The rare Arabian Oryx, a desert antelope dating from Biblical times, is believed to be the prototype of the mythical unicorn. Nearing extinction two decades ago, the World Wildlife Fund found three of the animals in 1962 and sent them to the Phoenix Zoo as the nucleus of a breeding herd in captivity. Today the Oryx population is nearing 200 and herds have been returned to breeding grounds in Israel and Jordan.

Copyright © 1980 by
The Oryx Press
2214 North Central at Encanto
Phoenix, Arizona 85004

Published simultaneously in Canada

Printed and Bound in the United States of America

Distributed outside North America by
Mansell Publishing
3 Bloomsbury Place
London WC1A 2QA, England
ISBN 0-7201-1601-5

Library of Congress Cataloging in Publication Data
Main entry under title:

Meeting the needs of the handicapped.

    Bibliography: p.
    Includes index.
    1. Handicapped children--Education--United States--Addresses, essays, lectures. I. Thomas, Carol H. II. Thomas, James L., 1945-
LC4015.M43   371.9   80-12504
ISBN 0-912700-54-8

Contents

Preface

Providing an appropriate education for all of our handicapped children is a monumental task requiring the cooperative efforts of individuals in many areas of education. As stated by Jasper Harvey, director of the Division of Personnel Preparation of the Bureau of Education for the Handicapped, "Appropriate implementation of Public Law 94-142 will require the concerted effort of many individuals—general and special educators and administrators, a myriad of support personnel, parents, siblings, and the children themselves."[1] It was this necessity for cooperation in providing appropriate programing for the handicapped which served as the impetus for the preparation of this book.

Meeting the Needs of the Handicapped has been compiled for use by teachers, librarians, media specialists, and administrators actively seeking ways in which the unique needs of the handicapped can be served in the programs offered by their schools. The editors have selected articles which appeared to offer the most knowledgeable approach to a particular subject area and which, for the most part, presented ideas that could be replicated in classrooms and school library media centers. The articles have been selected from educational journals published between 1973 and 1979. Each addresses one or more groups of handicapped students and offers suggestions for programs or activities appropriate to that population.

An effort was made to include articles covering as wide a range of curricular areas as possible. The content, of course, varies from section to section as not all topics dealing with each handicapping condition are given equal treatment in the literature. Additionally, the approaches described in these articles range in scope from the broad, such as a county-wide program to provide vocational training for mildly and moderately handicapped youth, to the far more limited, such as a talking calculator to aid blind students in making mathematical calculations.

Since the articles are, for the most part, directed towards specific groups of handicapped youth, the divisions of this book necessarily reflect those categories. This is not to imply that a program or activity successfully implemented with one group would not meet with success with another. On the contrary, it is hoped that the techniques and ideas presented in these articles will be adapted by the creative educator for children with other handicaps and levels of severity. This is particularly true for educational procedures being used with the mentally retarded, emotionally disturbed, and learning disabled, since many have been found to be equally successful with each type of child.

The categories of handicapped children discussed in this book are those defined in PL 94-142. Articles on the gifted student were not included as these *exceptional* children do not come under the provisions of PL 94-142. Part I provides clarification of aspects of the law as it affects educational programing including vocational education and school library media centers. The subject matter of the articles in Parts II through VI relate to the following: mentally retarded, learning disabled, emotionally disturbed, hard of hearing/deaf, visually handicapped, and orthopedically impaired. Part VII is devoted to articles concerning the provision of prevocational and vocational training to handicapped students. Each part contains introductory comments by the editors which define the population being addressed and highlight the articles.

NOTE

1. Jasper Harvey, "Legislative Intent and Progress," *Exceptional Children* 44 (1978): 237.

Introduction

Over the past decade the field of education has undergone significant changes, but none so drastic as those affecting the education of this country's eight million handicapped children. The first movement towards national programs to provide educational opportunities for the handicapped came in the mid-1960s with the passage of the Education Amendments of 1966. Although this legislation authorized a program of grants to states for expanding and improving their services to the handicapped,[1] it was estimated that, by the 1967-68 school year, only 33 percent of the handicapped were being served.[2]

Shortly thereafter, parents and advocate groups began to challenge the exclusion of handicapped children from the public schools. Many of these challenges took the form of lawsuits and resulted in the setting of precedents for access to free public education. Two of these cases received national attention. In 1971 the Pennsylvania Association for Retarded Children (PARC) alleged, in a class action suit, that the state had failed to provide for all school-aged retarded children. The final decision in the case decreed that Pennsylvania was to provide public education for retarded children between the ages of 6 and 21.[3]

The second case was a class action suit brought by parents in the District of Columbia on behalf of all handicapped children. The decision in *Mills* v. *Board of Education of the District of Columbia* resulted in a court order requiring an appropriate free public education for all school-aged children regardless of the severity of the handicap.[4] Besides the right to education, these and other suits also addressed issues of identification, classification, and placement procedures.[5]

Following the precedents established by the *PARC* and *Mills* decisions, individual states began to adopt mandatory legislation affecting their handicapped children. At the federal level, the establishment of full educational opportunities for the handicapped was given impetus by the passage of the Education Amendments of 1974. In spite of undeniable progress in educating exceptional children, however, as late as 1975 it was still estimated that over one million handicapped children were being excluded from public education and that 50 percent of the handicapped were not receiving appropriate educational services. Congress, therefore, extended the Education Amendments of 1974 by its passage in 1975 of Public Law (PL) 94-142, the Education for All Handicapped Children Act.[6]

The new law has been termed the "Bill of Rights for Handicapped Children." Its purpose is to "assure that all handicapped children have available to them, within the time periods specified, a free appropriate public education and related services designed to meet their unique needs."[7] A free and appropriate public education was to be available for every handicapped child, regardless of the severity of the handicap, between the ages of 3 and 18 by September 1, 1978 and for all handicapped individuals between the ages 3 and 21 by September 1, 1980 unless educating those children and youth in the age ranges from 3 to 5 and from 18 to 21 was inconsistent with existing state laws.

Among the major provisions of the law are those requiring education of the child in the least restrictive environment, procedures to protect the rights of the child and the parents, and the individualized education program (IEP). *Least restrictive environment* refers to educating the handicapped with the nonhandicapped to the maximum extent appropriate. For many mildly handicapped children this may mean full integration into the regular classroom, a practice generally referred to as *mainstreaming*. More severe handicapping conditions will require more specialized programing in order to provide an appropriate education. The underlying principle is that the handicapped child is to be placed in the program which is best suited to his/her special needs and as close as possible to the regular educational program.[8]

Procedural due process is guaranteed under the law so that the rights created by the Act are made available to the child, his/her parents or guardian, and the public schools. These rights include: written notice prior to identification, evaluation, placement, or change in placement of a child; opportunity to secure an independent evaluation of the child; access to relevant records; opportunity for an impartial hearing; and the right to appeal the decisions of the hearing.

One of the most significant provisions of the law and one relating directly to providing an *appropriate* education for each handicapped child is the requirement of an IEP. The IEP is a written statement of the educational program to be provided; it is developed through the cooperative efforts of a representative of the local educational agency, the child's teachers, the parents, and, whenever appropriate, the child. This document must contain a statement of the present level of educational performance, annual goals as well as short-term instructional objectives, specific educational services the child will receive to achieve these goals, the duration of services, and a means of evaluating whether the objectives are being achieved.

NOTES

1. Edwin Martin, ''A Helping Relationship: Federal Programs for Special Children,'' *Exceptional Children* 43 (November 1976): 132-5.

2. Jeffrey Zettel and Alan Abeson, ''Litigation, Law, and the Handicapped,'' *School Media Quarterly* 6 (Summer 1978): 234-45.

3. *Pennsylvania Association for Retarded Children* v. *Commonwealth of Pennsylvania*, F. Supp. 279 (E.D. Pa. 1972, Order, Injunction and Consent Agreement).

4. *Mills* v. *Board of Education of the District of Columbia*, 348 F. Supp. 866 (D.D.C., 1972).

5. C. H. Thomas and J. E. Smith, Jr., ''Education, Mental Retardation and the Law,'' *Enlightenment* 1 (1977): 23-8.

6. Public Law 94-142, Education for All Handicapped Children Act, November 29, 1975.

7. Ibid., Sec. 3c.

8. Ken Bierly, ''P.L. 94-142: Answers to the Questions You're Asking,'' *Instructor* 87 (April 1978): 63-5, 72-3.

Contributors

Sonya Abbye serves as Coordinator, Special Education Program for Neurologically Impaired and Emotionally Handicapped Students, Board of Education, New York, NY. She is currently working on her doctorate in school administration at Columbia University. She plans on opening a school for the learning disabled youngster in the near future. "The Learning-Disabled Child: Films for Social, Emotional, Language, and Sensory Needs" is reprinted with permission of the Editor, *Film Library Quarterly* (1976, vol. 9, no. 3, pp. 37-43). Copyright 1976 by the Film Library Information Council.

Bill Arnott has worked as an art therapist at the CED Mental Health Center in Gadsden, Alabama. He has his MA in Art Therapy from the University of Louisville (Kentucky) Institute of Expressive Therapies. "Film Making as a Therapeutic Tool" by Bill Arnott and Jeffrey Gushin is reprinted by permission from the *American Journal of Art Therapy* (October 1976, vol. 16, pp. 29-33). Copyright 1976 by Elinor Ulman.

Joseph Ballard is Assistant Director for Policy Implementation, Governmental Relations for the Council for Exceptional Children. "Public Law 94-142 and Section 504: What They Say about Rights and Protections" by Joseph Ballard and Jeffrey Zettel is reprinted from *Exceptional Children* (November 1977, vol. 44, pp. 177-84) by permission of the Council for Exceptional Children. Copyright 1977 by the Council for Exceptional Children, 1920 Association Drive, Reston, Virginia 22091.

Janice W. Bell is an art instructor at Mystic Oral School, Mystic, Connecticut. "Directed Creativity" is reprinted with permission of Davis Publications, Inc. from *School Arts* (February 1977, vol. 76, pp. 78-9). Copyright 1977 by Davis Publications, Inc.

Joel Beller is Assistant Principal (Supervision) in the science and special education departments at Francis Lewis High School in Flushing, New York. "Handicapped Students Learn a Helping Way of Life" is reprinted with permission from *Science Teacher* (October 1978, vol. 45, pp. 25-6). Copyright 1978 by the National Science Teachers Association.

Jane Biehl serves as Children's Consultant for the Mideastern Ohio Library Organization (MOLO). "Story Hours for the Deaf" is reprinted by permission from the *Ohio Media Spectrum* (1978, vol. 30, pp. 43-6).

Gweneth Blacklock-Brown is a private consultant in the area of services to the emotionally disturbed. "The Emotionally Disturbed Adolescent: Development of Program Alternatives in Secondary Education" by Richard L. McDowell and Gweneth Blacklock-Brown is reprinted by permission of *Focus on Exceptional Children* (September 1978, vol. 10, pp. 1-15). Copyright 1978 by Love Publishing Company.

Virginia L. Bruininks is Associate Professor of Special Education and Coordinator of the Teacher Training Program in Learning Disabilities, University of Minnesota, Minneapolis. "Designing Instructional Activities for Students with Language/Learning Disabilities" was originally published by the National Council of Teachers of English in *Language Arts* (February 1978, vol. 55, pp. 154-60). Copyright 1978 by the National Council of Teachers of English.

Marie Carbo is a learning disabilities specialist in District 24, Valley Stream, New York; President of Creative Teacher Publications, Williston Park, New York; and a curriculum consultant. "Teaching Reading with Talking Books" by Marie Carbo is reprinted from *Reading Teacher* (December 1978, vol. 32, pp. 267-73) by permission of the International Reading Association. Copyright 1978 by the International Reading Association.

Patricia T. Cegelka is Associate Professor, Department of Special Education, University of Kentucky. "Individualized Programing at the Secondary Level" by Patricia T. Cegelka and Misha W. Phillips Gover is reprinted from *Teaching Exceptional Children* (Spring 1978, vol. 10, pp. 84-7) by permission of the Council for Exceptional Children. Copyright 1978 by the Council for Exceptional Children, 1920 Association Drive, Reston, Virginia 22091.

Richard R. Champion is State Plan Officer, Bureau of Education for the Handicapped, US Office of Education. "The Talking Calculator Used with Blind Youth" is reprinted by permission from *Education of the Visually Handicapped* (Winter 1976/77, vol. 8, pp. 102-6). Copyright 1976/77 by the Association for Education of the Visually Handicapped, Inc.

Cynthia R. Chandler is Lead Teacher, Bulloch County Training Center, Statesboro, Georgia. " 'Babysitting' for Houseplants—Responsibility, Interest, and Enthusiasm Began to Grow" is reprinted from *Teaching Exceptional*

Children (Spring 1977, vol. 9, pp. 61-3) by permission of the Council for Exceptional Children. Copyright 1977 by the Council for Exceptional Children, 1920 Association Drive, Reston, Virginia 22091.

Eyler Robert Coates is formerly head of the Music Section, National Library Service for the Blind and Physically Handicapped, Library of Congress. He is now a library consultant living in San Francisco, California. ''Music for the Blind and Physically Handicapped from the Library of Congress'' is reprinted by permission from *American Music Teacher* (February 1976, vol. 25, pp. 21-4). Copyright 1976 Music Teachers National Association. This article has been revised by the author in collaboration with NLS staff.

Sandra B. Cohen is Associate Professor, Department of Special Education, University of Virginia in Charlottesville. ''Selecting a Reading Approach for the Mainstreamed Child'' by Sandra B. Cohen and Stephen P. Plaskon is reprinted from *Language Arts* (November/December 1978, vol. 55, pp. 966-70) by permission of the National Council of Teachers of English. Copyright 1978 by the National Council of Teachers of English.

''Creative Dramatics'' is reprinted by permission of the American Alliance for Health, Physical Education, Recreation, and Dance (AAHPERD) and the Unit on Programs for the Handicapped/Physical Education and Recreation for the Handicapped: Information and Research Utilization Center (IRUC). Published in *Practical Pointers* (September 1977, vol. 1, no. 4, 9 p.). ERIC Document No. ED 154 547.

Marion McC. Danforth is a parent educator interested in mathematics education. ''Aids for Learning Mathematics'' is reprinted from the *Arithmetic Teacher* (December 1978, vol. 26, pp. 26-7). Copyright 1978 by the National Council of Teachers of Mathematics. Used by permission.

Sharon Davis is employed by the Council for Exceptional Children as Project Director, Needs Assessment Project and Conventions and Training Unit. ''Federal Mandates for the Handicapped: Vocational Education Opportunity and Employment'' by Jane Ann Razeghi and Sharon Davis is reprinted from *Exceptional Children* (February 1979, vol. 45, pp. 353-9) by permission of the Council for Exceptional Children. Copyright 1979 by the Council for Exceptional Children, 1920 Association Drive, Reston, Virginia 22091.

Ellen J. Dehouske is on educational leave from St. Francis Hospital, Adolescent Crisis Intervention Unit in Pittsburgh, while working on her doctoral dissertation at the University of Pittsburgh in college teaching and child care/child development. "Original Writing: A Therapeutic Tool in Working with Disturbed Adolescents" is reprinted from *Teaching Exceptional Children* (Winter 1979, vol. 11, pp. 66-70) by permission of the Council for Exceptional Children. Copyright 1979 by the Council for Exceptional Children, 1920 Association Drive, Reston, Virginia 22091.

Stanley C. Diamond is Director, Mill Creek School of the Institute of Pennsylvania Hospital, Philadelphia. "A School Designed for Self Esteem" is reprinted from *Clearing House* (February 1974, vol. 48, pp. 342-6) by permission of the author and Heldref Publications. Copyright 1974 by Heldref Publications, 4000 Albemarle St., NW, Washington, DC 20016.

Eliza T. Dresang is presently a lecturer and doctoral student in the Graduate Library School, University of Wisconsin—Madison. "There Are No *Other* Children: Special Children in Library Media Centers" is reprinted by permission of the author. The article was originally published in *School Library Journal* (September 1977, vol. 24, pp. 19-23) by R. R. Bowker (a Xerox Company). Copyright 1977 by Xerox Corporation.

Charles P. Edwards is Reading Consultant, Division of Reading Effectiveness, Indiana Department of Public Instruction, Indianapolis, Indiana. "Special Education and the Media Center" by Michael A. Tulley, Charles P. Edwards, and Michael Olds is reprinted from *Hoosier School Libraries* (April 1978, vol. 17, no. 4, pp. 7-11).

Martha Efta is an EMR (educable mentally retarded) primary teacher in the Westlake School System, Westlake, Ohio. "Reading in Silence: A Chance to Read" is reprinted from *Teaching Exceptional Children* (Fall 1978, vol. 11, pp. 12-4) by permission of the Council for Exceptional Children. Copyright 1978 by the Council for Exceptional Children, 1920 Association Drive, Reston, Virginia 22091.

"Garden for the Blind" is reprinted by permission from *American Libraries* (September 1974, vol. 5, p. 409). Copyright 1974 by the American Library Association.

Louis Godla is Program Specialist, Bureau of Occupational and Adult Education, US Office of Education. A former vocational development director, supervisor, and teacher, he holds a master's degree and has completed coursework for a doctorate from the University of Maryland. "Program Changes to Accommodate Handicapped Students" is reprinted by permission of *American Vocational Journal* (March 1978, vol. 53, pp. 29-32). Copyright 1978 by the American Vocational Association, Inc.

Misha W. Phillips Gover is a speech pathologist with the Fayette County Schools, Lexington, Kentucky. "Individualized Programing at the Secondary Level" by Patricia T. Cegelka and Misha W. Phillips Gover is reprinted from *Teaching Exceptional Children* (Spring 1978, vol. 10, pp. 84-7) by permission of the Council for Exceptional Children. Copyright 1978 by the Council for Exceptional Children, 1920 Association Drive, Reston, Virginia 22091.

Jeffrey Gushin is currently attending the Kent School at the University of Louisville, Kentucky for a master's degree in Social Work. "Film Making as a Therapeutic Tool" by Bill Arnott and Jeffrey Gushin is reprinted by permission from *American Journal of Art Therapy* (October 1976, vol. 16, pp. 29-33). Copyright 1976 by Elinor Ulman.

Karen H. Harris is Associate Professor of Library Science at the University of New Orleans. She, along with Dr. Barbara Baskin, has conducted extensive consultant work in service to special children. They are joint editors of *The Special Child in the Library* and co-authors of *Notes from a Different Drummer; A Guide to Juvenile Fiction Portraying the Handicapped.* "Selecting Library Materials for Exceptional Children" is reprinted with permission of *School Media Quarterly* (Fall 1979, vol. 8, pp. 22-8). Copyright 1979 by the American Library Association.

John F. Henne is Media Specialist, Conway School District Elementary Schools, North Conway, New Hampshire. "Serving Visually Handicapped Children" is reprinted by permission of the author. The article was originally published in *School Library Journal* (December 1978, vol. 25, pp. 36-7) by R. R. Bowker (a Xerox Company). Copyright 1978 by Xerox Corporation.

Shirley A. Johnson is Director of Training at W. A. Howe Developmental Center in Tinley Park, Illinois. "A Toy Library for Developmentally Disabled Children" is reprinted from *Teaching Exceptional Children* (Fall 1978, vol. 11, pp. 26-8) by permission of the Council for Exceptional Children. Copyright 1978 by the Council for Exceptional Children, 1920 Association Drive, Reston, Virginia 22091.

Janet Klineman is Director of Early Education Programs at the Western Pennsylvania School for Blind Children. "They Opened Our Eyes: The Story of an Exploratory Art Program for Visually Impaired, Multiply Handicapped Children" by Judith Rubin and Jane Klineman is reprinted by permission from *Education of the Visually Handicapped* (December 1974, vol. 6, pp. 106-13). Copyright 1974 by Association for Education of the Visually Handicapped, Inc.

Dorothy Kobax is a psychiatric social worker in child guidance and a certified poetry therapist. She is presently Associate Director of Mid Way Counseling Center and Poetry Therapist at St. Clare's Hospital, New York. "Poetry Therapy" by Dorothy Kobax and Estelle Nisenson is reprinted by permission of the authors. The article has been published in *Activities for Emotional Development* by the Florida Learning Resources System/CROWN in Jacksonville, Florida and is an ERIC Document No. ED 133 957.

Robert L. Koegel is Associate Research Psychologist, Social Process Research Institute, and Associate Professor of the Autism, Speech and Hearing Center, University of California, Santa Barbara, California. "A Method for Integrating an Autistic Child into a Normal Public-School Classroom" by Dennis C. Russo and Robert L. Koegel is reprinted with permission from *Journal of Applied Behavior Analysis* (Winter 1977, vol. 10, no. 4, pp. 579-90). Copyright 1977 by the Society for the Exceptional Analysis of Behavior, Inc.

Barbara E. Lenkowsky is a remediation teacher with the Horizon School for Perceptual Development in Flushing, New York. "Bibliotherapy for the LD Adolescent" by Barbara E. Lenkowsky and Ronald S. Lenkowsky is reprinted by permission from *Academic Therapy* (November 1978, vol. 14, no. 2, pp. 179-85). Copyright 1978 by Academic Therapy Publications, Inc., San Rafael, California.

Ronald S. Lenkowsky is Director, Horizon Schools for Perceptual Development in Flushing, New York. "Bibliotherapy for the LD Adolescent" by Barbara E. Lenkowsky and Ronald S. Lenkowsky is reprinted by permission from *Academic Therapy* (November 1978, vol. 14, no. 2, pp. 179-85). Copyright 1978 by Academic Therapy Publications, Inc., San Rafael, California.

Hilda K. Limper is a retired librarian serving as a volunteer storyteller at the Strathmoor Presbyterian Church Library in Louisville, Kentucky. "Serving Mentally Retarded Children in Our Libraries" is reprinted from the *Catholic Library World* (April 1974, vol. 45, pp. 423-5). The article has also been published in Maryalls Strom's *Library Services to the Blind and Physically Handicapped* by Scarecrow Press, 1977.

Thomas J. Lombard is a consultant for School Psychological Services and Program Supervisor for the Statewide Preschool Screening Program for the Minnesota Department of Education, St. Paul, Minnesota. "A Prevocational Program for Secondary TMR Students: The Canby Project" by Thomas J. Lombard and Laird Schultz is reprinted by permission of *Journal for*

Special Educators (Spring 1978, vol. 14, pp. 173-8, 87). Copyright 1978 by the American Association of Special Educators, Inc.

Richard L. McDowell is Professor of Special Education, University of New Mexico. "The Emotionally Disturbed Adolescent: Development of Program Alternatives in Secondary Education" by Richard L. McDowell and Gweneth Blacklock-Brown is reprinted by permission of *Focus on Exceptional Children* (September 1978, vol. 10, pp. 1-15). Copyright 1978 by Love Publishing Company.

J. Paul Marcoux is Acting Director of Theatre at Boston College and Arts Consultant at the Gaebler School, Metropolitan State Hospital, Waltham, Massachusetts. "Helping Emotionally Disturbed Children through Creative Dramatics" is reprinted by permission from *Communication Education* (March 1976, vol. 25, pp. 174-7). Copyright 1976 by the Speech Communication Association.

Mary Jane Metcalf is a librarian at the Illinois School for the Deaf. Her responsibilities include purchasing and processing books and implementing the library program for grades K-12. "Helping Hearing Impaired Students" is reprinted by permission of the author. The article was originally published in *School Library Journal* (January 1979, vol. 25, pp. 27-9) by R. R. Bowker (a Xerox Company). Copyright 1979 by Xerox Corporation.

Allen Mori is Associate Professor and Director of Project Careers, Department of Special Education, University of Nevada, Las Vegas. "Annotated Bibliography of Prevocational and Vocationally Oriented Materials for Secondary Educable Mentally Handicapped Pupils" is reprinted by permission of *Education and Training of the Mentally Retarded* (February 1978, vol. 13, pp. 47-54). Copyright 1978 by the Division on Mental Retardation, the Council for Exceptional Children, 1920 Association Drive, Reston, Virginia 22091.

Doris W. Naiman is Associate Professor of Deafness Rehabilitation, New York University. "Picture Perfect: Photography Aids Deaf Children in Developing Communication Skills" is reprinted from *Teaching Exceptional Children* (Winter 1977, vol. 9, pp. 36-8) by permission of the Council for Exceptional Children. Copyright 1977 by the Council for Exceptional Children, 1920 Association Drive, Reston, Virginia 22091.

Richard S. Neel is Associate Professor, College of Education, University of Washington, Seattle. "How My Body Looks and Moves—Lessons in Self-Drawings" by Richard S. Neel and Debbie Schneider is reprinted from *Teaching Exceptional Children* (Winter 1978, vol. 10, pp. 38-9) by permission of the Council for Exceptional Children. Copyright 1978 by the Council for Exceptional Children, 1920 Association Drive, Reston, Virginia 22091.

Linda Nielsen is Assistant Professor, Educational Psychology, Wake Forest University, Winston-Salem, North Carolina. "Let's Make a Deal: Contingency Contracting with Adolescents" is reprinted with permission from *American Secondary Education* (April 1978, vol. 8, pp. 12-23). Copyright 1978 by Bowling Green State University, Bowling Green, Ohio.

Estelle Nisenson is a teacher at P.S. 49, Queens, New York. "Poetry Therapy" by Dorothy Kobax and Estelle Nisenson is reprinted by permission of the authors. The article has been published in *Activities for Emotional Development* by the Florida Learning Resources System/CROWN in Jacksonville, Florida and is an ERIC Document No. ED 133 957.

Madeleine Cohen Oakley is Co-chief of Reference Services, State Library of Massachusetts, Boston. Before receiving her MSLS from Columbia University in 1970, Ms. Oakley was for five years the physical therapist in a New York City [public] school unit for orthopedically handicapped children. "Juvenile Fiction about the Orthopedically Handicapped" is reprinted by permission of the American Library Association from *Top of the News* (November 1973, pp. 57-68). Copyright 1973 by the American Library Association.

Michael Olds is a media specialist at South Wayne Junior High School, Indianapolis, Indiana. He is the former editor of *Indiana Media Journal* (formerly *Hoosier School Libraries*). "Special Education and the Media Center" by Michael A. Tulley, Charles P. Edwards, and Michael Olds is reprinted from *Hoosier School Libraries* (April 1978, vol. 17, no. 4, pp. 7-11).

Salvatore J. Parlato, Jr. is National Coodinator, Captioned Educational Films for the Deaf and Evaluation Program, Rochester, New York, School for the Deaf. "Using Non-Verbal Films with the Deaf and Language-Impaired" originally appeared in *Sightlines* (Winter 1976/77, vol. 10, no. 2, pp. 10-1) published by the Educational Film Library Association. It is reprinted with permission of the publisher and the author. Copyright 1976/77 by the Educational Film Library Association, Inc.

Stephen P. Plaskon is Assistant Professor, Department of Curriculum and Instruction, University of Virginia, Charlottesville. "Selecting a Reading Approach for the Mainstreamed Child " by Sandra B. Cohen and Stephen P.

Jane Ann Razeghi is Education Coordinator for the American Coalition of Citizens with Disabilities. "Federal Mandates for the Handicapped: Vocational Education Opportunity and Employment" by Jane Ann Razeghi and Sharon Davis is reprinted from *Exceptional Children* (February 1979, vol. 45, pp. 353-9) by permission of the Council for Exceptional Children. Copyright 1979 by the Council for Exceptional Children, 1920 Association Drive, Reston, Virginia 22091.

Judith Rubin is an art therapist, Pittsburgh Child Guidance Center; Assistant Professor of Clinical Child Psychiatry, University of Pittsburgh; and President, American Art Therapy Association. "They Opened Our Eyes: The Story of an Exploratory Art Program for Visually Impaired, Multiply Handicapped Children" by Judith Rubin and Janet Klineman is reprinted with permission from *Education of the Visually Handicapped* (December 1974, vol. 6, pp. 106-13). Copyright 1974 by Association for Education of the Visually Handicapped, Inc.

Dennis C. Russo is Chief of Behavioral Psychology, Department of Psychiatry, Children's Hospital Medical Center, Boston, Massachusetts. "A Method for Integrating an Autistic Child into a Normal Public-School Classroom" by Dennis C. Russo and Robert L. Koegel is reprinted with permission from *Journal of Applied Behavior Analysis* (Winter 1977, vol. 10, no. 4, pp. 579-90). Copyright 1977 by the Society for the Exceptional Analysis of Behavior, Inc.

Debbie Schneider is an LLD (language learning disabled) resource teacher with the Everett Public Schools in Everett, Washington. "How My Body Looks and Moves—Lessons in Self-Drawings" by Richard S. Neel and Debbie Schneider is reprinted from *Teaching Exceptional Children* (Winter 1978, vol. 10, pp. 38-9) by permission of the Council for Exceptional Children. Copyright 1978 by the Council for Exceptional Children, 1920 Association Drive, Reston, Virginia 22091.

Laird Schultz is Coordinator for Special Education, secondary TMR (trainable mentally retarded) program, Canby Public Schools, Canby, Minnesota.

"A Prevocational Program for Secondary TMR Students: The Canby Project" by Thomas J. Lombard and Laird Schultz is reprinted by permission of *Journal for Special Educators* (Spring 1978, vol. 14, pp. 173-8,87). Copyright 1978 by the American Association of Special Educators, Inc.

Ruth Silver is Director, Center for Blind Children, Milwaukee, Wisconsin. She is the author of "Listening and Responding to Sounds and Language," a set of three records with a manual designed to teach auditory training and language comprehension to infants and young children with special needs. "Responding to Sound through Toys, the Environment, and Speech" is reprinted from *Teaching Exceptional Children* (Winter 1975, vol. 7, pp. 38-44) by permission of the Council for Exceptional Children. Copyright 1975 by the Council for Exceptional Children, 1920 Association Drive, Reston, Virginia 22091.

"Standard Criteria for the Selection and Evaluation of Instructional Material" was originally prepared by the National Center on Educational Media and Materials for the Handicapped working under the sponsorship of the US Office of Education. The material is an ERIC Document No. ED132 760 and is in the public domain.

Bill Stark is Director of Media Services, Illinois School for the Deaf. " 'Meanwhile . . .': A Look at Comic Books at Illinois School for the Deaf " is reprinted by permission from *American Annals of the Deaf* (October 1976, vol. 121, pp. 470-7). Copyright 1976 by Conference of Executives of American Schools for the Deaf, Inc. and Convention of American Instructors of the Deaf, Inc.

John D. Swisher is Professor of Counselor Education and Program Director, Center for Research on Human Resources in the Institute for Policy Research and Evaluation at The Pennsylvania State University. "Developmental Restaging: Meeting the Mental Health Needs of Handicapped Students in the Schools" is reprinted with permission from *Journal of School Health* (November 1978, vol. 48, pp. 548-50). Copyright 1978 by the American School Health Association, Kent, Ohio 44240.

Carol Ann Dodd Thornton is Associate Professor, Mathematics Department, Illinois State University. She conducts pre- and in-service courses with special and elementary education teachers and directs the Diagnostic and Development Center for the Mathematics Department at ISU. "Multiply Successes When Introducing Basic Multiplication Ideas to Visually Handicapped Children" is reprinted by permission from *Education of the Visually*

PART I

PROVIDING FOR ALL CHILDREN

Introductory Comments

The vocabularies of most educators have recently been expanded to include such terms as *least restrictive environment, due process, IEP, related services* and so on. These terms are found in numerous journal articles and are addressed in workshops, conferences, PTA meetings, and in-service training sessions. While they obviously have some relevance for everyone involved in the field of education, how they acquired their current import-ance and the implications of their meanings might be illusive in the lengthy pages of PL 94-142. For this reason, Part I was included in this text to provide a basis for understanding the major points of the law itself, how it specifically affects vocational education at the secondary level, and the ways in which the school library media center can expand its services to include all children.

For a concise overview of the law with regard to the rights of handicapped children, an article entitled "Public Law 94-142 and Section 504: What They Say about Rights and Protections" by Joseph Ballard and Jeffrey Zettel has been included. It clarifies, in a question-and-answer format, the major provisions of PL 94-142 and Section 504 of the Vocational Rehabilitation Act of 1973. References are made to sections of the Act or to the Section 504 regulations for readers interested in returning to the original source for additional information regarding specific provisions.

One of the provisions of PL 94-142 is that the schools are charged with preparing all students for eventual employment. This is to be accomplished for the handicapped student through the availability of vocational education programs. Fulfilling this requirement is an enormous task and necessitates the cooperation of administrators, and special, regular, and vocational educators. Large numbers of handicapped pupils at the secondary level are or will be involved in programs of prevocational and vocational training, a topic which Part VII of this book addresses. As a background to the types of programs described therein, an article titled "Federal Mandates for the Handicapped: Vocational Education Opportunity and Employment" is presented here in order to provide insight into the various aspects of recent legislation affecting vocational education. The article emphasizes that, while it is estimated that ten percent of the school population are handicapped, vocational education programs were serving less than two percent of the handicapped as of 1974. The authors, Jane Ann Razeghi and Sharon Davis, discuss the significance of this challenge.

The inclusion of a greater number of handicapped children into public school programs affects all school personnel including the media center specialist or librarian. The responsibility of this individual to include all children into the resources and programs of the library is aptly expressed by Eliza T. Dresang in "There Are No *Other* Children." In her words, "Librarians must not get caught up in dilemmas about whether to extend services to certain children or whether to limit service. It is the absolute right of every child in school to receive equal consideration." She sympathizes, however, with those who are anxious about serving unfamiliar children and offers sound suggestions for increasing one's understanding of certain groups or of individual children in order to adequately provide for their needs. The material, psychological, and intellectual needs of special children are discussed. The author also points out that meeting these needs does not necessarily entail the purchasing of new or adapted materials but rather requires a nontraditional approach to using materials and equipment already available.

Public Law 94-142 and Section 504: What They Say about Rights and Protections

by Joseph Ballard
and Jeffrey Zettel

BASIC THRUST, OBJECTIVES, AND TARGET POPULATIONS

What is PL 94-142?

PL 94-142, the Education for All Handicapped Children Act, is legislation passed by the United States Congress and signed into law by President Gerald R. Ford on November 29, 1975. The "94" indicates that this law was passed by the 94th Congress. The "142" indicates that this law was the 142nd law passed by that session of the Congress to be signed into law by the president.

What are the purposes of PL 94-142?

PL 94-142 can be said to have four major purposes:

- Guarantee the availability of special education programing to handicapped children and youth who require it.
- Assure fairness and appropriateness in decision making with regard to providing special education for handicapped children and youth.
- Establish clear management and auditing requirements and procedures regarding special education at all levels of government.
- Financially assist the efforts of state and local government through the use of federal funds (refer to Section 3 of the Act).

What is Section 504?

Section 504 is a basic civil rights provision with respect to terminating discrimination against America's handicapped citizens. Section 504 was enacted through the legislative vehicle PL 93-112, the Vocational Rehabilitation Act Amendments of 1973. Though Section 504 is brief in actual language, its implications are far-reaching. The statute reads:

> No otherwise qualified handicapped individual in the United States shall, solely by reason of his handicap, be excluded from the participation in, be denied the benefits of, or be subjected to discrimination under any program or activity receiving Federal financial assistance.

To whom do PL 94-142 and Section 504 apply?

PL 94-142 applies to all handicapped children who require special education and related services, ages 3 to 21 inclusive. Section 504 applies to all handicapped Americans regardless of age. Section 504 therefore applies to all handicapped children ages 3 to 21 with respect to their public education, both from the standpoint of the guarantee of an appropriate special education and from the standpoint of sheer regular program accessibility. Close coordination has thus been maintained between the provisions of PL 94-142 and those of the Section 504 regulations (refer to Section 611 of PL 94-142 and background statement of the Section 504 regulation).

What is the relationship of PL 94-142 to the older federal Education of the Handicapped Act (EHA)?

PL 94-142 is a complete revision of only Part B of the Education of the Handicapped Act. Part B was formerly that portion of EHA addressing the basic state grant program. The other components of the Act (Parts A-E) remain substantially unchanged and continue in operation. Parenthetically, all programs under the aegis of the EHA, including the PL 94-142 revision of Part B, are administered through the Bureau of Education for the Handicapped under the US Office of Education.

Was there a forerunner to PL 94-142?

Many of the major provisions of PL 94-142, such as the guarantee of due process procedures and the assurance of education in the least restrictive environment, were required in an earlier federal law—PL 93-380, the Education Amendments of 1974 (enacted August 21, 1974). PL 94-142 was enacted approximately one year and three months later, on November 29, 1975.

How are handicapped children defined for purposes of this Act?

Handicapped children are defined by the Act as children who are:

> mentally retarded, hard of hearing, deaf, orthopedically impaired, other health impaired, speech impaired, visually handicapped, seriously emotionally disturbed, or children with specific learning disabilities who by reason thereof require special education and related services.

This definition establishes a two-pronged criterion for determining child eligibility under the Act. The first is whether the child actually has one or more of the disabilities listed in the above definition. The second is whether the child requires special education and related services. Not all children who have a disability require special education; many are able and should attend school without any program modification (refer to Section 4 of the Act).

If a child has one or more of the disabilities listed in the preceding definition and also requires special education and related services, how does PL 94-142 define special education?

Special education is defined in PL 94-142 as:

> specially designed instruction, at no cost to parents or guardians, to meet the unique needs of a handicapped child, including classroom instruction, instruction in physical education, home instruction, and instruction in hospitals and institutions.

The key phrase in the above definition of special education is "specially designed instruction . . . to meet the unique needs of a handicapped child." Reemphasized, special education, according to statutory definition, is defined as being *special* and involving only instruction that is designed and directed to meet the unique needs of a handicapped child. For many children, therefore, special education will not be the totality of their education. Furthermore, this definition clearly implies that special education proceeds from the basic goals and expected outcomes of general education. Thus, intervention with a child does not occur because s/he is mentally retarded but because s/he has a unique educational need that requires specially designed instruction (refer to Section 4(a)(16) of the Act).

How are related services defined in PL 94-142?

Equally important to understand is the concept of related services that are defined in the Act as:

> transportation, and such developmental, corrective, and other supportive services (including speech pathology and audiology, psychological services, physical and occupational therapy, recreation, and medical and counseling services, except that such medical services shall be for diagnostic and evaluation purposes only) as may be required to assist a handicapped child to benefit from special education, and includes the early identification and assessment of handicapping conditions in children.

The key phrase here is "as required to assist the handicapped child to benefit from special education." This leads to a clear progression: a child is handicapped because s/he requires special education and related services; special education is the specially designed instruction to meet the child's unique needs; and related services are those additional services necessary in order for the child to benefit from special educational instruction (refer to Section 4(a)(17) of the Act).

RIGHTS AND PROTECTIONS

A Free Appropriate Education

What is the fundamental requirement of PL 94-142, from which all other requirements of this Act stem?

PL 94-142 requires that every state and its localities, if they were to continue to receive funds under this Act, must make available a free appropriate public education for all handicapped children aged 3 to 18 by the beginning of the school year (September 1) in 1978 and further orders the availability of such education to all children aged 3 to 21 by September 1, 1980 (refer to Section 3(c) of the Act).

What about preschool and young adults under PL 94-142?

For children in the 3 to 5 and 18 to 21 age ranges, however, this mandate does not apply if such a requirement is inconsistent with state law or practice or any court decree. Refer to regulations for further expatiation of this provision (Section 612 (2)(B) of the Act).

What does Section 504 say regarding the right to an education?

Section 504 makes essentially the same requirement. However, the 504 regulation says "shall provide." PL 94-142 says "a free appropriate public education *will be available.*"

The 504 regulation does not refer to specific age groups per se. Instead, it refers to "public elementary and secondary education," and, therefore, the traditional school-age population. With respect to that school-age population, the 504 regulation accedes to the September 1, 1978 date of PL 94-142 as the final and absolute deadline for the provisions of a free appropriate public education. However, the Section 504 regulation also precedes that requirement with the phrase *"at the earliest practicable time"* but in no event later than September 1, 1978. (Refer to #84.33(d) of the 504 regulation.)

What is required with respect to preschool and young adult programs under Section 504?

The 504 regulation appears simply to say that preschool and adult education programs will not discriminate on the basis of handicap, and further that such program accessibility is to take effect immediately. On the other hand, PL 94-142, as previously noted, explicitly states that there shall be available a free appropriate public education for children ages 3 through 5 and youth ages 18 through 21 unless such requirement is inconsistent with state law or practice or the order of any court. Again, PL 94-142 does not require such availability until September 1, 1978 (refer to #84.38 of the 504 regulation).

Since Section 504 and PL 94-142 are making, in essence, the same fundamental requirement of a free, appropriate public education, are federal monies authorized under Section 504 as they are under PL 94-142?

No. Section 504 is a civil rights statute, like Title VI of the Civil Rights Act of 1965 (race) and Title IX of the Education Amendments of 1972 (sex).

Must there be compliance with the fundamental requirement of PL 94-142 (as reiterated in Section 504 regulations) if PL 94-142 is not "fully funded"?

It is most important to note that compliance with this baseline guarantee of the availability of a free, appropriate public education is in no way dependent upon whether this Act receives appropriations at the top authorized ceilings, or in other words, is "fully funded." If a state accepts money under this Act, regardless of the amount of actual appropriations, it must comply with the aforementioned stipulation.

What does "free" education, as required in both PL 94-142 and Section 504, mean?

"Free" means the provision of education and related services at no cost to the handicapped person or to his/her parents or guardian, except for those largely incidental fees that are imposed on nonhandicapped persons or their parents or guardian (refer to #84.33(c)(1) of the 504 regulation).

What if a public placement is made in a public or private residential program?

If both the school and parents jointly agree that the most appropriate educational placement for the child is in a public or private residential facility, then such a program placement, including nonmedical care as well as room and board, shall be provided at no cost to the person or his/her parents or guardian (refer to #84.33(c)(3) of the 504 regulation).

Does "free" mean that no private funds can be used?

No. Private funds are not prohibited. To reiterate: there must be no cost to the handicapped person or to his/her parents or guardian.

What does "appropriate" education mean?

"Appropriate" is not defined as such, but rather receives its definition for each child through the mechanism of the written individualized education program (IEP) as required by PL 94-142. Therefore, what is agreed to by all parties becomes in fact the "appropriate" educational program for the particular child.

Individualized Education Programs

What are the basic concepts of the IEP?

The term *individualized education program* itself conveys important concepts that need to be specified. First, *individualized* means that the IEP must be addressed to the educational needs of a single child rather than a class or group of children. Second, *education* means that the IEP is limited to those elements of the child's education that are more specifically special education and related services as defined by the Act. Third, *program* means that the IEP is a statement of what will actually be provided to the child, as distinct from a plan that provides guidelines from which a program must subsequently be developed.

What are the basic components of an IEP?

The Act contains a specific definition describing the components of an IEP as:

> a written statement for each handicapped child developed in any meeting by a representative of the local education agency or an intermediate educational unit who shall be qualified to provide, or supervise the provision of, specially designed instruction to meet the unique needs of handicapped children, the teacher, the parents or guardian of such child, and whenever appropriate, such child, which statement shall include (A) a statement of the present levels of educational performance of such child, (B) a statement of annual goals, including short-term instructional objectives, (C) a statement of the specific educational services to be provided to such child, and the extent to which such child will be able to participate in regular educational programs, (D) the projected date for initiation and anticipated duration of such services, and (E) appropriate objective criteria and evaluation procedures and schedules for determining, on at least an annual basis, whether instructional objectives are being achieved.

(Refer to Section 4(a)(19) of the Act.)

May others be involved in the development of an IEP?

Good practice suggests that others frequently be involved. However, the law only requires four persons to be involved (i.e., the parents or guardians, the teacher or teachers of the child, a representative of the local educational agency or intermediate unit who is qualified to provide or supervise the provision of special education, and whenever appropriate, the child). If a related service person will be providing services, then it seems to make sense that s/he be as involved as the teacher. Also, good practice indicates that parents often want to bring an additional person familiar with the child to the meeting.

Who must be provided an IEP?

Each state and local educational agency shall insure that an IEP is provided for each handicapped child who is receiving or will receive special education, regardless of what institution or agency provides or will provide special education to the child: (a) The state educational agency shall insure that each local educational agency establishes and implements an IEP for each handicapped child; (b) The state educational agency shall require each public agency which provides special education or related services to a handicapped child to establish policies and procedures for developing, implementing, reviewing, maintaining, and evaluating an IEP for that child.

What must local and intermediate education agencies do regarding IEPs?

- Each local educational agency shall develop or revise, whichever is appropriate, an IEP for every handicapped child at the beginning of the school year and review and, if appropriate, revise its provisions periodically but not less than annually.
- Each local educational agency is responsible for initiating and conducting meetings for developing, reviewing, and revising a child's IEP.
- For a handicapped child who is receiving special education, a meeting must be held early enough so that the IEP is developed (or revised, as appropriate) by the beginning of the next school year.
- For a handicapped child who is not receiving special education, a meeting must be held within 30 days of a determination that the child is handicapped, or that the child will receive special education.

(Refer to Section 614(a)(5) of the Act.)

Do the IEP requirements apply to children in private schools and facilities?

Yes. The state educational agency shall insure that an IEP is developed, maintained, and evaluated for each child placed in a private school by the state educational agency or a local educational agency. The agency that places or refers a child shall insure that provision is made for a representative from the private school (which may be the child's teacher) to participate in each meeting. If the private school representative cannot attend a meeting, the agency shall use other methods to insure participation by the private school, including individual or conference telephone calls (refer to Section 613(a)(4)(B) of the Act).

Is the IEP an instructional plan?

No. The IEP is a management tool that is designed to assure that, when a child requires special education, the special education designed for that child is appropriate to his or her special learning needs and that the special education designed is actually delivered and monitored. An instructional plan reflects good educational practice by outlining the specifics necessary to effectively intervene in instruction. Documenting instructional plans is *not* mandated as part of the IEP requirements.

What procedures should educational agencies follow to involve parents in the development of their child's IEP?

- Each local educational agency shall take steps to insure that one or both of the parents of the handicapped child are present at each meeting or are afforded the opportunity to participate, including scheduling the meeting at a mutually agreed on time and place.
- If neither parent can attend, the local educational agency shall use other methods to insure parent participation, including individual or conference telephone calls.
- A meeting may be conducted without a parent in attendance if the local educational agency is unable to convince the parents that they should attend. In this case the local educational agency must have a record of its attempts to arrange a mutually agreed on time and place such as: (a) detailed records of telephone calls made or attempted and the results of those calls, (b) copies of correspondence sent to the parents and any responses received, and (c) detailed records of visits made to the parent's home or place of employment and the results of those visits.
- The local educational agency shall take whatever action is necessary to insure that the parent understands the proceedings at a meeting, including arranging for an interpreter for parents who are deaf or whose native language is other than English.

When must handicapped children be guaranteed the IEP?

- For handicapped children counted under the fiscal funding formula of PL 94-142, not later than the beginning of school year 1977-78.
- For all handicapped children in each state, regardless of the delivering agency, not later than the beginning of school year 1978-79.

What does Section 504 say with respect to the IEP?

As discussed, PL 94-142 requires the development and maintenance of individualized written education programs for all children. The 504 regulation cites the IEP as "one means" of meeting the standard of a free appropriate public education (refer to #84.33(b)(2) of the 504 regulation).

Least Restrictive Educational Environment

PL 94-142 requires that handicapped children receive a free appropriate public education in the least restrictive educational environment. What does this mean?

It is critical to note what this provision *is not:*

- It is not a provision for mainstreaming. In fact, the word is never used.
- It does not mandate that all handicapped children will be educated in the regular classroom.
- It does not abolish any particular educational environment, for instance, educational programing in a residential setting.

It is equally critical to note what this provision *does* mandate:

- Education with nonhandicapped children will be the governing objective "to the maximum extent appropriate."
- The IEP will be the management tool toward achievement of the maximum least restrictive environment and therefore shall be applied within the framework of meeting the "unique needs" of each child.
- The IEP document(s) must clearly "show cause" if and when one moves from least restrictive to more restrictive. The statute states that the following component must be included in the written statement accompanying the IEP "and the extent to which such child will be able to participate in regular educational programs."

(Refer to Section 612(5)(B) of the Act.)

Correspondingly, what does the Section 504 regulation say with respect to least restrictive educational environment?

The language of the 504 regulation is, in most important respects, nearly identical to the least restrictive statute in PL 94-142. There remains one notable distinction, however. The 504 regulation would seem to consider the "nearest placement to home" as an additional determinant of instructional placement in the least restrictive environment (refer to #84.34(a) of the 504 regulation).

Procedural Safeguards

Under PL 94-142, what happens if there is a failure to agree with respect to what constitutes an appropriate education for a particular child?

States must guarantee procedural safeguard mechanisms for children and their parents or guardians. Those provisions of previously existing law (PL 93-380, the Education Amendments of 1974) toward the guarantee of due process rights are further refined in PL 94-142, and their scope is substantially enlarged.

Basically, the state education agency must guarantee the maintenance of full due process procedures for all handicapped children within the state and their parents or guardian with respect to all matters of identification, evaluation, and educational placement whether it be the initiation or change of such placement, or the refusal to initiate or change. Interested individuals are strongly urged to read Section 615 of the Act (Procedural Safeguards) in its entirety.

It should be observed that the PL 94-142 refinements took effect in the first year under the new formula, that is, fiscal 1978 (school year 1977-78). In the meantime, those basic features of due process as authorized in the prior Act (PL 93-380) must be maintained by the states.

It should be further noted that, when the parents or guardian of a child are not known, are unavailable, or when the child is a legal ward of the state, the state education agency, local education agency, or intermediate education agency (as appropriate) must assign an individual to act as a *surrogate* for the child in all due process proceedings. Moreover, such assigned individual may not be an employee of the state educational agency, local education agency, or intermediate educational unit *involved* in the education or care of the particular child (refer to Section 615 of the Act).

Does the Section 504 regulation also require the maintenance of a procedural safeguards mechanism?

Yes. However, though most of the major principles of due process embodied in PL 94-142 are clearly present in the 504 regulation, *all* of the stipulations of PL 94-142 are treated only as "one means" of due process compliance under Section 504 (refer to #84.36 of the 504 regulation).

What does PL 94-142 say with respect to assessment of children?

PL 94-142 carries a provision that seeks to guarantee against assessment with respect to the question of a handicapping condition when such assessment procedures are racially or culturally discriminatory. The statute does not provide a comprehensive procedure of remedy with respect to potential discrimination but does make two clear and important stipulations in the direction of remedy:

- ''Such materials and procedures shall be provided in the child's native language or mode of communication.''
- ''No single procedure shall be the sole criterion for determining an appropriate educational program for a child.''

The provision, in effect, orders that assessment procedures be multifactored, multisourced, and carried out by qualified personnel. The regulations governing this provision should therefore be carefully reviewed (refer to Section 612(5)(C) of the Act).

What does the Section 504 regulation say with respect to the assessment of children?

The objectives of Section 504 and PL 94-142 are identical on this matter, and the regulatory language for both statutes are also identical (refer to #84.35 of the 504 regulation).

What does PL 94-142 say with respect to the confidentiality of data and information?

PL 94-142 contains a provision that addresses the question of abuses and potential abuses in school system record keeping with respect to handicapped children and their parents. PL 94-142, as did the prior PL 93-380, simply orders a remedy and does not go beyond. The governing statutes for this provision are contained in the larger Family Educational Rights and Privacy Act (often referred to as the *Buckley Amendments* after the author, US Senator James Buckley of New York). That measure sets forth both the access rights and privacy rights with respect to personal school records for all of the nation's children and youth, and their parents.

Thus, readers should study the Act itself (contained in PL 93-380), the accompanying regulations for the Buckley Amendments, and the modest addendums to those provisions contained in the regulations for PL 94-142 (refer to Section 617 (c) and Section 612 (2) (D) of the Act).

What then, in summary, are the rights and protections of PL 94-142 (which, for the most part, are also affirmed in Section 504) that must be guaranteed?

PL 94-142 makes a number of critical stipulations that must be adhered to by *both* the state and its local and intermediate educational agencies:

- Assurance of the availability of a free, appropriate public education for all handicapped children, such guarantee of availability no later than certain specified dates.

- Assurance of the maintenance of an individualized education program for all handicapped children.
- A guarantee of complete due procedural safeguards.
- The assurance of regular parent or guardian consultation.
- Assurance of special education being provided to all handicapped children in the "least restrictive" environment.
- Assurance of nondiscriminatory testing and evaluation.
- A guarantee of policies and procedures to protect the confidentiality of data and information.
- Assurance of an effective policy guaranteeing the right of all handicapped children to a free, appropriate public education *at no cost* to parents or guardian.
- Assurance of a surrogate to act for any child when parents or guardians are either unknown or unavailable or when such child is a legal ward of the state.

It is most important to observe that an official, written document containing all of these assurances is now required (in the form of an application) of *every* school district receiving its federal entitlement under PL 94-142. Correspondingly, such a public document also exists at the state level in the form of the annual state plan, which must be submitted to the US commissioner.

Federal Mandates for the Handicapped: Vocational Education Opportunity and Employment

by Jane Ann Razeghi
and Sharon Davis

PL 94-142

PL 94-142 indicates that vocational education should be made available to handicapped students. This law defines special education as specially designed instruction, at no cost to the parents, to meet the unique needs of a handicapped child. The definition does not stop there; it goes on to state:

> The term [*special education*] also includes vocational education if it consists of specially designed instruction, at no cost to the parent, to meet the unique needs of a handicapped student.[1]

Vocational education is defined as

> organized educational programs which are directly related to the preparation of individuals for paid or unpaid employment, or for additional preparation for a career requiring other than a baccalaureate or advanced degree.[2]

PL 94-142 notes that the above definition of vocational education is taken directly from the Vocational Education Act of 1963, as amended by PL 94-482, and that under this Act it may include industrial arts and consumer and homemaking education programs. In light of the above definitions, it is the intent of PL 94-142 that vocational education opportunity is an important part of full educational opportunity for handicapped students.

Vocational education for handicapped students is especially emphasized in the section concerning the availability of program options for handicapped students:

> Each public agency shall take steps to insure that its handicapped children have available to them the variety of educational programs and services available to nonhandicapped children in the area served by the agency, including art, music, industrial arts, consumer and homemaking education, and vocational education.[3]

This makes the case for vocational opportunity very clear. In the past, many of these program options have been closed to handicapped students. Many educators are not aware that these options are now open and should be considered in planning a student's individualized education program.

Immediately following the program options section is a section on nonacademic services. Little has been mentioned about this. Although this section does not specifically say "vocational youth organizations," the implications are obvious:

> Each public agency shall take steps to provide nonacademic and extracurricular services and activities in such manner as is necessary to afford handicapped children an equal opportunity for participation in those services and activities.[4]

> Nonacademic and extracurricular services and activities may include counseling services, athletics, transportation, health services, recreational activities, special interest groups or clubs sponsored by the public agency, referrals to agencies which provide assistance to handicapped persons, and employment of students, including both employment by the public agency and assistance in making outside employment available.[5]

This section should not be construed to mean that separate services, activities, or vocational youth organizations should be established specifically for handicapped students. On the contrary, such actions could be considered violations of Section 504, nondiscrimination on the basis of handicapped condition. Special educators should be aware of the vocational youth organizations that exist in many public high schools. These organizations include Distributive Education Clubs of America (DECA), Future Business Leaders of America (FBLA), Future Farmers of America (FFA), Future Homemakers of America (FHA), Office Education Association (OEA), and Vocational Industrial Clubs of America (VICA).

Special and regular educators often express concern about the integration of mentally retarded students in such organizations. These and other school activities can be accessed through the use of the "buddy" system or "big brother/sister" approach when a nonhandicapped student assists the handicapped student in the activity. Service clubs within the school often volunteer to meet students at the door, sit with them during the game, and provide socialization.

Employment is also stressed in the nonacademic services section. It would seem that the local education agency is advised to consider employing qualified handicapped individuals and to provide assistance to handicapped students in acquiring outside employment.

SECTION 504

Section 504, Nondiscrimination on the Basis of Handicap,[6] also affirms vocational education accessibility for handicapped students. Subpart D sets forth requirements for nondiscrimination in preschool, elementary, secondary, and adult education programs and activities, including secondary vocational education programs. The Office of Civil Rights monitors Section 504 and is presently in the process of preparing its compliance manual regarding vocational education for handicapped students. It is important for special educators to be aware of when the federal government is planning to determine the number of handicapped students in vocational education and whether or not discrimination against handicapped students exists.

PL 94-482

Vocational education is becoming more available and accessible to handicapped students. Probably one of the most important reasons for this is that states are now required to expend at least ten percent of their total federal allotment in vocational education for handicapped persons. States are required to use these funds "to the maximum extent possible to assist handicapped persons to participate in regular vocational education programs."[7] Such a statement parallels closely the least restrictive environment specifications of PL 94-142. Theoretically, if states do not spend at least ten percent of their federal funds on handicapped students, they could disqualify themselves from receiving the total federal allotment. This commitment of funds and the requirement to document their expenditures for handicapped students have caused state vocational education departments to take a closer look at the problems of handicapped students in their programs.

States must describe in their five-year plans for vocational education "the procedures for insuring that funds for vocational programs for handicapped persons are used in a manner consistent with"[8] the state plan for the Education of the Handicapped Act. Therefore, not only must there be a ten percent set-aside of vocational education funds for handicapped students, but also, such a set-aside must be used in accordance with the existing state plan for the Education of the Handicapped Act.

PL 94-482 mentions the importance of the individualized education program (IEP) and requires a statement in the five-year state plan for vocational education that describes

> how the program provided each handicapped child will be planned and coordinated in conformity with and as a part of the child's individualized educational program as required by the Education of the Handicapped Act.[9]

If special educators and the IEP team conclude that vocational education would benefit a particular handicapped student, then the vocational educator should be included in the development of that IEP. It is the vocational educator's task to define those activities in which the handicapped student will be participating and to identify the support services needed to carry out such activities in regular vocational programs.[10] There should be some interaction between the vocational educator who is to provide the instruction and the IEP team.

By accepting the state standards, a tremendous amount of duplication of services is avoided. PL 94-482 accepts the state standards for Education of the Handicapped Act, which reads as follows:

> Section 612(6) of the Education of the Handicapped Act requires that the State educational agency be responsible for ensuring that all educational programs for handicapped children within the State, including all of those groups administered by any other State or local agency, are under the general supervision of persons responsible for the educational programs for handicapped children in the State educational agency.[11]

Most states have designated that the identification and evaluation of handicapped students is to be accomplished through the Education of the Handicapped Act. PL 94-482 specifically states that any activity to assist the education of handicapped children must meet the educational standards of the state educational agency.

SECTION 503

Section 503 of the Rehabilitation Act of 1973[12] requires that every employer doing business with the federal government under a contract for more than $2,500 take "affirmative action" to recruit, hire, train, and promote handicapped individuals. Those businesses holding contracts of $50,000 or more and having at least 50 employees are required to develop and maintain an affirmative action program that sets forth policies and practices regarding the hiring of handicapped employees.

Affirmative action is intended to be a positive program to encourage employers to hire more handicapped persons. These programs should facilitate greater numbers of handicapped persons entering the job market. Business and industry, in their efforts to recruit qualified handicapped persons, will be looking to the local public schools' vocational education programs for assistance. If affirmative action is to be fully realized, educators must consider all the options available for training and preparing handicapped students for employment.

VOCATIONAL EDUCATION — WHAT IS IT?

Vocational education is defined by the US Office of Education (USOE) as organized educational programs that are directly related to the preparation of individuals for paid or unpaid employment or for additional preparation for a career requiring other than a baccalaureate or advanced degree. The nine vocational areas identified by the USOE are agriculture, distributive education, health occupations education, occupational home economics, consumer and homemaking education, office occupations, technical education, trade and industrial occupations, and industrial arts.

Handicapped students must have available to them the variety of vocational education programs and services available to nonhandicapped students. They may be placed in regular vocational education programs with special educational assistance or in specially designed separate programs. It must be emphasized that every effort should be made to ensure that handicapped students participate in regular vocational education programs and that only those students whose handicaps are such that they cannot achieve satisfactorily in the regular class even with special educational assistance are placed in special vocational education programs.

VOCATIONAL EDUCATION OPPORTUNITIES NEEDED FOR HANDICAPPED INDIVIDUALS

Most public school systems have vocational education programs in the comprehensive high school and/or in a regional vocational center. These programs provide training in 60 or more different skills, making it possible for some students to graduate into employment. Handicapped students have the right to this same range of options, but few handicapped individuals are presently being served. A 1976 Report to Congress states that of over 13 million individuals served in vocational education in 1974, less than two percent were handicapped. Ten percent of the school population is estimated to have handicapping conditions.[13] Handicapped persons tend to be limited to segregated programs that offer skill preparation for a limited range of occupations. The 1976 Report to Congress cites the example of a school district that provided a choice of only two vocational offerings to handicapped students in a separate program, while offering nonhandicapped students in the same district a choice of about 20 different career offerings and 130 different classes.[14]

In addition to offering few choices for vocational training, the segregated, specially designed vocational education programs usually prepare students for the lower skill occupations, such as hotel and motel aides, building maintenance, and service station attendants. Work experience programs may also be offered, but again, the on-the-job training they provide is in low skill occupations. The evidence indicates that those handicapped students who receive vocational education, whether through a segregated skill preparation program or through work experience, are not prepared for the wide variety of occupations for which the nonhandicapped are prepared.[15]

The need for expanding vocational education opportunities for handicapped individuals is also evident when the employment data for handicapped people are examined. Statistics on the educable mentally retarded indicate that only 21 percent of this population are fully employed when they finish school while 40 percent are underemployed and 26 percent are unemployed.[16] Other researchers report that 40 percent of all disabled adults are employed compared with 74 percent of the nondisabled population.[17] Shworles,[18] on the basis of students' records, predicted that by the end of 1977 about two million handicapped persons would be leaving school without the skills necessary for productive work.

While the unemployment figures are cause for concern, the underemployment of handicapped workers is also a serious situation. Handicapped workers are more frequently channeled into lower skill level jobs, which leads to their receiving lower average wages than those earned by nonhandicapped workers. Even taking into account that some handicapping conditions, such as mental retardation, can be expected to lead to lower skill jobs and lower income, there is evidence to suggest that many handicapped people cannot obtain jobs at a level commensurate with their ability. Biklen and Bogdan reported that ''according to US Census statistics, 85 percent of people with disabilities have incomes less than $7,000 and 52 percent of these make less than $2,000 per year.[19]

Economic considerations constitute a convincing rationale for expanding vocational education for handicapped individuals. Edwin Martin, US Office of Education Deputy Commissioner for the Bureau of Education for the Handicapped, estimates the cost of maintaining a person in an institution exceeds a quarter of a million dollars over a lifetime. By comparison, the cost-effectiveness of expanding vocational education for handicapped individuals is obvious.[20]

USOE POSITION STATEMENT

Recognizing that the education system can play a major role in preparing handicapped individuals to bridge the gap between education and work, the US Office of Education issued the following official statement in July 1978 on comprehensive vocational education for the handicapped: ''It is the position of the US Office of Education that an appropriate comprehensive vocational education will be available and accessible to every handicapped person.''[21]

Developed jointly by the Bureau of Education for the Handicapped (BEH) and the Bureau of Occupational and Adult Education (BOAE), the position statement is based on the following assumptions:

1. The provision of appropriate comprehensive vocational education for the handicapped is dependent upon all segments of the education system. Elementary, secondary, and adult education must provide the programs and services necessary for students to develop basic skills and make career choices. Vocational education must provide the education and training to develop occupational competencies.

2. Appropriate comprehensive vocational education for the handicapped must include cooperative relationships between the educational sector and the employment sector to facilitate the transition from school to work.

3. Appropriate comprehensive vocational education for handicapped persons will provide sequential educational instruction and training appropriate to the needs and progress of each handicapped individual.

4. Appropriate comprehensive vocational education will reduce the number of handicapped persons who are unemployed by providing the education needed for effective participation in the labor force. This also will assist employers to meet their affirmative action goals for employment of the handicapped.

5. Appropriate comprehensive vocational education will, to the maximum extent possible, identify and eliminate factors such as the attitudinal and environmental barriers, which determine to a large degree the impact that specific handicaps have on individuals.[22]

Plans for implementation of the official position are also being developed. These plans call for coordinating the activities of the two bureaus in such areas of shared responsibility as personnel training, program development and demonstration, dissemination of information, leadership training, and technical assistance.

COOPERATION WITH VOCATIONAL REHABILITATION

In addition to the interbureau agreement to cooperate in providing handicapped individuals with appropriate vocational education, the Office of Education has entered into an interagency agreement with the Rehabilitation Services Administration to plan and implement cooperative efforts that will prepare handicapped students for the world of work. The "memorandum of understanding" between the two agencies was made public in October 1977 and has provided impetus for states to establish systems for jointly providing services to handicapped students and for encouraging cooperative activities at the local level. The two federal agencies recognize that they have certain common responsibilities as providers of human services for handicapped persons. They are concerned that handicapped persons receive all the services they are eligible for under Public Laws 94-142, 94-482, and 93-112 and that the agencies administering these laws understand that eligibility under one law should not in and of itself result in a denial of complementary services under another of the laws. They are fully committed to aiding state and local agencies to engage in coordinated service delivery for handicapped persons.

The memorandum of understanding presents examples of activities that are appropriate for special education, vocational education, and vocational rehabilitation to assist handicapped individuals in preparing for and engaging in employment. Education and vocational rehabilitation agencies are encouraged to engage in a wide range of other cooperative endeavors, such as the following:

1. Consultation on development of state plans.
2. Personnel preparation and development.
3. Consultation on curriculum and program planning.
4. Joint operation of special programs designed to merge educational and vocational rehabilitation services in easing handicapped persons' entry into the world of work.

THE ROLE OF SPECIAL EDUCATION IN VOCATIONAL EDUCATION

In light of the federal mandates to provide appropriate vocational education for handicapped students and the directives for vocational education, special education, and vocational rehabilitation to cooperate in providing services, special educators need to become more involved. They cannot assume that vocational educators are totally responsible for the vocational education of handicapped students. Representatives of special education, vocational education and vocational rehabilitation must meet to set priorities, discuss needs and resources, and develop a plan for cooperation. The first step in creating or refining vocational education programing for handicapped students is to establish an administrative policy base to govern program operation. Because the provision of vocational education for handicapped students is relatively new to the American education system, many local education agencies have not yet adopted policies to guide the establishment of programs. Since written policies provide the basis for building and maintaining effective programs,[23] special educators can play an important part in ensuring that their local school system develops policies for vocational education of handicapped students.

Special educators can contribute to the vocational education of handicapped students in numerous ways. Special education can provide appropriate career awareness and exploration activities and prevocational instruction so that handicapped students will be prepared to participate in vocational assessment and vocational education. The handicapped adolescent typically lacks exposure to the world of work and needs to be provided with activities for development of career knowledge, basic occupational skills, and appropriate work attitudes and behaviors. Special education can also provide experiences to develop personal-social behaviors, which are an important part of success in an occupation. Basic academic skill development activities and training in independent living skills are also necessary in order for students to become suitably employed adults.

Special education can play a major role in the actual provision of vocational education for handicapped students by ensuring that vocational education is considered as an option in planning a student's IEP. Special education is responsible for the development, monitoring, and revision of IEPs for handicapped students and should ensure that appropriate vocational education representatives participate in the process to develop, monitor, and revise the vocational education component. If rehabilitation services are indicated, a vocational rehabilitation representative should be a part of the IEP development.

Special education should work with all personnel in developing and implementing policy concerning eligibility of handicapped students for regular vocational education. The persons who meet to plan the student's IEP must base their decision for placement on what is appropriate to meet the needs of that student. Eligibility requirements for regular vocational education should not automatically exclude on the basis of a handicap any student who can be reasonably accommodated. This may mean that entrance requirements may need to be modified, for in the past only those handicapped students most likely to succeed with little program adaptation have been admitted.

In order for a handicapped student to participate successfully in the regular vocational education program, all staff involved in the student's education must cooperate to provide appropriate, specially designed vocational instruction and related services in the regular class environment. Special education may provide many of the supportive (related) services needed by handicapped students to succeed in regular vocational education. Typical services include the following:[24]

1. Supportive instruction for individual students (individualized assistance in the classroom or laboratory) in cooperation with the regular instructor whenever necessary.

2. Remedial instruction in the basic academic skills on the basis of a student's need in a particular course.

3. Supportive educational services (assistance from interpreter, notetaker, direct reader, tutorial aide, bilingual specialist, or attendant for physically handicapped).

4. Specialized vocational counseling and guidance services.

5. Job placement and follow-up.

Special education may also provide special work-study programs for handicapped students in which students acquire actual job experience part of the school day. Work experience programs assist students in bridging the gap between school and work by helping them develop desirable social skills, work habits and attitudes, and entry level job skills. Ideally, such programs should not be the total vocational education provided to the student, but should complement the skill training provided in a vocational education program.

CONCLUSION

Now that vocational education is committed to providing handicapped students with job skills training, and now that business and industry are actively seeking handicapped individuals to employ, an environment has been created through which special educators can more effectively prepare these students. It will take the cooperation, concern, and efforts of many to ensure that handicapped students receive all the services necessary to achieve their employment potential. Special educators, who have always been concerned about the future welfare of handicapped students, may need to take the initiative in implementing these cooperative efforts. By planning and working together within the school and community, special and vocational educators, along with business and industry, will make vocational education a reality for handicapped students.

NOTES

1. *Federal Register*, Tuesday, August 23, 1977, Part II (Rules and regulations for amendments to Part B, Education for All Handicapped Children Act of 1975, PL 94-142, Education of handicapped children, Section 121a. 14(a)(3)).

2. Ibid. (Section 121a. 14(b)(3)).

3. Ibid. (Section 121a. 305).

4. Ibid. (Section 121a. 306(a)).

5. Ibid. (Section 121a. 306(b)).

6. *Federal Register*, Wednesday, May 4, 1977, Part IV (Rules and regulations for Section 504, Rehabilitation Act of 1973, PL 93-112, Non-discrimination on basis of handicap).

7. *Federal Register*, Monday, October 3, 1977, Part VI (Rules and regulations for Education Amendments of 1976, PL 94-482, Vocations education, state programs and commissioner's discretionary programs).

8. Ibid. (Section 104. 182(f)).

9. Ibid.

10. W. Halloran, et al. *Vocational Education for the Handicapped: Resource Guide to Federal Regulations* (Austin, TX: Texas Education Agency, Department of Special Education, 1978).

11. *Federal Register*, Monday, October 3, 1977, Part VI (Rules and regulations for Education Amendments of 1976, PL 94-482, Vocations education, state programs and commissioner's discretionary programs, Section 104.5(b)).

12. *Federal Register*, Friday, April 16, 1976 (Rules and regulations for Section 503, Rehabilitation Act of 1973, PL 93-112, Affirmative action obligations of contractors and subcontractors for handicapped workers).

13. "Training Educators for the Handicapped: A Need to Redirect Federal Programs." Report to Congress by the comptroller general of the United States, September 28, 1976.

14. Ibid.

15. S. Davis and F.J. Weintraub, "Beyond the Traditional Career Stereotyping," *Journal of Career Education* 5 (1978): 24-34.

16. M.D. Hightower, "Status Quo Is Certain Death," *Journal of Rehabilitation* 42 (1975): 2.

17. S.A. Levitan and R. Taggart, *Jobs for the Disabled* (Washington, DC: George Washington University Center for Manpower Policy Studies, 1976).

18. T.R. Shworles, "Increasing the Opportunities through Vocational Education," in *Vocational Education for Special Groups*, ed. James E. Wall (Washington, DC: American Vocational Association, 1976).

19. D. Biklen and R. Bogdan, "Handicapism in America," *WIN* (October 28, 1976): 11.

20. J.A. Razeghi and W. Halloran, "A New Picture of Vocational Education for the Handicapped," *School Shop*, Special Issue (April 1978): 50-3.

21. *Statement of Position of the US Office of Education on Appropriate Comprehensive Vocational Education for All Handicapped Persons* (Washington, DC: US Office of Education, 1978).

22. Ibid.

23. S. Davis and M. Ward, *Vocational Education of Handicapped Students: A Guide for Policy Development* (Reston, VA: Council for Exceptional Children, 1978).

24. Ibid.

REFERENCES

Abeson, A., and Zettel, J. "The End of the Quiet Revolution: The Education for All Handicapped Children Act of 1975." *Exceptional Children* 44 (1977): 114-28.

Ballard, J., and Zettel, J. "Public Law 94-142 and Section 504: What They Say about Rights and Protections." *Exceptional Children* 44 (1977): 177-85.

————. "Fiscal Arrangements of Public Law 94-142." *Exceptional Children* 44 (1978): 333-7.

————. "The Managerial Aspects of Public Law 94-142." *Exceptional Children* 44 (1978): 457-62.

"There Are No *Other* Children": Special Children in Library Media Centers

by Eliza T. Dresang

David is six years old. He is deaf, severely retarded, emotionally disturbed, and he spent the first three years of his life locked in a darkened room. A fictional character in a tale from the distant past? No. David is a real child, now living in Madison, Wisconsin with a foster mother and father who love him very much. He attends the Lapham Elementary School, enjoys learning in a classroom with an experienced teacher, joins in playground games with 350 other handicapped and nonhandicapped children, and makes a weekly trip to the media center. David happens to live in one of the states and school districts that has led the way in the education of exceptional children.

The Exceptional Education Law, which became effective in Wisconsin on August 9, 1973, was a forerunner of the national Education for All Handicapped Children Act (PL 94-142), which was passed in the fall of 1975 and became effective in 1978. These laws mandate that handicapped children with exceptional educational needs be educated in the least restrictive environment. The application of these laws means that many children who formerly received no public education or were segregated in separate buildings are now attending school with *typical* children and, as much as possible, are integrated into regular classrooms. (For a more detailed explanation of PL 94-142, see "We Can Grow," *School Library Journal* [May 1977], p.44 and *Early Years* [May 1977], pp.35-73).

In the fall of 1976, Lapham Elementary School was singled out by the National Association for Retarded Citizens as one site for the filming of *The Great Yellow Schooner to Byzantium,* which the association has distributed nationally without charge as part of its effort to increase awareness of what can be done when administrators, teachers, and students work together to provide the optimum education for everyone. (The "Great Yellow Schooner" is a school bus and "Byzantium" is a place where, according to the poet Yeats, everyone reaches his/her highest potential in life.) The handicaps of the 100 *special* students at Lapham may be physical, cognitive, or emotional and are recognized as only a part of the total makeup of each child.

Much effort is put into emphasizing the unique abilities and meeting the individual needs of all children in the school.

Because abilities, not disabilities, are accentuated at Lapham, *labels* of various children are referred to as seldom as possible. Terms like *mentally retarded, physically handicapped,* or *learning disabled* tell us very little about a child. Labeling promotes damaging stereotypes whether it concerns racial, sexual, or handicapped groups. (See the article by Glen G. Foster and John Salvia in *Exceptional Children* [May 1977], pp. 533-4.) I have applied labels sparingly in this article, and the ones I have used here should not be taken as terms that attempt to pinpoint specific personalities or abilities. Also, my use of the terms *special* or *exceptional* does not apply to gifted children.

Before late summer 1974, when I was hired as director of the Instructional Materials Center (IMC) at Lapham, I had had little experience in dealing with handicapped people. I once taught French to blind students, but never came into contact with special children. Moreover, many of the teachers who transferred to Lapham came from schools without media centers and they were as ignorant as I about what the IMC might offer them and their students. Our first year together was one of trial and error, but much progress has been made since then. In the past three years it has become increasingly clear to me that any type of educational program must be developed from an understanding of the needs of the children.

A FUNDAMENTAL NEED

The first and major step in the education of a special child is the recognition of his/her right (and notice I said *right* not privilege) to be served. Librarians must not get caught up in dilemmas about whether to extend service to certain children or whether to limit service. It is the absolute right of every child in a school to receive equal consideration.

As people tour our school and pass through the IMC they have been overheard saying, ''I would like to serve the handicapped students but I am already overworked, understaffed, and overextended. It would not be fair to the other children to try to serve this new group.'' The fallacy in this statement is that there are no ''other'' children. There should be a total IMC program. Media specialists must look at every child, at every need, and at every program in the school and then make across-the-board revisions in the library media center program. They must be inventive and skillful managers of time and resources and learn to look at familiar programs in new ways.

Fear of the unknown is common to all human beings and the thought of serving children with whom we are unfamiliar can produce feelings of anxiety. The most immediate and helpful sources of information about new students are their teachers. It is essential for the school media specialist to spend time with the teacher discussing each child before a special class arrives in the IMC for its first visit (usually these classes are small). They should also discuss the group's needs and expectations. I find it imperative to continue this talk with the teachers informally before school or in the lounge and then to arrange for more formal talks as a follow-up after working with the children for a few weeks. If a child seems more baffling or more difficult to reach than others, I read his/her file and make it a point to inquire specifically about that child's problems.

Reading seems an obvious step for library media specialists in preparing for this new type of service, but the problem is *what* to read. Only one book, *The Special Child in the Library*, edited by Barbara H. Baskin and Karen H. Harris, has been written on the subject of library service to exceptional children. Published by the American Library Association in 1976, the book is a compilation of articles, a number of which are outdated in terms of bibliographies and methods (e.g., mainstreaming is not mentioned). It has some helpful information but cannot be depended on for more recent developments.

On the other hand, too many books and articles concerning specific handicaps are published for the untrained person to be able to select the one or two most informative about a certain disability. Bibliographies of professional literature are numerous and extensive, but these are frequently not selective. You may prefer to consult a teacher or other specialist to guide your self-education.

Misinformation can be damaging and may produce false expectations of the children. Some books, for example, state that trainable mentally retarded (TMR) children cannot read; my own experience proves that this is far from universally true. Journals such as *Exceptional Children, Teaching Exceptional Children,* and *The Exceptional Parent* provide more current insights and more useful information.

The National Center on Educational Media and Materials for the Handicapped (NCEMMH) heads a national network of resource centers which provide information on materials, and sometimes the materials themselves, for educators of exceptional children. (See Part 6 of *The Special Child in the Library*, p. 163, for more detailed information.)

The National Instructional Materials Information Center (NIMIC) is a computerized bibliographical search service designed and implemented by NCEMMH. NCEMMH also publishes a newsletter, *Apropos*, to which media centers should subscribe. A fundamental responsibility of media specialists is to become familiar with the services and resources of NCEMMH and to convey this information to teachers.

MATERIAL NEEDS

There is no doubt that the physical size, shape, and arrangement of a library has an impact on its service to exceptional children. Most obviously this is true for physically handicapped students. A well-planned arrangement of furniture and shelves designed to accommodate children with special needs can promote their independence in using the library facilities.

Although the present state of restricted budgets would not permit major environmental changes in most media centers, small modifications are possible. For example, librarians can order revolving paperback racks that are only 46 inches high. These are accessible even to children seated in wheelchairs.

Beanbag chairs are favorite additions to the IMC at Lapham. After teachers in the orthopedic program saw how the beanbags could be molded to the bodies of the students, providing many more options for positioning, beanbags were purchased for each classroom. Our single, most useful piece of equipment has been the Singer Auto-Vance III. Because it has a large screen and is automatic, this machine allows a small group of children with special handicaps to gather around and view sound filmstrips without assistance. One of the next projects at Lapham is to work with the University of Wisconsin faculty in adapting our audiovisual machines for use by handicapped persons.

Special children do not need a myriad of new materials, either highly specialized or modified versions of those used by other IMC patrons. Take note of some of the filmstrips, records, and other products that many publishers are advertising for special children. They are frequently materials that we have used for years, now grouped under a new heading or title. It is most important to select the most appropriate items in an IMC for each child, whatever his/her *label*.

Occasionally an extension of resources is desirable. For Janice, a partially sighted, retarded student, I purchased a few extra books, some of which she can feel and smell and some with thick cardboard pages that won't rip easily. Recent acquisitions have included *I Am a Mouse* by Ole Risom (Golden, 1974), the Bowmar Manipulative Series, and a "scratch 'n sniff" book. We also use the Talking Books Program, a free program for both blind and physically handicapped people who are unable to use traditional book materials. On request, machinery and materials for the program are sent directly to the child's home or school. Complete information about both talking books and books in braille is available from the Library of Congress, National Library Service for the Blind and Physically Handicapped, 1291 Taylor St. NW, Washington, DC 20542.

It is important to note that most of the special children at Lapham can use the materials and equipment we already have and many of our regular students flock to any new item we receive for special students. Story books in sign language, published by Gallaudet College, 7th St. and Florida Ave. NE, Washington, DC 20002, are popular with hearing impaired children.

After the children become familiar with media center services and programs, they should be directed to other community library resources. Plan a class trip to the public library or ask the children's librarian to visit the school. Send notices to parents or guardians to inform them about resources in the area and how their children can make use of them.

PSYCHOLOGICAL NEEDS

A basic need of all people is to be able to communicate. Handicapped children often require inventive ways of communicating. A teacher of a TMR class at Lapham, Linda Hughes, has a group of students who, although they can hear normally, cannot speak. As an experiment this fall, Linda began using sign language with her class. The music teacher, the gym teacher, and I used the signs we knew. Within a few weeks, a very dramatic change took place in both the behavior and learning of these children because they could finally *speak*. (*Book*, incidentally, is one of the favorite signs of the class.) A high point for me came when Fred, a boy with whom I had had little hope of ever communicating verbally, turned to me and signed an entire sentence.

Some children who are too physically handicapped to sign or speak successfully, but who can read, use a communication board containing the most frequently used words in their vocabularies. They can point to a word they wish to use. When these children come to the IMC, I ask them questions that I know they can answer by using the communication board.

A final important means of communication is body language. All children are sensitive to approval, disapproval, warmth, or reserve. This type of nonverbal communication is accessible to every person, no matter what his/her abilities or disabilities are, and its power should not be under-estimated.

All children need a sense of accomplishment and self-worth. A media specialist is in an ideal position to recognize and reinforce positive aspects of personality. Some retarded people feel ashamed of the way they look. Evelyn Wieble, librarian at Northside Elementary School in Middleton, Wisconsin, helps retarded students at her school overcome this problem by asking them to bring small photographs of themselves to the media center.

Together they make and laminate personalized book marks. Sometimes simply being allowed to do something that other children do can be a great morale booster for a special child.

Books are unknown entities to children who have spent much of their lives in institutions struggling to learn the basic skills of survival. For these children, many weeks or even months of exposure to books may be necessary before they are ready to borrow a book of their own and be responsible for its return. As the right to check out books was extended to each class at Lapham, the pride and happiness the students felt was extraordinary to behold. Julie, a TMR student now reading on a second grade level, is allowed to take out extra books because of her improved reading ability—a special accomplishment for her. All classes now regularly check out books; I have never had a retarded student lose or damage a book.

Encouraging a feeling of self-worth and accomplishment in a child means allowing him/her to be as independent as possible. Once TMR children at Lapham learn to operate the simple equipment, they use the IMC individually as a reward for successful classroom behavior. Jerry, a child with severe cerebral palsy and a fierce drive for independence, has created ways of functioning without help. For example, he operates the remote control buttons of the carousel slide projector with his chin. Jane Besant, the IMC director at Hoyt School in Madison, trains educable retarded children as IMC aides.

It is especially important not to get bogged down with traditional uses of materials and equipment or with time-honored rules and regulations which limit the freedom of certain children. Emily can write her name, but she uses half a book card each time she does it; far better to spend the extra penny for a new card than to insist on writing "Emily" for her neatly on one line.

Linda, an orthopedically handicapped teenager, has some learning disabilities. She is in a class of students who may never be able to use a card catalog without assistance. Nonetheless, I decided to introduce all students to all aspects of the IMC. So one day last year each student picked a drawer from the catalog to look up a subject in which s/he was interested. Linda picked *Friendship*. We located the first three books listed for her to check out, and during the next 12 months she continued to read books on the topic, including easy and difficult books, fiction and nonfiction. The really exciting part of this incident is that Linda had been coming to the IMC for one entire year before this card catalog lesson occurred, and she had never checked out anything but cookbooks, despite my attempts to discover and promote other interests. If I had discounted her class because the students could not use the card catalog in the traditional manner, Linda might still be reading cookbooks. She has now finished all the entries on *Friendship* and has moved on to *Humor*.

Exceptional children do not want to seem *different* because they realize that in all the really important aspects of being human, they are not, in fact, different. So-called typical children can learn this very important fact by being with special children. In turn, special children can experience what society considers *normal* by playing and working with a nonhandicapped peer group. The interaction and togetherness of children who otherwise would have learned and lived apart is known as *mainstreaming*. The school media center is a perfect site for both informal and formal mainstreaming.

If an IMC is run on an unscheduled basis with children coming and going freely, informal mainstreaming takes place whenever special and regular children are present and are using the facilities together. On a recent Wednesday afternoon I observed several fourth and fifth graders working together on a research project, four second graders playing a game, a class of orthopedically handicapped children checking out books, three kindergartners reading with a parent volunteer, and seven emotionally disturbed students viewing a filmstrip with their teacher. (These students usually spend most of the day in a regular classroom and come to the IMC by themselves and once a week with their teacher.) It was an interesting picture of casual interaction and acceptance. All the children were learning something about each other.

Another type of mainstreaming can take place within more formalized or planned activities. At Lapham, in addition to using the IMC independently, the kindergarten, first, and second grades come to the IMC once a week on a scheduled basis, as do the ten classes of special children. An important operation this year has been the pairing of special and regular classes. Each week, a primary TMR class comes to the IMC along with a kindergarten class. The increase in attention span and responsiveness of the TMR children with this exposure to the kindergarten models has been remarkable. Most important, the children have become friends. Recently we had a *farm* day and acted out "The Farmer in the Dell." The children were free to choose whomever they wanted as the wife, child, nurse, cheese, etc. The children in the kindergarten chose children from the TMR class and vice versa. They do not fear one another and do not think of each other as bizarre or different.

When the IMC staff first encounters a new group of students, it finds that the children need to be convinced that an IMC is where they want to be. The more severe the child's handicap, the more difficult this will be. Librarians must become salespeople. It is our professional failure, not the fault of the place or resources, if we do not find a way to convey a feeling of belonging to all the children. We must discover what they enjoy and provide these experiences again and again and again, if necessary, until the IMC becomes a happy learning environment and each visit is a treat.

This past fall some new children joined a TMR class from which the higher achievers had recently graduated. For the first three or four weeks the new arrivals constantly disrupted the old-timers in the IMC, refusing to sit in seats (something never expected of them before), and remaining completely unresponsive to all my tricks of the trade (puppets, flannel board, filmstrips, music, storytelling, etc.). I was almost at my wit's end when suddenly I smelled the aroma of popcorn coming from a room down the hall. The next time this class appeared, I had *Brian Wildsmith's Circus* filmstrip and a popcorn popper on hand. I put the popcorn in the popper, and then showed a filmstrip while it popped. Many people, myself included, are suspicious of stories about dramatic changes, but a miracle occurred—from that day forward, I had the attention of the new children. Eventually, they became interested in other things I had to offer (and, they did not expect to get popcorn each time).

INTELLECTUAL NEEDS

The need for intellectual stimulation, support, and motivation may be overlooked in the case of special children because they may have so many other more obvious needs. Or, this omission may be the result of stereotyping. All physically handicapped children and their families have to fight the pervasive notion that the disabled cannot learn and progress. Similarly, people tend to refer to retarded persons as having the "minds of five-year-olds" as if they are unable to learn and will always remain at that intellectual level.

Exceptional children should be exposed to the best in children's literature and artistry on whatever level they can handle. Simple folktales, for example, can be read and then acted out. One of my favorite books, *The Very Hungry Caterpillar* by Eric Carle (Collins, 1969), was enjoyed by a class of severely retarded students. After the story, Maureen Ellsworth, the librarian, taught them to make paper butterflies. Mixed-media presentations are almost always desirable, but books should not be overlooked.

All school media librarians recognize the necessity of coordinating activities and programs with what occurs in the classrooms. With children who have some sort of impaired learning ability this is crucial, for it is through repetition that they learn. A conceptual approach—organizing units of study around a certain theme, reinforcing classroom activity with field trips—is most successful. If an unfamiliar subject is introduced, the same material should be used on several occasions.

After the emphasis I put on independence, it may seem contradictory to say that one of the most important things the IMC can offer children is a group experience. Because of their unique needs, some special children, particularly those who are severely retarded, have almost totally individualized instruction. In order to enjoy movies or plays or even television, these children must learn to listen attentively as members of a group. The IMC is a perfect place for reinforcing this skill. During group time, the concept that books are a source of pleasure is also introduced. When the media specialist reads aloud regularly, the size, shape, and contents of books become familiar to children who may have once considered them strange objects.

ACCURATE REPRESENTATION

Books dealing with exceptional children are now pouring off the presses. The media staff, even if there is not one special child in the school, needs to be aware of the inaccuracies of representation and the gross stereotypes that have existed in the past or are appearing again in some of these new books, both fiction and nonfiction. *Labels,* such as those to which I referred at the beginning of this article, are used carelessly. As with books portraying racist or sexist images, we should not run to the shelves with a zealous effort to discard in order to show that we are cognizant of the problem. We should learn to discriminate between the good and the poor titles now being published in such numbers and recommend the best ones to students and teachers.

Although many books now focus on special children as protagonists, exceptional children should be included in illustrations and texts that reflect society in general. Victor Fuchs, assistant director of NCEMMH, has pointed out that 99 out of 100 children's textbooks and nonprint materials fail to mention that exceptional persons exist. Close to ten percent of the population are almost completely ignored. Teachers and library media staff should insist that publishers be aware of this omission.

Teachers will ask media specialists for help in preparing a regular class to receive special children. Classroom materials must be previewed with a discerning eye before they are recommended to avoid stereotypes. Some excellent suggestions for preparing these children are also found in the May 1977 issue of *Early Years.*

PARENTAL SUPPORT

Parents of special children, in league with organized groups of handicapped persons, have been chiefly responsible for the legislation which is now requiring education for all children. Media specialists can provide support for these parents who have established their children's right to equal opportunities. This can be done in three ways. Perhaps the most important is to involve parents in school programs. Being a part of a *regular* school will be new to many parents, and they may be hesitant to volunteer for school activities. I use parent volunteers in book fairs, in PTA programs, on field trips, and for IMC routines. Second, as the media staff becomes more knowledgeable about which books are helpful and accurate, it can pass this information on to parents or start a professional collection. Third, the library can provide addresses of national and local organizations offering help and services to handicapped people. Order pamphlets from these organizations to have on hand so that parents can increase their knowledge.

SERVING ALL CHILDREN

The media center or IMC is one of the most positive things in education for exceptional children because the fundamental principle of an IMC is that different children learn in different ways. By presenting material in the medium and format most appropriate to the message being conveyed, each child can be accommodated. Remember that children who cannot see can hear; children who cannot hear can see; children who cannot understand abstraction and generalization can feel and handle and hold the concrete. Children who cannot relate to adults may relate to puppets and stuffed animals or to real animals. In the Lapham IMC we have three gerbils, six fish, and many stuffed animals and puppets. I begin almost every program by using a puppet to talk to the children.

In the IMC special children can increase their vocabularies, reinforce listening skills, and expand their knowledge of both commonplace and exotic things. For children whose mobility may be limited, vicarious experiences are essential. Perhaps more than anything else, a library media center can introduce exceptional children to lifelong sources of recreation, enjoyment, and stimulation.

ADDENDUM

NCEMMH and NIMIC no longer exist but have been replaced by the National Information Center for Special Education Materials (NICSEM), University of Southern California, University Park (RAN) 2d Floor, Los Angeles, CA 90007. NICSEM provides print bibliographies of commercially produced instructional materials for use with special children. It was patterned after the National Information Center for Education Materials (NICEM) indexes. The NICSEM database, available through DIALOG, contains over 36,000 items for use with special children.

MATERIAL SOURCES

Bowmar, Box 3623, Glendale, CA 91201. (Manipulative Books).
The Highsmith Company, P.O. Box 25, Highway 106 East, Fort Atkinson,
 WI 53538. (46-inch revolving paperback racks).
National Association for Retarded Citizens, 2709 Avenue E. East, Arlington,
 TX 76011. (*Great Yellow Schooner to Byzantium*).
Society for Visual Education, 1345 Diversey Pkwy., Chicago, IL 60614.
 (Singer Auto-Vance III).
Weston Woods Studio, Weston, CT 06880. (*Brian Wildsmith's Circus*).

PUBLICATIONS

Apropos. 2-3 yrs. National Center on Educational Media and Materials for
 the Handicapped (NCEMMH), Ohio State University, 220 West 12th
 Ave., Columbus, OH 43210.
Early Years. 9 yrs. Box 7414, Chicago, IL 60680.
Exceptional Children and *Teaching Exceptional Children*. 8 yrs. Quarterly.
 The Council for Exceptional Children, 1920 Association Dr., Reston,
 VA 20091.
Exceptional Parent. 6 yrs. Box 101, Back Bay Annex, Boston, MA 02117.

PART II
MENTALLY RETARDED STUDENTS

Introductory Comments

The mentally retarded are defined in the Education for All Handicapped Children Act as significantly subaverage in general intellectual functioning which exists concurrently with deficits in adaptive behavior, is manifested during the developmental period, and adversely affects a child's educational performance. Stated more simply, an individual under 18 years of age who scores markedly below average on an individual standardized intelligence test and displays social, sensory-motor, and academic skills far below those expected for his/her age range may be termed *mentally retarded*. As with other handicapping conditions, levels of severity range from mild to profound.

While all handicapped children now have the legal right to a "free appropriate public education," those children at the upper end of the continuum of retardation are still seen most often in the public schools. For this reason, as well as the scarcity of journal articles describing programs for the severely and profoundly retarded, the articles chosen for this section deal primarily with the mildly and moderately retarded student.

Even programs for these children are changing, however, with more and more mildly retarded or educable mentally retarded (EMR) youngsters being gradually integrated into certain aspects and sometimes all of the regular school program. Additionally, the moderately retarded or trainable mentally retarded (TMR) child is now less confined to a segregated special class environment.

The lead article in this section, "Selecting a Reading Approach for the Mainstreamed Child," was chosen for its practical approach to the problem of incorporating mildly retarded students into the regular class reading program. In order to select a method of teaching reading and appropriate supplementary materials, the teacher must have a basic understanding of the learning characteristics of the educable mentally retarded child. Sandra B. Cohen and Stephen P. Plaskon review these characteristics and use them to evaluate the six major approaches to the teaching of reading and the advantages and disadvantages of each for use with the EMR child.

Reading and the educable mentally retarded child is also the subject matter of "Reading in Silence: A Chance to Read," but in this article the topic is presented from a different perspective. In recent years many classrooms and even entire schools have initiated a policy of setting aside a specified time each day for students and teachers to read silently from material of their own choosing. Martha Efta's article describes her apprehension at attempting this activity with her highly active group of primary EMR students. She gives details of her gradual implementation of an adapted reading in silence (RIS) program, the rules she found necessary to make, and the means of handling infractions of those rules without interrupting the reading period.

The obvious benefits of practicing learned reading skills in a nonevaluative situation as well as deriving pleasure from materials of one's own selection need not, of course, be limited to EMR children. This approach could be used successfully with many types and age levels of handicapped youngsters as well as with groups integrating the regular and the special student.

The field of library science has long recognized the right of the handicapped to library service. The major journals are including, with increasing frequency, articles describing how the special needs of various groups of handicapped individuals may be served by the staff of public and school library media centers. In order to benefit from the resources of the library and the programs offered, its young users must develop listening skills early. This need is addressed by Hilda K. Limper in "Serving Mentally Retarded Children in Our Libraries." She gives suggestions for teaching these basic skills through the use of storytelling and reading aloud. Titles of books that she has found useful with different age levels of retarded students are incorporated into a discussion of meeting individual needs.

At the junior high level, Michael A. Tulley, Charles P. Edwards, and Michael Olds in "Special Education and the Media Center" describe a media program for EMR students developed through the cooperative efforts of the special education faculty and the media staff. While this particular program may not differ considerably from those of many other schools which tailor library orientation and supplemental activities to their special students, it clearly emphasizes the benefits that may be derived from ongoing communication between members of the school staff. By working closely with the teachers, the media center staff planned programs designed to prepare the EMR student to become capable and enthusiastic library users and, in some cases, media center assistants. Selection, preview, and post-use evaluation of new materials were also conducted as a cooperative effort so that the curricular and leisure needs of the special student could be given ample consideration.

The importance of play is an unquestionable part of the developmental years of any child, and toys are the acknowledged tools of play. Shirley A. Johnson in "A Toy Library for Developmentally Disabled Children" advocates including a toy library in classrooms housing retarded youngsters to be operated similarly to a regular library. She bases her ideas on the results of a program initiated at the Illinois Institute for Developmental Disabilities whereby a toy lending library was established for parents, paraprofessionals, and professionals working with developmentally disabled children. The recipients of the toys were moderately to profoundly retarded children aged 2 to 13. The operation of the library is described, and references on choosing safe toys are included. The thrust of the article, however, is the contention of the author that a similar program could be implemented within individual classrooms. Beyond the obvious benefit of having toys available for the handicapped child, the fundamentals of library use could be taught.

As toys provide a framework for imaginative play, the use of creative dramatics offers a vehicle for expression and communication. Although reprinted in this section on programs for the mentally retarded, "Creative Dramatics" offers a variety of ideas appropriate for all ages and abilities. Included are warm-up games and exercises, pantomime, presenting a story, and role playing. Suggestions are given to the leader in order to individualize the activities for the maximum benefit of the participants.

The development of an enjoyable, meaningful hobby is an important part of life, and perhaps it is even more important for those handicapped individuals whose lives are not as full as one might wish. In " 'Babysitting' for Houseplants," Cynthia R. Chandler relates her experience in helping her teenage trainable mentally retarded students to develop an interest in plants. Advertisements for the plant babysitting service in the school newspaper resulted in quickly turning a portion of the classroom into a greenhouse. Social skills and vocational training were acquired as job responsibilities increased and the interdependence of class members became more evident. Academic skills were also involved as plants had to be labeled and instructions and schedules for their care developed. As the author aptly points out, the introduction of a potential hobby or leisure-time activity into the classroom can contribute relevance to instruction in all areas of the curriculum.

Selecting a Reading Approach for the Mainstreamed Child

by Sandra B. Cohen
and Stephen P. Plaskon

A considerable amount of attention is being given to the return and mainte-nance of the educable mentally retarded in the regular classroom. Mainstream-ing programs which focus on the integration of regular and special education students are developing in school systems across the country. The passage of the Education for All Handicapped Children Act (PL 94-142) in 1975 man-dated that all educators become more involved in programing and adapting methods and materials to meet the needs of these students. This legislation prescribes only the general framework of instructional programing within the least restrictive environment, and does not specify either curriculum or methodology. However, it does have an impact on both of these areas since adjustments in instructional strategies will have to be made in order to successfully mainstream the educable mentally retarded. This fact will become increasingly apparent in the days ahead as teachers seek answers to many disturbing questions regarding differences among student learners.

READING AND THE EMR CHILD

Many regular classroom teachers will now be responsible for teaching mainstreamed educable mentally retarded children in their classes to read. Children who are unable to acquire proficiency in reading skills are often the same children who demonstrate learning difficulties in other academic areas. The term *educable mentally retarded* (EMR) refers to children who, during their school years, experience general learning problems due to lower intel-lectual ability level (below IQ 70) and inadequate social adjustment.

The basic objectives in a reading program for EMR children are the same as for intellectually normal students. The difference occurs in the degree to which they are emphasized. Specifically, the objectives are:

1. To develop a desire to read for information and pleasure.

2. To develop a basic sight vocabulary with emphasis on the child's existing language skills.

3. To develop skills in word analysis for independent reading.

For the EMR child objectives 1 and 2 are the most significant. Children must be motivated by a willingness to read throughout the learning experience in order to overcome the many intermittent frustrations they will most likely encounter, and the development of a functional sight vocabulary is important for children to gain independence as they grow older. Each of the first two objectives is essential for the child's growth and continuance in the reading program. Objective 3 is the one which is the most difficult to obtain. Most EMR children will achieve between a third and a sixth grade proficiency level in reading by the conclusion of their formal schooling. This means that with proper instruction the majority will function as literate adults able to adjust to contemporary demands.

Reading instruction is often beyond the reach of EMR children who have been mainstreamed into a regular class because the program is structured for groups of students without regard to specific learning problems. In order to successfully teach EMR children to read, it is imperative that the classroom teacher have an understanding of some general learning characteristics displayed by such children and their implications for the teaching of reading. By tailoring the reading program to the EMR child's individual needs, the teacher can provide a suitable approach to help the child overcome learning difficulties.

LEARNING CHARACTERISTICS OF THE EMR CHILD

The following learning characteristics are commonly associated with EMR students; however, the reader is cautioned that not all these traits are exhibited by every child, and even within children they vary in intensity.

1. The EMR child *learns best from concrete materials* which are meaningful to the child and the environment. Sight words and reading stories should pertain to experiences the child can relate to and which have relevance for daily life.

2. *Learning is related to the child's mental age (MA), while motivation is often related to chronological age (CA).* Materials selected for reading should be of high interest to the child but contain a controlled vocabulary.

3. *EMR children approach many learning situations expecting to fail*. Activities should be developed to provide successful reading experiences in order to eliminate the child's negative expectancies.

4. *Poor incidental learning skills* mean the child will not acquire a reading skill or concept without direct instruction. This places the responsibility for learning on the adequacy of the teaching plans. Make sure that reading skills are taught sequentially, allowing the child to progress from a learned skill to a more complex one.

5. *Small segments of material are remembered best*. Word lists should be short and stories and other experiences should be divided into manageable units. This allows the child to experience closure with a feeling of success.

6. *Poor retention* of reading skills and sight words can be alleviated by periodic review beyond the initial criterion learning. Reading practice should be distributed throughout the school day and not concentrated within a specified time block.

7. *An inability to transfer* concepts and knowledge results in skills being learned in isolation. Help the child generalize a concept's application by providing a variety of reading experiences.

8. Being *easily distractible*, the child won't always be able to focus upon relevant word stimuli. Attention needs to be trained. Emphasize similarities and differences among words and teach through a variety of modal experiences.

The EMR child learns at an early age the meaning of words and the power they provide. Such children hear words spoken in relation to the objects and activities around them and are eager to expand their world. Unfortunately, the stumbling blocks presented by learning difficulties can have a cumulative effect which will discourage involvement in the reading program. The effective reading teacher will be able to pinpoint specific learning problems and to identify the corresponding teaching implications.

ANALYZING READING PROGRAMS

Once the EMR child's learning characteristics are understood, the teacher can appropriately adjust the reading methods and materials employed. Beyond an understanding of the child's needs, the teacher must be aware of the philosophy and general approach of the reading program used in the classroom. As with normal youngsters, there is no one reading method or program that works best for the mainstreamed child.

The reading process may be insensible to the EMR child simply because the program structure does not meet learning needs. Elements of the philosophical and/or instructional framework of the reading program may not be suited to the manner by which the child acquires and retains information. Without an appropriate match between instructional strategies and learning strategies, a program is destined to encounter failure. Keeping in mind the specific learning characteristics of EMR students, it is possible to analyze the advantages and disadvantages of specific reading approaches. The majority of reading programs fall within the following classifications: a basal approach, linguistic approach, programed instruction approach, phonics approach, alphabetic approach, and language experience approach. Each of the six reading approaches has had an impact on public school programs, some being more successful than others. The analysis to follow should provide the reader with insight into the reasons for program effectiveness or ineffectiveness when considered in light of a broader range of the student population which includes the EMR group.

The advantages and disadvantages of the various reading approaches listed in the table on the following pages are applicable to many children other than the educable mentally retarded. Children of average intellectual ability often experience difficulties with specific approaches used in their classroom reading program. A two-step analysis, such as the one provided in this article, examining the learner's specific difficulties and needs and then delineating the structural advantages and disadvantages of the program in relation to these needs may suggest avenues of remediation for regular as well as special students.

The effectiveness of any reading program depends upon the teacher's ability to select, use, and adjust the approach to the needs of the students. The important ingredients for success in selecting a reading program for mainstreamed EMR children are: (1) awareness of the child's learning needs, (2) fundamental understanding of the reading process and the program's objectives, and (3) a willingness to work through each difficulty by adjusting the instructional program to appropriately match the individual learner.

REFERENCES

Gillespie, P. and Johnson, L. *Teaching Reading to the Mildly Retarded Child*. Columbus, OH: Charles E. Merrill, 1974.

Kirk, S.; Kliebhan, J.; and Lerner, J. *Teaching Reading to Slow and Disabled Learners*. Boston: Houghton Mifflin, 1978.

Matthes, Carole. *How Children Are Taught to Read*. Lincoln, NE: Educators Publications, 1977.

Advantages/Disadvantages of Six Reading Approaches

PROGRAMED INSTRUCTION

Advantages for EMR Children

1. The child is encouraged to proceed at his/her own pace with reinforcement provided at each learning step.
2. Continuous recording of the child's errors provides a learning profile for instructional planning.
3. Learning is designed for the individual child rather than for a group.
4. Instruction is provided in short units made up of many small segments.

Disadvantages for EMR Children

1. Most EMR children are not self-directed learners and, therefore, cannot initiate and pace their learning.
2. Many EMR children lose their initial high motivation and become distracted.
3. The repetitive material often becomes boring and loses the child's attention.
4. Short frames do not allow the EMR child to experience the flow of written language.
5. It is difficult to program advanced comprehension skills within the short frame structure.
6. The instructional frames do not lend themselves to interesting stories. The child does not develop a desire for reading.

ALPHABET

Advantages for EMR Children

1. Simplifies reading by making a direct sound-symbol association.
2. Programed for success which becomes both the reinforcer and the motivator.
3. There are no exceptions to the rule. Therefore, children may learn to read more rapidly than by other approaches.

Disadvantages for EMR Children

1. The child must make the transition from the alphabet approach (e.g., ITA) to the traditional orthography. This is often very difficult for the EMR child to do because of an inability to generalize.
2. The child sees the traditional alphabet outside of school and can become confused.
3. The program does not induce transfer from reading instruction to other academic areas.

PHONICS

Advantages for EMR Children

1. Emphasis upon word recognition leads to independent reading.
2. Increases interest in reading as the child learns to figure out new words.
3. Helps the child to associate sounds and printed letters representing them.

Disadvantages for EMR Children

1. Isolation of speech sounds is unnatural. EMR children often cannot blend the sounds to form complete words.
2. Child learns to read word by word. The EMR child becomes frustrated by new sounds and their blending.
3. Emphasis on word recognition is often at the expense of comprehension.
4. There are many exceptions to every rule. The EMR child may become confused, unable to differentiate the rule from the exception.

BASAL

Advantages for EMR Children

1. A sequentially ordered, comprehensive approach from early readiness to advanced reading levels.
2. Skills are divided into small units for systematic teaching.
3. Establishes a basic vocabulary repeated throughout the sequence.
4. Provides diagnostic tools for pinpointing strengths and weaknesses.
5. Gives the individual teacher guidance in establishing the reading program focus.
6. Many basals emphasize a sight word learning method.

Disadvantages for EMR Children

1. Organizes teaching reading for a group of children rather than for individual needs.
2. Limited vocabulary limits reading to only one basal series — de-emphasizes reading in content areas.
3. Stories and illustrations are often geared to the middle-class child. A majority of EMR children do not fit that description.
4. The material is often too difficult for the children at the lower end of the learning continuum. Using books designed for younger students reduces motivation.
5. Workbooks for skill development result in isolated learning. The EMR student is often unable to make a transfer from skill practice to the reading text.

LINGUISTIC

Advantages for EMR Children

1. Stresses the transition from spoken to written language by showing the child the relationship between phonemes and graphemes.
2. Arranges learning from familiar, phonemically regular words to ones of irregular spelling. This encourages recognition of consistent visual patterns.
3. Child learns to spell and read the word as a whole unit.
4. Creates an awareness of sentence structure so the child learns that words are arranged to form sentences.
5. Teaches reading by association with the child's natural language facility.

Disadvantages for EMR Children

1. Most teachers are not skilled enough in linguistics to develop the necessary program for individual learners.
2. Vocabulary is too controlled and does not approximate the child's speaking skills so that the EMR child has difficulty relating to it.
3. Creates word reading, losing the flow of the sentence.
4. Use of nonsense words for pattern practice is irrelevant and reduces comprehension training.
5. Emphasizes auditory memory skills which many EMR children are deficient in.

LANGUAGE EXPERIENCE

Advantages for EMR Children

1. Employs the child's current oral language abilities as the focus of the reading program.
2. Combines speaking, listening, and writing skills into the reading program.
3. Utilizes direct experiences so the child can relate to the written language form.
4. Adaptable to individual or small groups according to learner and teaching needs.
5. Flexible in style as it may involve narratives, descriptions, and/or recordings of event sequences. This allows an expansion of the child's reading style.

Disadvantages for EMR Children

1. Requires a prolonged attention span which is difficult for many EMR children.
2. May be limited to the child's speaking vocabulary and may not provide a structured enough approach to vocabulary development.
3. The LEA may not have enough consistency in vocabulary or control over syntax to teach and reinforce sequential skills for the EMR child.
4. Relies heavily upon the child's own experiences and ability to relate them.

Reading in Silence:
A Chance to Read

"RIS will now begin!" announces the student leader, having previously checked to see if I am comfortably seated with book in hand. Within moments 16 books open and silence prevails in room 106, a normally active, bustling group of educable mentally retarded children ranging in age from seven to ten years. Only the ticking of the timer and the rustling of pages can be heard. Everyone is "reading."

FINDING THE RIGHT NAME

Reading in silence (RIS) is my class-adapted name for the practice of silent reading without interruption for a predetermined period of time. RIS is representative of USSR, an acronym for uninterrupted sustained silent reading as introduced by Lyman C. Hunt, Jr. of the University of Vermont in the early 1960s. Other names include Robert McCracken's sustained silent reading (SSR)[1] and Marvin Oliver's high intensity practice (HIP).[2]

For several months, the children repeatedly asked for clarification of the USSR acronym. Simpler, more understandable terminology to describe this daily practice seemed necessary. The children responded by offering alternate names which were then posted and voted upon. RIS received a unanimous vote.

GIVING STUDENTS A CHANCE TO PRACTICE READING

Teachers of slow learners know that reinforcement is an integral part of learning any skill. RIS provides an opportunity to personally integrate skills. It is *not* a total reading program. It *is*, simply, an activity providing the children with the opportunity to practice their reading skills privately.

Too often we instruct and assume that the children will practice. But how often do we consistently provide the opportunity for practice? RIS is an attempt to do so.

SETTING UP THE RULES

RIS encompasses the practice of the total reading act including the integration of the reader's sight word vocabulary, decoding skills, comprehension, background experiences, and degree of enjoyment. It can easily be incorporated into any program. The general rules, as concisely outlined by McCracken,[3] are as follows:

1. Each student must read silently.
2. The teacher reads adult fare materials, thus setting an example.
3. Each student selects a single book, magazine, or newspaper. No book changing during the period is permitted. A wide range of materials must be available.
4. A timer is used.
5. There are absolutely no reports or records of any kind required.
6. The teacher should begin with a whole class or large group of heterogeneous students.

Ganz and Theofield[4] also offered helpful suggestions in beginning a sustained reading program.

I first heard about these ideas in a graduate course. The professor seemed enthusiastic about the idea and assured us we would feel the same once we tried it. As I listened to the description of this assignment, I became apprehensive. "It'll never work in my class! My hyperactive children and nonreaders will never last 3 minutes! When can I fit it into the schedule?" After giving serious thought to the rules outlined above, I decided to amend them slightly with my children. Explanation of the practice was discussed, and this more simplified procedure was introduced and posted.

1. Choose any books you wish (with a limit of three).
2. Stay in your seats. (Later the option to sit anywhere was incorporated.)
3. Read silently.
4. Teacher reads; guests read.

We *sustained* for 3 minutes the first day with no infractions. A minute was added every other day until a period of 13 minutes was reached. This seems to be the limit for a silent reading session with this group of primary children.

Even though there are certain guidelines for RIS, we also allow for flexibility. Presently, RIS begins after the noon recess break. This seems to be a good time for the children and me to reorient ourselves to the classroom atmosphere. We will assemble our reading material and show our readiness by placing the signal flag (a square labeled RIS stapled to a straw) on our desks. The student leader for the week checks all signals, puts the sign out on the door ("Silent reading in progress. If you come in, bring a book!"), and signals for all to "find your places." The timer is set. "RIS will now begin!" I vary the time interval from 10 to 13 minutes depending on the daily classroom climate, which fluctuates from a settling calm to an energetic whirlwind.

DEALING WITH INFRACTIONS

Occasional infractions do occur including the whispering to a neighbor or reading aloud. Instead of ending RIS period at the moment of interruption as suggested by Frank Greene[5] and others, the student leader quietly and calmly walks to the reader and removes the book. If the reader has previously selected another book, he may continue reading with the second book. If he has not selected another book, he must quietly sit and wait for the buzzer. In this way, the continuation of RIS for the allotted time allows the students who do follow the rules to continue to read with little interruption. When the timer buzzes, the leader announces "RIS is now over."

To provide added incentive, RIS is tied into our behavior modification system. The student leader is responsible for awarding a point to all readers who have followed the established rules. In order to earn his/her point, the student leader must organize and carry out the RIS procedures and address himself/herself to any major infractions.

SEEING EXCITING CHANGES IN STUDENTS

From the onset of RIS, the students have demonstrated some exciting and favorable behavior changes such as independent decision making, self-discipline, sharing, student leadership, student interaction, and broadened reading interests. The enthusiastic rush to select their day's reading materials following noon recess is indicative of the children's interest and eagerness for RIS. The children seem to delight in the adultlike responsibility of selecting their own reading matter.

Materials provided in the classroom include newspapers, magazines, encyclopedias, picture books, controlled beginning vocabulary readers, and library books. Students have offered books such as comic books, sports program booklets, and discarded textbooks from an older brother or sister.

It is interesting to watch the sharing of the different types of materials among the children. Book chatter and bartering occur, and developing salesmanship abilities are evident in comments such as "You've *got* to read this one; it's so funny" and "Oh, there are two copies of this book. Do you want one?"

Independent decision making plays an important role in the personal development of all children, especially slow learners. The self-selection of reading materials for RIS affords them such an opportunity.

When children are given time to practice reading in school, they are also in control of their reading pace and style. One may opt to flip through a selection prior to reading it, read the conclusion first, or read only the intriguing parts. Using their own personal combination of reading strategies, they attempt to find meaning and enjoyment from print without adult or peer intervention. RIS is for enjoyment and not for answering teacher questions or worksheet problems. Many become absorbed in their reading matter and appear disappointed when the timer buzzes. "Oh, I read *this* far?" is a delightful comment to hear.

Sharing an interesting picture or story situation with the total class has become a daily spinoff activity from RIS. "This Dr. Seuss book has the funniest person in it who does the craziest things" and "Here's a picture in this encyclopedia of Jaws, the great whale. He's out looking for food!" are spontaneous "book reports" of an enjoyable nature.

As a result of RIS, "attention span increases, self-discipline improves, self-selection of reading materials becomes more sophisticated, acceptance and enjoyment of reading improves, and reading skills are refined and extended."[6] My students, many of whom are hyperactive and some of whom are nonreaders, appear to enjoy the quietness of RIS and the opportunity to read. *Reading* for children who daily put forth *so* much effort into learning a single sound or a new sight word is indicative of a beginning reader's positive experience with RIS. "I really like RIS because it's so quiet and peaceful" and "Nobody is walking around, so I don't get mixed up" suggest that RIS is positively affecting the entire learning atmosphere.

SHARING AND MODELING

Sharing and modeling are integral components of RIS. Not only the sharing of materials has occurred but also the sharing of reading spots. Children are found under the television stand, behind the piano, and squeezed together on a carpet. As I delve more deeply into my current novel, sharing an occasional picture or a situation from my book seems to be appreciated. My reading behavior is being mirrored. Children have made and are using their own special bookmarks.

One day a nonreader, who consistently flipped pages as he hurried through book after book, was so engrossed in watching a friend read that he sat immobile, staring for the entire RIS period. Modeling the reading behavior of his friend, he began, in subsequent RIS periods, to scan, through use of his finger, each sentence word by word.

In addition, many student leaders have demonstrated exceptional leadership capabilities as they organize the daily RIS proceedings, thus serving as role models for subsequent student leaders. When weekly jobs are awarded, this leadership role is the most coveted position.

MEASURING THE EFFECTS

Is this daily activity effective? Are the children learning? One study compared reading achievement over ten weeks using sustained silent reading versus selected commercial practice materials commonly used as supplement to a basal instructional program.[7] Findings on the Metropolitan Achievement Test indicated that "SSR as a form of practice was neither more or less effective than a multi-material form of practice."[8]

Future researchers should consider the effects of SSR on the reading interests, skills, and behavioral changes of children. It will be important for all investigators to follow a uniform set of guidelines, such as those outlined by McCracken.[9] The length of the study should be appropriate, so as to allow for the integration of reading skills. If we, as educators, believe in individual differences in learning styles and instructional methodology, we need to use statistical measures that will determine the compatibility between RIS and changes in individual children.

RIS is as much a part of our day as handwriting, arithmetic, and lunch, and the children question if they think it has been forgotten. "Oh, we've *got* to have RIS today; I want to finish my book" and "I told my friend I'd sit by him today" are heard in their pleas for RIS. The children and I really look forward to the opportunity to read silently and without interruption. Although it is difficult to measure, I am observing exciting changes in reading interests, self-discipline, decision making, sharing, student interaction, and student leadership. Sustained silent reading can be a dynamic, enriching, positive experience for you and your students.

NOTES

1. R.A. McCracken, "Initiating Sustained Silent Reading," *Journal of Reading* 14 (1971): 521-4, 582-3.

2. M.E. Oliver, ''High Intensity Practice: The Right to Enjoy Reading,'' *Education* 91 (1970): 69-71.

3. McCracken, ''Initiating Sustained Silent Reading.''

4. P. Ganz and M.B. Theofield, ''Suggestions for Starting SSR,'' *Journal of Reading* 17 (1974): 614-6.

5. F.P. Greene, ''High Intensity Practice,'' Course handout from Syracuse University Clinic, 1971.

6. Oliver, ''High Intensity Practice,'' p. 69.

7. H.M. Evans and C. Towner, ''Sustained Silent Reading: Does It Increase Skills?'' *Reading Teacher* 29 (1975): 155-6.

8. Ibid., p. 156.

9. McCracken, ''Initiating Sustained Silent Reading.''

Serving Mentally Retarded Children in Our Libraries

by Hilda K. Limper

All too often children's librarians are concerned mainly with serving normal children in their libraries and neglect the children who have special reading needs and who could benefit from services which are tailored to meet these needs. By far the largest single group of handicapped children is that of the mentally retarded; and since they are found in almost every community, and most children's librarians at times have opportunity for contact with them, this article will be concerned mainly with library services to this group of children.

TEACH THE CHILD TO LISTEN

First of all, it is necessary to accept these children who, though they have definite limitations, can become contributing members of society. The educable mentally retarded child has an IQ ranging from 50 to 75, and has some potential for book learning. We can contribute to his/her realization of this potential by providing him/her and his/her teachers with suitable materials. We can have a part in making taxpayers instead of tax users of the educable mentally retarded.

The educable retarded children learn to read, albeit more slowly than normal children, and seldom above the fourth grade level. During the pre-reading period, books can play an important role in language development and the readiness program when used for storytelling and reading aloud. I'll always remember the words of a speaker I heard at a conference on the education of retarded children some years ago. "Teach the child to listen," he said, "and then give him something worth listening to." Retarded children do listen to well-selected and well-read or -told stories, and we often hear the same response from them that we get from normal children after a story: "Read it again" or "Read us another story."

It is best to start with realistic stories or those in some way related to the children's experiences. Gradually more fanciful stories can be added, but long complicated fairy tales or fantasies are seldom suitable.

Along with the *stories* we use with educable retarded children during their prereading and early reading period, we give them books on shapes and colors. Dr. Norris Haring says in his *Teaching Reading to Mentally Retarded Children:* "Our first consideration, regardless of the child's age on entering the reading program, is to determine his ability to distinguish forms such as circles, squares, and triangles. To strengthen this ability we use activities that involve the sorting of color and form." A book such as Fredun Shapur's *Round and Round and Square* can be used to advantage to help the child distinguish shapes as well as colors. Others which serve in this capacity are Blossom Budney's *A Kiss Is Round*, Seymour Reit's *Round Things Everywhere*, Ed Emberley's *Wing on a Flea*, and John Reiss' *Color and Numbers*. Another book on color concepts and color combinations is *Little Blue and Little Yellow*. Tana Hoban's book, *Push-pull, Empty-full* is another good concept book showing opposites like 'over' versus 'under', 'up' versus 'down', etc. We've successfully used Helen Buckley's *Grandfather and I* for creative dramatics and taught the children something about the concept of hurrying versus leisurely activity.

INVOLVE THE CHILD IN CREATIVE ACTIVITIES

Many books lend themselves to creative activities where children draw or cut out figures of book characters (if the teacher makes the model) to encourage eye-hand coordination, for this also promotes reading readiness. One of our classes made a collage figure of Curious George holding aloft the bunch of balloons, each balloon having been cut out separately. This took a great deal of eye-hand coordination, and thus enhanced development in the children. The *Curious George* stories, incidentally, are great favorites among retarded children, as are *Harry, the Dirty Dog* and sequels and the *Billy and Blaze* stories.

SATISFY THE INDIVIDUAL'S NEEDS

Naturally, the older retarded readers of teen age are the most difficult age group for whom to supply books they can read and which they find interesting. Many of them do like animal and nature books, and several publishers have made available easy books in this category. Follett's Beginning Science series has such useful titles as *Snakes, Robins, Alligator*

Hole, Birds That Hunt, Insects and *Hummingbirds*. The Crowell Let's-Read-and-Find-Out series also has good, well-illustrated titles in this category—among them *Giraffes at Home, Spider Silk, It's Nesting Time, The Blue Whale, Rain and Hail, Flash, Crash, Rumble and Roar*, and several titles on astronomy and space.

The Garrard Junior Science Books have such useful books as the *Junior Science Book of Stars* and the *Junior Science Book of Beavers*. The Random House Gateway Books offer titles like *The Friendly Dolphins*, and *All Kinds of Seals*. *The Sun, the Moon, and the Stars* is in their Easy to Read series.

Franklin Watts has a useful series they call Let's Find Out About, and includes both nature subjects and biography. The ones on snakes and birds are particularly useful as are the biographies of Lyndon Johnson, Abraham Lincoln, and Thomas Edison.

We find that the easy brief biographies make good reading for junior high retardates. Several publishers now offer such biographies which have largely supplanted the Bobbs-Merrill Childhood Stories of Famous Americans series. The Crowell series is probably the best for teenage retardates and offers such popular subjects as Wilt Chamberlain, Jackie Robinson, Jim Thorpe, Samuel Clemens, and Marian Anderson. The Putnam Beginning to Read series offers such modern subjects as Lyndon Johnson and John F. Kennedy, and historical figures like Daniel Boone, Abraham Lincoln, and Sam Houston. The Garrard Discovery Books are a little longer, but still easy and include such women as Annie Oakley, Florence Nightingale, and Eleanor Roosevelt and men like the Wright brothers and Frederick Douglass.

Retarded boys are not exceptional when it comes to an interest in racing cars and motorcycles. They ask for books on these subjects more often than almost anything else. Edward Radlauer has contributed a number of books in the field which some of the boys can manage and like. They include *On the Drag Strip, Karting Challenge, Scramble Cycle*, and *Mini-bike Challenge*. They are well illustrated with color photographs and are fairly easy books of information in the story form. A little similar and quite simple is *Drag Racing* by Julie Morgan.

Fiction on the same subjects is available in the Checkered Flag series by Field Enterprises Educational Publications. Although the stories are mostly acceptable, the textbook format is against them. The covers are not inviting and don't indicate the content of the individual titles. The stories cover both auto and motorcycle racing, yet all have the same checkerboard cover. The best of the series are probably *Scramble, Smashup*, and *The Riddler*—the latter having a slight mystery.

Fiction, generally, is more of a problem than nonfiction for the older retarded reader. Some of the less mature readers will read the easy Coatsworth titles and books by Clyde Bulla, Patricia Lauber, Miriam Mason, Margaret Johnson, and Matthew Christopher. In fact, we served one home-bound retarded girl in her late teens who likes frontier stories, and was quite happy with Coatsworth's *Sod House* and *Dancing Tom,* Mason's *Caroline and Her Kettle Named Maud* and Dalgliesh's *Courage of Sarah Noble.* For the mystery fans we have successfully used Frederic Martin's *Mystery under the Fugitive House* and *Mystery at Monkey Run,* Mary Adrian's *Fire House Mystery* and *Skin Diving Mystery,* Rambeau's Morgan Bay mysteries, Bulla's *Ghost on Windy Hill,* and Warner's *Snowbound Mystery.* But for those who want modern teenage stories, there is a dearth of material available, for even the Doubleday Signal books are too difficult for them. We hope that in time publishers will respond to the need.

Since September 1973 we have made available a revision of our list of books for retarded children. The booklet contains four separate lists, three for the different age groups of educable mentally retarded children, and one list for trainable retarded. The booklet, entitled *Books for Mentally Retarded Children* (1977, 6th printing), is available for $1 from the Exceptional Children's Division of the Public Library of Cincinnati and Hamilton County, 800 Vine Street, Cincinnati, OH 45202.

Many of the books listed are also suitable for deaf children and those with learning disabilities since they are educationally retarded and need easy materials. We urge those of you who have the opportunity to serve any of these special children to do so with the knowledge that it is definitely worthwhile.

It is through reaching out
that a child grows and
finds out who s/he is.
For some children this is
exceptionally difficult.
In what ways can the
library help such children
to reach out?

Special Education and the Media Center

by Michael A. Tulley,
Charles P. Edwards,
and Michael Olds

It is a popular misconception that educable mentally retarded (EMR) students cannot take full advantage of resources available in the media center. While certain obstacles do exist which inhibit full utilization of the media center (MC), at South Wayne Junior High School in Indianapolis we have developed a program which makes use of the media center an integral part of the special education curriculum.

At South Wayne it is the intention of the EMR staff to provide educational experiences similar to those of the other students. Use of the resources available through the media center is, of course, a vital element of the regular curriculum. In addition, the media center itself is a very popular facility with South Wayne students because of the diversity of recreational and instructional activities made available to them. It was this desire to provide the entire scope of available services and resources of the media center which led the special education faculty and the media staff to develop a media center program from which EMR students could also benefit.

The secondary special education program at South Wayne consists of two teachers in a team setting. The number of students is generally 20 to 25. Students' abilities fall within the EMR range of intellectual functioning. (For our purposes, the EMR IQ category is 55 to 80.) The special education teachers use two adjoining open space classrooms which can be altered physically into larger or smaller units as needed. There is also access to a self-contained classroom. All classroom space is situated physically close to the MC. Students have access, through mainstream scheduling, to art, music, home economics, and industrial arts teachers. The special education staff is responsible for four academic subject areas: English/reading, math, social studies, and science.

Students are in assigned grade levels 7, 8, and 9. Levels of functioning, mental ages, and curriculum fall into the upper elementary level (grades 3 through 6).

Instructional classes are formed heterogeneously with the criteria being ability, age, and grade level. Within that framework, most work is individualized to fit students' needs as determined by periodic individualized education program (IEP) sessions. Emphasis is placed on prevocational skill formation.

The MC staff meets regularly with the special education staff, and that cooperation has made possible the following components of our program:

1. Team planning;
2. Formation of a media center introduction and orientation sessions designed especially for EMR students;
3. Materials selection, purchase, and evaluation;
4. Materials exchange with other media centers;
5. Formation of educationally oriented supplemental activities for students' independent study periods; and
6. Videotape recording for performance evaluation.

South Wayne principal Dr. Duane Fleener, long a proponent of the team concept in education, provides the time and structure necessary for interdepartmental cooperation. Within that framework, we enjoy the flexibility which allows for diversity of curriculum. During a typical team planning session, discussion involves the use of instructional materials and alternative methods of instruction.

One of the first products of these team planning sessions was the creation of an introductory orientation to the MC, designed and geared exclusively for the EMR students. Conducted early in the school year, these sessions included instruction in the use of the card catalog, arrangement of materials, and services and resources available through the MC. In addition to informal discussions designed to acquaint the EMR students with the media staff, activities included hands-on experiences with shelving materials, perusing low readability reference materials, and operating several types of audiovisual and production equipment.

The use of individualized instruction, repetition, and ability grouping distinguishes the EMR library skills program from the one used with other students. The orientation program has been so successful that, for the first time, some EMR students have served as media center assistants this year. The students have exhibited a strong desire to learn the operations of the media center and, as a result, have come to be very valued employees.

Prior to the purchase of new materials, the following process is implemented. The special education staff defines and identifies curricular needs and relates them to the media staff.

The media staff provides catalogs and other selection tools. At team planning sessions, the media staff and special education staff develop a list of possible purchases. After priorities are assigned, many of the items are ordered for preview.

The media staff offers advice for possible use of the materials in the classrooms. A post-use evaluation determines the desirability of the materials in terms of effectiveness, student acceptance, and curricular relevance. The media staff and special education staff use this evaluation as the basis for determining which materials shall be purchased.

The media staff and special education staff had an excellent opportunity this past school year to cooperate in the purchase of instructional materials when they collaborated to prepare a program for utilization of ESEA Title IV B funds. This allowed for the maximum exploitation of our diverse talents: the media staff's knowledge of materials and the special education staff's understanding of the needs and abilities of the students.

To achieve the desired degree of individualization, it is necessary to have access to materials from a wide range of levels. Toward that end, the media center staff assists the special education faculty in obtaining materials from other sources. Among the sources which are utilized are the school corporation motion picture library, the Indianapolis/Marion County Public Library Film Library, and commercial sources.

The media center staff also initiated an interlibrary loan program which makes a variety of print and nonprint materials from elementary school media centers in the school corporation available for use by the EMR students in our building. Such an arrangement provides for maximum use of all funds and materials at the school system level. Special education and media staff members maintain a file of materials borrowed from outside sources which are noted for desirability and include suggestions for future use.

At South Wayne, the EMR students are given study time equal to that of other students; this time may be used in one of several ways. Visiting the media center is one of the student's many options.

For students who choose the media center, the same number of options are available to them as the other students enjoy. Sixteen-millimeter motion pictures concerning a wide variety of educational and interesting subjects are shown to students in the media center. Audiotapes, including recordings of all types of popular music, are available to students to listen to at individual wet [with electrical power] carrels.

Educational games, including many popular board games, may be used in the media center. Students may choose to use one of the typewriters located in the media center to complete an assignment. The periodical browsing area offers a variety of current, popular magazines and newspapers. Filmstrip, slide, and audiotape presentations may be viewed by all students on one of the media previewers located throughout the media center. Media staff members are always available to assist students in selecting materials for recreational reading and locating materials for completing assignments. EMR students seem to enjoy the opportunity to visit the media center and, as a result, often take advantage of the resources available.

One method employed to evaluate classroom and material effectiveness is the videotaping of unrehearsed classroom performances, including reading group sessions, oral recitations, and role playing situations. The videotapes are used to allow the teachers to critique the students' performances and the success of various instructional methods.

The tapes are also submitted to outside consultants, including university instructors and other educators, for their reactions and suggestions. Students welcome the opportunity to review their own performances in individual and group settings.

Achieving equal educational opportunities for EMR students is still beyond reality in many school settings. A totally effective curriculum will depend upon the ability to approach the least restrictive environment which allows for the realization of maximum potential. Utilization of the valuable resources of the media center and cooperation with the special education staff are important steps toward that goal.

A Toy Library for Developmentally Disabled Children

by Shirley A. Johnson

Classroom teachers of developmentally disabled children are constantly looking for new and effective ways of providing these children with rewarding and meaningful learning experiences. This article offers ideas for the implementation of an alternative program in the typical classroom setting.

Play is as natural and important for the child as work is for the adult; therefore, it is imperative that the classroom teacher capitalize on the learning potential in play. Play provides the vehicle through which the child is learning to learn. It helps the child gain confidence through discovering how to come to terms with the world, to cope with life's tasks, and to master skills. A child's play is his/her way of exploring and experimenting while s/he builds up relations with the world and with himself/herself.

Play, both solitary and group play, contributes to a child's intellectual development. Piaget[1] has suggested that intelligence develops as the individual constructs a cognitive framework, which Piaget terms *logico-mathematical*. This framework is the result of the child's exploratory, thinking, and knowing activities and is important for the construction and memory of knowledge.

THE ROLE OF TOYS IN PLAY

One of the most effective tools that can be used in the classroom to encourage play is the toy. Retarded children have been helped to master skills and develop confidence with toy practice.[2]

A unique way to make toys available in the classroom is to develop a toy library. In addition to providing a medium in which learning can take place, a toy library also prepares the child with prerequisite skills that are required when using a regular library in the community.

Experts recognize four main types of play that contribute to well-balanced learning experiences for children:

1. Active/physical play.
2. Manipulative, constructive, creative, and scientific play.
3. Imitative, imaginative, dramatic play.
4. Social play.

The toys in a toy library should be appropriate for and encourage these four main types of play.

TOY LIBRARY OPERATIONS

On the basis of these ideas, the Education Program Development section of Illinois Institute for Developmental Disabilities housed a toy lending library for nine months. The library was opened to parents, guardians, paraprofessionals, and professionals who had or who worked with developmentally disabled children. The day-by-day operation of the library was modeled after traditional public libraries, but housed toys instead of books.

The toys could be used in the library or checked out of the library for instructional use. The checkout period for each toy was three weeks. At the end of the period, the toy had to either be returned to the library or checked out for another three-week period.

An activity file was kept on each toy in the toy library. When a toy was checked out of the library, an activity card was given to the person checking out the toy. This card offered ideas as to how the toy might be used. (See Figure 1.) Also, someone was always available during the open hours of the toy library to give demonstrations to teachers and parents on how each toy could be used.

Toys for a child's age level and interest encourage play for which the toys are designed and thus reduce the chances for accidents. In choosing safe toys for the library, particular attention was given to *Abbreviated Staff Analysis to Toy Injuries* (P 1300 series, excluding P 1313), *Consumer Product Safety Commission, September 25, 1973 Report* and the *Banned Products* (Special Holiday Issue) Volume III, Part I, October 1, 1974, all published by the US Government Printing Office.

A toy library newsletter was published monthly and featured topics such as "Homemade Toys," "Toy of the Month," and "Why Play?"

THE LIBRARY CONTENTS

Commercial toys were intentionally chosen over homemade toys in order to evaluate the appropriateness of commercial toys for the developmentally disabled child.

Figure 1 Sample Activity Card

RUBBER KINDERGARTEN BALLS A person sits or stands behind the child directing him/her in the activity as needed.

ROLLING

1. Two persons and the child sit on the floor facing each other. The child sits between the legs of person 1 with his/her legs opened. Person 2 faces person 1 and the child with his/her legs opened. The ball is rolled between person 2 and the child. The child is assisted by person 1 if needed.

2. The child sits between the legs of a person facing the wall. The ball is rolled against the wall by the child and rolls back to the child. This activity is continued in this manner. The person assists the child as needed. One may start the activity two to three feet away from the wall, and as the child's skills improve the distance between the wall and the child may be increased.

3. The child rolls the ball at a target (e.g., a milk carton, large plastic bottle, or opened box). This activity may be done sitting or standing.

BOUNCING

1. This activity may be done standing or sitting.

THROWING

1. The child throws the ball to another person.

2. The child throws the ball against the wall.

3. The child throws the ball into a box, wastebasket, plastic clothes basket, etc.

4. The child throws the ball at a target (e.g., a milk carton, large plastic bottle, or opened box). This activity may be done sitting or standing.

5. The child practices throwing overhand and underhand with another person.

CATCHING

1. The child catches the ball when someone else throws it.

2. The child throws the ball against a wall and catches its.

KICKING (OUTDOOR ACTIVITY)

1. The child practices toe kicking.

2. The child kicks with the sides of his feet.

3. The child directs the kick toward a target (e.g., milk cartons, a line, or boxes).

The children who used the library were mostly profound, severe, and trainable handicapped children between the ages of two and thirteen years. The toys in the library were recommended for children between the ages of zero and nine years and were available in six categories:

1. Balls (12)
2. Blocks (20)
3. Colors (67)
4. Noisemakers (27)
5. Shapes (49)
6. Wheels (18)

The number after each category indicates the number of toys in the library of that particular category. For example, there were 12 different types of balls in the library. Some of the toys may have been included in more than one category. For example, the clutch ball was included in the noisemakers category as well as the balls category.

THE SIX-MONTH REPORT

The six-month report revealed that 943 individuals visited the toy library. Each toy was evaluated in the following areas: self-initiated play, play initiated by someone other than the child, solitary play, group play, and the number of times that each toy was checked out of the library.

The individuals who returned the toys to the library evaluated the toys as poor, fair, or good. See Figure 2 for details on the number of children observed interacting with toys in the different areas of play.

At the end of the first six months, the circulation statistics disclosed that 444 toys had been checked out of the toy library by the children who used it. Parents and/or professional staff (e.g., teachers, speech and language specialists, occupational therapists, physical therapists) checked out 226 toys, which were used in instructional programs for the developmentally disabled child. Statistics also showed that in 771 instances the toys were involved in self-initiated play, 221 instances in play initiated by others (an adult or another child), 712 instances in solitary play, and 131 instances in group play. Evaluations of the toys revealed 226 good ratings, 22 fair, and 10 poor.

On the basis of number of interactions, certain preferred toys were selected. The preferred toy in each of the six areas is as follows:

- Balls: Pom Pom Game
- Blocks: Educubes
- Colors: Take Apart Car
- Noisemakers: Pocket Radio Music Box
- Shapes: Gingerbread Game
- Wheels: Take Apart Game

Figure 2 Data Collected during the Three-Month Follow-up Period.

Category	June	July	August
TYPE OF PLAY			
SELF-INITIATED PLAY			
Females	60	49	38
Males	52	22	30
PLAY INITIATED BY OTHERS	9	15	12
(Adult or Another Child)	103		
SOLITARY PLAY			
Females		56	28
Males		21	25
GROUP PLAY	17	7	11
TOYS CHECKED OUT			
Females	4	0	3
Males	3	0	4
Adults	28	27	22
EVALUATION OF TOYS			
Good	54	26	62
Fair	3	1	1
Poor	4	3	0
PREFERRED TOYS	Lock 'N Stack Blocks	Actions Blocks	Take Apart Car
VISITOR'S SCORE	88	100	40

The toy interacted with most in the above categories was the Take Apart Car (produced by Playskool). This toy is recommended for children between the ages of three to six years. It is a wheel toy that also provides for color recognition stimulation. The child learns how to take the toy apart and how to rebuild it. Here, one can capitalize on the concepts of part and whole.

The Pom Pom Game (produced by Fisher-Price) is recommended for children three years or older. It is an excellent game for two, three, or four persons to play at the same time. There are seven assorted plastic balls, and the first person to get the seven balls in the basket is the winner. The game aids in developing coordination and manual dexterity, reinforces color recognition, and offers exciting entertainment.

Educubes (produced by Learning Products, Inc.) are multifunctional, colorful giant building blocks. The giant cubes are tough and sturdy and are not harmed by enthusiastic use. The cubes come in red, blue, yellow, orange, and green. These blocks are recommended for preschool age to six years of age. Color recognition and construction and building skills can be developed through the use of these giant cubes.

The Pocket Radio Music Box (produced by Fisher-Price) is a durable toy that provides one the opportunity to listen to a tune while watching a picture story that corresponds to the tune. It has a plastic front, a rear wooden case, and a carrying strap. This radio enhances listening skills and is recommended for children between the ages of one to five years.

The Gingerbread Game (produced by Romper Room) is recommended for children between two-and-one-half to six years of age. The Gingerbread Game consists of a plastic house and four gingerbread figures. Small decorative shapes can be dispensed from the house and fitted into the matching shape depressions in the gingerbread figures. This is an excellent game for teaching and reinforcing shape and color discrimination skills. However, one primary deficiency of this game is that it is not durable.

Of the five most preferred toys, four of them had the property of color and one was a noisemaker. The toys least interacted with were the Wiffle Ball, Thing Puzzle, and Punch-A-Shape. The least durable toys were found to be Close 'N Play Automatic Phono and Jukebox (these two produced distorted sounds); Turn-Gear and Gingerbread Game were made of plastic material that cracked easily. The other 143 toys were found to be quite durable for the children who visited the library.

The individuals who used the library were cooperative in returning the toys which they checked out. There were only four toys that were checked out of the toy library and not returned.

See Figure 2 for a three-month follow-up report on the library.

AN INEXPENSIVE, SUCCESSFUL APPROACH

The toy library was found to be an inexpensive way of providing appropriate toys for developmentally disabled children. Often, parents could not afford to buy toys, did not know the appropriate toys to buy, or found it impractical to obtain all the toys that their child may have shown an interest in and all the toys that could aid the child in developing skills. Therefore, parents, classroom teachers, speech therapists, and occupational therapists saw the toy library as a practical alternative in offering a large variety of selectively chosen toys for developmentally disabled children.

As a classroom teacher, you and your children will find that the toy library provides an exciting environment in which to learn and offers a unique approach in providing instructional materials to the developmentally disabled child.

NOTES

1. J. Piaget, *Play, Dreams, and Imitation in Childhood* (New York: W.W. Norton, 1962). First published in French in 1946.

2. I. Cleper, *Growing Up with Toys* (Minneapolis, MN: Augsburg Publishing House, 1974).

Creative Dramatics

by the American Alliance for Health, Physical Education, Recreation, and Dance (AAHPERD)

The term *creative dramatics* implies acting out situations without formal or strict guidelines. The focus is on expression of one's feelings and working cooperatively with others. *Participation*, rather than finished *product*, is emphasized.

Creative dramatics can contribute to development of:

- Verbal and nonverbal communication skills,
- Respect for others' attempts at expression and communication,
- Body awareness,
- Body coordination,
- Listening skills,
- Sensory awareness,
- Individuality within a group setting, and
- Imagination.

Other values of creative dramatics experiences are:

- Opportunities for freedom of expression;
- Acceptable outlet for tension; and
- Participation in a successful, fun experience.

A wide variety of activities are possible in a creative dramatics program for individuals of all ages and abilities. For example, individuals who cannot speak can pantomime stories; persons with severe movement restrictions may perform as narrators; very young or severely retarded children can present simple stories or mimes; older individuals may want to write and improve their own dramatic productions. All activities included here can be varied to suit the ages and abilities of participants.

WARM-UP GAMES AND EXERCISES

These activities help creative dramatics participants become more aware of their senses and bodies. Such awareness is extremely important as a prelude to more sophisticated activities. Exercises generally are conducted in a circle or with participants scattered around the room.

EXERCISE 1. *Listen* for all the sounds around you; each person in turn tells what s/he has heard.

EXERCISE 2. *Look* around the room and list all that you have seen after a specified period of time.

EXERCISE 3. With a partner, *study* what the partner is wearing; the partner changes three things; what has been changed?

EXERCISE 4. *Touch* various objects (a ball bearing, dirt, sandpaper, a lizard) and *name the feeling* they give you.

EXERCISE 5. With hands behind back, *feel* various objects and *identify* them.

EXERCISE 6. *Identify* various *sounds* created by the leader (pebbles being dropped in a pail of water, light switch turned on/off, sweeping a floor, taking a wrapper off candy).

EXERCISE 7. Using the whole body, *pretend* to be a ballet dancer, inchworm, puppet on a string, racing car, rolling ball.

EXERCISE 8. Using only *fingers* and hands, be a butterfly, a snowstorm, three people walking together.

Leadership Hints

Since there are no right or wrong answers in creative dramatics, these activities are particularly good for groups that mix individuals of differing abilities. The leader should be sure to encourage different approaches to the same exercise. For example, in Exercise 4 recognize that not all participants will derive the same sensation from touching the same object, and discourage stereotyped responses by saying, "Who gets a different feeling from touching the dirt?" In exercises like 1 and 2 the leader can prevent competition from developing by asking each person in turn to name one thing that s/he has seen or heard, rather than letting each participant recite a list of all things seen/heard.

Several retarded, speech impaired, or withdrawn participants may have had little experience in expressing themselves in a group. Some individuals may not know how to respond, even to activities that allow a wide range of responses. It may be best to start these individuals in small groups with simple movement exploration activities to involve them in learning about parts of their bodies, movement, basic motor skills, and simple language and commands. Warm-up games and exercises can then be used to reinforce language concepts. For example, instead of having these participants identify sounds that they cannot see, show them a pail filled with water, drop pebbles in it, and have them name these objects; as language skills are acquired, use the exercises to elicit simple verbal responses.

When physically handicapped participants are involved, especially those having severe mobility limitations, use Exercise 7 to encourage movement and develop motor abilities. Again, since no response is right or wrong, recognize all attempts at movement, perhaps having participants explain why they chose a particular approach.

Exercises 1, 4, 5, and 6 are good for helping visually impaired persons strengthen their other senses, as well as preparing them for additional creative dramatics experiences. When having these individuals act out words or situations (as in Exercises 7 and 8), be sure you are using concepts with which they are familiar and can call upon past experience to perform.

PANTOMIME

Formation for these activities is the same as for warm-up games and exercises—all in a circle or scattered about the room. All individuals participate simultaneously and without verbalization, which makes pantomime particularly suitable for withdrawn and speech handicapped persons. Some individuals undoubtedly express themselves *best* this way.

Some examples of activities using pantomime are:

- Participants are all mirrors and must reflect motions and expressions made by the leader; this can be done with partners, too.
- Let's pretend to be

  — a spaceship blasting off,   — flipping pancakes,
  — cooked and uncooked spaghetti,   — playing basketball together,
  — combing our hair,   — cutting and raking grass, or
  — riding a bumpy subway,   — a taxi driver.

Leadership Hints

Be sure to draw upon experiences familiar to participants when creating pantomimes, especially with very young or low functioning children. Keep activities simple and short until participants become more adept and at ease.

As individuals becomes less inhibited and embarrassed, half the group could serve as audience and half as performers, with individuals eventually performing alone. In some activities, such as mirroring, participants could eventually act as group leaders.

ORFF-SCHULWERK

This approach to creative dramatics began as a simplified approach to music and rhythm for the classroom. Originally introduced into the German school system by Carl Orff, the Orff-Schulwerk process was intended for children ages five through twelve. However, it has been successfully used with mentally retarded teens and adults. The process has also been used in a variety of settings—therapeutic, clinical, recreational, as well as educational.

Orff-Schulwerk starts with an idea, then expands on it through four processes:

- Improvisation,
- Selectivity,
- Fulfillment, and
- Closure.

A good example of the way in which these processes mesh is presented by the drama-music program at the Recreation Center for the Handicapped (207 Skyline Blvd., San Francisco, California 24132). At the beginning of an activity session with the Day Trippers, a group of 25 moderately mentally retarded adults, participants were asked if they had heard anything about a recent major fire in San Francisco. Several said they had, and this stimulated a discussion about how fires start. A pantomime fire was built in the middle of the circle, with the leader warning the group not to get too close. This evolved into a chant:

If you get too close,
You can burn your pants;
If you burn your pants
It'll make you dance.

To the beat of a drum, each participant in turn did a fire dance around the imaginary fire. After each had danced, it was suggested that as a closure the fire be put out. The group tightly encircled the fire and blew it out.

In this particular example *improvisation* involved exploration of the concept of fire. *Selectivity* occurred as participants, guided by the leader, decided upon the best way to build the story. In acting out the fire story participants achieved *fulfillment,* and *closure* was achieved naturally because the story had a definite end.

Leadership Hints

All kinds of ideas can be expanded into Orff-Schulwerk experiences, with both participants and leader developing chants and using rhythm instruments to accentuate the chanting and movement. Activities can be simplified for severely retarded participants and easily expanded and made more complex according to participants' abilities and creativity. When accompanied by the beat of a drum, deaf individuals can also take part, either by speaking or signing chants. There is no right or wrong—only the assumption that every individual is capable of creative growth.

PRESENTING A STORY

For people of all ages, acting out a story read by the leader is great fun. Some highly professional productions have been developed from what was originally a spontaneous interpretation of a story-reading. Short stories with plenty of action are particularly effective.

The reason acting out stories can be so successful is that it is a non-threatening kind of activity. Emotions and situations which the participants must act out are not *their* emotions or predicaments, but the feelings and expressions of a character in a story. In addition, this activity truly allows each to participate fully according to his/her own abilities. Those with freedom of movement can act; those with severely limited movement can make, arrange, and set up simple props. In some presentations, severely handicapped persons in wheelchairs have actually become parts of the scenery, such as the sun moving across the horizon or a car or bus passing by.

Some of the methods of acting out stories include:

- The leader pauses while reading a story and the whole group acts out the particular action demanded;

- The leader assigns parts (or participants choose), and participants only act out parts of the story dealing with their particular character;

- The leader tells the whole story, the group divides it into scenes, and each scene is acted out;

- The group makes up stories to act out;

- The leader starts reading a story and asks the group, "And what happened next?" The whole group or individuals then act out the story's conclusion;

- Group acts out musical stories, either simultaneously or by assigning a part to each participant ("Peter and the Wolf," for example).

Leadership Hints

Story narration must take participants' abilities into account. The narrator should read slowly enough for the slowest participant and be alert to repeat cues if necessary.

A part of the activity can be found for every participant, despite speech, mobility, or other limitations or apprehension to participate. Those who cannot read can act out parts; those who have severely limited movement can serve as narrators; those who are apprehensive to act may be assigned a group walk-on part; all can enjoy simple behind-the-scenes activities, such as locating props, designing scenery, and making costumes. Often participants themselves can suggest or develop adaptations that permit them to take part in the activity. Certainly, no individual should be denied participation in these activities based on disability.

In terms of props, scenery, and costumes, these may make a story presentation more realistic for the players but should not *overwhelm*. The most successful approaches have been those utilizing the merest hint of scenery and costumes. For example, players wearing wide-brimmed hats with brightly colored towels draped over their shoulders stand in front of a brightly painted cardboard archway to set the scene in Mexico; waves cut out of cardboard and painted blue are pasted to two chairs, suggesting that participants are in rowboats; one player becomes a snow-capped mountain by draping an old blue sheet with a white circle painted in the middle over herself and her wheelchair.

Presenting a story can be easily adapted to ages of participants by selecting stories from different reading levels. The leader can find a wide variety of suitable stories among the plays and short stories in the public library. Or, participants can adapt or write their own stories. When involving mentally retarded participants, the leader should always consider chronological age rather than mental age in selecting stories. Better to rewrite an adult's story with simpler words than to have a group of mentally retarded adults acting out a children's fairy tale.

ROLE PLAYING

Adolescents, adults, and individuals who have trouble handling their emotions or dealing with problems may enjoy this creative activity. In treatment settings for emotionally disturbed, behavior disordered, or mentally ill persons, role playing assumes a place with the other adjunctive therapies as a treatment modality. In such settings supervised role playing sessions have been found successful in helping participants face their problems, understand why other people act the way they do, and develop new ways of dealing with difficult situations.

Role playing can also be a fun addition to the recreational creative dramatics program, however. In this sense, it often borders on improvisation as players select situations, occupations, and people to characterize.

Some activities for role playing include:

- Individuals choose and attempt to portray a character, such as a courtroom judge, teacher, waiter/waitress;
- Two or more individuals act out a situation selected by the leader or chosen by the group;
- The leader describes a situation, then asks the whole group to act out what they would do if it happened to them.

Leadership Hints

Unless supervised by a psychologist or trained psychodrama specialist, role playing should never be approached as a psychotherapeutic exercise. The leader might open the door to a situation that s/he is totally unprepared to adequately cope with and cause undue distress to a participant.

Even when role playing activities are recreational, the leader should never imply that the session is being held to examine participants' problems. It would be more appropriate for the leader to hold "What Bugs Me Is..." sessions in which each participant assumes the role of a character in a particularly annoying situation. This activity is both fun and cathartic for participants. The leader might also keep a box full of role play ideas written on pieces of paper; individuals draw from the box and then present the particular idea.

OTHER RELATED ACTIVITIES

The creative dramatics activities presented suggest numerous possibilities for complementary activities.

- *Making Masks*. Use paper bags, newspapers, tempera paints, inexpensive masks from toy shops as bases for more elaborate creations, and chicken wire covered with papier-mâché; these can be colorfully painted and built upon using one's imagination. Many times individuals who fear performing before a group will more readily participate when protected by a mask. Cerebral palsied individuals who are self-conscious about facial distortions sometimes feel more comfortable when wearing a mask in initial creative dramatics activities.

- *Make Up*. Grease paint sticks are best for this, but be sure to first apply a thin layer of cream to each person's face. Be sure no one is allergic to such makeup.

- *Dressing Up*. Old clothes, long lengths of remnants, and a box of old hats can form the base of a costume collection. Participants might be asked to play the character that a certain hat or outfit suggests.

- *Making Scenery*. Use cardboard boxes, powdered paints, various-sized brushes, chalk, felt-tip markers, rolls of plain paper, and recycled junk (polystyrene, tissue paper, cans, cardboard tubes, newspaper, string).

REFERENCES

Gillies, Emily. *Creative Dramatics for All Children*. Washington, DC: Association for Childhood Education International, 1973.

Jennings, Sue. *Remedial Drama*. New York: Theatre Arts Books, 1973.

Morgan, David. "Orff-Schulwerk: An Adaptation for Drama for Retarded Participants." In *The Best of Challenge*, vol. 3, pp. 16-8. Washington, DC: AAHPERD, 1977.

"Babysitting" for Houseplants—Responsibility, Interest, and Enthusiasm Began to Grow

by Cynthia R. Chandler

Teenage trainable mentally retarded students often lack one of the most vital parts of a fulfilled life—an enjoyable, meaningful hobby to fill leisure time hours. It is very important at this point in their development that these students find new avenues of interest. A classroom greenhouse, complete with a plant babysitting service to create the necessary stock, provided trainable mentally retarded teenage students with an enthusiastically received outlet for the development of productive leisure time activity. Advertisements for the plant babysitting service appeared in the school's daily bulletin, and response from the school faculty was overwhelming. The plants added a new feeling of life in the classroom and provided an educational experience the students will carry with them throughout their lives.

The students in our classroom range from 12 to 18 years of age, with mental ages from 3 to 7 years. Handicaps included cerebral palsy, brain injury, and Down's syndrome.

The general goal of this babysitting project, which lasted from mid-October to mid-March, was to introduce the students to an interesting and rewarding activity that could fill leisure time at home and in school. Social skills and competencies were also stressed throughout the unit process with an emphasis on job responsibilities, working with others, and obeying rules.

The students acquired many special skills and performed specialized tasks throughout the project. Among the several appointed duties were labeling each plant with the owner's name, watering according to pre-scribed schedules, fertilizing, pruning, repotting, grafting, controlling harmful pests, controlling temperature, rooting, and identifying the various types of plants.

Self-realization and economic efficiency were also important goals since the basic concern for the children is to help them realize whatever potentials they possess and make contributions to society. With these goals in mind, the students can capitalize on their potentials and be ready to make their contributions to the world of work. They begin to recognize the mutual interdependence of people. In each area specific behavioral objectives were listed.

As each new plant arrived, the students alternated the duty of labeling the containers with the owner's name and the plant's identity. The teacher aide also kept a complete list of every plant and owner in the plant record notebook. A language experience story was written about each new plant, which served as a reference for care. Each student made his/her own plant notebook and kept a copy of all the experience stories along with his/her original artwork. As these stories unfolded, a pattern of care became apparent. Some of the plants needed more water than others, and many required extra sunlight. It was decided at that point to divide the plants into special categories.

The classroom greenhouse was located along the fully windowed wall on the north side of the building, and bright indirect sunlight shone on the plants all day. Thus, those plants requiring four or more hours of direct sunlight per day were moved into the hallway twice a week for their sunbath. Plants requiring moist soil at all times were grouped together and watered slightly on Monday, Wednesday, and Friday. Further groupings were also deemed necessary, such as a cacti and succulent division that required a minimum amount of water. Most of the other plants were watered once or twice a week and were seldom moved except for a turn toward the sun.

The morning period from 9:15 until 10:00 was set aside for unit development. During this time the students wrote their stories and carried out their specific plant care duties. Other interesting aspects of this unit included field trips to a nursery, a plant shop, and a florist. A local horticulturist also visited the classroom and gave many helpful hints. News of our classroom greenhouse spread throughout the school and community, and visitors from the community added their excitement to the project. They also expressed their appreciation to the students for giving such loving care to the plants.

The classroom greenhouse provided concrete experiences that motivated these students to learn. Basic concepts and skills were reinforced through daily routine; social competencies were acquired during the teamwork process; and vocational training was acquired with each new duty assigned. Above all, the students had a real hobby—something special, something that would live and grow, something that depended on them. A sense of worth and a positive self-concept blossomed in each student as a result of this most successful project.

PART III
LEARNING DISABLED STUDENTS

Introductory Comments

According to the definition found in PL 94-142, specific learning disability refers to a disorder in one or more of the basic psychological processes involved in understanding or in using spoken or written language, which may manifest itself in an imperfect ability to listen, think, speak, read, write, spell, or to do mathematical calculations. The term includes such conditions as perceptual handicaps, brain injury, minimal brain dysfunction, dyslexia, and developmental aphasia. The term does not include children who have learning problems which are primarily the result of visual, hearing, or motor handicaps; mental retardation; or environmental, cultural, or economic disadvantages.

As is evident from the definition, a number of children identified as learning disabled may exhibit quite diverse problems. Characteristics usually attributed to this group, however, include hyperactivity, perceptual-motor impairments, deficits of coordination, disorders of attention or memory, and impulsivity. Disorders of language are also characteristic of many learning disabled children and may vary from relatively mild to severe.

In "Designing Instructional Activities for Students with Language/ Learning Disabilities," Virginia L. Bruininks briefly reviews major theories of language development as a background for offering classroom teachers strategies for helping students with language problems. For students with severe language disabilities, the author advocates the direct teaching of semantic relationships utilizing the *cloze procedure*. For the less severely language impaired, a model is presented for structuring the learning task according to the degree of difficulty of the stimuli presented and the type and level of response required from the student.

Many learning disabled children have difficulty with reading. "Teaching Reading with Talking Books" is one teacher's solution to the problem of finding a reading method for her learning disabled students who exhibited memory and attention difficulties as well as auditory perception deficiencies. Marie Carbo describes in detail the characteristics that a reading program for this type of student must offer, and she relates how she incorporated each of these into her talking book method. In essence, talking books are books which are recorded on tape by the teacher. Unlike commercially recorded books, the books used in Ms. Carbo's recordings are tailored to the particular child for whom the book is being taped in terms of reading level, interest appeal, length of phrases, and reading rate. The success and popularity of the method resulted in the programing of talking books and the use of trained volunteers to work with large numbers of children.

"Aids for Learning Mathematics" is not so much a program as it is a refresher of sound teaching practices. Marion McC. Danforth reiterates the importance, especially for the handicapped child, of clarifying objectives, having the student verbalize his/her thought process, recording types of errors, and varying the instructional technique by relating these principles to the problems and progress of a learning disabled junior high student.

The need for direct training of self-awareness and identification of body parts is not limited to learning disabled youngsters. There is reason to suspect, however, that these individuals, because of perceptual-motor or other difficulties, may not possess clear or realistic images of their own bodies. In "How My Body Looks and Moves—Lessons in Self-Drawings," Richard S. Neel and Debbie Schneider describe a three-week program that involves a sequence of eight units. The accuracy with which each child drew a self-portrait was used as a pretest and again as an evaluation of the program's effectiveness. Similar programs can be easily implemented by following the detailed lesson descriptions provided.

One method available to teachers for motivating students is that of contingency contracting. While this technique is most often used with students of elementary age, Linda Nielsen offers support for its use with older learning disabled students in "Let's Make A Deal: Contingency Contracting with Adolescents." This article does not give the ways and means for setting up a contract program, but instead relates the outcome of a one-year project in which five teachers utilized academic and social contingency contracts with learning disabled high school students. A question-and-answer format covers the major aspects of the project, and offers the combined opinions of the teachers and students involved.

Bibliotherapy is usually depicted as a process of dynamic interaction between the personality of the reader and literature. Purposes vary from being able to identify with characters having problems similar to one's own to personality and behavior change. Barbara E. and Ronald S. Lenkowsky advocate the use of bibliotherapy with the learning disabled in their article "Bibliotherapy for the LD Adolescent." It is their belief that this is a technique that could be used by classroom teachers to facilitate personal, social, and emotional growth.

A similar philosophy is held by Sonya Abbye in "The Learning Disabled Child . . . Films for Social, Emotional, Language, and Sensory Needs." Instead of using books alone, she suggests the use of films to deal affectively with the social and emotional needs of the learning disabled and offers an annotated list of films for children from ages 5 to 14. Two additional annotated lists contain films to aid with language development and the five senses.

Designing Instructional Activities for Students with Language/Learning Disabilities

by Virginia L. Bruininks

The "right to education" directives from the courts and in recent public law require that all handicapped children receive an education appropriate to their needs and offered in the least restrictive environment. Increasingly, students with language/learning disabilities will be taught in regular classrooms, and their needs must be met with proper teaching strategies. Most of these students require relatively slight modification in instructional procedures because they have learned the basic rules of language usage. Some, however, need a systematic language development program because of severe language problems evidenced by consistent errors in meaning (semantics) and/or sentence structure (syntax). This article first presents a rationale and specific suggestions for planning a language development program for students with severe language problems. Important principles of instruction are then discussed. These principles may also be used effectively to modify the regular curriculum for students with less severe language/learning disabilities.

PLANNING A LANGUAGE DEVELOPMENT PROGRAM

Instruction of students who have failed to learn basic rules of language usage should be based upon available knowledge about language acquisition. There is little agreement among theorists, however, about the process of language acquisition. The behaviorist model suggests that language acquisition is a process of reinforced imitative behavior.[1-4] Critics of this position feel that behaviorism explains only a small portion of language behavior and fails to account for (a) why all children exhibit much the same pattern of development, (b) how they construct novel utterances even in the earliest days of language use, and (c) the ways they master abstract relationships that are not apparent in the utterances they hear. Critics argue further that only morphology (e.g., forms and grammatical inflections of words for tense changes, number changes, person changes) is learned through imitation.[5]

An alternative conception to the behaviorist position is the nativist model of language acquisition. This view holds that language emerges during the maturational process[6] and that the child possesses either some innate linguistic knowledge[7,8] or some innate ability to learn language.[9] Critics of these positions maintain that theorists of the nativist orientation actually say very little about the mechanisms of language acquisition and that their claims are not based on convincing evidence.

As these debates continue, new theories of language development are being introduced which occupy some sort of middle ground between the behaviorist and nativist positions, not denying some elements of innateness such as cognitive ability, but rather focusing on the learning of adult sentence structure.[10,11] A sharp distinction is made between (a) semantic relations or understandings based on events infants see and experience in their environment, and (b) grammatical relations which are purely syntactic rules for formulating sentences. Children observe people or objects acting on other people or objects and then observe how adults express these relations in speech. Gradually children learn to code their semantic understandings into the grammatical sentence form of the language they hear. Buium, Rynders, and Turnure[12] conclude that "while the child is equipped with innate means to symbolically represent his experiences in such terms as agent-action, possession, etc., the rules of rearrangement, expansion, and combination of these relational concepts are not innate but subject to learning principles."[13]

One of the learning principles which apparently plays an important role in the development of semantic concepts is reinforcement. Brown, Cazden, and Bellugi[14] found that if the meaning of the child's utterance corresponds to reality, adults are rewarding; otherwise, the child receives a nonrewarding response from adults. This concept of the use of reinforcement is quite different from the idea of reinforcing imitative language behavior, for here reinforcement is not rewarded by adults on the basis of speech patterns (grammar), but rather on the basis of meaning the child communicates (semantics).

The development of semantic concepts is central to language development in the natural language-learning environment. Then the rules of rearrangement, expansion, and combination of semantic concepts are learned. Traditionally, language training programs in the schools have not directly taught semantic relationships, but for children with severe language problems, this should be the primary focus in instruction.

TEACHING STUDENTS WITH SEVERE LANGUAGE PROBLEMS

The development of semantic concepts and semantic relationships should be the content of language instruction for students with severe language problems. Activities to teach semantic relationships can easily be designed by the classroom teacher using the *cloze procedure*. This technique was introduced by Taylor[15] to measure the readability of narrative material. It is based on the principle of Gestalt closure, which involves a postulated human impulse or need to complete a structure by supplying a missing element. In the cloze procedure, sentences are constructed with selected words deleted, and the student is required to supply the missing element either orally or in writing. Examples are presented below.

> Dad can drive the (run - car).
> Dad can drive the _____.

Using the cloze procedure to teach semantic relations, the teacher constructs sentences with selected semantic parts missing. The following plan for use of this technique has been found effective in improving students' use of language on structured language tasks and in spontaneous speech.[16]

As the basic instructional task in the language development program, a nine-sentence story is developed following a pattern in which increasingly difficult semantic concepts are stressed. Table 1 presents a basic pattern for the story. The italicized word in the pattern and in the example is omitted when these sentences are presented to the student, and the instructional task requires the student to supply the appropriate semantic concept.

Sentences in the story pattern can be presented in a variety of ways to suit the abilities of individual students. For example, an auditory stimulus with a picture cue could be provided, with a spoken response required from the student. In this case someone might show the student a picture of a yellow cat drinking milk in a school kitchen and read each sentence in the story pattern to the student, omitting the italicized word in each sentence (as illustrated in Table 1). The instructional task could also be organized to provide a visual (word) stimulus and require a spoken response from the student by presenting the sentences to the student in written form, or a visual (word) stimulus could be provided with a written response required from the student. Written words used as visual stimuli should be at the student's reading level, for the instructional objective is language development, and the task should not be made more difficult for the student by using words that cannot be read easily.

The reinforcement of semantic choices that correspond to reality is very important, for this is the way children appear to learn language in the natural language-learning environment. A response generated by the student should be judged correct and rewarded if it has meaning that corresponds to reality, even if it is not the word that is expected in the story pattern. In this case, the teacher should then present the story pattern again. For example, the story pattern is:

> "The man drives. The man drives the boat. The young man drives. The young man drives the boat," and so on.

On the last sentence, the student is to supply the word "boat," but instead says, "The young man drives the car." The teacher would say something like, "That's right—now listen again and say another word. The man drives. The man drives the boat. The young man drives. The young man drives the ____." If the student again says "car," the teacher would say, "That's right, or you could say: the young man drives the boat. Say the young man drives the boat."

Instructional tasks based on the basic pattern of semantic concepts can also be varied to meet the needs of the student with severe language/learning disabilities by altering the level of abstraction required in the student's response. Table 1 shows the instructional task developed at the recall level because the student must generate the missing semantic concept: for example, "The cat drinks ____." If a student were unable to respond correctly, the language task could be restructured to become a recognition level task,

TABLE 1   Suggested Pattern for Teaching Selected Semantic Relations

	Pattern of Presentation of Semantic Concepts	Examples
Simple	Agent - Action	The cat drinks.
	Agent - Action - *Patient*	The cat drinks *milk*.
	Modifier - Agent - Action	The *yellow* cat drinks.
	Modifier - Agent - *Action* - Patient	The yellow cat *drinks* milk.
	Modifier - Agent - Action - *Possessive* - Patient	The yellow cat drinks *his* milk.
	Modifier - Agent - Action - Possessive - *Modifier* - Patient	The yellow cat drinks his *warm* milk.
	Modifier - Agent - Action - Possessive - Modifier - Patient - *Locative*	The yellow cat drinks his warm milk *in the kitchen*.
	Modifier - Agent - *Recurrence* - Action - Possessive - Modifier - Patient - Locative	The yellow cat *always* drinks his warm milk in the kitchen.
Complex	Modifier - Agent - Recurrence - Action - Possessive - Modifier - Patient - *Possessive* - Locative	The yellow cat always drinks his warm milk in the *school's* kitchen.

which is easier. At the recognition level of abstraction, options are presented from which the student chooses the correct response. For example, "The cat drinks (ride - milk)." Initially word options themselves should represent different semantic concepts, but later choices should be introduced so that the major concern is correspondence to reality. For example, "The cat drinks (dogs - milk)."

The modifications of instructional tasks which have been discussed are based upon certain principles of instruction. These principles are elaborated in the following section because they may be used effectively to modify the regular curriculum for students with less severe language/learning disabilities.

TEACHING STUDENTS WITH LESS SEVERE LANGUAGE PROBLEMS

The first consideration in the development of any instructional task for students with language problems is the structure of the learning task. The task may (a) present an auditory stimulus and require a spoken response, (b) present an auditory stimulus and require a written response, (c) present a visual stimulus and require a spoken response, and (d) present a visual stimulus and require a written response. In general, tasks which present an auditory stimulus and require a spoken response are the easiest to perform because abilities in listening and speaking precede the development of reading and writing skills. When a student fails to perform an instructional task, the teacher should alter the stimulus and/or response mode to more simple levels until the student can perform the task. For example, if a student is unable to respond in writing, the task should be presented again giving an opportunity to respond orally.

A second consideration in the presentation of instructional tasks is the level of abstraction required in the student's response. This relates to processes which must occur as the student (a) integrates stimuli with past experience to give them meaning and (b) formulates an appropriate response. Responses required of students can vary greatly from simple discrimination tasks to complex tasks requiring reasoning and critical evaluation. For example, when teachers ask, "What number comes after three?," they are requesting a recall response from the student. When teachers ask, "What number comes after three—four or ten?," they are requesting a recognition response from the student. The recognition task is a simpler task because the symbols for the correct response do not have to be remembered, only the correct response. In contrast, at the recall level the student has to remember both the correct response and the correct verbal symbols for expressing that response.

Table 2 presents the hierarchies of difficulty for stimuli, response modes, and levels of abstraction required in responses on instructional tasks. These listings proceed downward from simple to complex levels.

When a student is unable to perform an instructional task, the teacher should systematically vary the stimulus (section I of Table 2) by presenting progressively less difficult stimuli until the task can be performed accurately. For example, if a student is unable to read the printed word "ball" from a flashcard (visual stimulus—spoken response), the teacher should give an auditory cue such as "You can play with it." If the student does not respond, a picture of a ball can be presented with the word, and so on. The same process for presenting less difficult stimuli would be followed for auditory stimuli.

If the teacher has reached the most basic stimulus level and the student has been unable to perform the task, the teacher should return to the original

TABLE 2   Hierarchies of Difficulty for Stimuli, Response Modes, and Levels of Abstraction in Responses

	I		II	III
	Stimuli		Response Modes	Levels of Abstraction
	Auditory	Visual		
Simple	Word With Concrete Cue	Concrete Object With Auditory Cue	Gestural	Discrimination
	Word With Picture Cue	Concrete Object Only	Spoken	Recognition
	Word Only	Picture With Auditory Cue	Written	Recall
		Picture Only		Comprehension
		Printed Word With Auditory Cue		Application
		Printed Word Only		Analysis
				Synthesis
Complex				Evaluation

level of stimulus presentation and systematically vary response modes (section II of Table 2) so that the task is restructured to require progressively less difficult responses. Using the previous example, the teacher would present the printed word "ball" again on the flashcard and say "Show me this word," requiring a gestural rather than a spoken response, and would again systematically vary the stimulus if an accurate response were not achieved.

Since gesturing is the most basic response level, if the student is still unable to perform the task, the teacher would then lower the level of abstraction (section III of Table 2) from the recall to the recognition level and ask, "Is it ball or book?" as the original printed word stimulus is presented. Still, at the recognition level, section I of Table 2 should then be varied so that less difficult stimuli are presented if the student is unable to answer correctly. The picture of the ball would be shown, and the teacher would again ask, "Is it ball or book?" If necessary a real ball could be displayed, and the teacher would again ask, "Is it ball or book?"

In the unlikely event that the student has still not responded correctly and the most basic level of abstraction in section III of Table 2 is reached, the teacher would finally present the task in its simplest form: (a) show the ball and say "This is ball," (b) show another object such as a book and say "This is book," and then (c) say "Show me ball." If the student is able to respond, the teacher would then proceed "up" the hierarchies of difficulty by systematically making the task more difficult as long as the student could respond correctly. Approximately 85 percent mastery at one level of task difficulty should be evidenced by the student before the teacher introduces the next highest level of task difficulty.

The previous example has shown how information in Table 2 can be used as an aid in teaching students with language problems in any curriculum area. The process of systematically varying stimulus, response mode, and level of abstraction is also a very useful assessment technique for the teacher. Careful record keeping of (a) the stimulus most likely to elicit a response from the student at each level of response difficulty, and (b) the level of abstraction at which the student is able to perform should reveal the best instructional strategy to use in teaching the student. Careful design of instructional tasks will then allow most students with language problems to succeed in the regular classroom curriculum.

NOTES

1. M.D.S. Braine, "On Learning the Grammatical Order of Words," *Psychological Reviews* 70 (1963): 323-48; idem, "The Ontogeny of English Phrase Structure: The First Phase," *Language* 39 (1963): 1-13; idem, "On

the Basis of Phrase Structure: A Reply to Bever, Fodor, and Weksel," *Psychological Reviews* 72 (1965): 483-92.

2. J. Jenkins and D. Palermo, "Mediation Processes and the Acquisition of Linguistic Structure," in "The Acquisition of Language," ed. U. Bellugi and R.W. Brown, *Monographs of the Society of Research in Child Development* 29 (1964): 141-69.

3. B.F. Skinner, *Verbal Behavior* (New York: Appleton-Century-Crofts, 1957).

4. A.W. Staats and C.K. Staats, "A Comparison of the Development of Speech and Reading Behavior with Implications for Research," *Child Development* 33 (1962): 831-46; *Language, Learning, and Cognition* (New York: Holt, Rinehart, and Winston, 1968).

5. J.B. Carroll and R.O. Freedle, *Language Comprehension and the Acquisition of Knowledge* (New York: John Wiley and Sons, 1972).

6. E.H. Lenneberg, *Biological Foundations of Language* (New York: John Wiley and Sons, 1967).

7. N.A. Chomsky, *Syntactic Structures* (The Hague: Mouton, 1957).

8. D. McNeill, "Developmental Psycholinguistics," in *The Genesis of Language: A Psycholinguistic Approach*, eds. F. Smith and G.A. Miller (Cambridge, MA: Massachusetts Institute of Technology Press, 1966); idem, *The Acquisition of Language: The Study of Developmental Psycholinguistics* (New York: Harper and Row, 1970); idem, "The Development of Language," in *Carmichael's Manual of Child Psychology*, ed. P.A. Mussen (New York: Wiley and Sons, 1970).

9. D.I. Slobin, "Grammatical Transformations and Sentence Comprehension in Childhood and Adulthood," *Journal of Verbal Learning and Verbal Behavior* 5 (1966): 219-27; "The Acquisition of Russian as a Native Language," in *The Genesis of Language*, eds. F. Smith and G.A. Miller (Cambridge, MA: MIT Press, 1966).

10. R. Brown, *A First Language: The Early Stages* (Cambridge, MA: Harvard University Press, 1973).

11. I.M. Schlesinger, "Production of Utterances and Language Acquisition," in *The Otogenesis of Grammar: A Theoretical Symposium*, eds. C.A. Ferguson and D.I. Slobin (New York: Academic Press, 1971).

12. N. Buium, J. Rynders, and J. Turnure, *A Semantic-Relational-Concepts Based Theory of Language Acquisition as Applied to Down's Syndrome Children: Implications for a Language Enhancement Program*, Research, Development, and Demonstration Center in Education of Handicapped Children, Research Report No. 62 (Minneapolis: University of Minnesota, 1974).

13. Ibid., p. 3.

14. R. Brown, C.B. Cazden, and U. Bellugi, "The Child's Grammar from 1-11," in *Minnesota Symposium on Child Psychology*, ed. J.B. Hill (Minneapolis: University of Minnesota Press, 1968).

15. W.L. Taylor, "Cloze Procedure: A New Tool for Measuring Readability," *Journalism Quarterly* 30 (1953): 415.

16. S.K. Jordan, "A Field Test of the Reinehr Language Development Program One," Master's paper. University of Minnesota, 1975.

Teaching Reading with Talking Books

by Marie Carbo

If you have agonized with students who struggle and stumble as they read, expending their energies merely deciphering words, barely comprehending, this article is for you. You may find the three *talking book* reading methods described here useful in helping these students become more fluent readers with better comprehension.

For three years I have used talking books (specially tape recorded books) to teach reading to children with severe learning handicaps, including the learning disabled, educable retarded, emotionally disturbed, and severely speech impaired. All of the students have made substantial gains in comprehension, word recognition, and word meaning. Moreover, after the talking book experience, some of the children appear to have understood intuitively and applied phonics rules without formal phonics instruction. Talking books seem to serve as a readiness activity for phonics instruction by enabling students to develop a basic sight vocabulary from which phonics rules may be drawn.

Teaching reading with talking books appears to be particularly effective with youngsters who have memory problems and/or difficulty learning to read through the phonics approach, and for older students who, after repeated failure, have been turned off to reading. Talking books enable older students with some reading skills to read material on their language comprehension level and to integrate the rate, rhythm, and natural flow of language necessary for good comprehension. In addition, with talking books, students make fewer reading errors and the possibility of forming incorrect reading patterns is diminished. From the very beginning, talking books provide youngsters with the correct reading model to imitate. And, as a result, the success which youngsters experience with the talking book method builds their self-confidence and makes them more willing to invest further effort in learning to read.

SEARCHING FOR A SPECIAL METHOD

The talking book reading methods were initially designed for eight learning disabled students of average intelligence, in grades two to six, who had memory problems, attention difficulties, and most importantly, auditory perception deficiencies. They could not easily discriminate between the sounds represented by letters (much as a tone-deaf person cannot discriminate between musical notes), nor could they easily blend sounds to form words. Furthermore, their attention and memory problems made it difficult for them to remember whole words. Therefore, their sight vocabulary was minimal. When these youngsters, who were reading two to four years below grade level, tried to read a page of print, they did not see words which formed sentences and paragraphs. Instead, they saw a page with hundreds of individual letters which had to be deciphered, remembered, and then blended in the correct sequence to form words—an impossible task for them.

It was regrettable that many of these children had been exposed to intensive phonics instruction early in their schooling. Lerner has cautioned against the continuous use of a phonics approach with a youngster who has a serious defect in the auditory modality because it may lead to "frustration, failure, and a dislike of reading and the teacher."[1] Evidently, at some critical point in the learning process, many of these learning disabled students had been taught to read through their weakest modality. It was no wonder that they perceived the reading process as a series of endless, unrelated obstacles to be surmounted. They were, therefore, poor readers in the most basic sense; they did not understand that the fundamental purpose of reading is thought communication.

I sought a special reading method for these learning disabled students which would utilize their individual learning styles, as recommended by Dunn and Dunn.[2] The method, I concluded, would have to possess these characteristics: (1) multisensory, to compensate for their perception deficits; (2) high interest, to hold their attention; (3) in context, to increase their comprehension; (4) highly structured with instant feedback, to promote steady growth and feelings of security; and (5) fail-safe, to improve their self-concept. In addition, sufficient repetition, which could be controlled by the student, would be needed to overcome memory deficiencies.

I knew that research had demonstrated that the process of reading aloud to children produced growth in vocabulary, word knowledge, and visual decoding.[3-5] Moreover, Heckelman had used his "neurological impress method" to improve reading skills.[6] (In Heckelman's method an instructor is positioned behind the student. The student holds the book to be read, while the instructor traces his/her fingers below the words, reading the words aloud with the student. The neurological impress method did eliminate the need to rely on the phonic skills of students; printed words would not have to be deciphered. Instead, students could see and hear the words within the context of a story.)

Heckelman's method, however, might not provide sufficient repetition, and many of the learning disabled students might be embarrassed if they had to learn in the presence of an instructor. Tape recorded books seemed to be the answer, since a student could read along with the voice of a recorded instructor and could in this way learn the passage in private. Furthermore, students would be assured of success with talking books since they would read aloud only after a tape recording had provided sufficient repetition to enable learning to take place.

As a beginning step, I observed how the eight students used commercially recorded books. Although Carol Chomsky would later report reading gains using commercially recorded books with average third graders,[7] these learning disabled students could not keep their places in the story and, therefore, had no way of associating what they heard with the printed words on the page. Special recording procedures had to be developed in order to transform tape recorded books into reading lessons, and to allow these handicapped students to associate the printed words with the words spoken on the tape recording. Consequently, I devised three recording techniques which synchronized for the student the printed words with the tape recorded words, and the *talking book* method was born.

RECORDING TECHNIQUES

1. *Cueing the listener*. I numbered the book pages consecutively (if they were not already numbered) and cued the youngster for whom I was recording by stating the page number before reading the page. Next, I paused long enough to allow the listener to turn to the correct page, look at the pictures, and find the first line of print.

2. *Phrase reading*. I recorded the material with particular emphasis on clarity, expression, and logical phrasing. The latter seemed to help the students to assimilate natural word groupings and lessen their tendency to read word by word.

3. *Tactual reinforcement*. To help the children keep pace with the taped reading and focus better on the task, I instructed them to move their finger under the words as they heard them. Part of a talking book recording is reproduced below. Notice that the page cues are consistently reduced until only the page number is stated.

Book Number Eight
The Little King, the Little Queen and the Little Monster
Open the book to page one. [long pause]
Move your finger under the words as you hear them.
Page one [pause]
There was/ a little boy/ who had always/ wished to be king.
Turn to page three. [pause]
So that night/ the Good Fairy came/ and asked,/ "What is your wish?"/ And
the little boy/ told her,/ "I wish/ to be a king."/
Page five [pause]
The Good Fairy/ granted the little boy's wish./
Six. [pause]

Sound effects were not used on any of the recordings in order to reduce the
possibility of auditory distractions and, thereby, to increase the student's
focus on the spoken and printed words.

RECORDING ENTIRE BOOKS

This method helped the students associate printed language with spoken
language, train their eyes to move from left to right, improve their reading
rate and rhythm, and experience the enjoyment of understanding and discussing books. The eight learning disabled students learned through this method
for three months, and, on an achievement test, made the following gains in
word recognition: time lapse–3 months; average gain–3 months; highest
gain–5 months; lowest gain–2 months. Of course, these are rough measures;
but they indicate definite improvement in students who previously had
shown severely below average gains on similar tests.

I recorded 30 paperback books ranging in reading level from second to
fifth grade. Each book was numbered and then recorded on one side of a
tape cassette which had the corresponding number. The eight students were
permitted to select freely from among the books.

Most of the students were able to follow the recording visually (seeing
the words), aurally (hearing the words), and tactually (tracing the words with
their fingers). All of the children enjoyed the recorded books and discussed
them with interest and good comprehension after working with the tapes.

For many of the students this was a major breakthrough. They began to
understand that reading can be stimulating and enjoyable—perhaps a skill
worthy of effort. Moreover, some of the youngsters were even able to read a
book without the accompanying tape after listening to it several times. This
was a feat they had never before accomplished and one that made them proud.

This first method can be used by both classroom teachers and specialists.
It increases reading enjoyment and comprehension, helps youngsters associate printed language with spoken language, and lets them experience
the enjoyment of reading and understanding an entire book.

RECORDING PARTS OF BOOKS

The objectives of the second talking book method were identical to the first, with this important addition: to enable students to read material on their language comprehension level with correct pacing, phrasing, voice inflection, and rate, regardless of their low reading ability.

The real potential of the talking book method became more evident when individual tape recordings were made for the eight learning disabled students. In only three months, the gains in word recognition were phenomenal, especially when compared to past performance. What is more, the highest gains were made by sixth graders who, for the first time, were able to read material on or near their grade level even though their actual reading level was three and four years below grade level. Note the extraordinary gains: time lapse–3 months; average gain–8 months; highest gain–15 months; lowest gain–4 months.

On a daily basis, I made tape recordings of parts of my books for each student. The choice of books varied according to the age and reading level of the child. Children who were beginning to read were assigned basal readers with a controlled vocabulary, while the students in grades four through six were permitted to select books closer to their language comprehension level rather than their reading level.

When tape recording for a student, both my reading rate and phrase length depended upon the reading ability of the potential listener. For example, if an upper grader with poor reading skills chose a difficult book, I recorded the selection using short word groups (two to four words), at a slower than usual rate, and in small quantities (as little as one paragraph). The length of the recorded passage (from one paragraph to about five pages) was dependent upon the amount of material that the potential listener could digest in one sitting and then read back to me with relative ease, as observed on several trials. As the youngster's reading improved, I gradually quickened my recording pace, lengthened the phrases, and increased the quantity. If a student chose a book below his/her reading level (which was unusual), then I recorded the material at a normal rate in longer phrases, and in larger quantities. To summarize, when recording for a child, I considered (1) the extent of his/her interest in the book, (2) the maximum phrase length s/he could assimilate, (3) the maximum reading rate at which s/he could follow, and (4) the amount of material s/he could digest in one sitting.

Every day the students received their individual tape recording and book. The students usually chose to listen to their tape three to four times. When a child read a passage back to me, I helped to focus his/her attention on phrases instead of individual words by visibly surrounding each phrase with my thumb and index finger to form a semicircle above the phrase to be read. This visual phrasing reinforced the auditory phrasing on the recording and helped to lessen reversals and word by word readings.

After the students listened to their individually recorded books, they were able to read the material back to me. It was a delight to hear the change in their oral reading. Instead of their previous slow, hesitant, labored reading, they now read with enthusiasm and expression, appropriately altering their voice and pacing to suit the mood of the passage. They understood, enjoyed, and could read their books.

The greatest gain in word recognition (15 months) was made by Tommy, a sixth grade boy reading on a 2.2 level. Prior to working with the tapes, he had faltered and stumbled over second grade words while his body actually shook with fear and discomfort. Understandably, he hated to read. Because a beloved teacher had once read *Charlotte's Web* to him, he asked me to record his favorite chapter from this book. I recorded one paragraph on each cassette side so that Tommy could choose to read either one or two paragraphs daily. The first time that he listened to a recording (five times) and then read the passage silently to himself (twice), he was able to read the passage to me perfectly, with excellent expression and without fear. After this momentous event, Tommy worked hard. At last he knew he was capable of learning to read and was willing to give it all he could. The result was a 15-month gain in word recognition at the end of only three months. Every learning disabled child in the program experienced immediate success with his/her individually recorded books.

This second method can also be used by both classroom teachers and specialists. Since individual tape recordings are time-consuming to make for large numbers of students, teachers might want to assemble a group of volunteers and train them in the recording techniques described here. Pair each volunteer with one student so the volunteer assumes recording responsibility for that student. Assign material to be recorded to each volunteer on a regular basis.

PROGRAMING TAPE RECORDED BOOKS

The third reading method combined strategies used in both the first and second methods. In order to avoid having to erase each student's tape each night to record new material, I decided to program talking books. Each book would be sequenced, with small gradations of difficulty between successive books, and then recorded in small segments, since this strategy had been so successful in the second method. Programing allowed for the accumulation of permanent book recordings with supplementary materials such as activity cards, games, audio cards, and reading skills exercises. Furthermore, since individual tape recordings no longer had to be made, greater numbers of students could participate, and new entrants could be diagnosed and easily and accurately assigned appropriate talking book materials. After three months, the eight students made excellent gains in word recognition, although the gains were not as large as they had been with the personalized tape recordings: time lapse–3 months; average gain–6 months; highest gain–9 months; lowest gain–3 months.

I selected and sequenced in order of difficulty 100 high-interest paperback books (ranging from first to fifth grade). I recorded each book in small segments so that every child in the program could successfully complete one tape recording at a sitting. I noted on a chart the number of the cassette side and the pages recorded on it. A short book might require only two tape sides, a longer book as many as ten. This crucial recording of small amounts would later eliminate virtually all feelings of frustration or failure on the part of the students. Every child would be capable of completing at least one tape cassette per day, or approximately one to three books per week.

Record keeping was accurate and minimal. I duplicated a chart of the books and had only to color in the box on the chart which corresponded to the book and tape side read by the youngster, indicate the date, and then make notations about the student's reading progress. Individual programs were written for the students on a weekly basis, and even the most severely disabled students had no difficulty following them, or locating and returning materials. "Book 15(3)" written on a child's program simply meant "book number fifteen, tape side three."

EFFICIENT SYSTEM

This third method helped the youngsters improve their reading skills substantially and evolved into an efficient and smooth-running system. As new youngsters entered the program, they could be tested and immediately assigned appropriate materials. The permanently recorded materials and high degree of organization made it possible to train volunteers to work with the children. Not only was one-to-one instruction provided for each youngster through the taped readings, but, in addition, volunteers worked individually with the students on the games, skills, lessons, and activities which were devised to accompany the recorded books.

Programed talking books can be used by a classroom teacher but are most suitable for use by a specialist working with large numbers of students. This method allows the specialist to program materials that are ideal for his/her students and to develop a smooth, workable, stable program in which children can make steady, substantial reading progress.

Each of the talking book reading methods proved to be successful with the eight learning disabled students described in this article and with other youngsters with severe learning handicaps. Repeatedly in the past three years I have seen nonreaders and poor readers transformed into enthusiastic learners after their first experience with talking books.

A supplementary programed and tape recorded word study skills program is used after the youngsters have developed both a sight vocabulary and security in and affection for books. It is important to note that none of the three talking book strategies requires phonic skills. They do provide high-interest, in-context material with adequate repetition, and allow the student to determine when s/he is ready to perform.

With talking books, students can experience immediate success. I have found that the talking book method has what Roswell and Natchez[8] term a "psychotherapeutic" effect on the personalities of the students. Not only have all the youngsters made excellent gains in reading compared to previous performance, but they have become more interested in reading, more willing to try, and more helpful toward one another.

NOTES

1. Janet Lerner, *Children with Learning Disabilities* (Boston: Houghton Mifflin, 1971).
2. Rita Dunn and Kenneth Dunn, *Educator's Self-Teaching Guide to Individualizing Instructional Programs* (West Nyack, NY: Parker Publishing, 1975).
3. D. Cohen, "Effect of Literature on Vocabulary and Reading," *Elementary English* 45 (1968): 209-13.
4. G. Baily, "The Use of a Library Resource Program for Improvement of Language Abilities of Disadvantaged First Grade Pupils of an Urban Community," (PhD diss., Boston College, 1970).
5. Carol Chomsky, "Stages in Language Development and Reading Exposure," *Harvard Educational Review* 42 (1972):1-33.
6. R.G. Heckelman, "A Neurological Impress Method of Reading Instruction," *Academic Therapy* 44 (1969): 277-82.
7. Carol Chomsky, "After Decoding:What?" *Language Arts* 53 (1976): 288-96.
8. Florence Roswell and Gladys Natchez, *Reading Disability: Diagnosis and Treatment* (New York: Basic Books, 1964).

Aids for Learning Mathematics

by Marion McC. Danforth

Mike, a seventh-grader with a visual memory deficit, had an excellent grasp of logical reasoning and problem-solving principles, yet he was unable to perform basic mathematical operations. In my efforts to meet Mike's special needs as a learning disabled child, I found some procedures that are good teaching practices in the regular classroom.

Give a concise statement of the specific objective for each session.

When a lesson had to be repeated because of a weakness in a certain area, Mike benefited from being aware of the source of his errors. Making him aware may have been as simple a procedure as stating, "Mike, today we will work on the division of fractions again. During yesterday's assignment you seemed to have difficulty remembering to invert the divisor." When he was beginning a new assignment, Mike relied on seeing the logical relationship between successive lessons. The statement of an objective also lends itself to directing the thought process needed for the particular learning situation. It is a mistake to assume that each individual mentally fills in the unspoken or unwritten logical gaps of a teacher's presentation.

Have the student verbalize his/her thought process in working specific problems.

This procedure is important in determining sources of errors as well as in helping the individual to comprehend the process being used. In listening to the student verbalize the nature of his/her difficulty, the teacher becomes more aware of the student's thought process and can better direct remediation in any reasoning and operational deficiency. An individual may not be aware of an error in his/her approach until s/he verbalizes his/her attempts at problem solving or his/her operational process. Verbalization is also important in reinforcing memory. (Care must be taken, however, to avoid reinforcing errors.) Because Mike's specific learning deficit is in visual memory, it is essential for him to use verbalization or reauditorialization as a learning aid.

Keep an error-analysis card.

Errors on worksheets are frequently crossed off as carelessness, particularly in matters of simple addition, subtraction, multiplication, or division. A careful record of these mistakes, however, often reveals patterns. For example, if 6×7 occurs five times on an error record, the student obviously has difficulty with this item and needs reinforcement on recall. If $6 \times 7 = 43$ occurs several times, the student has probably entered this as a rote fact which s/he is erroneously reinforcing.

Use analogies to emphasize numerical relationships.

The relationship between logical thinking and the use of analogies is important as a problem-solving technique. Mike often could grasp the numerical relationship in simple mathematical situations, which he could apply in more complex problems after direction. For example, a given problem might state that the area of a rectangular piece of land is 288 square meters, one side is 12 meters, and it is necessary to find the other side. I would first review with Mike information that we had previously investigated regarding area. Then, presented with an example, such as two sides of a rectangular figure were 2 and 4, Mike stated that the area was 8 square units and orally explained by what process he had obtained the solution. Given a second example, a rectangular figure with an area of 20 and one side of 5, Mike would verbalize the relationship between the side and area in the first example and conclude that 4 was the solution to the second example. This process was enhanced by using figures of rectangles drawn on graph paper squares where the solution could be visually seen. Finally, encountering the given problem, Mike would verbalize his independent observations on its solution and compute the answer.

A second use of analogy is that of visual reference. Given problems of multiplication and division of fractions, an example of each type of computation was given for visual reinforcement.

Present directions in several different ways.

Analogies on mathematical operations or problem-solving techniques should also supplement simple verbal and written statements of instructions. Individuals processing information through different modalities may rely on one modality or a combination of several before successfully grasping the meanings of instructions. Mike also benefited from orally repeating and interpreting given instructions before beginning assignments.

Use concrete materials and real-world situations for presentation of a lesson.

Although the use of manipulative materials has been encouraged repeatedly, the practice is less used as the child leaves the primary or elementary levels. The fact is that many seventh- and eighth-graders may still require this type of activity. Manipulating objects increases understanding and indicates the practicality of certain mathematical procedures. Sawing a piece of lumber into fractional parts will have the same effect as cutting strips of paper, and yet the former appeals to an adolescent stage of development.

Neither mathematical identification of a decimal part with a fraction ($1/2 = 1 \div 2 = 0.5$) nor presentation of money as a decimal system seemed to convince Mike that a decimal like 0.5 was less than a whole. Using the idea of a gasoline pump, however, Mike immediately understood that the hose was only gradually releasing gasoline, and that tenths were being used as a measure until a whole gallon was pumped into the tank. Watching a moving odometer had the same effect. The practicality of multiplying decimals and the value of rounding off numbers in an answer was reinforced when Mike used labels from meat packages. Multiplying the price per pound and the number of pounds as given to the nearest tenth, Mike calculated the price and checked his answer against the price as marked.

Develop aids for avoiding errors.

Circling mathematical signs on a worksheet in color codes helps the student who has difficulty discriminating between the signs or making a transition from one operation to another. When presented with a review worksheet on mixed operations, multiplication and division of fractions, for example, Mike would grasp the first sign and consistently use this throughout the assignment. Because Mike had not developed automatic responses to some operational processes, he would concentrate on the correct procedure for the first problem encountered. His thought process would then become set for the remaining problems. The use of the color-coded visual aid helped him make the necessary transition in thinking.

Remove frustration from the learning situation.

When I assisted Mike in working a series of problems presented on a worksheet, I found that he would often be frustrated, not by the problem at hand, but by the number of problems on the page, the apparent difficulty of a problem in the next row, or the visual distraction of other numbers in adjoining problems. By placing each problem on a separate slip of paper, the size of the paper depending on the amount of computation needed, these distractions were eliminated. If Mike's rate of working was slower than anticipated, the activity was terminated at a point when he was achieving success. Thus Mike was not left with the feeling that he had an unfinished worksheet. In other words, Mike would experience the positive reinforcement of successful closure.

There will always be those students who achieve success without the reinforcing practices described here and, hopefully, these will be in the majority. But for the few who are meeting continual failure, we need to look for aids to learning. Many of these procedures can be handled by the student, such as keeping an error-analysis card, or color-coding operational signs before beginning an assignment. All of the suggested practices are intended to provide the individual with a successful experience in mathematics.

How My Body Looks and Moves—Lessons in Self-Drawings

by Richard S. Neel and Debbie Schneider

Self-drawings have been used for many years in the assessment of the abilities and feelings of children. They are often used to help determine what a child is capable of doing or to determine why the child is doing it. It is believed that self-drawings reflect more than the ability to draw or the awareness of how the body looks and moves. Many children, however, have never been taught how their bodies look or move. This is especially true for young children or for children who are handicapped. Through eight lessons, teachers can increase some children's self-awareness by directly teaching them about their bodies and how they move.

PROCEDURE

A group of children with learning disabilities was selected from a resource room in a suburban area of a large metropolitan city. The children began the project by drawing pictures of themselves. Each drawing was reviewed and the errors and omissions were noted. This information was used to design a program sequence that provided direct instruction to remedy each type of error.

The instruction phase consisted of eight units and the program required three weeks to complete. The materials needed include: a full-length mirror; a chalk board; butcher paper; 3×5 inch cards; 8×11 inch newsprint paper; two large (3×5 feet) pieces of tagboard; a camera; and some pens, paints, and chalk.

Lesson 1

Lesson 1 consisted of a naming exercise. First, the teacher named a part of the body and the children pointed to the appropriate part of their own bodies. The members of the group usually corrected each other's mistakes. Occasionally, the teacher had to mediate or clarify responses. When each member could point to each body part (e.g., head, neck, trunk, leg, knee, ankle, etc.) consistently, the process was reversed. The teacher pointed to a body part and the children named it. This was repeated often so that each child had ample practice.

Lesson 2

The teacher began Lesson 2 with a brief review of the tasks of Lesson 1. A few of the children required correction (e.g., the word *trunk* was forgotten). On the whole, however, the retention was good. Then the tasks of Lesson 1 were repeated, but with the children's eyes closed. This new task presented few problems to any of the children. Finally, the teacher drew around each of the children as they lay on butcher paper and the children cut out their own images. During the remainder of the project, the children worked on painting their cutouts. Photographs of each child were also taken and displayed next to their cutouts as a model for painting.

Lesson 3

The teacher placed the names of body parts on 3×5 inch cards. The children practiced saying the words and placing them on the correct part of their cutouts. Initially, this exercise went fairly slowly, as would be expected. The teacher repeated the exercise in each subsequent lesson until each child could read each word in isolation and correctly place the card on the cutout.

Lesson 4

Lesson 4 was designed to allow the children to explore how their bodies moved and to have fun. They discovered the ways each body part could move, and they were asked to touch one part to another. "Touch your left hand to your right knee." As they progressed the challenge was increased. "Touch your left hand behind your right leg to your right toe." Lesson 4 ended with the direction to, "Touch your left elbow to your right ear."

Lesson 5

In the fifth session the children were divided into pairs. One child touched one body part to another and the other child imitated what s/he saw. The process was then reversed. Toward the end of the lesson, one child was instructed to give oral directions and the other child carried them out. This activity served as a review of the previous lessons.

Lesson 6

For this lesson the teacher created a life-size puzzle of a boy and girl out of tagboard. Each cut was made so that the specific body parts (e.g., arms, hand, trunk, neck, etc.) were separate. Each child was then given a chance to put a puzzle together. The teacher drew the children's attention to where the parts fit in relation to each other.

Lesson 7

On the seventh lesson each child identified pictures of body parts that were cut from catalogs and mounted on cards. Each child was encouraged to identify the specific characteristics that differentiate one part from the others. Fingers and toes were easy, of course. However, the children were also able to differentiate between knees and elbows by noticing the thickness and shape of each.

Lesson 8

For the final lesson, the teacher worked individually with each child at the chalkboard, drawing a picture of the child. Proportion and detail were stressed. Each child compared his/her chalk drawing with the cutout s/he had finished by this time.

CONCLUSION

After the instructional part of the program was finished, each child drew another self-portrait. All pictures showed improvement in the inclusion of detail and correct proportions. There was also a noticeable improvement in the accuracy of body part connections (see Figures 1 and 2).

The teacher in this program found that she could teach the children to draw a more accurate self-portrait. Their initial attempts to draw self-portraits were, perhaps, the result of a lack of experience and a lack of awareness of their bodies. These results suggest that caution should be used in interpreting single measures of any behavior because they might change over a short period of time, as evidenced by the children's self-portraits.

FIGURE 1   **FIGURE 2**

Let's Make a Deal: Contingency Contracting with Adolescents

by Linda Nielsen

RATIONALE

The popularity of contingency contracting as an option to motivate under-achievers seems questionable among high school personnel. Though numerous studies have demonstrated the efficacy of contracts to enhance the academic achievement of elementary students, fewer have implemented the method with high school populations (Table 1). Perhaps this paucity is further evidence of the contention that adolescents are too frequently an ignored group in educational research.[1-3] While high school teachers request educational alternatives to dispel student apathy, others suggest a relationship between learning disabilities, school failure, and delinquency.[4,5] Thus the demand for motivational techniques remains appreciable.

Project Acumen was designed to address some of these needs by training high school teachers to develop programs for underachieving adolescents with learning disabilities. Academic and social contingency contracts were utilized intermittently throughout the year by the five teachers in the project.[6]

METHOD

Student and Teacher Samples

The project served a total of 150 male and female adolescents in the tenth through twelfth grades of a southeastern rural high school. All students had been assigned to intact classes for underachievers on the basis of the previous English teacher's recommendation. Ages ranged from 15 to 19, with 54 percent of the sample male and 46 percent female. Reading achievement level was preprimer through eleventh grade with a mean of

Table 1   Successful Programs Utilizing Contracts with Adolescents

Conduct Modified	Reference
Public school setting:	
Social and study conduct	Webb and Cormier, 1973
	Williams and Long, 1973
Homework completion	Pollack, Azaroff and Williams, 1972
Academic achievement	Anandam & Williams, 1971; George and Kendall, 1976; Glynn, 1970; Panyan, Neerinox & Landers, 1976; Staats, Minke, Goodwin, & Landeen, 1967; Williams, Long and Yoakley, 1972
Social conduct of LD students	Broden, Hall, Dunlap, and Clark, 1970
Academic achievement with LD	Nolen, Kunzelman, Haring, 1967; Knapczyk and Livingston, 1973; Stark, 1976
Psychiatric setting:	
Social and achievement	Clark, Boyd, Macrae, 1975; Kaufman and O'Leary, 1972; Mainprize, 1977; Gormly and Nattoli, 1971
Social conduct	Burchard and Berrera, 1972; Kris and Schiff, 1969
Room cleaning	Aitchison and Green, 1974
Delinquent home setting:	
Tests on evening news broadcasts	Tyler and Brown, 1968
Achievement & class attention	Stein, Ball, Conn, Haran, Striver, 1976
Achievement & attendance	Holt and Hobbs, 1976
Attendance	MacDonald, Gallimore & MacDonald, 1970
IQ and reading scores	Rice, 1970
Homework, punctuality, grammar, social	Liberman, Ferris, Salgado, 1975; Phillips, 1968
Reintegration to public schools	Martin, Burkholder, Rosenthall, 1968
Attending counseling sessions	Schwitzelbel and Kolb, 1964
Locus of control & self-concept	Eitzen, 1975
Academic and social conduct	Bailey, Timbers & Phillips, 1970; Cohen and Filipczak, 1971; Christen & McKinnon, 1977
Social conduct	Phillips, Wolf, Fixsen, 1973; Meichenbaum, Bowers, and Ross, 1968
Curfew & attendance	Alexander, Corbett and Smigel, 1976
Job corps:	
Job performance & quality	Pierce and Risley, 1974
Reading skills	Clark, Lachowicz and Wolf, 1968

eighth grade for 58 seniors, sixth grade for 32 juniors, and seventh grade for 60 sophomores. Thirty-two percent had previously failed one academic year in school, and 4 percent had failed two years. Ten percent of the students were black, and 30 percent were employed part time.

After the first nine weeks of school, teacher ratings on a Likert scale indicated that 14 percent of the students were perceived as "extremely disruptive" and 25 percent as "sometimes disruptive." Only 24 percent of the students had perfect attendance during the first nine weeks of school, with a range of from 1 to 22 days absent. In addition, many of the students exhibited behaviors labeled in previous research as characteristic of learning disabled persons: hyperactivity, short attention span, inability to follow directions, lack of motivation, easily distracted, test anxiety, underachievement in more than one academic area, and inconsistency in work output.

Four English teachers had requested a consultant to assist them with underachievers and were, therefore, chosen as the grant recipients. The fifth person, a first year teacher, was required to participate since all the learning disabled sophomores designated within the grant's funding had been assigned to her. The teachers' ages were 42, 29, 29, 27, and 22 with years of teaching experience 10, 8, 7, 6, and none, respectively. None of the teachers had completed any special education courses and only experienced teachers had attended one or two in-service programs on teaching exceptional students or poor readers. One teacher was finishing her master's degree in language arts education and another had completed six hours of graduate coursework in English literature.

Procedure

At the end of the academic year the five teachers submitted notebooks in which questions and experiences with contracts throughout the year had been recorded. These records were compiled by the project consultant into a set of guidelines for educators. The students responded anonymously to a survey composed of open-ended questions and specific statements assessing the contract method. Results were computed into percentages on the basis of grade level and sex. Student responses to open-ended questions were ranked according to frequency.

RESULTS AND DISCUSSION

Students considered the contracts fair, worthwhile, and preferable to other teaching methods (Table 2). Females generally rated contracts more positively than males, probably reflecting their greater achievement within a system which required self-discipline, deficient among more of the male students. No consistent trends or differences existed between the three grade levels.

Students' reasons for enjoying the contracts were ranked respectively by frequency: (1) working at my own pace without being nagged, (2) knowing exactly what was expected of me, (3) being able to improve my course grade, (4) working alone, (5) earning free time for completing the work, (6) receiving individual teacher attention, and (7) choosing from a variety of activities. Students' recommended improvements were: (1) increase the time allowed to complete the contract, (2) award more points for each daily activity, (3) lessen the amount of work required, (4) provide more group instruction beforehand, (5) include greater variety among contract options, (6) allow more oral work for contract credit, (7) decrease the points for the final contract test, and (8) design some small group activities on the contract.

TABLE 2   Student Opinions of Academic Contracts*

Response	Soph. N-26	Junior N-28	Senior N-29	Soph. N-22	Junior N-27	Senior N-24
I learned nothing	7%	—	—	—	—	—
I learned a usual amount	86%	50%	62%	60%	57%	50%
I learned a lot	7%	50%	38%	40%	43%	50%
Contracts were fair	70%	92%	86%	100%	95%	92%
I prefer contracts to regular class	65%	72%	75%	60%	90%	80%
I want another contract	74%	72%	80%	60%	90%	92%
I want to design my own contract	38%	28%	49%	27%	33%	45%
N=156		Males			Females	

*Grade 10—2-week contract on a novel
 Grade 11—2-week contract on job interviewing
 Grade—3-week contract on grammer

Teachers' concerns and experiences were compiled into the following question-and-answer guideline:

Why should I exert the effort to design contracts rather than using my present methods?

Contracting has repeatedly demonstrated its ability to improve academic and social conduct, especially for underachieving or disruptive students (see Table 1). Contracts clarify to students, parents, and administrators what the objectives are. This can often calm irate students who feel they are being discriminated against, since the criteria are written beforehand and are more objectively graded. Contracts ease the grading procedure and often remove the subjective element from evaluation. You are already using contracts at present: plans and grading methods stored "in your head" which are supposedly understood clearly by students. Contracting only means transferring these unwritten plans to paper, so all students will understand the contingencies.

How can I decrease the time invested in designing contracts?

Contracts do not require elaborate mimeographed documents in which you invest more time than other teaching methods. Simple contracts can be written on the board or posted on a bulletin board. Brief contracts (Figure 1) are merely copies of weekly lesson plans. Also, teachers can design contracts together or exchange contracts which are kept in a mutual file for the department.

FIGURE 1 Simplified Weekly Contract

Points I earned	Maximum Points Possible	Activity
	5	Attendance: 1 per day
	10	Test: 1 per question (see list of possible questions)
	10	Theme: 2 for each criterion met (see list of evaluation criteria)
	6	Class participation in discussion: 2 per discussion, 1 for any comment, and 2 for several comments
	5	Homework: 1 per question correct
	36	Total Possible
A=32	B=30 C=26 D=22	

Other teachers criticize me for rewarding my students with "free days" or games which they have earned by completing a contract. How do I cope with their criticism?

Perhaps these phrases will be useful with nonsupportive colleagues: "I reward students for appropriate social behaviors which effect their academic learning. Tangible and frequent rewards are effective with disadvantaged and underachieving students to increase their academic skills." " 'Bribery' is a payoff for illegal or undesirable behavior. But receiving a reward for good behavior is like our paycheck each month for teaching—a payoff for good work or desirable conduct." "Disruptions and constant nagging each day used to consume much of my instructional time in class. Using a contract and rewards like games or free days saves me and the students much time which is otherwise wasted through nagging." "My eventual goal is to make the activities in my class so intrinsically reinforcing that no other rewards will be necessary. But at this point my underachievers are so unmotivated that they will not persist at any task without some enticement. I will begin with them at this level and hope eventually to remove rewards if students ever become self-motivated." "I simply cannot ignore in good conscience the abundant amount of research which substantiates the success of contracting. I like my students and want to do whatever I can to help them to learn academic skills."

How will contracts allow me to explain individually to students who are learning the material incorrectly or inadequately on their own?

Deliver lectures, or whatever methods you are presently using, to explain difficult materials at the beginning of a class period or on designated days of the week. Contracting does not imply that the teacher must never engage in whole group instruction. Include these group methods in the contract. For example, one point on the contract would be awarded to all those who attend class on the day you are lecturing.

Won't the lack of peer competition decrease learning since contracts allow many students to achieve A's and B's?

Research does not support the myth that peer competition enhances academic achievement for students who are underachieving, unmotivated, anxious, academically unskilled, or previous school failures.[7]

Can I administer an additional test after the contract is complete for students who earned poor grades on the contract?

·This in inconsistent with the philosophy of contracting, since students will quickly learn to mistrust the terms of a predetermined contract once you have modified it afterwards. They will henceforth badger you at the end of each contract to let them earn extra points. Better alternatives, if students do not master the content, are: (1) create another contract which will reteach the materials, (2) consider whether your first contract contained goals which were too far beyond students' skill levels or whether the time limit was too brief, (3) offer students the option to retake tests on any contract, *but* the extra studying will not be during class time and the makeup exam will not consume class time designated for other activities.

Students' grades still seem low on the unit contract tests. How do I know this method was really better?

To assess the success of contracts you would need a *control* group of students being taught by traditional methods in order to fairly evaluate the contracts' success. Research which has included these controls demonstrates the superiority of contracts over other approaches, with the most significant differences noted for underachievers and least significant differences with academically successful students (Table 1). Furthermore, benefits accrue which may not be assessed by mere grading methods — primarily, improvements in student attitude.

How do I find materials at a low enough academic level to individualize contracts for lowest and highest skilled students?

Any material which you are presently using can be individualized to some degree in a contract by varying several factors which are within the teacher's control: time limits, quantity of material, *aids* available (books, instruments, teacher assistance, peer help) and the method or medium through which the acquired knowledge will be evaluated. Individualizing can also mean incorporating various learning modalities into your contract (Table 3).

How do I reply when students complain that their contracts are different from their peers and that this is "unfair"?

These sample comments should suffice. "My role as a teacher is not to reteach you material which you already have mastered. The materials being presented on your contract are introducing you to new skills for which others may not yet be ready." "You seem to feel that you are being treated unjustly or unfairly. I do not believe it would be just or fair for you to earn an *A* by doing work in a book which you can easily read while someone else will have to learn many new words just to complete the book. I am giving you material from which you can learn new skills. That seems very fair to me." "Do you think that it would be fair for you to earn $6,000 a year

TABLE 3   Contract Activities

Primarily Auditory	Primarily Visual	Primarily Kinesthetic
Student oral reading	Films	Producing a movie
Teacher instruction	Flash cards	Puppet theater
Class discussion	Notes on board	Role playing
Guest lecture	Board games	Field trip
Quiz games	Written desk work	Learning centers
Records and tapes	Programed materials	Building mobiles
Student debate	Silent reading	Nonwritten projects
Student speeches	Creating scrapbooks or written projects	Designing book jackets
Guest interview	Written themes	Creating bulletin boards
Drills and questions		Using globes, equipment, manipulative materials
		Acting plays
		Camera assignments

working every day of the week building highways while I earned $15,000 for working one day a week delivering newspapers? I am giving you a reward for work which you can complete in one day because of your abilities, while someone else will need more time to earn the reward for that amount of work. We do not all come into this class with the same skills.''

What about students who aren't self-disciplined enough to work independently on a contract?

Contracting often requires introduction, since students are accustomed to traditional appoaches in which they have not been given practice in self-control and responsibility. Ways to teach students how to develop self-discipline during contracting are: (1) introduce the concept initially by providing one or two day contracts, (2) enumerate the problems which might arise, and establish a social behavior contract for those who disrupt others while they should be working on the academic contract, (3) use *backup* reinforcers to entice students to be more self-disciplined. Some students will not find earning points on the contract very rewarding; but social backup reinforcers are often effective (Table 4).

TABLE 4   Potential Reinforcers for Adolescents

Listening to the radio (ear phones or plug to avoid disturbance)
Solving puzzles: crossword, manipulative, riddles
Reading comics, sports magazines, newspapers, car brochures, love stories
Listening to records (students choice from home)
Talking to friends
Playing a game
Writing notes
Sitting in a comfortable chair or at the teacher's desk
Choosing seats near friends
Returning equipment to media center
Being read to by the teacher
Assisting the teacher: grade paper or tutor
Drawing at the board
Creating a bulletin board on topic of own choice
Drawing overhead transparencies
Looking at old school yearbooks
Conducting class outside
Performing for peers: musical or skill demonstration
Sitting on a mattress in the room
Threading a projector
Watching television
Primping
Exclusion from homework
Building a mobile
Telling jokes
Taking a nap
Tape recording own voice
Watching old silent movies
Leaving early for lunch
Playing in the gym if free time is earned
Field trips or guest speakers
Taking photographs around campus
Having creative work displayed in the room

What happens when I run out of ideas for contracts?

Contracting is not a panacea and should not be used as a continual substitute for other teaching techniques. Let students suggest ideas. The responsibility should not be yours constantly to entertain students or allow them to blame you when they become bored. When they complain of boredom with a contract, reply: "I am only one person. There are 35 of you. On this contract, therefore, you will design your weekly activities. Write your contract now and submit it to me at the end of class for my approval.'' Also, brainstorm with other teachers for contract ideas (Table 3).

How do I record students' work? The task of monitoring and grading seems overwhelming with the contract method.

Include your daily or weekly grading checklist on the contract itself (Figure 1). Do not feel compelled to grade all work for quality. Some points may be awarded merely for the completion of a daily assignment and a simple check in a grade book will suffice as recording. Grade intermittently for quality. For example, of three papers which a student may write for a weekly contract, credit would be awarded for completion of each paper, but only one would be randomly selected for quality and content grading.

What if the school has a policy that students with excused absences must be allowed to make up work? How can I include points for attendance as part of my contract then?

Rewarding attendance can still be included on a contract without violating the school's policy and while still reinforcing regular attendance. Simply include a variety of activities on a weekly contract which a student could complete outside of class in order to compensate for points otherwise earned by attendance. The option is much less pleasant to most students than simply earning points for daily attendance; but if you do value attendance, reward it within your contract system.

What about students who set their contract goals excessively high or low in relation to their actual abilities?

Inability to set realistic goals is a common characteristic among students with low achievement needs. These students will choose tasks which ensure predictable outcomes, regardless of whether the result is success or failure. In contrast, students with high achievement needs elect tasks of intermediate difficulty and are motivated by occasional failure to achieve the goal.[8-10] Some programs have been designed to teach students goal-setting skills[11,12] by requiring them to outline a goal checklist and record daily their progress. Contracting and consequent feedback regarding goal attainment is an alternate method for learning goal-setting skills; but the acquisition requires time and practice.

CONCLUSION

Obviously, contingency contracting is only one alternative available to teachers and is not intended to become a substitute for other motivational options. Counseling, values clarification, bibliotherapy, parent programs, peer control, educational games, dietary alterations, teacher praise, peer tutoring, computer programs, videotaping, modeling, curriculum materials, teacher expectations, school environments, and instructional style have all been identified as potential contributors to student motivation. Likewise, training programs for achievement motivation, locus of control, self-modification, and goal setting have demonstrated their value. In contrast to other approaches, however, contingency contracting can be implemented without extensive teacher training, additional expenses, staff enlargement, administrative involvement or mechanical assistance. With continued publicity and research, it is hoped that contracting will become a more popular method for enhancing adolescent motivation and achievement.

NOTES

1. *Learning Disabilities: The Link to Delinquency but Schools Should Do More Now*, Department of Health, Education and Welfare, March 1977, GGD-7697.

2. J. Lipsitz, *Growing Up Forgotten* (Lexington, MA: Lexington Books, 1977).

3. J. McMillan, "Factors Affecting the Development of Pupil Attitudes toward School Subjects," *Psychology in the Schools* 13 (1976): 322-5.

4. E. Gagne, "Educating Delinquents: Review of Research," *Journal of Special Education* 11 (1977): 13-27.

5. *Learning Disabilities: The Link to Delinquency*.

6. For a complete explanation of contingency contracting, see R. Williams and K. Anadam's *Cooperative Classroom Management* (Columbus, OH: Charles E. Merrill, 1974).

7. D. Johnson and R. Johnson, "Instructional Goal Structures: Cooperative, Competitive or Individualistic," *Review of Educational Research* 2 (1974): 213-40.

8. J. Atkinson, *Motives in Fantasy, Action, and Society* (Princeton, NJ: Van Nostrand, 1958).

9. A Kukla, "Performance as a Function of Resultant Achievement Motivation, Perceived Ability, and Perceived Difficulty," *Journal of Research in Personality* 7 (1974): 374-83.

10. B. Weiner, *Theories of Motivation* (Chicago: Rand-McNally, 1972).

11. R. Bradley and J. Gaa, "Domain Specifics Aspects of Locus of Control: Implications for Modifying Locus of Control Orientation," *Journal of School Psychology* 15 (1977): 18-24.

12. E. Gagne, "Motivating the Disabled Learner," *Academic Therapy* 10 (1975): 361-2.

Bibliotherapy for the LD Adolescent

by Barbara E. Lenkowsky
and Ronald S. Lenkowsky

The belief that reading can change an individual's attitudes and behavior is not new. Ancient civilizations considered books an important influence in shaping the values of youth. The classics' primary objective was character training. Indeed, the basic objective of early American education was the inculcation of desirable character traits and moral values. Today, reading programs, although reflective of behavioral expectations, have generally moved away from the concept of actively changing attitudes.

The learning disabled adolescent, however, brings special attitude problems to the classroom. These result from his/her experiences of academic and social failure, from the increasing pressures of secondary education, and from adolescence itself. Teachers of this age group are aware of these problems, but they often lack effective emotional support and relief techniques. We are offering the concept of bibliotherapy as a possible classroom method to help meet these personal, social, and emotional needs.

WHAT IS BIBLIOTHERAPY?

Bibliotherapy can help adolescents understand themselves by providing them with literature relevant to their personal problems and developmental needs at the appropriate time. Preventative bibliotherapy prepares teenagers to cope with problems of adjustment.[1] Both constructs are applicable only to the classroom or remedial reading experience.

Research on the bibliotherapy hypothesis is both incomplete and inconclusive. Its validity for the normal learner is not clear. Nevertheless, as special educators, we have come to recognize the potential importance of this concept in our classrooms. We view bibliotherapy for the learning disabled as:

> . . . a process of dynamic interaction between the personality of the reader and literature . . . which may be utilized for personality assessment, adjustment

and growth . . . [it] lies within the province of every teacher . . . [and] does not assume that every teacher must be a skilled therapist . . . Rather, it conveys the idea that all teachers must be aware of the effects upon children and must realize that through literature most children can be helped to solve the developmental problems of adjustment they face.[2]

HOW DOES BIBLIOTHERAPY WORK?

The *therapy* in bibliotherapy denotes a three-step hypothesis. Bibliotherapy proceeds from identification to catharsis to insight.

Identification with characters, situations, or elements of a story is the first step in this process. Identification helps the reader realize that s/he is not the first person to encounter a particular problem, and it enables him/her to vicariously relive a particular experience. Thus, the reader is able to view his/her problem from a different perspective, which promotes personality adjustment and growth.

The second step is catharsis, or the release of tension. We suggest that the reader gratifies his/her impulses or desires (even the socially unacceptable drives) by his/her identification with the actions of the story characters. This gratification results in tension reduction and overall relaxation (catharsis).

Insight is the final phase. By achieving insight the reader understands, modifies, and changes his/her attitudes and behaviors. Bibliotherapeutic intervention's goal will be to gain insight, and it is the responsibility of the teacher to guide students toward it.

WHY BIBLIOTHERAPY FOR THE LEARNING DISABLED ADOLESCENT?

Bibliotherapy is consistent with the general goals of education and reading. Furthermore, it is similarly consistent with the theory that a positive self-concept is essential to learning. Certainly, this should be inherent in education for the learning disabled. We have observed, and believe most teachers will agree, that learning disabled adolescents are especially aware of their own feelings of inferiority, failure, and impotence. And they often express these feelings if a supportive, interested teacher provides them with an opportunity to do so. In utilizing an individualized reading technique with our classes, it was apparent that students often used reading conferences, developed as comprehension checks, for personal guidance. Our pupils expressed empathy for characters, identified with situations they read, and were delighted to discover fictional and factual stories whose characters experienced problems similar or comparable to their own. Reading such stories reinforced their feelings of *normalcy* and helped the students to realize that they were not alone in facing adolescence's problems and the special problems created by their disabilities. The pupils enjoyed this identification and eagerly awaited their conference time to request additional books relevant to their needs. Thus, we chanced upon a motivational source for previously reluctant readers, which we regarded as a new beneficial technique, as well as a *therapeutic* aid for these teenagers.

The teacher's role in individualized reading is to foster comprehension, to guide students to topics that interest them, and to encourage students to read pupil-selected materials. To fulfill this role, the teacher must often administer formal and informal interest inventories. This enables him/her to select trade books, magazines, and other materials for the classroom library that will motivate the students to read. These same inventories will also reveal the students' problems and concerns, and they will allow the teacher to select books of higher interest and greater therapeutic value.

In addition, teachers of learning disabled adolescents realize that the selection of reading materials is complicated by the need to find books and stories which are highly interesting yet have a lowered vocabulary. The learning disableds' reading skill limitations often negate the teacher's ability to guide a student to a book or story which s/he knows would be a source of identification and insight, if the student could read it. Fortunately, bibliotherapy does not require silent reading, although this is obviously one goal. The teacher can accomplish bibliotherapy by reading out loud to the individual or to the class. Thus, it is an appropriate method for poor or nonreaders. The teacher may also substitute taped presentations of stories or books which can be either commercially available or teacher-made. (We found that our students enjoyed using *talking books* which are usually employed with blind and visually impaired youth.) Finally, bibliotherapy can be accomplished through group discussion, if a student brings to his/her classmates' attention a particularly meaningful book, and if the class then wishes to read it and discuss its meaning for them. This group aspect of bibliotherapy is particularly useful with adolescents, and research exists to confirm the importance of peer group opinion to adolescents.

Bonnie

To briefly illustrate the process, we will consider Bonnie, a tall, pretty, 15-year-old with a reading level just above grade six. When we assessed her interests for individualized reading (mostly by observing her selections and by asking after each book conference), it was soon apparent that her greatest (and only) passion was sports. It was equally obvious that she had very few friends, no boyfriends, and little self-confidence. We used a problem checklist to verify the observations and found that Bonnie, who had never dated, was significantly concerned about dating and boys. She felt that she never would date with her "personality," academic, and appearance problems. To Bonnie, athletics seemed to offer the only chance she had to excel in anything (she was good); and, since she was convinced that she was unattractive, further rejection by boys because she was "an athlete" was irrelevant.

We used this information to direct her to a short story book of the high interest–low vocabulary type which happened to contain a story entitled, "Red."[3] The plot of this quickly readable story concerns an adolescent girl who seems to excel only at basketball and is unable to make friends or to date. She is unable to do so, that is, until the school basketball captain observes her practicing by herself, is amazed by her prowess, and asks to join her. The open-ended story leaves room for the reader to imagine what occurs next but it also reveals enough to convey the growth in the girl's confidence and happiness.

Bonnie reported in her next book conference that she had particularly enjoyed that story, and we discussed its meaning and relevance to her life and feelings. We talked about being athletic and attractive and using one to enhance the other. We recommended another short story entitled "Kiss the Ref,"[4] and, when she completed it, she was excited and anxious to talk more about using her skill to improve her social life.

Although we did not have additional applicable books and stories on her level, we were nevertheless able to move forward by reading to Bonnie. A national magazine had published an interview with tennis star Billie Jean King in which she freely spoke of her childhood struggle to be attractive and athletic, competitive and "feminine." This interview prompted many conversations with Bonnie in which we learned what concerns and special problems she was feeling. Consequently, this enabled us to continue to direct her to reading material important in improving her concept of self, her confidence, and her outlook. In this way, bibliotherapy has enabled us to begin helping Bonnie in more significant ways than by merely trying to tell her or to reassure her of her competence and attractiveness.

SUGGESTIONS AND NEEDS IN IMPLEMENTING BIBLIOTHERAPY

Any classroom teacher or reading teacher can begin a bibliotherapy program. We have found that consultation with school librarians, psychologists, social workers, and guidance counselors is important to expand the scope and effectiveness of such programs. Although much research confirmation is necessary, interdisciplinary cooperation can help isolate specific pupil variables which would be amenable to the bibliotherapeutic approach. Cooperation can also provide direction in the search for meaningful materials.

Although we have collected lists of books written by and about the handicapped, these are too often unrelated to the learning disableds' very specific problems. A great need exists for professionals, parents, and publishers to fill this vacuum with materials which explore the intrapersonal ramifications of being learning disabled. Even more helpful would be the development of a collection of fiction or biography by and about those who have overcome, compensated for, or come to grips with their own learning dysfunctions. The lack of such books is still a weakness in bibliotherapy, although our students were interested in and gained insight from stories concerning emotional and social problems.

The adolescent's teacher needs to be familiar with the literature centered on the varied trials and experiences of children from 12 to 19. If a teacher wishes to obtain this information, s/he must collect anthologies (most useful with edited comments and suggestions), contact publishers for assistance, join book clubs, and, most important, read. Although these efforts are sometimes time consuming, we have found them to be rewarding. Our expanded knowledge has enabled us to better guide our pupils through bibliotherapy; and through this process we have helped them to help themselves adapt and cope with their own problems.

CONCLUSION

We have found that bibliotherapy is compatible with our classroom reading programs and with the goal of self-concept and behavioral improvement for the learning disabled adolescent. Student feedback and problem inventories have shown us that bibliotherapy appears effective. We recognize the need for an objective study which would further expand the bibliotherapy concept with this population and we are preparing such a study.

NOTES

1. D. Russell and C. Shrodes, "Contributions of Research in Bibliotherapy to the Language Arts Program," *School Review* 58 (1950): 335-42, 411-20.
2. Ibid., p. 335.
3. J.A. Bacon, "Red," in *Don't Die Baby* (Columbus, OH: Xerox Education Publications, 1974), pp. 47-56.
4. M. Katz, M. Chakeres, and M. Bromberg, "Kiss the Ref," in *Real Stories: Book A* (New York: Globe Book, 1973), pp. 133-9.

REFERENCES

Anglin, E. and Lipscomb, E. "Sixes Can Take a Giant Step." *Elementary English* 40 (1963): 174-82.

Arbuthnot, M.H. *Children and Books*. 3d ed. Chicago: Scott-Foresman, 1964.

Edwards, B.S. "Therapeutic Value of Reading." *Elementary English* 49 (1972): 213-7.

Elkins, D. "Students Face Their Problems." *English Journal* 38 (1949): 498-503.

Kircher, C.J. *Character Formation through Books: A Bibliography.* Washington, DC: Catholic University of America Press, 1952.

Reading Ladders for Human Relations. 4th ed. Washington, DC: American Council on Education, 1963.

Shrodes, C. "Bibliotherapy." *Reading Teacher* 9 (1955): 24-9.

Spache, G.D. "Using Books to Help Solve Children's Problems." In *Good Books for Poor Readers*. Champaign, IL: Garrard Publishing, 1974.

Weingarten, S. "Developmental Values in Voluntary Reading." *School Review* 62 (1954): 222-30.

The Learning Disabled Child: Films for Social, Emotional, Language, and Sensory Needs

by Sonya Abbye

The term *learning disabled* can encompass any of the perceptual areas and interfere in many ways with the learning process. Reading, physical-motor, visual-motor, and language areas can be affected. It is difficult to profile the learning disabled child, who is usually of average or above average intelligence and in many ways appears normal. Some areas of his/her perception may be affected, while others are unaffected. Unless a child is severely impaired, his/her deficiencies are usually amorphous and subtle. Perhaps herein lies the problem. A learning disabled child may go through primary grades undiagnosed or incorrectly diagnosed. A bright child can be labeled lazy or dull. Bizarre behavior and hyperactivity can be attributed to poor discipline or a just plain "bad" child.

Because of late or inaccurate diagnosis, or adult ignorance, frustration mounts and a youngster often develops a poor self-image. School becomes a place associated with failure. Teachers become enemies; books and written material are sources of more frustration and failure.

In order to combat such barriers, alternate means of breaking through to the learning disabled must be explored. Incorporating film programs into the regular course of the school day is one way. Enlisting the aid of public libraries and outside child-oriented organizations may also prove helpful. Many public libraries have special programs for school children and can accommodate the learning disabled if sufficient preparation time is given. Effective programs combining film with lavishly illustrated books can be designed. Libraries can provide after-school help as well and frequently hold family film programs in the evening.

When I first saw a group of severely impaired youngsters engrossed with the events on screen, I was amazed. Hyperactivity diminished; common fights and outbursts happened less often. The children seemed to be happy and far more tractable. What was the magic formula? What happens to a child when the lights are turned down and the projector is turned on? Perhaps the simplest explanation is the reduction of anxiety. Films and television are associated with recreation. Films are fun. Children don't feel called upon to perform and hence may relax and enjoy themselves. How can their enthusiasm and enjoyment be used to help them overcome learning disabilities?

Based on my work in the classroom, and in order to help those working with the learning disabled child, I have assembled a series of films which is divided into three areas: *social and emotional needs, language development* and a special series of films on the *five senses*. Some films are found in more than one category. Most of the films have been used with groups of children ages 5 to 14. Age levels are based on classroom use. The films have been evaluated for quality of language, visual appeal, and narrative strength, i.e, is the story line easy to follow or too confusing?

SOCIAL AND EMOTIONAL NEEDS

A learning disabled child feels isolated, caught up in a world s/he barely understands; s/he has painful, confused feelings. Films help a child become aware of those feelings and begin the complicated process of problem solving. The films in the following list deal sensitively with many problems that arise, not only those dealing with learning disability, but also those which occur in the natural process of growing up. It's one thing to realize that the "kid" sitting next to you has a problem, but when a stranger on the screen experiences the same sense of loss and bewilderment, it is much more affective by making certain problems universal. The child feels less alone. When such a film is discussed in small groups, many hidden feelings surface. Important bonds may form between group members and adults. Adults gain insights into children and find ways to reach them.

Almost Everyone Does color 14 min. Wombat.
By Gene Feldman, 1970.
> This film was used with older children from ages 10 to 13. It focuses on drugs, drinking, smoking, and pill-taking as means of dealing with problems. Children are encouraged to offer alternatives.

Circus: Serrina Becomes an Acrobat color 11 min. EBEC.
Produced by Encyclopaedia Brittanica, 1972.
> An exciting presentation of a young girl training to be an acrobat with the circus. It shows her successes and failures, and the learning processes unfold. Used successfully with youngsters from ages 5 to 9 and can be used with older children.

Elsa and Her Cubs   color   31 min.   Benchmark.
By Raquil Sobel, 1970.
> A touching story of the friendship between the Adamsons and the lioness Elsa. Many sensitive areas such as friendship, love, and death are brought up. Has been used effectively with age groups from 5 to 14.

Evan's Corner   color   24 min.   BFA.
By Conrad Rothman, 1969.
> A story about a black child who is from a large family and feels pressure to find a place to call his own. Children can identify with his feelings and realize it's not so bad to want to be alone at times. This was used with youngsters from ages 9 to 14. Adapted from the book by Elizabeth Starr Hill.

Eye of the Storm   color   25 min.   Xerox.
By William Peters for ABC News, 1970.
> A superb film which documents the experience of a third grade teacher's efforts to show her class the problems of prejudice and discrimination. "One day the blue-eyed children were told they were superior to the brown-eyed children." Implications for use in classrooms are vast. Differences and similarities in people can be discussed. Differences in race, religion, height, weight, and ability can all be brought to light. A group of 10-year-old boys were inspired to lengthy discussions and creative writing after having seen this film.

Helen Keller and Her Teacher   color   27 min.   McGraw-Hill.
By Noah Keen, 1970.
> An excellent dramatization of the developing relationship between Helen and her teacher Annie Sullivan. Shows the trials, errors, and pains they share before the initial breakthrough. Helen's problems seem insurmountable and yet the film goes on to discuss the success story of these determined women. A beautiful film for children and people of all ages.

Help I'm Shrinking   color   10 min.   Films Inc.
By Barbara Dourmaskin, 1975.
> A delightful cartoon about a 7-year-old girl who feels incapable of doing anything. She feels helpless and small and every time she says, "I can't," she shrinks until she is the size of a butterfly. This film was shown to a group of 7- to 9-year-old boys who began to chant "You can do it," at the end of the film. There was a great sense that they were saying "they could too"!

J.T.   color   51 min.   Carousel.
By Robert Young, 1969.
> An excellent story for children of all ages. It deals with a lonely Harlem boy who, having stolen a radio, hides in an abandoned building. There he finds a sick cat which he nurses back to health. It is a tender story that shows J.T.'s growing sense of responsibility. It takes place at Christmas time but can be used anytime during the year.

Just Awful   color   8 min.   Oxford.

By Morland Latchford, 1972.

> About a little boy who cuts his finger in a playground accident. His fear is communicated by the expression on his face and the words, "I feel just awful." What makes you feel just awful? It's a good question to ask 5- to 9-year-olds. Should the little boy be scared of going to the school nurse? Would you be scared? The answer will surprise you. Adaptation of a book by Alma Whitney.

L'Adolescence   black & white   22 min.   Macmillan.

By Vladimir Forgency, 1966.

> Follows the activities of a 14-year-old girl as she tries to become a professional dancer. She experiences disappointment when she is turned down by a ballet company. Should she give up or try again? This film seems to work well with young children and older girls. French with English subtitles.

Lady of the Light   color   19 min.   Walt Disney.

By Walt Disney Productions, 1965.

> A film without dialogue about a lonely lighthouse keeper's daughter who sends out requests for mail in bottles and receives many responses. A new world of friendship opens up to her. How important is friendship? What is a friend? These were questions asked of groups of children ages five through nine.

Not Me   black & white   51 min.   McGraw-Hill.

By Allen Savage, 1970.

> A powerfully dramatized "but authentic chronicle of the addiction of a 13-year-old youth from an urban ghetto, resulting in his death from an overdose of heroin." It leaves an audience spellbound. Shown to children from ages 10 to 14, as this seems to be an age group that will benefit from it.

Pets: A Boy and His Dog   color   11 min.   BFA.

By Gabor Kalman, 1969.

> A sensitive treatment of the love of a boy for his dog. Even though the dog loses out in a pet show, the love remains. Again a child is faced with disappointment and finds ways to overcome it. Used with children from ages 9 to 11, but would be good with younger children also.

Skinny & Fatty   black & white   45 min.   McGraw-Hill.

By N. Terao, 1959.

> Shown effectively to youngsters aged 5 to 14. Despite its 45-minute length, interest was maintained throughout. It is the story of two Japanese school boys: one who seems to excel at everything, the other who is shy and awkward and familiar with failure. It is the kind of film that all children can relate to. Children, again, can think about or discuss feelings about friendship; about differences; about prejudices; and, if the environment is right, about failure. Japanese dialogue dubbed in English.

White Mane   black & white   39 min.   McGraw-Hill.

By Albert Lamorisse, 1953.

> A sensitive, poetic depiction of a young boy's devotion to a wild white horse. Follows the boy's often frustrating attempts to control the horse. Useful with children from ages 5 to 14.

LANGUAGE DEVELOPMENT

Many of the films in this list were used with severely language-impaired children. These are the ones who need to be helped to look, listen, and feel. These children respond, in many cases, to silent films which encourage expressive language. They were able to add dialogue by watching for particular cues: facial expressions; body movements; and, in some instances, background music. They were encouraged to make associations between actions and reactions, between different people and things, and to relate them to everyday life.

Many films were used to tap such language areas as storytelling, sequencing of events, absurdities, etc. Questions with *who, what, where, how,* and *why* were answered with little effort on the part of the child. The following films are all excellent for developing language abilities.

Harold and the Purple Crayon   color   10 min.   Weston Woods.
By David Piel, 1959.
> Based on a character in a book by Crocket Johnson, Harold is a delightfully animated character who can draw in his surroundings wherever he goes. A terrific film for work with young children who need help in categorization, classification, sequencing, fallacies, etc. After showing the film you can do the following types of exercises with groups. You can use the blackboard and take turns giving the children chalk. "If you were Harold and you wanted to be on a farm, beach, supermarket, or zoo, what could you draw?" The teacher can draw inappropriate things and see if the children can pick them out. Does an elephant belong on Harold's farm? It's a fun game which the children love.

Harold's Fairy Tale   color   8 min.   Weston Woods.
By Morton Schindel, 1974.
> In this adventure Harold's travels take him to an enchanted garden where nothing grows. He encounters giants and witches and finds a happy ending. Another appealing film for young children. Retelling the story through pictures and experience stories can be a valuable language exercise.

A Kite Story   color   25 min.   Churchill.
By Pieter Van Deusen, 1970.
> A fantasy adventure without words about a young boy who discovers a kite-maker who helps him to make a kite. The kite is quite plain and is soon forsaken for a glittering one. It is a colorful film which can appeal to children from ages 5 to 10. In this type of film, children can be encouraged to provide dialogue for the characters, e.g., they can pick one character, the boy, or the kite and offer a sentence or more for them in different sequences in the film. When working with older children, the exercise can be transferred to writing.

Moonbird   color   10 min.   Films Inc.
By John Hubley, 1959.
> An amusing tale of two little boys who venture into the night seeking the "moonbird." It is animated and uses very little language. It uses sounds and vocalizations effectively to generate feelings. Children can be asked to devise

their own imaginary animals and characters. Where would you look for them? What would it look like? Good for language arts programs, creative writing, and illustrating for older children; storytelling and sequencing for young children.

On the Twelfth Day   color   21 min.   Films Inc.
By Wendy Toye, 1964.
An imaginative film drawn by Ronald Searle, which "takes off" on the well-known Christmas carol, "The Twelve Days of Christmas." It brings a multitude of gifts and many results to the screen. Children delight in the repetition of song and the visual absurdities. What's so funny about a polka dotted cow? Ask the children.

One A.M.   black & white   14 min.   Blackhawk.
By Charlie Chaplin, 1916, Silent.
"In this early Charlie Chaplin film, Charlie returns home from a night on the town, in evening dress and high silk hat." He then finds himself in many incredible situations. Children are encouraged to read subtitles through the laughter. This kind of film is good for kids of all ages. Children can add their own language with episodes or feelings generated by the character.

The Pawnshop   black & white   21 min.   Blackhawk.
By Charlie Chaplin, 1916, Silent.
Considered one of Chaplin's best films. It concerns Charlie's escapades as an employee in a pawnshop. Children are delighted by the antics and the bigger-than-life gestures and facial expressions which aid comprehension and inspire expressive language.

People Soup   color   13 min.   LCA.
By Alan Arkin, 1961.
Amusingly follows the antics of two young boys as they experiment in the kitchen. After they taste their concoctions, one turns into a chicken and the other turns into a sheepdog. This is a quality film which can be used for many language areas. Sequencing and especially storytelling exercises can be developed for the youngest children.

A Picture for Harold's Room   color   6 min.   Weston Woods.
By Morton Schindel, 1971.
Another story about Harold, the little boy who draws things that become real. For suggestions, see *Harold and the Purple Crayon*.

The Red Balloon   color   34 min.   Macmillan.
By Albert Lamorisse, 1956.
A moving and beautifully photographed film about a young boy's attachment to a magic balloon. Done without words, the film captivates children with its highly visual and fantastic adventures of the boy and his balloon. Children can be motivated to provide language for the film.

The Rink   black & white   15 min.   Blackhawk.
By Charlie Chaplin, 1916, Silent.
Charlie Chaplin is a waiter who spends his spare time at a roller skating rink. Laughter and mayhem combine in many fast-moving sequences. Can be used with children of all ages.

Second Hundred Years   black & white   30 min.   Blackhawk.
1921, Silent.
>   Stan Laurel and Oliver Hardy are shown as cellmates trying to dig their way out of prison. Children make associations to derive the humor. They are encouraged to read subtitles and to generate language.

The Tramp   black & white   25 min.   Blackhawk.
By Charlie Chaplin, 1915, Silent.
>   "This is the first film by Charlie Chaplin in which pathos was evident and the first one to end on a note of sadness." Children can empathize with "The Tramp," a lovable, well-meaning character for whom nothing goes right. Children are motivated to read subtitles and to look for more than surface meanings; for children of all ages.

Two Tars   black & white   22 min.   Blackhawk.
1928, Silent.
>   Follows the antics of Laurel and Hardy, who are sailors on shore leave. Vintage automobiles stuck in a colossal traffic jam provide the humor in this delightful film. Children take pleasure in retelling the story and providing dialogue for these incredible characters.

FILMS FOR FIVE SENSES

As further encouragement for work with the handicapped, my experiment with *Helen Keller and Her Teacher* demonstrates how readily a program may develop. I showed the film to a group of severely language-impaired 5- to 7-year-olds. Their responses were very enthusiastic. Many of the youngsters began to reenact Helen's movements. They closed their eyes, walking with outstretched arms. They asked many, many questions. The result of the enthusiasm was a series of films and activities about the five senses. They played guessing games that involved isolating the senses and testing their validity. Interest and energy remained at high levels throughout the program, and they asked to see the films again and again.

Bread   black & white   8 min.   Eccentric.
By Craig Umanoff, 1953.
>   A highly tactile film demonstrating the making of a traditional Jewish challa.

Dragon Stew   color   13 min.   BFA.
By Robert Konikow, 1972.
>   An animated tale about a "con" man cook who must make a stew out of a dragon. The dragon's voice was particularly appealing and helped with auditory awareness. The film was a particular favorite which easily held the children's attention.

Helen Keller and Her Teacher   color   27 min.   McGraw-Hill.
By Noah Keen, 1970.
> Excellent dramatization of the developing relationship between deaf and blind Helen Keller and her persevering teacher, Annie Sullivan.

In a Spring Garden   color   6 min.   Weston Woods.
By Cynthia Freitag, 1967.
> A collection of Japanese haiku, short poems about nature, showing the creatures and sounds one might find in a garden on a spring day.

Kittens Are Born   color   10 min.   McGraw-Hill.
By Susan and Hugh Johnston, 1971.
> Explicit live-action film of kittens being born. Excellent photography contributes to strong visual impact. Quiet background music is soothing.

On the Twelfth Day   color   11 min.   Films Inc.
By Wendy Toye, 1964.
> An imaginative film drawn by Ronald Searle, which "takes off" on the well-known Christmas carol, "The Twelve Days of Christmas." The repetition and visual absurdities make it particularly good with younger children.

One Day at Teton Marsh   color   47 min.   Walt Disney.
By Walt Disney Productions, 1966.
> Animal life in a marsh, with emphasis on a family of otters. Taken from the Sally Carrighar book of the same title. Appealing visual and auditory aspects. Especially good on small, hard-to-hear noises like crickets and water sounds.

PART IV

EMOTIONALLY DISTURBED STUDENTS

Introductory Comments

Emotionally impaired, behavior disordered or *emotionally disturbed* (ED) are the terms most frequently used to describe the child who exhibits one or more of the following characteristics over a long period of time and to a marked extent: (a) an inability to learn which cannot be explained by intellectual, sensory, or health factors; (b) an inability to build or maintain satisfactory interpersonal relationships with peers and teachers; (c) inappropriate types of behavior or feelings under normal circumstances; (d) a general pervasive mood of unhappiness or depression; and (e) a tendency to develop physical symptoms or fears associated with personal or school problems. Behavior disorders may range from mild, transient problems to the more profound, chronic disorders of schizophrenia and autism.

The first article in this section does not describe a program per se but presents a philosophy of dealing with students whose common characteristic is that they have made a less than satisfactory adjustment to situations involving school and community. In "A School Designed for Self-Esteem," Stanley C. Diamond characterizes this type of student as "ego deficient"— one who has had little opportunity to experience success. Towards the goal of eliminating the "loser-syndrome," the author enumerates what he considers to be the key ingredients necessary to enable students to consider themselves important, valued, and successful. While the article is directed mainly towards those educators working with the emotionally disturbed student, the ideas presented have relevance for all children served in the schools.

Educational opportunities for autistic children have generally been limited to a one-to-one teaching situation or to a special class environment with other autistic or seriously disturbed students. The feasibility of integrating such a child into a regular classroom with the use of behavioral techniques is explored in "A Method for Integrating an Autistic Child into a Normal Public-School Classroom." Dennis C. Russo and Robert L. Koegel report the results of a 55-week study covering two school years in which a five-year-old girl attended a regular kindergarten and first grade. A therapist was utilized to administer a system of token reinforcement for managing social behaviors, reducing self-stimulatory behavior, and increasing verbal response to command. The regular teacher was trained by the therapist and eventually took over dispensing tokens and social reinforcement.

The next four articles in this section describe techniques which have been used with preadolescent and adolescent emotionally disturbed youngsters. While each conveys a totally different approach, the underlying common goal is that of providing a vehicle for communication and expression of feelings in as nonthreatening an environment as possible. J. Paul Marcoux, in "Helping Emotionally Disturbed Children through Creative Dramatics," advocates the use of dramatics to facilitate creative expression within a controlled environment. He describes several specific activities which have been used successfully with different age levels of students. Although the exemplary program described in this article was conducted at a special school serving the emotionally disturbed, many of the principles of creative dramatics are applicable to other classrooms in which the teacher wishes to promote affective as well as cognitive learning.

One of the many pleasures derived from reading or hearing poetry is that a mood is rapidly created through the use of words and rhythm. Dorothy Kobax and Estelle Nisenson capitalize on this quality in the program they describe in "Poetry Therapy." A poem dealing with a particular subject is read and becomes a "springboard" for group discussion of feelings about the topic. An illustration is included. This technique, as well as the two following, is described as therapeutic because it attempts to facilitate a change in attitude or behavior of the individuals involved. As such, its use in conjunction with professionals trained in the area of emotional disturbance is advocated.

In "Original Writing: A Therapeutic Tool in Working with Disturbed Adolescents," Ellen J. Dehouske shows how the choice of appropriate writing tasks allows students to communicate their feelings and concerns. One of the least anxiety-producing techniques involved having the student draw small figures using their thumbprints as bodies. A sequence of four thumbprint pictures was then captioned in the same manner as a cartoon to tell a story. By presenting examples of responses to various writing assignments, the author stresses the necessity of employing patience rather than pressure, accepting instead of evaluating the writing produced, and knowing when a particular subject becomes too sensitive for a child to pursue.

Another method to encourage creative expression among emotionally disturbed youngsters is proposed by Bill Arnott and Jeffrey Gushin in "Film Making as a Therapeutic Tool." Four preadolescent boys participated in a seven-week workshop in which each boy wrote, directed, and filmed his own story. The article describes the physical structuring of events as well as the method of utilizing the story as a projection of the child's own feelings and behaviors. In many ways the project contributed to the social or personal development of each of the boys involved. The authors also relate the limitations of their approach and offer suggestions for designing a smoother and perhaps more fruitful venture.

A School Designed for Self-Esteem

by Stanley C. Diamond

Adolescents who are considered emotionally disturbed by educators, psychologists, and others for whom labeling is a solemn professional duty fall into a number of categories depending on the behavior they manifest. Among the familiar classifications are the depressives, the character disorders, the psychotics, and those suffering from what is now termed *adjustment reaction*. The problem one faces in designing a school program for such a variety of young people is that their differences are far greater than their similarities. As a matter of fact, a deeply depressed teenager, who may be involved as well in extensive drug use, is as different from his/her peer who cannot enter a classroom without the onset of debilitating anxiety or who cannot sit for more than a few moments at a time in an educational setting as either of these youngsters is from the more typical student who functions without special notice in the thousands of classrooms across the country. A paranoid schizophrenic stands out no less in the midst of a group of hostile, acting-out students than s/he would in a random grouping of adolescents. Even if one wished to group such students solely according to psychological diagnosis, it would be economically unfeasible in any but the most mammoth school system. The result is that we who work with emotionally disturbed young people in the classroom must somehow develop a special program which is addressed to the similarities that exist in a basically heterogeneous group.

In seeking to point a way toward resolving that dilemma, I would contend that the anxious youngster, as well as the withdrawn, the impulse ridden, and the dreamer, generally have one characteristic in common which is frequently enough present to be taken into account for planning—they are all *losers*. By this I mean that their adjustment in family, peer, and classroom settings has usually left them without the degree of fulfillment and self-satisfaction that enables them to see themselves as important or valuable or that allows them to view the future, perhaps even the very next task, as a potentially successful one. Any school, special or otherwise, which purports to deal effectively with such young people has to program for change in this quintessential aspect of their humanity. No amount of remediation alone can compensate for previous failures, nor will any adolescent's attitude toward learning be modified until that young person alters his/her self-perception as a learner.

What is obvious in this connection is that success is an important new experience that the ego-deficient student we are describing here must have. Certainly the special-education sensitivity toward utilizing tailor-made materials and setting realistic goals so that a student can complete a task without the concomitant exasperation that so many experience in school is a necessary element in a proper learning environment. Equally valuable are the techniques of careful educational diagnosis, special remediation in basic skills, individually prescribed learning programs, small group settings, and the other familiar components of the special-education package. Although these approaches may well impede greater erosion of a youngster's self-image and perhaps even make for some positive change, they do not strike me as sufficient for so critical an undertaking.

How, then, can one approach still more directly and effectively the task of eliminating the loser syndrome which generally accompanies and perpetuates the particular emotional disturbance that handicaps our student? He has already been defined, labeled, and likely placed in a hospital or special classroom so an already severe case of ego deficiency has been exacerbated markedly. For the purpose of this discussion, I intend to deal only with what happens to students who are grouped together and will not enter the tempting debate about how grouping can be most effective. In essence, my proposal is simply that we deal with each of our students without reference to his/her problem, except when that difficulty manifests itself in a way that clearly interferes with the learning process. At such a point, sensitive, special techniques may well be in order; otherwise, they probably are not. This is really no more nor less than we do in general education when we are designing schools which work and which have a real impact on the students who attend them. We just have to be a bit better at the job when the adolescents are needier and more sensitive to the injuries customarily sustained in a crudely operated educational setting.

Some of the ingredients which are most helpful in enabling a student (special or otherwise) to consider himself/herself important, valued, and successful are outlined here. For the ego-deficient youngster in a special-education setting, they may be matters of sanity or debilitation, life or death.

1. *Choice.* Any school for adolescents which does not offer students the opportunity to participate in the modification and design of significant aspects of the environment in which they learn is transmitting an attitude toward students which devalues them as community members and tells them their job is to be exclusively passive recipients of the wisdom of some important persons. I cannot imagine any more effective way than this of reinforcing the loser syndrome.

There is a risk, of course, that the choices which our students make may not be as wise for them as those we would have imposed; I suggest that this is a very small gamble even when we have fine diagnostic tools at hand, and much of the current educational literature supports such a point of view. The extent and nature of the choices can be modified in line with the student's ability to handle decision making. For a few, openness itself is danger and anxiety producing, and such youngsters must be nurtured slowly upon its fruit. To whatever extent a young person can make choices, s/he should have real ones to make.

2. *Justice*. A good classroom is one in which the self-esteem of the participants remains undiminished in spite of the natural tensions of learning tasks. Of course, in order to make this possible, a staff of secure and open adults is a requisite. When a student feels an injustice has been committed, s/he must have a right to be heard on the matter and to confront the perpetrator of the alleged injustice so that the issue may be resolved. The student's problem and the teacher's position are irrelevant considerations in respect to any adult behavior toward a young person which is humiliating, denigrating, or patently unfair. A teacher does have special responsibilities in the classroom which students do not, but there is never a responsibility so vital that it necessitates or justifies making a young person feel less important.

3. *Self-examination*. Evaluation of performance and behavior should be a process whereby all members of a school community learn something about themselves and not merely a series of judgments in shorthand of students by the staff. When a teacher describes what a young person has and has not yet learned, that fulfills quite adequately whatever responsibility s/he bears for evaluating his/her student. No class or school rating, no honor roll, no numerical or letter grades, no special award has a useful place in a process which seeks to inform and not to coerce.

Since I believe that human beings learn many important things from being evaluated by others, it necessarily follows that such a principle must be lived out in a school community with real consistency. If students can profit from accurate feedback about their performance, so can teachers; indeed, even directors of schools. People should be required to evaluate themselves and each other in any situation which has potential for their growth. The message to be conveyed by such an arrangement is that the student is vital in this process also and that his/her opinion is an essential and valued one. The result is a bonus for all.

4. *Community*. I use this vague and overworked term here for lack of a more specific one to describe the sense an individual has of belonging to a defined group. Group allegiance and participation which results in growthful experience for the participant can only be attained if s/he also feels needed

and valued by the community to which s/he belongs. That is indeed a difficult arrangement to insure. Nonetheless, we must commit ourselves to searching for ways in which students can so perceive their environment in school.

My earlier comments regarding choice making are relevant to this issue. Students should be involved in as many essential decisions about the school as is possible, perhaps even to the extreme of participation in the staff hiring process. Though a few alternative programs in general education allow for extensive student involvement in "school matters," emotionally disturbed adolescents are too often regarded as cripples in the area of decision making and have yet to get their just share of such an eminently sensible development in contemporary education. But that is precisely what it means to be important, is it not?

Within a real community, real dialogue exists and that should be the case on such school issues as rules, parties, behavior which affects others, and all matters of interest to the group at large. Space which is basically used only by the students can and should be designed and decorated by them and not dressed up by professionals for visitors. If possible, a separate and private area for each student is highly desirable; perhaps some small rooms can be offices which house a number of students and serve as places for study and storage of personal belongings. Common spaces, especially lounges and halls, should be decorated and arranged in line with the wishes of both the students and the staff who use these areas. I am sure the reader can supply a list of his/her own to further implement the notion of community outlined here.

5. *Trust.* Unless we can bring ourselves to risk a great deal with youngsters whose manner and background are not particularly trustworthy, we incur the even greater hazard of augmenting their already plentiful distrust of themselves. I suggest here no ongoing, naive acceptance of obviously implausible tales on the part of students shown to be harming themselves or the community; no youngster profits by easy manipulation of the adults responsible for his/her welfare. Behavior must be dealt with and not ignored.

At the same time, however, the policy of the school can be to open doors rather than to lock them. We can encourage guests to inquire of the students about the school, not only of the adults. If a visitor wishes to observe a class, that can be checked out with the groups as well as with the teacher; students will also know whether they feel like being on display that particular period. If we are truly willing to extend trust to adolescents, each and every one of us can find meaningful ways to do so.

6. *Honesty.* There is nothing which distances an adolescent more certainly than manipulation on the part of an adult. If people interact in the school in an emotionally open manner, sharing their love as well as their anger, their joy as well as their sadness, the staff may transmit an essential lesson about the validity and humanity of all those feelings. Students may learn to

experience emotions free of the guilt which is engendered in most students at school when they are deemed "hostile," "surly," "uncooperative," and all the other adjectives with which they are so quickly labeled. A lesson that most youngsters never learn in an educational setting except in a punitive and often authoritarian manner is how one can handle unpleasant or antisocial feelings.

There is, of course, much risk in this approach also. Teachers will have to be themselves with each other and with the director as well as others connected with the school. Few staff members will arrive ready to start right in on this but most will have the capacity to grow into an emotionally open environment. The reader may note here that some teachers are well off hiding the pervasive bitterness, hostility toward children, or destructive anger they possess; my answer to that concern is that such people have no right to work with young people in any event, and certainly not with those who are already so hypersensitive to hurt as the students we are discussing here.

7. *Intimacy*. A school should remain so small that no person walks the halls a stranger. This is perhaps the most difficult suggestion to follow, for economically it may not be attainable, especially in a large public school system. Where such a problem exists, however, smaller, self-contained units or mini-schools may be the answer. Once the school becomes so large that we do not know from day to day how each member of the community is doing and feeling, we are likely to deal with our "stranger-student" in an arbitrary manner, often seeing the rule or the issue as more important than the person. This is precisely the opposite of the goal we have set for ourselves. Even small numbers can make for strangeness, however, unless students and teachers are free to spend some time with one another without a business agenda between them. It may even be worth a period less of formal instruction each day to have members of the school community randomly available to one another for sitting around, walking about, and just being people.

8. *Order*. Any institution needs some structure and some rules in order to function successfully and provide the service for which it is intended. Schools are no exception to this. Rules do have special meaning for adolescents, though, be they disturbed, disturbing, or just plain "normal." The fewer the rules, the better. At the same time, it is important to take seriously the ones which do exist. Priorities should also be clear so that the confusion which results from dealing with a youngster in the same manner when s/he hurts another as we do when s/he mumbles some profanity does not becloud our student's sense of what is important and what is trivial. We will probably need to think hard on this question ourselves. At least half the rules I have encountered in most schools are quite unnecessary to the successful operation of that school's program.

In summary, then, if there is any special task which the teacher of emotionally disturbed young people is obligated to fulfill, it is that of helping his/her students grow toward a level of self-awareness and self-esteem which enables them to conceive of coping successfully with the world in which they live and the future they are to experience. My contention is that the kind of school which is best for emotionally disturbed adolescents is special in its sensitivity, its warmth, and its integrity, but is basically just a very, very good school.

A Method for Integrating an Autistic Child into a Normal Public-School Classroom

by Dennis C. Russo
and Robert L. Koegel

In the past, reviews of the literature on autism have discussed, as a central weakness in remediation of the disorder, the lack of available and effective classroom education programs and the almost total exclusion of the autistic child from public-school programs.[1-4] Recently, however, significant strides have been made toward providing effective educational opportunities for these children. Increased public awareness and interest in autism, legal actions filed on behalf of the autistic child and his/her right to an education, and recent research on the development of an educational technology specifically for teaching autistic children have resulted in many classrooms being established and new curricula devised.

The research on placing the autistic child into the mainstream of the educational environment has thus far fallen into two general categories: (1) the one-to-one teaching situation, and (2) the formation of special-education classes solely for groups of autistic children.

One-to-one teaching situations, as documented in the literature, have been extremely productive in developing skills in autistic children. For example, programs for teaching conversational speech,[5-7] generalized imitation,[8,9] and appropriate play,[10] as well as the control of inappropriate behaviors,[11,12] have been utilized for some time. Further, Koegel, Russo, and Rincover[13] have developed procedures that are empirically effective in training teachers to work with autistic children in such one-to-one situations. While, undeniably, one-to-one therapy procedures are important in the remediation of problem behaviors and the teaching of new adaptive behaviors, the major problem with implementing such an approach in a public-school system has been that of cost.

The second line of research, focusing on the development of special classes for autistic children, has attempted to increase the number of children with whom a given teacher can work. In recent years, several investigators have suggested guidelines for such classes.[14-19] Further, Koegel and Rincover[20] reported systematic data showing that it is possible gradually to increase the size of such classes to at least eight children per teacher.

While such classes have been effective and are becoming more widely available, they still present a potential problem, in that in most cases they are composed solely of autistic children. Thus, such classes may be merely another form of exclusion. By placing every autistic child in a classroom made up entirely of autistic children, we may deprive those children of several possible benefits, including the influence of appropriate role models and the exposure to a nonautistic curriculum taught in regular classrooms.

As a third alternative, the present study systematically investigated the feasibility of integrating an autistic child into a normal public-school classroom.

METHOD

Subject

A five-year-old girl, who had received a primary diagnosis of autism from an agency not associated with this study, served as the subject. She evidenced relative lack of appropriate verbal behavior, rarely initiating verbal interactions with the teacher or the other children in her public-school kindergarten class, and generally failing to respond to the questions or commands of others. When she did engage in speech, it was generally out of context with her activity, or characterized by pronoun reversal. For instance, when asking for a drink of water, she would say: "You want a drink of water."

The child's classroom behavior consisted of a small repertoire of generally inappropriate actions. She would often stand up in the middle of a work period and walk about the room, twirling a large feather, a flower, or a handkerchief that she persistently carried with her. When she did interact with the teacher, she would ask, repetitively and without regard to classroom activities, to get either a drink of water or a tissue. If these requests were not met, a tantrum ensued, with screaming and physical withdrawal from the other people in the room.

In general, the child remained aloof, rarely interacting with anyone. Her behavioral repertoire consisted primarily of bizarre autistic mannerisms and stereotyped behaviors. She engaged in frequent repetitive finger manipulations in front of her eyes and rhythmic manipulations of the objects she carried. She would also frequently masturbate in class. The baseline data reported below give a more empirical measurement of the child's pretreatment behavior.

Although the child's verbal and social behaviors were minimal, the fact that such behaviors were evidenced at all by an autistic child suggested to us that she would show relatively good response to treatment. Nevertheless, because of her relative lack of appropriate behavior and relative abundance of inappropriate autistic mannerisms, school officials had made the decision that typifies the fate of autistic children: to exclude her from the school system. The child was, however, allowed to remain in school for the course of this investigation.

Settings

The entire investigation was conducted in the kindergarten and first-grade classrooms of an elementary school in Santa Barbara, California. In addition to the child and the therapist, present in both classrooms were an observer to record data, a teacher, a teacher's aid, and 20 to 30 normal children. The children attended school from 9:00 a.m. to 2:30 p.m., five days a week. Each classroom was equipped with tables and chairs, and a rug on which all of the children sat during story and discussion times. The rooms, each 9.1 by 9.1 meters, contained toys, blocks, and other usual materials.

Design and Definitions

A multiple-baseline design across behaviors was employed to assess the effects of treatment by the therapist on the behavior of the child in each classroom. Implementation of the treatment program by the classroom teachers was instituted simultaneously across behaviors. A brief reversal on social behavior was also instituted to assess the maintenance of treatment gains by the untrained kindergarten teacher.

Three target behaviors were selected on the basis of the following criteria: (1) that school officials demanded the behaviors be modified if the child was to remain in school, and (2) that they were characteristic deficits of autistic children. The definitions and instructions used by the observers for recording target behaviors are listed below.

Social behavior. Any response involving direct interaction with another person. The major criterion for including a response in this category was that the behavior would not be occurring if another person were not present. Examples of the behavior were saying hello to another student, borrowing a toy from a child, sharing candy, etc. Social behavior was measured by frequency of occurrence during the session, with each instance recorded by a check on the data sheet.

Self-stimulation. Any stereotyped movement, e.g., rocking, repetitive finger movements, rhythmic manipulation of objects (feather, flower, hand-kerchief, etc.), and gazing at objects such as pencils or lights. Much of the child's self-stimulatory behavior was of a subtle nature, such as repetitive finger movements in the lap, and persistent, repetitive scratching and pulling of socks and other clothing. This behavior was measured by duration: every time an incidence of self-stimulation was observed, the observer started a stopwatch and allowed it to run until the offset of the behavior. Seconds of self-stimulation were kept cumulatively for each observation session and divided by the total session time to obtain the percentage of session time occupied by self-stimulatory behavior.

Verbal response to command. Any appropriate verbal response to a verbal stimulus presented by the teacher or therapist. A verbal stimulus was any statement (e.g., ''What color is this?'') that required a verbal response from the child. This stimulus may have been directed to the child individually, or toward the entire class, requiring a group response. An appropriate verbal response was any verbal statement made within five seconds of the verbal stimulus that provided the type of response requested (e.g., the name of a color, ''I don't know''), whether correct or incorrect. Each verbal stimulus, the response or lack of response, and whether or not the response was appropriate were recorded on the data sheet. This behavior was measured by the percentage of verbal stimuli responded to appropriately in each session.

Observation and Measurement

All observers had previous training in the general observation and recording of behavior, and had successfully completed one undergraduate course in the area of autism. Before observation in the classroom, observers were taught the definitions and scoring procedures, as well as the procedures for and the importance of unobtrusive observation. None of the observers were informed of the purpose of the study.

Measures were recorded in three four-minute time samples per session, each separated by nine minutes of no recording, giving a total measurement time of twelve minutes per session. Two measurement sessions were conducted each week throughout all conditions. Measurement sessions began at 9:30 a.m. All three target behaviors were recorded simultaneously during each session. Observers indicated each occurrence of social behavior, kept a cumulative record of self-stimulation on the stopwatch, and recorded each verbal stimulus and the child's response during each four-minute sample.

EXPERIMENT I

The procedure for evaluating the child's behaviors, therapist treatment, and transfer of the program to the kindergarten teacher is presented below.

Baseline

Measurements were taken of the child's behavior in the kindergarten classroom with 20 to 30 other children present, before any intervention. The teacher was instructed to continue regular classroom activities. No attempt was made to manipulate reinforcement contingencies. At the start of this condition, the therapist was introduced to the class as another teacher who would be visiting often in the future. During the class period, the therapist sat next to the child in the last row of children, to habituate both the child and the rest of the class to his presence, but he interacted with neither the child nor her classmates.

Treatment by the Therapist

In order to dispense rewards easily and unobtrusively within the classroom, it was decided to employ a token economy.[21,22] The child received three one-hour pretaining sessions to establish tokens as reinforcers. These sessions were conducted after school during the third week of the baseline condition, in a small room (1.8 by 2.4 meters) at the University of California, Santa Barbara. During the sessions, the child was intermittently handed a white poker chip and prompted to exchange it for a food reward (one piece of candy, one potato chip, etc.). Token deliveries were not contingent on any specific behavior by the child. When she began to trade tokens for food without prompting, and saved at least three tokens for ten minutes, the token program was implemented in the classroom during subsequent treatment conditions.

Treatment of social behavior in the classroom was begun in Week 4. Each occurrence of social behavior by the child during the session was followed by the presentation of a token and appropriate verbal feedback (e.g., "Good girl!") by the therapist. As in the previous condition, the therapist sat quietly next to the child and interacted with her only when social behaviors occurred. One-hour treatment sessions were carried out twice a week, beginning at 9:20 a.m., while the teacher continued to conduct the class according to her regular procedures. During the session, the child saved tokens in a cellophane bag attached to her dress. After the session, she was able to redeem her tokens at the "store," a small area at the rear of the classroom. After three weeks of treatment of social behavior by the therapist, the baseline condition was reinstated during Weeks 7 to 9, and treatment by the therapist was begun again in Week 10. This reversal was used to assess the effects of therapist treatment on social behavior.

Treatment of self-stimulation was begun in Week 10, concurrently with the second treatment of social behavior. During this condition, each occurrence of self-stimulatory behavior was followed by the removal of tokens and an abrupt verbal statement, "No." The absence of self-stimulatory behavior for progressively longer intervals produced the contingent presentation of a token and the verbal statement, "Good sitting." In the early stages of treatment, a prompting procedure was used to control self-stimulation. The therapist restrained the child from this behavior by placing his hands on the child's when she began to self-stimulate. The restraint was then faded gradually, and longer and longer periods (ultimately about 15 minutes) of no self-stimulatory behavior were shaped. The close physical proximity of the therapist, the use of a systematic shaping program, and the position of the child and therapist in the back of the room allowed the procedure to be conducted with a minimum of disruption to the class.

Beginning with Week 13, treatment was begun on verbal response to command. The therapist awarded the child a token every time she answered a question requiring a verbal response, whether the question was directed specifically toward her or toward the class as a whole, and regardless of whether the response was correct or incorrect. At first, the therapist prompted the child with the command, "Answer the question!" If she did not respond within 5 seconds she was prompted with the correct response and rewarded for repeating it. The prompt was then faded by increasing the interval between the teacher's verbal statement and the therapist's prompt. While initially the procedure required 15 to 20 seconds to produce a response, the necessity of waiting for a response or prompting it was a common occurrence among the other pupils in the class.

Training of the Teacher by the Therapist

The teacher was trained during Weeks 14 and 15, while regular morning measurement and treatment sessions by the therapist were continued. The teacher-training procedure included several components (general instruction, practice, and feedback) reported by Koegel, Russo, and Rincover[23] as effective in training teachers in generalized behavior-modification skills with autistic children. These components, demonstrated effective in one-to-one teaching situations, were adapted for use in the public-school classroom in the present study. Training of the teacher involved four steps:

(1) The teacher received general training in behavioral techniques. The following materials were used to acquaint the teacher with the behavioral approach, define terms, and present behavior-change strategies: *Teaching/ Discipline*,[24] *Parents Are Teachers*,[25] and Volumes 1, 2, and 3 of the *Managing Behavior* series.[26] Three one-hour sessions were required for the teacher and therapist to discuss the materials and review test questions.

(2) The therapist discussed with the teacher the operational definitions and specific contingencies operative on the child. During two one-hour

sessions, the therapist and teacher discussed each of the definitions, the teacher was asked to describe examples of the child's behavior, and the therapist provided feedback and questions. At this time, the teacher also received a complete explanation of the token economy.

(3) With the therapist present, the teacher identified occurrences of the child's target behaviors. While an aide ran the class, the child was observed during three one-hour afternoon periods of free play and story time. When the teacher observed one of the target behaviors, she explained the behavior, how it fit the definition, and the applicable token administration procedure. The therapist provided feedback and pointed out instances of target behaviors that the teacher had missed.

(4) The teacher, under the therapist's supervision, began administering social reinforcement. During three additional afternoon periods, the teacher provided verbal praise to the child for social behavior, quiet sitting, and verbal responding.

During Week 14, concurrent with the training of the teacher, the therapist began systematically to reduce the density of token reinforcement. From an initial rate of one token given for every occurrence of appropriate behavior, as defined, and the removal of one token for each instance of self-stimulation, the therapist began giving tokens on an intermittent basis. Social reinforcement (e.g., "Good girl") and saying "No" contingent on self-stimulation were continued at each occurrence of the target behaviors. As the fading of tokens continued, the therapist maintained behaviors by social reinforcement, while providing tokens for intervals of appropriate behavior (e.g., sitting quietly for ten minutes, playing for several minutes with another child, responding appropriately to questions during a class activity).

During Week 15, under the therapist's direction, the teacher began to provide social reinforcement and tokens for appropriate behavior, and to remove tokens contingent on self-stimulation. The child was moved to the front of the classroom to facilitate these interactions, with the therapist initially remaining close to her. The therapist was present at least four days each week during the fading of tokens and transfer of the program to the teacher (Weeks 14 and 15), to ensure a smooth transition. By putting the aide in charge of the class during parts of the school day, the teacher was able to spend more time with the child during the transfer. The therapist provided feedback to the teacher during each break in school activities.

Treatment by the Trained Kindergarten Teacher without the Therapist's Assistance

Beginning with Week 16, the teacher totally took over treatment, carrying out the token program throughout the school day. The teacher was told to remain in close proximity to the child and to provide frequent, specific social feedback, with periodic tokens during breaks (about every 30 to 45 minutes). Instances of self-stimulation continued to be followed by the immediate removal of tokens. On a sheet she kept with her, the teacher was asked to note why she had given tokens and the times at which they were administered. She reviewed this information with the therapist each day, either in person or by telephone. While maintaining control of the child's behavior with social feedback, the teacher increased the response requirement for tokens over a 14-day period by lengthening the time between token presentations. Eventually, the teacher was able to dispense tokens twice a day (once before lunch and once before the day ended) with a brief explanation to the child as to why she was receiving them. However, verbal feedback continued to be presented immediately after appropriate behaviors.

Observations during this condition were made twice each week on selected weeks, in the manner previously described. The therapist continued to visit the classroom at least twice a week during the first five weeks and once a week during the remaining five weeks.

Reliability

Over the course of the experiment, 135 reliability measures were obtained. At least two reliability sessions occurred in each condition for each of the three target behaviors. In each reliability session, observations were made independently by two observers during three four-minute blocks spaced nine minutes apart. Observers were said to be reliable if agreement on each behavior recorded within a given four-minute block was 80 percent or better. Reliability was calculated by dividing the lower number of units (occurrences or seconds) recorded for a particular behavior by the higher number of units recorded for the behavior, and multiplying the quotient by 100. Forty-four of the 45 measures for social behavior were above 80 percent (mean reliability = 89.2 percent per session; range = 67 percent to 100 percent). All of the reliability measures for self-stimulation were above 80 percent (mean = 92.1 percent; range = 85 percent to 99 percent), as were those for verbal response to command (mean = 93.2 percent; range = 83 percent to 100 percent).

RESULTS

Figure 1 shows the results of Experiment I across conditions for each of the three behaviors measured in the kindergarten classroom. The data reveal changes in the child's classroom behavior on all measures. First, consider the child's social behavior. During the three weeks of baseline, she consistently emitted fewer than four social behaviors per session. When the therapist introduced token reinforcement in Week 4, the child's social behaviors immediately increased with a mean of 11.5 recorded during Week 6. Beginning with Week 7, a brief reversal (Baseline 2) was instituted to assess the reinforcing effects of the tokens. The child's rate of social behavior dropped to 5.5 per week in Week 7, and remained consistently below the treatment rate during the three weeks of this condition. In Week 10, when the therapist reinstituted token reinforcement (Retreatment), the child's social behaviors again increased, reaching an average of 13 per session, and a high of 17.5 in Week 14. Measurements of the child's behavior in the Trained Teacher condition occurred in Weeks 16 to 25. Throughout the ten weeks of this condition, the child's rate of social behavior remained as high as or higher than during treatment by the therapist.

The child's self-stimulatory behavior was measured during the same period. The occurrence of self-stimulation ranged from 27 percent to 54 percent during the nine weeks of baseline. It decreased to 19 percent during the first session of treatment by the therapist (Week 10), and continued to decrease to a low of 3 percent during Week 14. During the Treatment by the Trained Teacher condition, the child's rate of self-stimulatory behavior was maintained at a level similar to that achieved during the Treatment by the Therapist condition (range = 8 percent to 14 percent).

The child's verbal response to command also showed systematic improvement. During baseline, appropriate verbal responses showed great variability, ranging from 8 percent to 68 percent, with a mean of 35 percent appropriate responses per session. Beginning with the first session of treatment by the therapist, in Week 13, the child's percentage of appropriate verbal responses rose to 97 percent and ranged between 68 percent and 100 percent during the three weeks of treatment. A steady high rate of appropriate responses was maintained during the Treatment by the Trained Teacher condition. The child's rate of appropriate verbal responses was low during baseline, improved during treatment by the therapist, and reached a consistent level of 100 percent for the final eight weeks of treatment by the trained teacher.

EXPERIMENT II: FOLLOW-UP

On the kindergarten teacher's recommendation, the child was graduated at the end of the term to the first grade and a new teacher. However, during the first week of the new term, the school reported that the child's classroom behavior was again unmanageable and requested additional treatment for her. In order to ascertain whether the changes induced in the kindergarten

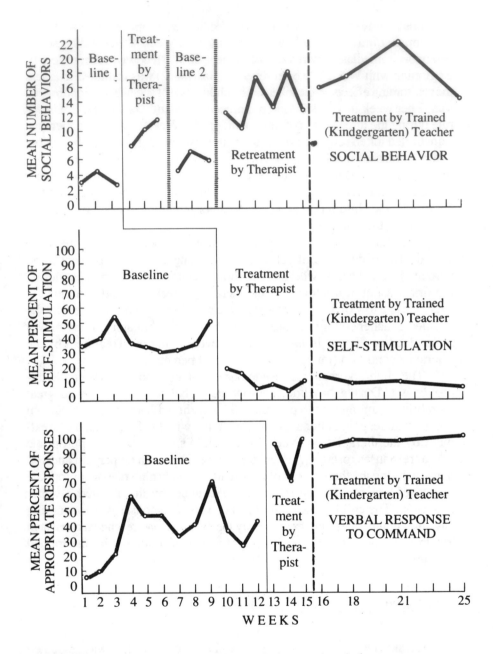

FIGURE 1 Social behavior, self-stimulation, and verbal response to command the normal kindergarten classroom during baseline, treatment by the therapist, and treatment by the trained kindergarten teacher. All three behaviors were measured simultaneously.

classroom had, in fact, not been maintained after the summer vacation and the introduction of a new teacher and class, measures were again taken on the three target behaviors. Definitions of target behaviors, design of the investigation (with the exception of a reversal on social behavior), and recording and observation procedures were identical to those described previously.

Baseline in the First Grade

This condition was procedurally identical to the Baseline 1 condition in Experiment I. Measurements of the child's classroom behavior were begun during the second week of the first-grade term.

Retreatment by the Therapist

Retreatment of social behavior by the therapist was begun in Week 40 (as measured from the start of Experiment I). The procedures utilized were identical to those described in Experiment I, except for the fact that no token pretraining was given.

Treatment of self-stimulation, begun in Week 43, was conducted concurrently with treatment of social behavior. The procedures for treatment of self-stimulation were the same as those described in Experiment I.

A high, steady rate of appropriate verbal responses were observed between Weeks 37 and 46. Since this percentage was within the range of responses achieved during treatment of this behavior in Experiment I, no further treatment of verbal response to command was undertaken.

Training of the Teacher by the Therapist

The first-grade teacher was trained under the same procedure as the kindergarten teacher. During Week 46, she was trained to recognize the occurrences of the target behaviors in the classroom, to present and remove tokens, and to provide social feedback.

Treatment by the Trained First-Grade Teacher
without the Therapist's Assistance

Beginning in Week 47, the first-grade teacher took over treatment. Since treatment by the therapist in Experiment II involved reestablishing previously functional contingencies, the first-grade teacher took over on the final contingencies, using social reinforcement to provide immediate feedback to the child and dispensing tokens twice daily (before lunch and at the end of the school day). Otherwise, procedures were identical to those of Experiment I.

Reliability

At least two reliability sessions were held in each condition. Reliability, calculated as before, was over 80 percent for each category.

RESULTS

Data on treatment during the child's first-grade year are presented in Figure 2. Baseline measures indicated that the child's social behaviors had decreased and her rate of self-stimulation had increased since treatment in kindergarten. Verbal response to command, however, had remained stable at previous treatment levels.

Retreatment by the therapist on social behavior and self-stimulation, using previously established contingencies, was sufficient to restore improved levels of the behaviors. Social behavior increased to over 12 responses per session, and self-stimulation decreased to three percent by Week 46.

The child was monitored for 10 weeks after the training of the first-grade teacher (Weeks 47 to 55). Her behaviors were maintained in the same range as during the Retreatment by the Therapist condition, with social behavior ranging between 12 and 16 responses per session and self-stimulation remaining below ten percent.

DISCUSSION

The present results may be summarized as follows. First, the child showed considerable improvement in classroom performance for each of the three behaviors treated. Her final performance on each of these behaviors was more than adequate, as judged by school officials, to ensure her continuation in the public schools. Second, training the kindergarten teacher in behavior-modification techniques seemed sufficient to enable her to maintain all of the treatment behaviors over a ten-week formal measurement period, which was the remainder of the academic year. The concreteness of the token procedure, coupled with the increased response requirement for obtaining a token, appeared to provide a means for maintaining strong behavioral control without constant teacher attention. Third, recurrence of problems with two of the target behaviors at the onset of the first-grade year was rapidly

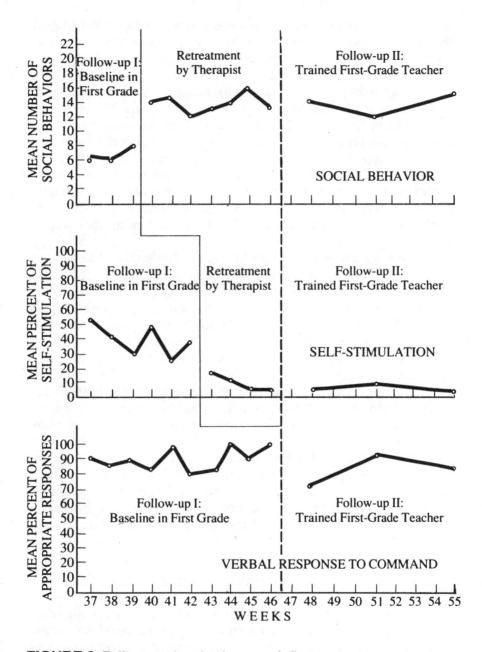

FIGURE 2 Follow-up data in the normal first-grade classroom during baseline, retreatment by the therapist on social behavior and self-stimulation, and treatment by the trained first-grade teacher. All three behaviors were measured simultaneously.

remediated by the therapist and maintained after the training of the first-grade teacher. No further problems were reported by the school through the remainder of that year, nor during the child's second- and third-grade years when she had different teachers.

It may be important to note that the behavior change induced by the therapist was maintained after the training of the teachers. The brief return to baseline in Experiment I, and the lack of maintenance of two target behaviors that necessitated retreatment in the first-grade classroom, lend additional support to the notion that training facilitated maintenance. The introduction of the therapist in a one-to-one situation within the broader context of the classroom allowed for intensive treatment to bring the child's autistic behaviors under control. After such control was established and the teacher was trained, the child's behavior was maintained with little disruption to classroom routine.

A recent study has shed some light on the importance of the development of maintenance environments to the long-term success of behavior modification with autistic children. Lovaas, Koegel, Simmons, and Long[27] provided extensive follow-up data which show that when autistic children are discharged from a behavior-modification treatment program, their continued improvement is to a large extent a function of the post-treatment environment. Children who were discharged to state hospitals regressed. Children who were discharged to their parents' care (after the parents received some training in basic principles of behavior modification) continued to improve. The present results imply that training classroom teachers contributed to the maintenance of treatment behaviors. This is particularly true because two of the three behaviors deteriorated when the child entered first grade with a new teacher. However, it is also possible that the thin partial-reinforcement schedule used during the final stages of treatment may have contributed to the maintenance results (compare Koegel and Rincover).[28] Research on variables contributing to treatment durability is still in its infancy, and continued research in this area will undoubtedly prove very important.

Generality of Results

Autistic children have previously been excluded from public-school programs, or in some cases are given only the option of a special autism class. The significance of this study lies in its suggestion that school teachers can easily learn to teach at least some autistic children in regular classrooms. Although much research is still necessary, we expect that a fairly large number of autistic children may be able to benefit from the treatment described here.

Using the procedures outlined here, four additional autistic children have been placed in normal public-school classes. Table 1 describes the characteristics and placements of these children. All were fairly advanced, in that they had some minimal social and verbal behavior at the time of their placements. In each case, the abilities of the particular child were matched to those of the class, and deficits remediated with one-to-one training in the classroom before the program was transferred to the teacher. Each of the four children was given extensive pretreatment, using the procedures described by Koegel and Rincover[29,30] before placement was attempted. Therefore, this study suggests that, in addition to higher-level autistic children, some lower-level autistic children trained in a class composed solely of autistic children might upon "graduation" (achievement of a minimal appropriate behavioral repertoire) be placed in a normal classroom among children who provide more appropriate role models. A study of the conditions and child characteristics resulting in successful placements may prove to be both interesting and beneficial for the future education of autistic children.

TABLE 1 Characteristics and Placements of Four Additional Autistic Children Placed in Normal Classrooms. Procedures Used Were Similar to Those Described in the Study.

Child	Pre-treatment	Age at Placement	Verbal Behavior at Placement	Placement	Curriculum Level	Duration of Placement
1	1 yr.	5 yr.	Some Conversational Speech (3- to 5-yr. level)	Kindergarten	Same	1 yr.
2	2 yr.	10 yr.	Able to express simple one-sentence demands— *e.g.,* "I want candy," or "I want bathroom."	Fifth Grade	First-Second Grade	1 yr.
3	2 yr.	6 yr.	Some Conversational Speech (3- to 5-yr. level)	Kindergarten	Same	1 yr.
4	2 yr.	6 yr.	Able to express simple one-sentence demands— *e.g.,* "I want outside," or "I want candy."	Kindergarten	Same	1 yr.

NOTES

1. J.L. Brown, "Follow-up of Children with Atypical Development (Infantile Psychosis)," *American Journal of Orthopsychiatry* 33 (1963): 855-61.

2. O.I. Lovaas and R.L. Koegel, *Behavior Modification in Education, NSSE Yearbook* (Chicago, IL: University of Chicago Press, 1973).

3. O.I. Lovaas, L. Schreibman, and R.L. Koegel, "A Behavior Modification Approach to the Treatment of Autistic Children," *Journal of Autism and Childhood Schizophrenia* 4 (1974): 111-29.

4. M. Rutter, "The Description and Classification of Infantile Autism," in *Infantile Autism,* eds. D.W. Churchill, G.D. Alpern, and M.K. DeMyer (Springfield, IL: Charles C. Thomas, 1971), pp. 8-28.

5. F.M. Hewett, "Teaching Speech to an Autistic Child through Operant Conditioning," *American Journal of Orthopsychiatry* 35 (1965): 927-36.

6. O.I. Lovaas, "A Program for the Establishment of Speech in Autistic Children," in *Early Childhood Autism,* ed. J. Wing (London: Pergamon, 1966).

7. T.R. Risley and M.M. Wolf, "Establishing Functional Speech in Echololic Children," *Behaviour Research and Therapy* 5 (1967): 73-88.

8. O.I. Lovaas, L. Freitas, K. Nelson, and K. Whalen, "The Establishment of Imitation and Its Use for the Development of Complex Behavior in Schizophrenic Children," *Behaviour Research and Therapy* 5 (1967): 171-81.

9. J.R. Metz, "Conditioning Generalized Imitation in Autistic Children," *Journal of Experimental Child Psychology* 2 (1965): 389-99.

10. R.L. Koegel, P.B. Firestone, K.W. Kramme, and G. Dunlap, "Increasing Spontaneous Play by Suppressing Self-Stimulation in Autistic Children," *Journal of Applied Behavior Analysis* 7 (1974): 521-8.

11. R.L. Koegel and A. Covert, "The Relationship of Self-Stimulation to Learning in Autistic Children," *Journal of Applied Behavior Analysis* 5 (1972): 381-7.

12. M.M. Wolf, T. Risley, and H. Mees, "Application of Operant Conditioning Procedures to the Behavior Problems of an Autistic Child," *Behaviour Research and Therapy* 1 (1964): 305-12.

13. R.L. Koegel, D.C. Russo, and A. Rincover, "Assessing and Training Teachers in the Generalized Use of Behavior Modification with Autistic Children," *Journal of Applied Behavior Analysis* 10 (1977): 197-205.

14. S. Elgar, "The Autistic Child," *Slow Learning Child* 13 (1966): 91-102.

15. W.I. Halpern, "The Schooling of Autistic Children: Preliminary Findings," *American Journal of Orthopsychiatry* 40 (1970): 665-71.

16. R.L. Hamblin et al., *Humanization Process* (New York: John Wiley & Sons, 1971).

17. J. Harper, "Establishment of an Educational Programme for a Group of Autistic Children," *Slow Learning Child* 16 (1969): 3-14.

18. G.L. Martin et al., "Operant Conditioning of Kindergarten Class Behavior in Autistic Children," *Behaviour Research and Therapy* 6 (1968): 281-94.

19. E. Rabb and F.M. Hewett, "Development of Appropriate Classroom Behaviors in a Severely Disturbed Group of Institutionalized Children with a Behavior Modification Model," *American Journal of Orthopsychiatry* 37 (1967): 313-4.

20. R.L. Koegel and A. Rincover, "Treatment of Psychotic Children in a Classroom Environment: I. Learning in a Large Group," *Journal of Applied Behavior Analysis* 7 (1974): 49-59.

21. A.E. Kazdin and R.R. Bootzin, "The Token Economy: An Evaluative Review," *Journal of Applied Behavior Analysis* 5 (1972): 343-72.

22. K.D. O'Leary and R. Drabman, "Token Reinforcement Programs in the Classroom: A Review," *Psychological Bulletin* 75 (1971): 379-98.

23. Koegel, Russo, and Rincover, "Assessing and Training Teachers."

24. C.H. Madsen, Jr., and C.K. Madsen, *Teaching/Discipline* (Boston: Allyn & Bacon, 1970).

25. W.C. Becker, *Parents Are Teachers* (Champaign, IL: Research Press, 1971).

26. R.V. Hall, *Managing Behavior,* vols. 1-3 (Lawrence, KS: H. & H. Publishing, 1971).

27. O.I. Lovaas, R.L. Koegel, J.Q. Simmons, and J.S. Long, "Some Generalizations and Follow-up Results on Autistic Children," *Journal of Applied Behavior Analysis* 6 (1973): 131-64.

28. R.L. Koegel and A. Rincover, "Research on the Difference between Generalization and Maintenance in Extra-Therapy Responding," *Journal of Applied Behavior Analysis* 10 (1977): 1-12.

29. Koegel and Rincover, "Treatment of Psychotic Children."

30. A. Rincover and R.L. Koegel, "Classroom Treatment of Autistic Children: II. Individualized Instruction in a Group," *Journal of Abnormal Child Psychiatry* 5 (1977): 113-26.

Helping Emotionally Disturbed Children through Creative Dramatics

by J. Paul Marcoux

Since the whole process of education involves a continuous examination of new goals and a reevaluation of existing goals, the classroom teacher is not immune to the effects of state and national goal-setting commissions and committees. Like other specialists, classroom teachers of speech communication and theatre take their cues from the findings of such groups while assessing their own students' needs and abilities.

In 1971, the combined task forces on educational goals for Massachusetts reported that "education should provide each learner with various opportunities to nurture interests, to discover and to develop natural talents, and to express values and feelings through various media."[1] This goal is a direct challenge to the teacher of speech communication and theatre at all grade levels. The challenge becomes even more obvious when dealing with the child with special needs, especially the child whose emotional and mental health is in some questionable state. A closer look at "difficult students" might prompt us to label them *emotionally disturbed*. Labeling children is convenient for teachers but not very helpful for children, particularly with regard to educational planning. In point of fact, we don't know how many children can be labeled *emotionally disturbed*. According to incidence studies, figures vary from less than one percent to upwards of ten percent of the school population depending on wide differences in criteria and points of view.[2] In any case, what is of paramount concern to classroom teachers is that every year they face a number of children whose sociopsychological makeup interferes in some way with the learning process. Some of these children may need to be taught in special programs such as hospital schools and day care centers, but many more remain in our regular classrooms.

If these children are to make educational progress, we must learn to recognize their special needs, and we must be willing to manipulate the teaching process accordingly. Most classroom teachers have developed their own techniques for identifying special needs and have learned to adapt their programs to accommodate a variety of individual problems. However, it is also true that few teachers consider affective learning when engaged in educational planning. The tendency is to stress cognition as an end in itself.

All children need to be taught to feel as well as to know. All children need to experience and explore their environment with their hearts as well as with their minds. This is no less true for exceptional children. Since handicapped children are not partial persons, we must teach them as whole human beings, regardless of their individual degree of exceptionality.

Creative dramatics offers some interesting possibilities in pursuing this goal. Nearly all children take to drama with ease and delight perhaps because it appeals to their natural mimetic sense. It is an activity in which each and every child can succeed on some level of expectation. It has proven positive effects on the creativity of children.[3] Considering these factors, it is not surprising to find more and more teachers using creative dramatics in a variety of ways and as an alternative to cognition-oriented learning.

An example is an experimental program in creative dramatics which is being developed for the school department of the Gaebler Children's Unit of the Metropolitan State Hospital in Waltham, Massachusetts.[4] The Gaebler School services some 200 children per year in a variety of categories ranging from residential treatment to diagnostic work-ups and adjustment counseling for nonresidents. The full-time school program maintains an average daily attendance of about 100 children, ages seven to sixteen. Of this number, 30 to 40 are residents of the Children's Unit, while the remainder are in a variety of day care programs specifically tailored to meet individual needs.

There is a wide range of problems among the children. Some are severely disturbed, suffering from clinically demonstrated mental illness, while others have severe to mild personality disorders. Still other children have a variety of behavior problems which make it difficult or impossible for them to function in ordinary school settings. About 20 percent of the children are court referrals, while the remainder have been referred to the Gaebler program through mental health agencies and public school officials.[5] An active transition program has had marked success in returning to their own schools an encouraging number of children who are better able to cope with everyday stress and frustration.

The most significant reason that creative dramatics fits into the curriculum of the Gaebler School is that the activity provides opportunities for creative expression within a controlled environment. Children with emotional problems need such opportunities since their academic and behavior management programs are in most cases and of necessity highly structured. Because the drama program is approached from an educational and recreational rather than therapeutic point of view, it provides needed escape valves while developing important skills and abilities. The program also caters to the children's need for approval and ego satisfaction.

From this standpoint, creative dramatics has been of significant value for a majority of the children at the Gaebler School. Many children in the program have shown improvement in their ability to concentrate and to focus on a single task at a time. Progress has been noted in some children's verbal skills and in their desire to communicate. Some children have responded well to exploratory exercises involving multisensory experiences leading to keener sense awareness. Carefully selected, reward-oriented theatre games have improved social behavior among the children. There is evidence to indicate that certain children working with pantomime and improvisation are better able to use their imaginations for constructive purposes.

The gains mentioned above are related to the most common behavioral characteristics of emotionally disturbed children. One educator has described such children as "inattentive, withdrawn, aggressive, nonconforming, disorganized, immature, and unable to get along with others."[6] It is in precisely these areas that creative dramatics can make a contribution. Carefully planned drama activities can advance behavioral goals as well as serve the educational needs of children with emotional problems. The Gaebler School experiment indicates clearly that such activities become an integral part of the total program and that, encouraged by the success of the specialist, classroom teachers soon learn to utilize such activities in their own work with the children.

An experienced teacher's own imagination and enthusiasm is undoubtedly the best source of ideas for creative dramatics. The Gaebler School experiment has shown that emotionally disturbed children respond most readily to theatre activity when it is presented with honesty and gusto. For example, the teacher comes into the classroom carrying a large roll of some imaginary substance under one arm. S/He announces that s/he has found a magic carpet and asks the children if they would like to take a trip with him/her. S/He unrolls the "carpet" and invites three or four children to join him/her. Off they go to a witch's cave or a giant's castle or a magic forest. On a prearranged signal, the travelers return to the magic carpet. The carpet picks up another load; this time they're off to the moon or a far-away planet. Eventually, there are four or five groups, each with a student leader, developing ideas according to their own locales.

The teacher can easily rearrange the groups or change the locales, and the "carpet" serves as a focal point for each group. Story lines and short scenes can be developed on each "trip." Children will "become" whatever their own imaginations and the teacher's allow. Such flexibility is important; but, at the same time, the activity must incorporate controls to avoid excessive energy releases. Unusual signals such as the clash of small cymbals or the sound of a slide whistle can provide these controls. Severely disturbed children respond well to such signals, especially if they are accompanied by a pleasurable countermeasure such as a trip on the magic carpet.

Other devices work equally well. All children love to be animals, plants, or inanimate objects. They enjoy making sounds for their own sake or responding physically to music or even assuming the characteristics of natural forces. One class at the Gaebler School found a group of nine- and ten-year-olds having a delightful time being the wind and snow which come to cover the flowers in the Selfish Giant's garden. This particular activity was developed into a performance of the Oscar Wilde fairy tale; but educationally speaking, the class activity was probably of equal merit.

Some children with emotional problems find it difficult to enter such imaginary worlds. They may need warm-up exercises. Rhythm games, mimed reaction to words (Halloween, gypsy, yo-yo, hurricane, etc.), and simple tension/relaxation games may be useful in this respect. Try frozen tag, but have the children freeze as something or someone. Use bright scarves or old hats or lengths of colored jersey to prod the children's imaginations.

At Gaebler, we found that older children (especially boys) enjoy more contemporary situations. Television programs and news items can stimulate highly imaginative dramatic play. Three older boys at the Gaebler School developed a series of black-out skits on air and noise pollution which were eventually submitted to a local television station for possible airing. A group of adolescent students enjoyed working up unusual "who-what-where" situations by listing each separately and then scrambling them. The resulting combinations were often very amusing. Imagine a 14-year-old trying to improvise an 80-year-old man (who?), riding a bicycle (what?), at the bottom of a pool (where?)! Since the audience (the remainder of the class) had to discover the combination entirely on the basis of the student's pantomime, the entire class became very much aware of nonverbal communication and the part it plays in our everyday lives. Behaviorally, the class had been given an acceptable substitute for a disorganized, disruptive atmosphere. The task was reward oriented (communicating the idea to the audience), mildly competitive, and simply too interesting to ignore.

In summary, creative dramatics can serve the teacher in a number of ways. It has been demonstrated that as an activity for emotionally disturbed children it encourages better communication, develops imagination and creativity, and provides opportunities for increased sense awareness. From a behavioral standpoint, creative dramatics provides opportunities for group participation and cooperation, creates opportunities for the controlled release of energy, and encourages ego-satisfying activity within the framework of peer approval. On a theoretical level, creative dramatics may be viewed as an alternative means of encouraging effective learning while enhancing a more positive approach to behavior management and control. Whereas it is difficult to validate such claims empirically, there is sufficient descriptive evidence, particularly as a result of the Gaebler School program and other similar experiments, to warrant further study and to encourage classroom teachers to incorporate creative dramatics into their educational planning and decision making, especially when considering a child with emotional problems.

NOTES

1. Commonwealth of Massachusetts, Board of Education, *Educational Goals for Massachusetts* (September 1971), p. 13.

2. N.W. Morse Long and R. Newman, *Conflict in the Classroom: The Education of Emotionally Disturbed Children,* 2d ed. (Belmont, CA: Wadsworth, 1971). This text stresses this diversity while advocating individualization of instruction.

3. Toni Schmidt, Elissa Goforth, and Kathy Drew, "Creative Dramatics and Creativity," *Educational Theatre Journal* (March 1975): 111-4.

4. Established in 1945, this facility was the first publicly supported psychiatric hospital for children in the country. It is administered by the Massachusetts Department of Mental Health with special support grants from other state and federal agencies.

5. Statistics are taken from Roland L. Nuttall, "Evaluation of the Gaebler School, Gaebler Children's Unit, Metropolitan State Hospital, 1971-2," (Boston: January 1973).

6. Frank M. Hewitt, *The Emotionally Disturbed Child in the Classroom* (Boston: Allyn & Bacon, 1968), p. 3.

Poetry Therapy

by Dorothy Kobax
and Estelle Nisenson

Helping a child solve emotional problems by putting his/her own creative ideas to work is a process we are using at Public School 49 in Queens, New York. We call it *poetry therapy*. It's based on the idea that the concepts, inspirations, moods, sounds, and rhythms in poetry can be used to supplement traditional clinical treatment. With a team approach, a psychiatric social worker and a language arts elementary teacher worked with five emotionally disturbed eight-year-olds who had shown symptoms of acting-out behavior, anxiety, withdrawal, and regression.

We began by explaining to the children that poems often tell how people feel and we were interested in hearing how certain poems made them feel. We added that the poems were specifically chosen to try to help them talk about why they thought good or bad things in school and at home. Over and over it was emphasized that our poetry sessions were not a class and that there were no marks or tests involved. The poems selected were geared to children of various ages. They dealt with the usual fears, joys, questions, and attitudes of children. Some were humorous, others were sad—all were provocative and challenging.

Reading a poem served as a springboard for discussion at each session. As leaders, we encouraged even the simplest responses and acknowledged all contributions favorably. Children were also encouraged to react to each other's comments and digress from the original theme of the poem to any other topics they wanted to discuss. Our goal was to direct the children's thought from their initial, superficial responses to a deeper level, where more feeling, emotion, and genuine release of anxieties could be verbalized. Printing a portion of a session demonstrates our method best. The poem used in the example that follows is "Andre" by Gwendolyn Brooks.

Andre

I had a dream last night. I dreamed
I had to pick a mother out.

I had to choose a father, too.
At first, I wondered what to do.
There were so many there, it seemed,
Short and tall and thin and stout.
But just before I sprang awake,
I knew what parents I would take.
And this surprised and made me glad:
They were the ones I always had.

Dialog

Bill: I don't like this poem.
Tom: Me neither.
Leader: What don't you like about it?
Bill: I don't know. I just don't like it.
Leader: Does anybody else not like it?

(Group agreement that they did not like the poem.)

Leader: Does the poem upset you?
Jane: It makes me feel bad.
Leader: Maybe you feel afraid to admit that sometimes you also wanted to change your mothers and fathers. (Long silence)
Leader: When you are angry, perhaps you wish you could pick new parents.
Mark: Well, once my father made me mad and I wanted to run away.
Leader: Did you want a different father?
Mark: For a little while I did.
Leader: When I was a little girl, my mother was very strict with me and many times I wished I had different parents.
Tom: It makes me scared to think about it.
Leader: You mean scared that you are a bad person if you wish that sometimes?
Mike: I wish I could get rid of my sisters.

(Group agrees in unison that they would like to pick new brothers and sisters.)

Leader: You don't seem so upset about picking new brothers and sisters. But suppose we give you a chance to pick.
(We go around the room.)
Bill: Parents that leave me alone.
Mark: Parents that don't holler.
Tom: Parents that let me do what I want.
Mike: Parents that listen to me.
Jane: Parents that don't get so mad.
Leader: Aren't your own parents ever the way you want them to be?

(Group agrees that sometimes they are.)

Leader: It looks like you want to tell us about it.
Bill: I got mad at the girl next to me—I took her pen to get even.

Jane: Why don't you just tell her you were angry and not steal?

Bill: Well, maybe. But I'm not going to give it back.

Leader: Do you feel better now that you've told us?

Bill: I guess so.

Leader: It was very brave of Bill to tell us about something he didn't like to do. Maybe he told us so he wouldn't have to tell his real parents.

Tom: Yes, we're good parents because we don't bawl him out or holler at him.

(Group reacts with laughter and relief.)

COMMENTS

The poem served as a way for the boy who had stolen to air the thought on his mind. The poem also enabled the group to understand that negative feelings about one's parents could be expressed without punishment. Each child became aware that he wasn't alone in having those kind of feelings.

Poetry therapy need not be limited to small groups. It can be effectively used with whole classes to focus on such issues as ethics, commitments, responsibilities, life-styles, and spiritual awareness.

Original Writing: A Therapeutic Tool in Working with Disturbed Adolescents

by Ellen J. Dehouske

Many disturbed adolescents have a desperate need to communicate and feel that they have been deprived this by parents, teachers, and peers. Often, when they are given the opportunity, they freeze or yell "Leave me alone." They seem to leave many rap sessions feeling frustrated, angry, isolated, and lonely. However, these adolescents can often express their concerns through original writing tasks.

Original writing is inherently therapeutic. It is exciting to observe students as they discover the appealing qualities of this form of self-expression. The students seem to find it private and soothing; they have a chance to express their fears, anxieties, miseries, and uglinesses; and it is up to them to share their writing with others. Creative writing can be a disguise for self-revelation. Students do not have to be spontaneous, think quickly, or be able to socialize; all they need is a means of recording their thoughts. Over the course of several months, a student's writings become a personal record of progress.

THE CLASSROOM ENVIRONMENT

A workshop setting with typewriters, tape recorders, notebooks, art supplies, and several work areas communicates to students that all types of writing are acceptable. Such a setting allows students to become more attuned to their individual writing personalities. (At times, the tape recorder plays soft music to encourage a relaxed atmosphere.) To dispel anxiety, new students are assigned writing tasks that offer a disguise and introduce them to the notion of original writing. The thumbprint stories, animal stories, and line character stories discussed in this article are examples of this. As students become less anxious, they gain the freedom to explore their own personal avenues of writing.

The writing class encourages a climate of respect. Almost every student has something to say and it is hoped that s/he will state it honestly and will find it meaningful. Initially, students need to know that they are expected to write but that they do not have to write about personal topics. The teacher's evaluation should convey the positive note, "This is fine," so that students are encouraged, shown acceptance, and invited to establish a trusting relationship. No matter how simple, guarded, clichéd, or artsy a writer's beginning, if s/he is accepted and respected, the writing will reflect more personal and troublesome issues after a period of time.

The teacher should respond to the concerns students bring with them to class and channel these into meaningful writing tasks. It is essential to be willing to wait, allowing students to reveal themselves at their own pace; to be willing to hold back and listen rather than judge; and to be willing to back off, dropping a subject when the squirming student indicates it is a too-sensitive area. Students need the opportunity and space to explore their problems. In this classroom environment, students will begin producing original writings filled with personal statements about themselves, their feelings, and their conflicts.

BEHAVIORS, ATTITUDES, AND PROBLEM-SOLVING SKILLS

Although some students will not speak directly about their personal concerns and feelings, their writings unfold self-revealing information. For example, Tom, a 16-year-old, was usually nonverbal about personal issues. He used the four-sequence thumbprint story to experiment with solutions to his problem. In actuality, Tom ran away from home and lived in a tree house for several months—one of a number of crucial actions that resulted in his hospitalization. In his story (see Figure 1) "The Runaways," the characters considered running away but decided to return home instead. Although the story was simple and concrete and the style was rigid and guarded, Tom did show that he could solve problems and that he was trying to seek a more acceptable solution than escape.

Another nonverbal student, George, was a 17-year-old who had failed school, unexpectedly, in his junior year. He was depressed and withdrawn. In class, George usually could not verbalize. His face showed confusion and he seemed to be trying to recapture some thought. He seemed afraid of the confusion yet afraid to admit to it. His thumbprint story (see Figure 2) took him a whole week of 45-minute classes. He spent a great deal of time sitting and thinking before he made each new addition. However, George's story, "Jim Gets a Car," did show that he could think through a problem to

FIGURE 1 The Runaways

One day a policeman was walking along the sidewalk.

He noticed two runaways.

The policeman started to chase them and they ran away from him.

The runaways finally decided to go back home because they didn't want to get caught by the police.

FIGURE 2 Jim Gets a Car

One day Jim bought a car. He was happy with it.

Then one day, he got a flat.

Jim decided to do something about it, to fix it.

Now Jim is happy once again.

a solution, even though it was on a very concrete, literal level. The story also revealed his feelings and attitudes toward hospitalization.

George was asked to write another story, this time using an animal character and giving a moral. His fable, "Bark, Dog," gave insight into his nonverbal state:

> There was a dog who would not bark. His name was Duke. His master did everything he could, but Duke would not bark. He felt more intelligent if he didn't. So his master decided to give Duke to a friend of his. Now Duke has fun all day playing and barking.
>
> Moral: Keep your dog, he'll bark eventually.

Students were asked to include a moral to their stories in order to lessen the possibility of misinterpretations. The moral also showed a student's desired focus. At times, some students' written morals had little to do with the story but a lot to do with themselves.

Two students, Rob and Beth, were quite articulate, personable, and perceptive of human behavior. Yet, both were guarded about their private selves. Externally, they demonstrated positive, objective strengths but internally they saw themselves as losers. Rob wrote a story with lines as characters, entitled, "Little Lost Line," to illustrate his attitude:

> Once, a while back, there was a little deformed line in the midst of all the straight lines. He felt all out of place and all the straight lines laughed at him. One day he decided to have an operation to straighten himself out. While he was out of town having his operation, someone stepped on something and bent all of the straight lines in town, and everyone laughed at him.
>
> *Moral:* You can't win.

Beth used the four-sequence thumbprint story to illustrate her attitude toward life. (See Figure 3.)

For both Rob and Beth, merely positively reinforcing their accomplishments was of little value. It was necessary to deal with their negative self-perceptions.

Through original writings, students seem to express their feelings and concerns. Sometimes students will present what they have written and ask "Is this okay?" When answered with "Are you satisfied?" they seem to cope with the resulting anxiety and even enjoy the opportunity for self-expression. As their self-esteem increases, many students become excited and proud when their stories are published in the class magazine. It is healthy for them to uncover their attitudes, emotions, and problem-solving skills. Simultaneously, this information is useful to the staff in helping to construct an individualized program for each student. The following two case studies will illustrate these ideas more thoroughly.

FIGURE 3 Tommy's Haircut

One day, when Tommy Green Thumb woke up. He was happy til his father came in and said, "You have to get your hair cut."

Well, that made Tommy's hair stand up. He was very sad. That made his dad happy cause his dad was mean.

Tommy's on his way home from his haircut. He is now happy because he likes it.

Tommy's girlfriend doesn't.

NEW DIRECTION: JACK

Jack was a 16-year-old, learning disabled student whose learning disabilities had gone undiagnosed for many years. He had a poor self-concept. Initially, when Jack needed help, he called "Iron Man" to the rescue. Iron Man was the hero in all his original writings and stories; he righted all wrongs and did all the things that Jack wished he could do. Jack frequently could be observed assuming the all-powerful pose of Iron Man during the day.

One writing task Jack performed was the creation of a children's storybook, a task that many immature students find to be safe and nonthreatening. The student could then choose to do the illustrations with traced or freehand drawings. Jack chose to trace Iron Man but he drew the boy, the ma and pa, and the "bad guys" in his own hand (see Figure 4). Both the drawings and the story revealed his poor self-concept, his immaturity, and his fantasy wish: to have the strength of a superhero.

Jack needed to write about Iron Man and was permitted to do so. Nearly one month later, he expressed a problem with his fantasy through a "Dear Abby" letter in our school magazine. ("Dear Abby" letters are a part of our monthly magazine, published by the writing classes. If some students

FIGURE 4 How Iron Man Came to Be

requested to answer an "Abby" column, all the other students were asked to write letters with silly or serious problems.) Jack submitted the following:

Dear Abby:
> I have a terrible problem, I think I'm Iron Man. All the kids are bothering me—not to mention any names like W.M. Please help me.
>
> Signed,
> Iron Man

Jack received the following answer from "Abby":

Dear Iron Man:
> Maybe one night you should take a good look at yourself in the mirror. Don't you realize Iron Man isn't everything! I bet you he's got a lot of problems. Haven't you ever wondered why he wore a mask? It's to hide those dreaded worry wrinkles. The kids are upset 'cause they would rather have you be yourself, and they're sick of the same old Iron Man front. Give it a try.
>
> —Abby

This letter, along with other pieces that Jack was writing, suggest that he was feeling strong enough and good enough about himself to dare to deal with the ineffectualness of his Iron Man identity. Through writing, Jack had signaled the fact that he was considering taking his next step. A program to deal with this could now be initiated.

The staff jointly began reinforcing Jack's responses and ignoring or negatively reinforcing his Iron Man comments. In writing, Jack requested the opportunity to write another children's storybook. I suggested that he consider the topic, "How Iron Man Faded into the Past." Jack accepted the challenge and developed a story in which Iron Man was wiped out by repeated attacks from the child care staff. Iron Man was weak and returned to his laboratory and maybe would make a new super charged battery. The story ended at that point.

Several months later, Jack was wondering whether he should quit school and join the army; he was learning how to play guitar for his band. He had made much progress. There was no mention of Iron Man; Jack was feeling better about being himself.

ESTABLISHING TRUST: MATT

Nov. 6

Hello. I would like to introduce you to a quiet person, me. My name is Matt. I am 16 years old and live in S_____ Township. At this moment I am at St. Francis Mental Health Clinic getting help with my problems. I feel it has helped me a great deal. Time is passing very quickly for me here. I am interested in electronics and hope to work in the field of computer repair.

I am satisfied with being quiet but sometimes I wish I was noisier. So I could get my better opinions across.

This place has helped me accept reality more readily. It also helps make it so sometimes when I want to say something I will at least try to say it.

Matt entered the classroom following a second genuine suicide attempt. He was cautious about relating to his peers. Although he was tolerant and understanding of others, he rarely made himself known to us. He chose individual assignments. He did not seem to know how to engage in socializing. The only times he shared himself were when he and I were chatting over academics.

It was important to discover what was going on inside of him and yet there were several hindrances. Matt found social situations so anxiety provoking that they had to be presented in small doses initially, until he could deal with them more effectively. It also was essential to know his pressure points before social situations could be constructed without being overly demanding.

I decided to try journal writing with Matt. He made entries several times weekly. I stressed that he was to say as much as he wished and that I would respond to his comments through writing. Matt's comments helped suggest the next topic for his journal. For example, Matt's page after his introduction read: "What are the most difficult problems you see in relating to others?"

The most difficult problems in relating to others is knowing what to say, how to say it, and "reactions." With me I do not want to say something wrong, and have their feelings hurt. Sometimes hurting someone's feelings is unavoidable, but if it is not necessary to hurt someone I will not. You also must react properly. I mean, for instance, don't laugh when someone says something which is not meant to be funny. Another problem is you should show concern with a person, but "not always" too much concern. Some people do not like too much "concern" because they feel you are just doing it for no "good" reason. It really just depends on the person, which causes problems in relating.

Matt and I were establishing an active line of communication:

Me: Matt —
You appear to be very sensitive to other's feelings. I wonder, do you ever share this lovely, sensitive self with others so they get to know you? You know, it seems that the small hurts and awkwardnesses are worth it with those few people who interest you as potential friends. If people appeal to you, chances are they have the same fears and sensitivities. Give them credit, too!

Matt: Do you think you could explain more.

And so the journal continued as an active, therapeutic writing experience. My role developed from listener to active participant. Matt always had the option of writing anything he wished or of responding to my comments if he preferred this.

Nov. 13

My biggest problem in relating to people is trying to talk. Sometimes I have a hard time making people understand what I really want to say. It is difficult getting people to understand what my true intentions are. The only way I try to solve this problem is keep talking until I do get my idea across. I try never to give up, but yet sometimes I do.

Another problem I have is "copping out." I do this a lot and I should really try harder not to, but yet, for me, it is getting difficult. I do not know why I am trying to get out of everything but yet I do. I wish I wouldn't.

Matt's writing was circular: he kept going round and round about his inability to communicate, but he would never get beyond obscure generalities. So, we kept on:

Nov. 19

It is hard to say something important. I mean it is good to talk but if there is no meaning in what I say there is no use saying it. Words should be used for meaning not just to waste time. If there is nothing to be said why say something. It is good to talk things out, but if someone does not want to talk, why FORCE THEM. Words should be said when they fit not as an added extra. In some instances people need a little push to get started doing what they should do, like you're doing now, pushing me so I write more, but you can't push a person too hard or they will drop too fast.

Here, Matt asked me to back off—I was pressing too hard. So, the journal was withdrawn for a time. However, one day, Matt entered the classroom, quite obviously upset. He wrote the following article for the class magazine:

Could you imagine yourself being dead. What would it be like. Would you be reincarnated? If so as what. Or do you think that when you are dead there is some place you go. If so where and what would you do when you get there. Would you have eternal happiness or would you have eternal hell. There are many possibilities of what could happen to you. It is up to you, what you believe. Where will you go, you'll have to wait till your death to find out.

Because there were other students present, and because Matt and I had a private channel for communication, I quietly walked up to him with his journal and said, "Matt, you seem upset and I cannot talk to you now. Perhaps you would be willing to write in your journal and tell me why you seem so concerned with death today? Then, you might feel better just because you wrote it down. And, if you wish, we could talk about it, later." And, Matt wrote:

It seems to me that this death is not physical but mental. My mind is confused. I love my father and wish I could show this love. Without sharing this love I feel down. Right now I am trying to get help with this problem with my counselor, but it does not seem to be working. I am going to go fishing with my dad on Sunday but I do not know how this is going to turn out. I wish I knew in advance. If only I could do something to show him I really love him. My mother I love too and with her it is easier to show her that I love her but I still have difficulty. Right now I am trying to withdraw from reality so I can think what I am going to do. I need more time to think but yet I do not know how long it's going to take me or how long I have left.

Matt began really using his journal. He almost seemed compelled to express his feelings and confusions.

It took several months, but Matt was coming to trust me, as he illustrated through personal issues he discussed in his journal. We then moved from using the journal occasionally, to not using it at all. Of course, Matt was always writing for the magazine so he continued to communicate his thoughts and feelings:

> Imagine being a dictionary. Just think, you could have all the words known. You would be, almost, the most brilliant thing alive. The only thing is, you could not express your knowledge unless someone wanted to use you. You would be able to tell a person what "zounds" is ("zounds"—an oath expressing surprise or anger). If you were a foreign dictionary, you would be a great help to people by teaching them a different language, but, again, you have to be opened. So, it would be nice being a dictionary if you did not mind being used only when necessary!

Now, Matt began participating in controlled social situations. Initially, Matt showed anxiety when presented with social situations, but he trusted—and tried. He began doing small group tasks that demanded socializing within structure. Soon, he began responding to girls, and gentle teasing helped him to ease into encounters. Generally, the journal ceased being a route for therapy. Nevertheless, the journal was a valuable tool in allowing Matt to discuss important issues privately and to establish a trusting relationship—one that would encourage and guide him in socializing.

FINAL COMMENTS

Within the setting of a nonthreatening class, original writing gives students an opportunity to express their concerns, to work through their conflicts, to share themselves with others, and to take pride in their writing. Original writing allows students, in their own way and in their own time, to reveal their feelings to themselves, to the teacher, and to others. Original writing can work as a tool to tap adolescents' need to express themselves and to develop good feelings about themselves. Whether through thumbprint stories or through larger books and journals, students' writings give insights into their concerns, lead to further topics for exploration, suggest problems that can be dealt with through classroom structure, and help to establish a personal line of communication between students and teacher. However, the teacher must be willing to put forth a great deal of time, energy, and thought in order to listen to the students, decode their messages, and weigh teacher responses therapeutically.

Film Making as a Therapeutic Tool

by Bill Arnott
and Jeffrey Gushin

Film making combines a highly personal form of expression with communication to others on a large scale. It also affords the opportunity to combine many forms of expression to represent thoughts and feelings in new and unique ways. The visual portion of a film offers untold possibilities. In particular, animated films can be designed around the filming of art works created for the purpose in a variety of media, such as sculpture, painting, and drawing. As an integral part of both standard and animated films, sound, too, can serve as an effective vehicle for expression in the form of dialogue, effects, and music.

For many years film techniques were thought to be too complex for use with children and mental patients, but recently many schools and art centers have successfully incorporated film making into their programs. Bader and Muller reported on the making of several movies by patients at the Lausanne University Psychiatric Clinic in Switzerland,[1] and Fox and Wortman wrote of their use of film making as a therapeutic tool with students in a course on "Psychology of the Person" at Northwestern University.[2]

The basic mechanics of camera operation and editing are simple enough for children as young as ten years old to understand, and, given some experience with equipment, such children have demonstrated their ability to make films.[3] Exposure to television and cartoons has familiarized children with such basic film techniques as long-, medium-, and close-range shots; voice-overs; and montage. Animation is a particularly suitable form for children in that frames are photographed singly at whatever pace the child can manage. What has been thought of as a disadvantage of film work with children—the delay caused by processing—can be used to encourage disciplined behavior and planning and to develop impulse control. This is especially desirable for children in whom impulsiveness and demand for immediate gratification are pronounced.

In the balance of this paper we will describe our experience in conducting a seven-week workshop for a small group of preadolescent boys with behavioral problems. Under our supervision each boy wrote his own story and directed its filming, often assisted by other group members. One or the other of us discussed privately with each boy the content of his film in an effort to promote his self-awareness and our understanding of them.

BACKGROUND

The film-making workshop took place at a special residential school which drew students from the public-school systems of three counties surrounding a medium-sized city. The special school served as a diagnostic and treatment center for elementary school children of average or above-average academic potential who were unable to function in a regular classroom because of emotional, behavioral, or learning difficulties. The film-making group operated independently of regular school activities, and the four boys who participated, after having been recommended for the workshop by their teachers on the basis of expressed interest, attended voluntarily.

The equipment which the boys used in the workshop consisted of a Canon Super 8 movie camera, with an adaptor for single-frame exposure (used for animation); a Kodak Standard 8 millimeter Brownie movie camera; an Emdeko Dual 8 millimeter projector; a Baia Dual 8 millimeter reviewer and splicer; two tripods; a projection screen; lights and light stands; and assorted other basic film equipment. Also available were standard art materials, such as crayons, chalk, felt-tip pens, paint, brushes, paper, cardboard, scissors, and glue.

The group met once a week for a two-hour session in a large room in the basement of the school. Although filming was not restricted to this area, all the planning, editing, and viewing took place here.

In the first session the functions and operation of the camera and projector were explained and a short film on techniques was shown. During the following session, a practice film was shot with each member taking a turn behind the camera. At the next session the group viewed the film and got suggestions on how to improve techniques. The next step was for each boy to write a story and make drawings of scenes for his film. Each was asked to read his story to the group and to explain what his drawings were meant to illustrate. The group then voted on which story to film first.

The following ground rules were established during these early sessions: There was to be no fighting or rough play during the film class. Equipment was to be handled with care. Each member would have a turn to make his movie, with the rest of the group helping, and while filming his story he was the director, responsible for final decisions on how the movie was to be filmed and what roles other members would play in its production.

The instructors tried to remain as unobtrusive as possible during the filming, interceding only when they thought it was necessary to maintain order or offer information. If a boy violated any of the rules, he would be removed from the room for a time. When the group became uncontrollable, all production would be stopped and a group meeting held to determine the source of the problems and effective ways of dealing with them.

After each boy had viewed his unedited film, he discussed it privately with one of the instructors in a manner and for purposes which will be explained below. Then the boy proceeded to edit his film into its final form.

A THEORETICAL CONSIDERATION

In an effort to learn as much as we could about each boy in the workshop and, more important, to help him to see, understand, and possibly even modify his behavior, our discussion of each boy's film with him proceeded along the lines of Richard Gardner's storytelling reconstruction therapy.[4] With Gardner's method the therapist, after hearing the child's story and attempting to analyze it for unconscious pathological content, unresolved conflicts, and irrational attitudes projected by the child onto his characters, says, "Now I have a story I would like to tell you." The therapist then reconstructs the story, using the same characters, but gives it a different outcome. Gardner theorizes that a child is more likely to gain insight into his own behavior by bypassing his conscious ego through the device of seeing his own characters, with whom he unconsciously identifies, behave differently. According to Gardner's theory, the child internalizes the therapist's proposed solution to the child's conflicts by accepting as his own the qualities ascribed to his characters by the therapist. Our procedure in the film-making workshop differed from Gardner's in that instead of ourselves providing the children with alternate resolutions to their stories, we encouraged the children to invent their own.

The film medium lent itself well to this process, and we organized our procedures to make the most of the opportunities it offered. In making his movie each boy had an excellent opportunity to project his feelings and behavior onto his characters and those children who played the part of his characters and literally to see his emotions externalized. We chose the moment when the boy had viewed his rough version to talk privately with him about those emotions on the premise that he would be particularly open at this time to such discussion and the gaining of insights. The process of editing the rough version of the film into its finished form served as a natural occasion for modifying the original story line if a boy chose to do so. Of course, each boy could make changes at any time throughout the making of his film.

In our analysis of each boy's story we looked for psychological content that might relate to his behavioral problems. We expected each boy to project his conflicts into his story and to identify with at least one of the characters. The boy's assignment to a character of the hero's role, his identification or nonidentification with this character, and his proposed solution to the projected conflict were especially considered. We felt it would be more helpful if each boy made his own discoveries and found his own rational solutions. Our role was to stimulate insight by asking him to think of as many different endings and morals to his story as he could. When each boy viewed his completed movie, we asked him what he would change if he were to do it again, whether or not he wanted to alter his moral or add new ones, and what movie he would choose to make next.

THE STORIES

Following is a brief description of each boy, his story, the moral he applied to it, and a discussion of the possible significance of his movie in relation to the boy's background and behavior.

David, age 9, was the youngest member of the group. He was immature, hyperactive, and inclined to watch rather than to participate. He continually tried to get people to do things for him. He did not get along well with the other boys, possibly because he was younger than they. Despite his resentment of group authority, he would grudgingly abide by group decisions.

The other three boys based their movies on their stories, but David, after writing the story and moral which are given below, decided instead to make an unrehearsed film.

The Tennessee Dog

It was a cloudy day. The Tennessee Dog was laying out in the yard and then another dog came along. He got up and played with him. Then another dog came along and all three played. Each one jumped over each other. They played leap frog. They keep on playing and then another dog came along and the Tennessee Dog fought with it and the Tennessee Dog got his nose torn off. He went home and never played with other dogs again anymore. He fought with dogs from then on. Moral: Never fight with dogs.

We might rewrite David's story as follows, making him the central character, to better understand how he feels about himself in relation to others: "It was a cloudy day. I was lying in the yard. Along came a boy; we played together; another boy came along and I fought with him. He tore my nose off and I went home and I'll never play with anyone again. Getting my nose torn off justifies my being aggressive. Moral: So don't be aggressive."

David lets his hero character, the Tennessee Dog, suffer a defeat and offers this experience as justification for later aggressive behavior. We were able to observe a direct parallel to his story in David's effort to maintain equal standing with the other (older) boys in the group. His aggressive behavior continually put him at odds with his peers. Especially with Eddie, he consistently resorted to name-calling, a self-defeating tactic to use against Eddie who was wittier and always succeeded in outdoing David. The exchange would certainly have led to fights, had we not intervened. David's moral contradicts the content of his story. This seems to reflect his uncertainty about how to handle his feelings appropriately.

When we talked with David about his story and suggested to him that the Tennessee Dog might get lonely if he didn't play with any dogs, he changed that part of the story and let the Tennessee Dog play with some of his friends. Later he decided not to film this story. Instead he made a spontaneous film about his hamster and other things that interested him, such as a smokestack, tall trees, moving machinery, and an empty swimming pool. He called his movie, "My Hamster and All the Interesting Things." He said he wanted his next movie to be an animated film about racing.

Gino, age 11, was fairly well adjusted but mildly hyperactive and had a short attention span and wandering thought processes. At times Gino was aggressive, more so verbally then physically. He showed considerable maturity in social relationships and had a good imagination. He was the most respected member of the group.

The Boy Who Never Came Home

It was a hot day, nobody was around. A boy was very sad trying to seesaw. He walked into the woods and saw a man chopping wood. The man called the boy and then grabbed him. He put him in his office. A policeman found him later. Moral: Never go outside without someone with you.

While composing this narrative, Gino decided to rewrite it in the first person. It was as though he realized that he was writing a story about himself. Later, while working on the film editor, he told us that the plot was similar to an experience that he had when he was younger. He had gotten lost and his mother called the police. His sister then found him. When he arrived home, his mother spanked him and told him not to go out alone anymore. She warned him that something terrible could happen to him. Although Gino seemed to understand the relationship between his film and his earlier experience, after viewing the film he said he did not want to alter it. He wanted, rather, to make a new film showing the actual incident as it had occurred when he was a young child.

Eddie, age 10, was very hyperactive, rarely staying with an activity for more than a minute. He was immature and indecisive and frequently quarreled and fought with others. Always wanting his own way, Eddie resented and rejected group decisions and authority. His tendency to interfere with his peers' work and to disregard their rights made him unpopular. Eddie had many original ideas but could seldom carry them out.

Bad Man's Bluff

Eddie presented his story in drawings, comic book style, rather than as a written narrative. A robber hides behind a tree, jumps out and robs a man, and then escapes by dashing into the woods. However, he drops his coat which a policeman finds and uses to track him down. Moral: The good guys always win.

We think Eddie's hero character was "the good guy" or policeman in the story, but Eddie himself identified with the "bad guy" or bandit. Again a conflict over aggression and expression of hostility appears, as in David's story. To the extent Eddie identified with the bandit, he probably felt relieved that someone (the hero character) exercised control over his (the robber's) previously uncontrolled aggression. While working on the film editor, Eddie said he felt fairly satisfied with his movie, although he would have liked to refilm certain sequences of bad footage. He talked about good guys and bad guys and said that he and his peers were good guys but didn't know how to avoid getting into trouble. We discussed whether it was worth getting into trouble at the expense of being punished. He said that it wasn't worth it, but that he had difficulty controlling his anger when provoked by others.

Mark, age 10, was withdrawn, immature for his age, hypersensitive, and reacted with unrealistic anxiety to simple problems. His social relations were poor; he was more interested in mechanical objects and how they worked than in people. Often he acted in a passive-aggressive manner. He resented authority—always wanting to have his own way—and anything that reminded him of school. He preferred to work alone rather than with others.

Racing

One car was speeding over one road and another car was speeding over another road. The two roads came together and the two cars crashed into one another. Moral: Drive carefully—Don't litter.

Mark went about filming in a supercautious, compulsive manner. He considered for another movie a story about two people who, when crossing a street, are hit by an ice cream truck and taken to the hospital with broken legs and arms. The moral of that story was, "Watch where you're walking; don't cross the street when the sign says don't walk." Both stories clearly reflect Mark's fearfulness, his excessive anxiety about himself.

On the whole, the boys' stories and morals center on punishment—a display of aggression which the boys considered justified and acceptable. The bad guys of their stories—bandits and kidnappers—roundly deserve the harsh beatings they get from the good guys. And the heroes turn out to be more aggressive in redressing wrongs than are the villains in committing them. We think that the boys actually identified to some extent with all three characters in such stories: villain, victim, and hero. The behavior of the characters is usually reinforced by the morals, which may be restated as "You get just what you deserve when you don't go by the rules." We tried to encourage the boys to take a somewhat less harsh approach to punishment than they demonstrated in their stories and not to use another's aggression as justification for their own often more violent aggression.

OBSERVATIONS OF BEHAVIOR

Because there was little advance information on which to base evaluation of behavioral change, we had to rely on our own observations. We saw no major alteration of individual behavior patterns, but occasionally we felt a particular member had gained some insight or made a favorable change—at least, for the moment—in his usual style of behaving. The boys' teachers informed us that the boys were excited about their film work and talked to their classmates about it. Our observations of the boys' behavior is organized under the following headings: group interaction, problem solving, and impulse control.

Group Interaction

The workshop was so structured as to encourage development of skills in group relations in several ways. First, the boys had to decide as a group the order in which the stories would be filmed. Eddie tried to get around the group's decision to film Gino's story first, but eventually he realized he would have to accept the decision or be left out. Also, each person in directing his own film had to enlist the aid of other group members if he needed help. Everyone participated and had a role in both Gino's and Eddie's films. But Mark found, in filming his animated movie, that working with more than one other individual caused problems and interfered with the job. And because David's film did not require any actors, he was able to work well with only one assistant. Thus, Mark and David assisted each other in filming while Gino and Eddie worked on editing their own films.

Often, while making the first two films, the actors came to the instructors to ask permission to do something or to complain about someone. They were referred to the director. When the director complained about lack of cooperation, he was told that he was in charge and must use his authority to get the group's cooperation. Gradually the actors grew to respect the authority of the director, even if they disagreed with him, because they knew that, eventually, they would get their turn at directing. It was difficult for the boys to adjust to the idea that one of their peers was in authority.

Gino and Eddie came to realize that they must not only assert themselves but also be willing to make compromises and concessions if they were to gain the cooperation of the others. Eddie seemed to gain some insight into his own behavior as a result of his experience. After shooting his film he told the instructors that he probably irritates people who want his attention in the same way the other boys had irritated him. Although he was not ready to change, at least he understood the others' reaction to him.

When Mark began filming his animated movie, he operated the camera while Gino and David moved the cars. This arrangement didn't work, and eventually David left to do other work. Mark continued to have difficulty and soon asked Gino to leave so he could work by himself. Because he had the right to make his film as he chose, he was allowed to work on his own. However, after several minutes of running back and forth from the cars to the camera to shoot two frames of film at a time, he realized that in order to finish his film on time he needed someone to help him. Thus, Mark saw that he had to compromise and ask for help when he could not work effectively alone.

David had a similar experience while directing his film, with Eddie assisting. They did not get along well and there was much arguing. But since Eddie was the only person available at the time and David could not handle the hamster and man the camera at the same time, he had to rely on Eddie for help.

Problem Solving

The numerous procedures of film making demanded that the boys solve many problems. Each boy had to conceive and put his story on paper and plan its execution. This process forced the boys to think ahead—to have some conception of the final product to guide them when they began shooting. There was some resistance to doing this as it reminded them of schoolwork. However, when they began shooting they found it useful to refer to their written (or, in the case of Mark, cartoon) versions.

Before shooting, the story was run through and the actors assigned their parts. Then each scene was rehearsed and followed by the camera without any film being exposed. This preparation of each scene, besides being necessary to a smoothly running film, gave the directors the opportunity to think of new ideas and make creative use of the camera.

When a problem occurred in trying to shoot some especially difficult scene, the cameraman would have to work out alternative methods of shooting. Decisions had to be made also about lighting, location, camera range, props, costumes, and so forth. Thus, group members became more aware of the complexity of the film process and the necessity for planning.

Screening the films gave the boys a chance to view their work and judge the results, thereby reinforcing the importance of well-considered planning before shooting. Viewing also fostered self-esteem and provided incentive for doing further work.

Editing the films also posed some problems. Each boy worked separately on his own movie with the aid of an instructor. Here he had to make decisions about what to keep and what to cut. Although editing can be tedious, the boys were able to follow through and do most of their own editing and splicing.

Gino, the most creative, enjoyed the editing and changed some scenes around in the process. The others were mainly interested in eliminating bad footage and attaching their titles. Most were worried about taking too much out, and had to be reminded that a film would not be interesting if it had a lot of unnecessary or bad footage in it. Eddie had a difficult time attending to this task; he worked only for short periods. We allowed this rather than force him to the point where he would lose interest in his work.

Impulse Control

Various aspects of film making, coupled with other means of dealing with the group, were used to foster the development of impulse control. We hoped that the boys' interest would serve as an incentive for appropriate behavior, thereby lessening the need for strong external controls. We wished to provide as free an environment as possible. However, the group needed constant reminders of the rules, even though the boys had agreed to accept them. To control aggressive or destructive behavior, the threat of temporary removal from the room had to be used. Occasionally, as a last resort, we used the token system which prevailed in their regular classes. Usually, however, threat of removal was sufficient.

Several procedures inherent in making films demand the control of impulses. First, the boys had to take turns filming their movies, and since they themselves determined the order of shooting, they could not blame the instructors for partiality. Eddie had difficulty accepting that he had to wait to make his movie but, after assuming his role in the first movie, he forgot about having to be first. The need for planning and rehearsing each film also served as a check to impulsive behavior. The boys could not go out and impulsively start shooting and achieve the results they wanted. The delay caused by processing the film also forced the group to wait before they could see the outcome of their work.

Mark, who was excessively anxious, doubted that the camera was working right when he was using it. He needed constant reassurance that it was functioning properly. When the instructors were not nearby, he could not refrain from the impulse to assure himself that the film was moving by opening the camera door. He did this despite having been told in the beginning session that opening the door would expose and ruin the film. When Mark's film was screened a week after he shot it, he saw that the camera had indeed been working well and that, by opening the camera to check the film, he had ruined some otherwise good footage. Since his film was animated, it had required a lot of time and work. This experience served as an excellent lesson for Mark on the wisdom of controlling his impulses.

CONCLUDING REMARKS

Had we had more time, we would have tried other possibilities with this group. For instance, each boy could have written another story and, instead of assuming the role of director and cameraman, could have chosen a particular role to play in his own movie. It would be interesting to see each boy acting out one of his own characters. Another possibility would be a film created as a joint effort, rather than under the directorship of one person.

Although we felt that using film with these children resulted in some benefits, several special problems may have limited our success. The physical conditions were restricting. At the beginning of each session we had to set up all the equipment and at the end of the session we had to put it away. A room set aside exclusively for film making would be much more workable. Because of limited space, we brought out art materials only as we needed them. The group might have made far more use of such materials if they had been more readily available.

Perhaps a less complex camera, such as a Kodak Instamatic, would have been more suited to children of this age. Time and money posed other problems. Had there been more equipment to go around and more time, each boy could have taken more pains in shooting his film.

Because of their age, the boys in this workshop were interested for the most part in just going out and shooting what they saw, as opposed to thinking out a story and working in a group. Our workshop approach might be more successful in larger groups and with children 13 years of age or older.

This venture might best be regarded as a pilot study which, with some of the above-mentioned changes instituted, could serve as the model for a useful program of film making as therapy.

NOTES

1. "Therapeutic Art Programs around the World: Film Making in a Swiss Psychiatric Hospital," *American Journal of Art Therapy* 11 (July 1972): 185-9. See also C. Muller and A. Bader, "The Cinema and the Mental Patient: A New Form of Group Therapy," *Current Psychiatric Therapies* 1 (1968): 169-72.

2. Carol Fox and Camille B. Wortman, "A Therapeutic Use of Film with University Students," *American Journal of Art Therapy* 15 (October 1975): 19-21.

3. We found the following books helpful in working in film making with children: Y. Anderson, *Teaching Film Animation to Children* (New York: Van Nostrand Reinhold, 1970) and J. Lidstone and D. McIntosh, *Children as Filmmakers* (New York: Van Nostrand Reinhold, 1970).

4. Richard Gardner, *Therapeutic Communication with Children: The Mutual Story Telling Technique* (New York: Science House, 1971).

PART V

HARD OF HEARING/DEAF STUDENTS

Introductory Comments

The extent to which a child's hearing is impaired determines his/her specific classification as a handicapped student. Those children having an impairment so severe that their hearing is nonfunctional for the purposes of educational performance are referred to as *deaf*. The child who, although not deaf, has a hearing impairment, either permanent or fluctuating, which is severe enough to adversely affect his/her educational performance is termed *hard of hearing*. Additionally, a severe impairment present at birth is generally more debilitating than one which occurs after the child has begun to acquire oral language.

The articles in this section attempt to acquaint the reader with a variety of services and resources that are available to the hearing impaired population. Equally important are the ways in which these children can be integrated into the mainstream of education by modifying techniques that have been proved successful in encouraging the deaf and hard of hearing to communicate with the world around them.

Effective use of the library and its resources is especially critical for individuals who do not have full use of their sense of hearing and, therefore, lack access to many forms of mass media. Library skills should be taught early and, as Mary Jane Metcalf states in "Helping Hearing Impaired Students," librarians and media specialists have a responsibility to develop and implement programs to meet their needs. In her article she reviews some of the characteristics of hearing impaired children and incorporates these into ways in which library skills can be taught, storytelling activities conducted, and reading encouraged.

Because sharing books and storytelling is very much a part of the elementary program, a separate article on this topic has been included. Although the program Jane Biehl describes in "Story Hours for the Deaf" was conducted as a service of a public library, the techniques she used are applicable in a public school setting. Educators who desire to work with children who use signed English but have no training in sign language themselves might enlist the help of other school staff, older deaf students, or parents of deaf youngsters to help with this aspect of the story hours.

The utilization of comic books as a motivation to read is slowly becoming a more acceptable practice. The added benefit for the deaf student is that most comic books emphasize conversational dialogue rather than literary narrative, have an abundance of picture cues, and provide liberal contact with idioms which are often confusing to deaf individuals who have had little exposure to them. In " 'Meanwhile...': A Look at Comic Books at Illinois School for the Deaf," Bill Stark attempts to dispel some of the stigma surrounding their use by explaining the standards set forth by the comic code authority for controlling content. The author also explains how the media center selects and uses comics and provides details of activities that involve supplying new dialogue for comic illustrations; acting out the roles of the characters; and producing sequential, captioned slide stories.

It is often necessary to use supplementary materials and other equipment to encourage interaction and communication among hearing handicapped children. In "Picture Perfect: Photography Aids Deaf Children in Developing Communication Skills," Doris W. Naiman relates how the use of Polaroid cameras with 20 deaf children, ages 9 to 16, accomplished this objective. The four-week project began with individual instruction on the use of the camera. Each child had access to a camera and was supplied with two rolls of film a week. The picture-taking process greatly facilitated interaction as the students asked friends, family, and even community members to be subjects for their pictures. The pictures themselves became the subject of much communication both at home and at school and led to many follow-up activities. The author relates a number of other beneficial outcomes of the project for individual students.

In choosing the pictures they wanted to take, the deaf children described by Naiman were able to express themselves in a situation structured for success. In "Directed Creativity," Janice Bell also states the necessity of providing a secure base from which a child may gain the confidence to creatively express himself/herself. In order to diminish the hesitation and discomfort many children experience in facing a blank page, she structured her art lesson on color by giving uniform instructions designed to yield identical products. Additional instructions to the seven- and eight-year-old deaf and brain damaged youngsters also led to similarity of design while they discovered that a new color had been created. Thereafter, additional materials were introduced without further directions, and originality prevailed for the remainder of the activity.

The final article on the hearing impaired offers a means of acquainting deaf students and deaf adults with the ongoing issues of day-to-day life. In "Using Non-Verbal Films with the Deaf and Language-Impaired," Salvatore J. Parlato, Jr. has compiled a guide to relatively recent films which do not rely on the spoken word to convey their message. Some of the topics covered by the films are deafness, love, old age, ecology, and personal health.

Helping Hearing Impaired Students

by Mary Jane Metcalf

Because of the nature of deafness, hearing impaired children do not have access to the same sources of information as their hearing counterparts. Many messages from radio, television, and other forms of mass media are unaccessible to the deaf. Therefore, it is essential that libraries help disseminate the world's fund of information to the hearing impaired. Librarians can and should provide the means for children with this handicap to study and learn independently. Hearing impaired children can and must be taught how to use a library to its fullest extent.

In many instances hearing impaired children are retarded in the language arts, specifically reading. This retardation varies according to the degree of hearing loss. Students with moderate hearing losses typically use run-on sentences and omit prepositions, plural suffixes, and tense suffixes. The language of profoundly deaf students is typified by the omission of conjunctions, articles of speech, and prepositions, or an incorrect choice of prepositions or articles.

Reading problems quite naturally follow language retardation. These problems are not just due to a limited vocabulary. Hearing impaired children have difficulty with syntactical structure, idiomatic expressions, and multiple meanings—things which are not always controlled in so-called high interest/low vocabulary books. For example, when one of our high school teachers showed a filmstrip to her literature class, one frame included a caption that read, "She made a mad dash down the stairs." When the teacher asked the students what "mad dash" meant, they said it meant "angry soap."

AVENUES OF LEARNING

Children with significant hearing losses learn primarily by sight. For this reason ideas and concepts must be presented in a visual format in order for the children to understand them. An illustration showing a person writing at a desk aids in making the meaning of the word *author* much clearer than just a written, spoken, or signed definition can.

Conversely, instructing with pictures alone may not suffice because hearing impaired children have some difficulty interpreting illustrations. Their language handicaps make it difficult for them to infer reactions, conversations, or events which are not specifically depicted in the illustrations. In order for hearing impaired children with significant hearing losses to understand a concept or story, librarians should use both pictures and total communication (using spoken and manual communication) simultaneously.

Hearing impaired children often have different interests than those of their hearing counterparts. The extent of this difference is open to argument but there is no question that differences do exist. There are children whose interest and maturity levels are practically the same as those of their hearing peers, and there are hearing impaired children whose interests and maturity levels are much lower than what is considered the norm for their age levels.

STORYTELLING

Storytelling is an experience of which no child should be deprived. It gives children important cultural knowledge, expands their experience, and stimulates their interest in books. For this reason, storytelling is a major part of my program for kindergarten through junior high.

Hearing impaired children can derive almost as many benefits from a storytelling session as hearing children. However, a lot depends upon which method of storytelling is used. Every method I use is visual in nature. The reason is that hearing impaired children miss the pleasurable sounds, such as jingles, the cadence of rhymes, and vocal inflections which are a part of storytelling sessions for hearing children. During early childhood and the lower grades, hearing impaired children are dependent upon the adults around them for the presentation and interpretation of all types of literature. They *need* to have the visual experience in order to enjoy and understand the story. Parents of the hearing impaired should be encouraged to tell stories at home and read and talk about the library books that their children bring home.

Visual mediums for storytelling include films, filmstrips, slides, and the flannel board. I have found that some of these methods are more effective than others. (See Table 1.)

Because slide stories and flannel board stories meet more of the necessary requirements for hearing impaired children, the children understand stories in these mediums better than those told on film or filmstrips (and they can be more actively involved in the story as it is being told). Slide and flannel board stories can be locally produced. This gives the storyteller control over what content is included.

I have used each of the four methods singly and in combination to increase the children's understanding and enjoyment of a story. For example,

TABLE 1   Comparisons of Visual Mediums

Qualities	Films	Filmstrips	Slides	Flannel Board
Shows motion	yes	—	—	yes*
Allows ample time for explanation	—	yes	yes	yes
Script can be adapted to different abilities	—	—	yes	yes
Shows actual pictures from the book	yes**	yes**	yes	—

  *dependent on teacher manipulation
 **dependent on the film or filmstrip used

"The Brave Little Indian," a participation story, is presented in a slide format and is a very simple story about an Indian boy who goes hunting for a bear. After I have twice presented the slide story, I run the film "Little Hiawatha" showing Hiawatha, as a boy, looking for a bear. This is a perfect combination because the children are treated to a repetition of the story and the story is told through the use of two mediums.

For another storytelling unit based on Aileen Brothers' *Sad Mrs. Sam Sack* (Follett), I use slides and a flannel board. Because the slides do not fully show the effects of the actions of this woman who fills her house with animals, flannel board figures are used to enhance the visualization of the story. This visualization increases understanding.

LIBRARY INSTRUCTION

The library skills K-8 curriculum that I created is designed to prepare students to use the library with a minimum of assistance once they reach high school. Every lesson is planned to teach one library skill or concept at a time followed by review exercises. The number of review exercises depends upon the complexity of the concept or skill and the capabilities of the children. For example, in discussing the meaning of book titles, I show the students some books, point out the titles, and then have them find and tell me the titles of other books. This lesson is reviewed before going on to the next step. However, teaching other areas in a library skills curriculum (e.g., use of the card catalog) is much more difficult and will take much longer to get across to students.

Because hearing impaired children learn visually, I use visual material with every lesson. Overhead transparencies are used extensively because they are easily viewed by the entire class. I don't find that commercially produced audio materials such as cassette tapes are useful with the hearing impaired or deaf students.

In teaching library skills to hearing impaired children, I find these points are helpful to remember:

- Get teachers involved in what you are doing since they can reinforce the skills you are teaching.
- Teach one skill at a time.
- Repeat a statement two or three different ways if students do not understand it the first time and review lessons.
- Always use visuals and total communication.
- Provide individualized instruction.
- Be sure to repeat or review lessons and to teach the most basic library skills.

USING THE CATALOG

Even though hearing impaired students are taught to use the card catalog, their language retardation makes it difficult for them to find materials. The card catalog should contain many *see* references from simple terms to the more difficult subject headings. For example, a hearing impaired child might not think to look under the heading AUTOMOBILES if s/he is looking for a book about cars. Frequently, the children cannot spell a subject they are interested in. If this is the case, they will probably approach the librarian and start describing the subject and the librarian will often have to determine what they want and spell the word for them.

At the Illinois School for the Deaf, we devised our own simplified subject heading list based on *Sears List of Subject Headings,* 11th ed., by Barbara M. Westby (Wilson, 1977). Instead of using AUTOMOBILES, we use CARS AND TRUCKS. We use very few of the standard subdivisions because our students simply do not know what the terms mean. The standard subdivisions just make a complicated tool even more complicated to use.

If your card catalog cannot be tailored to meet the needs of a few hearing impaired children, remember that these children need much more assistance in using card catalogs than other students.

READING PROGRAMS

It is very important to constantly encourage hearing impaired students to read. Because of their language handicap, they frequently become reluctant readers. Many just look at pictures but do not try to read the text. How do I persuade these children to actually read their books? One approach is to institute some kind of reward program whereby the students receive recognition for every book read. In checking on whether or not the books have actually been read, we consider the ability of each child. The amount of cooperation received from their teachers is also important. If you choose to require book reports as a method of checking, then leniency is required! From my experience, most hearing impaired children have great difficulty writing coherent book reports. If you insist on grammatically correct book reports, writing assignments will be very tedious for the children and will take all of the enjoyment out of the incentive program. It's better to have students give oral book reports.

Teachers are an invaluable source of assistance in a reading incentive program. They know the abilities of their students; they can assist in deciding what evaluation method to use; and some teachers might even be willing to use class time to help in determining suitable books for students and follow-up reading evaluations.

MATERIALS AND AIDS

Because hearing impaired children can be easily discouraged, they should be provided with books that are readable for them, meet their interest/maturity level, and contain visuals that reinforce the text. Although there are numerous so-called high interest/low vocabulary books on the market, many of them contain too many difficult language patterns and sentence structures. They do not have sufficient illustrations. I have found that books with a wide disparity between interest levels and reading levels (e.g., eighth grade interest/third grade reading), usually are illustrated and are easier for the students to read.

One particular type of high interest/low vocabulary reading material (that has long been anathema to librarians, educators, and parents) is comic books. Although they were once condemned, comics are used as valuable tools in the constant struggle to attract reluctant readers. Comics have such a universal appeal that now some textbooks are published in comic book formats. Two such educational series are *Awareness Pictorial Books* (Davco Publishers) and *Career Awareness Program* (King Features). Our library has educational comics, Classic Comics, and popular comic books (Donald Duck, Batman, etc.) that are sold at newsstands. All of them are useful in encouraging students to read.

I use four book selection aids in finding appropriate materials. They are: Spache's *Good Reading for Poor Readers*, Strang's *Gateways to Readable Books*, McCarr's *Materials Useful for Deaf/Hearing Impaired*, and the teachers' suggestions. Some excellent high interest/low vocabulary books are listed in these sources. Two reading series that I purchased upon the recommendation of a teacher were Scholastic's *Sprint Books* and *Action Books*. Not only do these have grade levels ranging from 2.0 to 3.9, an interest range of grades 7 to 12, and a mature format, but they are well illustrated.

Periodical collections and reference collections do not need to be altered for hearing impaired students. However, librarians should remember that these children will seek help in understanding the language in the periodicals and reference books.

Audiovisual collections should be supplemented with films which have been captioned for the hearing impaired. To date, approximately 900 educational and 700 general interest and theatrical 16-millimeter films have been captioned and are available on a free loan basis to any agency serving the hearing impaired. For information on the captioned films program write to: Captioned Films and Telecommunications Branch, Bureau of Education for the Handicapped, United States Office of Education, Washington, DC 20202.

Librarians who have not already done so may want to purchase professional books on deafness. There are numerous books which overview the pathology of deafness, the methods of instruction and communication, and relevant topics to inform parents, teachers, and others working with the hearing impaired. The chief sources of professional books (and books in sign language) are:

> Alexander Graham Bell
> Association for the Deaf, Inc.
> 3417 Volta Place, NW
> Washington, DC 20007
>
> Gallaudet College Bookstore
> Gallaudet College
> Washington, DC 20002
>
> National Association of the Deaf
> 814 Thayer Avenue
> Silver Spring, MD 20910

DISCIPLINE

A common misconception is that our library is quieter than other school libraries because hearing impaired children supposedly cannot talk. It seems that hearing people equate deafness with an absence of vocal chords. Actually, our library is noisier than many other libraries. The reasons are that hearing impaired children can talk or make vocal sounds because they have the same anatomical apparatus as hearing people; hearing impaired children have difficulty controlling the loudness of their voices because they cannot hear themselves; staff talk loudly to children with residual hearing as a part of total communication; and, in order to get the attention of another student at the same table, a student will often rap on the table and the vibrations attract the other student's attention.

The handicap of deafness demands *awareness, understanding, patience* and *tolerance* in a library setting. It is crucial that hearing impaired children *use* their library resources. A librarian's attitude toward them and skill in developing and implementing the library programs to meet their needs, can drastically affect a child's future use of libraries.

SELECTION AIDS

McCarr, Dorothy. *Materials Useful for Deaf/Hearing Impaired: An Annotated Bibliography*, 1976. (Available from Dormac, Inc., Box 1622, Lake Oswego, OR 97034.)

Spache, George D. *Good Reading for Poor Readers*. Champaign, IL: Garrard, 1974.

Strang, Ruth. *Gateways to Readable Books,* New York: Wilson, 1975.

PUBLISHERS' ADDRESSES

Davco Publishers, 5425 Fargo Ave., Skokie, IL 60076.

Follett Publishing Company, 1010 W. Washington Blvd., Chicago, IL 60607.

King Features, Educational Division, Dept. 1254, 235 East 45th St., New York, NY 10017.

Scholastic Book Services, 904 Sylvan Ave., Englewood Cliffs, NJ 17632.

Story Hours for the Deaf

by Jane Biehl

The Main Children's Room of the Akron-Summit County Public Library has storytelling for the deaf in sign language. Deaf people from the entire county are represented in the audience. Deaf children, their hearing brothers and sisters, and occasionally their parents all attend the story hours. The ages of the children range from five-year-olds to teenagers. The story hours are sponsored once a month during the school year and once a week during the summer months. Miss Jane Biehl, Children's Librarian, conducts the story hours with occasional help from deaf mothers and deaf teenagers who volunteer their aid. Miss Biehl can both speak and tell stories in sign language.

The techniques which can be used in a story hour for deaf children are varied. The storyteller should be alert and try to discover new techniques which will appeal to the children. The following methods have been successful.

VISUALS

The storyteller for deaf children must use visual methods as much as possible. This includes flannel boards, pictures, visual objects, tell and draw stories, and any other resources available.

An introduction to the story before actually telling it is imperative. The storyteller can write the title of the story on the board or show the children the book. S/He should explain (beforehand) parts of the story which may be difficult for the children to understand. Sometimes there are several different signs used for the same word—at least three different signs mean 'Santa Claus'. The storyteller can ask the children which sign they use most often for a certain word, thus feeling confident that the children are familiar with their particular sign.

WATCH THE AUDIENCE

One must watch the children closely during the story hour to be sure that all of them comprehend the story. If a puzzled look appears on a child's face, repetition of a sentence may be necessary. The storyteller may even choose to stop the story and ask the child outright if s/he understands. The story-teller should never proceed until s/he is confident that all the ideas in the story are understood by the entire group.

ACT IT OUT

Acting out the story is advantageous. In *The Snowy Day* by Ezra J. Keats, the storyteller is most effective if s/he lies down on the floor and 'makes angels' in the snow just like Peter! Not only do children enjoy watching the storyteller, but they better understand the story when accompanied with actions.

Participation by the children during the story hour should constantly be encouraged. Even routine questions like "What do you think happened next?" help immensely to keep their attention on the storyteller. The participation also helps the newcomers to the story hour to overcome any initial shyness they may experience when confronted with a new situation. If a book is used in a story hour, the storyteller should find one with large, bright pictures. No story should be used which involves poetry, songs, or rhythm, since sounds mean nothing to a deaf child. The plot should be very simple. Books should not be used which have lengthy descriptions or lots of phrases; otherwise the deaf child can become confused. Often preschool picture books work well with school-age deaf children because of the simplicity of plot and large bright pictures which they contain.

TECHNIQUES

There are several approaches one may use for the actual story hour. A combination of different techniques may be used for the same story.

One method is to have a volunteer tell a story. Sign language itself is very expressive and many deaf people become excellent storytellers. The hearing storyteller can then interpret the story for the hearing people in the audience. This is an excellent way to get older deaf teenagers involved in helping, too.

Simultaneous storytelling should be used only with a sophisticated or older group of children who know signs very well. This method is very fast and allows no extra time for repetition or for stopping the story to explain parts which may be confusing. Two hearing storytellers are involved, and deaf and hearing children are included in the same group. One storyteller gives a story to a group of hearing children, while the other storyteller interprets and tells the same story to the deaf children at the same time. This works on the same principle as an interpreter for the deaf in a church service.

When the storyteller speaks and signs both, several different methods can be used. One way is to tell a story from a picture book by signing and then pointing to the pictures in the book. A child is always eager to volunteer to hold the book and turn the pages for the storyteller. This also benefits the child who needs to feel helpful and important.

The storyteller can also use visual objects and/or pictures instead of a book. An example would be to tell the story *Ask Mr. Bear* by Marjorie Flack. The storyteller can use a L'eggs egg, blanket, pillow, feather, and cheese to demonstrate the objects used in the story. Pictures may be shown of a hen, goat, sheep, goose, and bear.

The storyteller may decide to use a combination of a picture book and visual objects. The storyteller first shows the children the object, then points to the picture in the book, thus increasing the children's understanding of the story.

'Cut and tell' stories such as those from the book *Paper-Cutting* by Eric Hawkesworth are very effective. The storyteller proceeds slowly by signing part of the story, then cutting parts of the paper, and then repeating the process. This enables the child to watch the story develop in front of his/her eyes.

'Tell and draw' stories from the series by that title by Margaret Oldfield are similar to the cut and tell stories. The storyteller tells part of the story in signs, then draws a section of the picture on the blackboard. S/He then signs a little more of the story, and draws another section of the picture. The children can visualize the picture being drawn and see for themselves what character or animal is portrayed at the end.

One of the most effective and commonly used methods of storytelling to deaf children is the flannel board. When old books are discarded, the pictures can be used to make excellent flannel boards. The storyteller may prefer to make his/her own flannel board stories from felt or construction paper. Paul Anderson's books *Storytelling with the Flannel Board* (volumes 1 and 2) can be invaluable aids to the storyteller. These books include instructions and patterns for making flannel board stories. With experience, the storyteller soon will be able to discover other favorite stories which can be converted into flannel board stories.

When using a flannel board with deaf children the storyteller signs part of the story, then places the appropriate flannel piece on the board. The process is repeated until the story is told. The children can follow the action of the story easily with the flannel pieces directly in front of them.

CONCLUSION

Storytelling to deaf children requires much preparation, practice, and patience on the part of the storyteller. Experiments can fail and problems of communication may arise. However, the time will come when the storyteller fathoms a look of jubilation on a deaf child's face as the youngster comprehends and understands a story, when the child laughs out loud at a funny picture, or when the child claps at the end of the story. When these reactions occur, all the efforts are extremely worthwhile. Indeed, this will be one of the most heartwarming experiences the storyteller will ever know.

"Meanwhile...": A Look at Comic Books at Illinois School for the Deaf

by Bill Stark

"Odd as it seems, I would say comic books significantly contributed to my language development. I used to have stacks and stacks of comic books and traded them with hearing kids. Perhaps, subconsciously, I learned dialogue, which I consider crucial in language development. Instead of discouraging me, my parents would give me money to buy and collect classics comics, which in turn spurred me to borrow classic books from the library as I grew older."[1]

The above is but one of many testimonies from deaf adults crediting their reading of comic books as a significant factor in their language development. It is also through comics that many deaf persons first experienced interest and enjoyment in reading.

The pictures in sequence format of comic books make them a visual form of language and thus a 'natural' for use with the deaf. However, many programs for the deaf, including our own, have hesitated to use them. It wasn't until 1968 that we began very timidly and on a small scale to introduce comic books into our library and our classrooms.

WHY DID IT TAKE US SO LONG?

There has long been a comic book stigma. Much of the criticism, focusing on subject matter treatment and quality of writing, is a holdover from decades ago.

In 1948, public outcry against the crime-infested, sex-saturated tales promoted publishers to hire censors and tone down the violence. Six years later the Comics Association of America was formed. This association, which represents 80 percent of the comic book industry, adopted the comics code. The comics code authority, an agency which operates apart from the comic industry, has the responsibility for enforcing the code and keeping a rein on comic book content. Reviewing comic books prior to their publication, its aim is "to make certain that comics are reasonably acceptable, morally, to reasonable people.''[2] To receive the code's seal of approval (see Figure 1), comic books have to adhere to strict standards concerning editorial matter; dialogue; costume; and treatment of subjects such as religion, race, sex, marriage, and violence.

Sex is one of the subjects which is perpetually a topic of criticism in any reading material. The comics code states that illicit sex relations are not to be portrayed, rape shall not be shown or suggested, and sexual perversion or any inference to same is strictly forbidden. The treatment of sex in comic books has been likened to the attitude toward sex in the 1950s. For example, it made national news recently when Clark Kent kissed Lois Lane. Unlike the 1950s, but consistent with our times, today's romance comics often picture a more involved and aggressive female. A boy may receive karate assistance from his girlfriend if the bully kicks sand in his face at the beach.

In respect to violence, the comics code states that no gory or gruesome crime, depravity, or excessive bloodshed shall be permitted. While there are many scenes with fistfights and earthshaking wrestling matches, bloodshed and killing are mainly shadowy suggestions even in war comics. There is never any mistaking who the heroes are in comics, and the villains always meet their just end as a result of their ill-gotten gains. Horror or terror comics, according to the comics code, must be handled in the classic tradition of Frankenstein, Dracula, and similar literary works written by Edgar Allan Poe, Sir Arthur Conan Doyle, and other respected authors. Considering the format of comic books, they seem to be reasonably successful in achieving this goal. In comparison to movies and television, comic book treatment of violence is relatively mild.

For years there have been those who have said that comic books are vulgar and poorly written. These critics have tended to favor the preservation

**FIGURE 1
Comics Code Seal
of Approval**

Comic books which meet the comics code standards bear this seal in the upper right-hand corner of their cover.

of literary form at the expense of substance. Characters' words spoken in overhead balloons are precise and have been more likened to a sound track than a documentation. Having the economy of a telegram, they promote imagery and realism. 'Good English' out of the mouth of a comic book character caught in a catastrophic situation would be unbelievable. It is the very fact that comic books contain inventive language and slang that gives them a currency and widens their appeal to young people. Scaling the height of a tower in pursuit of a villain, Batman is suspicious of something he sees and states, "If that's a coincidence, I'm Henry Kissinger." Archie's frustration at being unable to loosen the collar of his shirt is expressed as an 'expletive deleted.'

WHAT TYPES OF COMICS DO WE USE AT ILLINOIS SCHOOL FOR THE DEAF (ISD)?

The majority of the comics we select are of the following types: classics and classics junior, animated cartoon, humor, science fiction, and teenage adventure. To a lesser extent we choose detective, mystery, romance, war, western, and superhero types.

Most of our comic books come from the nearly 100 individual comic book titles published by major newsstand comic publishers. These publishers include Marvel Comics (world's largest), DC Comics, National Comics, Dell Comics, Gold Key, Harvey Comics, Archie Comics, King Features, Chartlon Comics, Warren Publications, Skyworld, and Classic Comics.

In addition to newsstand comics, we select a few other titles which are available from church groups and special interest groups. Alcoholics Anonymous, The American Cancer Society, The American Dental Association, and B.F. Goodrich are a few examples of publishers of special types of comics.

Several of the comic book publishers have expanded their scope. Just issued (or soon to be) are separate especially prepared comics to aid reading programs. A packet of materials on Marvel Comics' Spiderman contains a special reader, picture sequence cards, and other reading aids.

Some publishing companies have begun to copy the successful comic book format. An especially good series in that format is the *Now Age Illustrated* by Pendulum Press. This series, with vocabulary based on the Dale-Chall list, is beautifully illustrated and familiarizes the reader with great characters and stories from European and American literature.

WHY COMICS IN OUR LIBRARY?

Comics long ago infiltrated our school and were looking for a place in the library. We have comics in our library because our deaf children read them!

Deaf children *want* to read them and don't have to be forced to check them out. We can only add a resounding "Amen!" to the following statement by the Orlando Public Library. "Do we need any other justification other than the fact that kids read them? If they were reading cereal boxes, that would be the most sensible thing to fill the library with."[3]

To increase their life span, we have laminated all the pages and covers of classic and classic junior comics. Other comics have only their front and back covers laminated. All comics are also given a special binding. Even with this treatment, comics are read and reread until they are ragged!

We have seen no evidence that the presence of comics adversely affects our book circulation. Quite the contrary. For example, our high school language arts teachers have testified that the reading of classics comics has led students to read simply written versions of the classics themselves.

In the selection of comics for the library, we follow the following guidelines: First, we are cautious not to compare comics with any other type of literature. They should be judged on their own merit. Second, we try to select those comics which are visually appealing. Third, we apply our usual selection policy considerations as set forth in the *Library Bill of Rights* of the American Library Association. These considerations include the provision of materials to enrich and support the curriculum, taking into account the varied interest, ability, and maturity levels of the students we serve. Comics are also reviewed very closely as to their treatment of subjects such as ideology, race, religion, and sex.

School libraries can make a start on their collection by obtaining distributors' catalogs from local newsstands. Comic book publishers will often furnish lists of their titles. The Comics Code Authority, 41 East 42nd Street, New York, NY 10017, is an excellent source of information on comics.

WHY COMICS IN OUR CLASSROOMS?

We have comics in our classrooms for the same reason they are in the library. Deaf children read them! Perhaps they read comic books because they are unrelated to past reading failures. Or, perhaps they are simply attracted to comics because they are pictorial and colorful.

Comics are used in our junior high school reading programs as one of the nontext reading motivation materials. Students are given an opportunity to write book reports on the comics for extra grade points. For these optional book reports, Thermofax overhead transparencies are made from the pages of certain comics. (These turn out surprisingly well!) Then students come up to the front of the class and, reading the transparencies, act out the roles. At times the balloons are left blank, and the students supply their own vocabulary.

This is also a good opportunity for changing direct discourse to indirect and for summarizing or moralizing a story.

Comic books are replete with idioms. From Bugs Bunny wondering how to get Elmer Fudd "back down to earth" to the Hulk bemoaning the fact that he is getting "punch drunk," the comics afford numerous opportunities to teachers.

Comics have been used at our school to introduce deaf children to fairy tales, Aesop's fables, nursery rhymes, and classical literature. Pictorial classics and classics junior comics help children begin to understand these works of literature which are very difficult in their original form. Classic comics are themselves sometimes difficult to read, so we've produced slide series based on these comics. Writing our own language, we've produced sequentially captioned slide stories. In sequential captioning, the caption is presented first, followed by the visual. (Slide copies from comics are excellent!) The teacher using such a slide series story will first project a caption and ask a student to read and interpret it (in gestures, signs, or pantomime). The teacher then projects the visual so that the class can see whether or not the caption was correctly interpreted. This visual is usually just one frame from the comic page. It is important that each visual actually illustrates the sentence or sentences on the preceding caption. Although a story told with sequentially captioned slides is not truly programed instruction, it can have many things in common with a programed lesson. First of all, the material is presented in small, logical steps. Second, the student has frequent opportunity to respond (to the meaning of the printed word). The student gets immediate feedback to his/her interpretation of the caption because the visual which follows it either does or does not confirm his/her interpretation. Some teachers initially voiced doubts about using sequentially captioned slides, as they were concerned that sequential captions would confuse their students. These same teachers later reported that their students were not confused at all. Several teachers even felt that students learned more by reading sequentially captioned slides than by reading traditionally captioned slides. We've been delighted to see these slide stories motivate students to read the comics themselves or simply written versions of the literary works upon which the comics are based. The story, or simple version, we write is sometimes handed out separately to students as a reading lesson (see Figure 2).

"MEANWHILE..."

Within the limits of propriety, anything a deaf child reads is an educational tool. The assumption that reading is an end in itself is self-defeating. Deaf children read material that gives them pleasure and satisfies their quest for knowledge and understanding of the world. Material like that can be found in comic books!

FIGURE 2 A Completion Exercise Based on the Slide Series Story, "War of the Worlds."

WAR OF THE WORLDS

An astronomer in London, England, saw a strange thing through his telescope. A brilliant flash of gas was shooting from Mars toward the earth. When it was close to earth, it _____ like a falling star.

The meteorite (falling star) _____ in the country, just outside London. A man went to look for it. He found it. It was not a meteorite. It was a spaceship!

By nightfall, many _____ people had gathered around the spaceship. Then, a strange thing happened. The lid of the spaceship unscrewed and _____ off. A tentacle emerged. More tentacles emerged. It was a monster from Mars! There were other Martian monsters just like it.

People ran to hiding places and watched the Martians. The Martians erected a strange machine. A beam of light flickered out from the machine. The people were afraid. They _____ a white flag to show they wanted peace. Suddenly, blinding flashes of light struck at the people and the landscape! Many people were killed.

One survivor went _____ into the city of London. He told people about the Martians. They laughed at him _____ they didn't believe his strange story.

Then, other space ships came through the sky. The Martians began to attack the cities. People _____ to escape. Nothing could stop the Martians. There was no place that was really safe. Everything was _____ and desolate. Everything seemed hopeless. But then a strange thing _____. Everything became quiet. The monsters stopped their machines. A man began looking around to see what had happened. The monsters were dead. They had been killed by some of the smallest living things on earth -- germs.

tried	happened	ruined	waved	fell
looked	back	because	landed	curious

NOTES

1. Frank Bowe, "The DA Interview: Dr. Allen E. Sussman," *The Deaf American* (July-August 1974): 7-11.

2. John L. Goldwater, *Americana in Four Colors* (New York: Comics Magazine Association of America, 1974).

3. Will Eisner, "Comic Books in the Library," *Library Journal* (October 14, 1974): 2703-7.

Picture Perfect: Photography Aids Deaf Children in Developing Communication Skills

by Doris W. Naiman

Individual use of a camera is a joyful and effective way to help deaf children increase interpersonal communication. While taking the photographs and while showing them, children are stimulated to interact more with other children at school and with parents and siblings at home.

New York University's Deafness Research and Training Center conducted a photography project with children ages 9 through 16 in four classes at New York City's Public School JHS 47 for the Deaf. Financed by grants from New York University's Deans' Committee, the Polaroid Foundation, and Marge Neikrug of Neikrug Galleries, the project produced results positive enough to encourage teachers to use this technique.

The project included children in regular classes and children who had been placed in special classes because they exhibited patterns of maladaptive behavior severe enough to interfere with their ability to function and learn in regular classes for the deaf. The behavior of the children in special classes ranged from extreme lack of control and hyperactivity to almost complete unresponsiveness and withdrawal from interaction. Many had developed neither language nor a way to communicate.

Individual student photography with cameras seemed a promising approach because it offers a nonverbal, nonacademic way in which children can achieve success, express themselves, and communicate.

WHAT WE WANTED TO DO

The overall objective was to provide an additional mode of communication for the 20 deaf children involved in the project. Specific behavioral goals for each child were set for the first four weeks of the project. These included:

1. To learn how to operate the camera.
2. To take at least 20 photographs at school.
3. To take at least 20 photographs at home or outside of school.
4. To show the photographs to classmates and teachers.
5. To show the photographs to family and friends at home.
6. To talk, write, sign, or pantomine about the photographs to classmates and teachers.
7. To talk, write, sign, or pantomime about the photographs to family and friends at home.

In preparation for the project, conferences were held with administrators and teachers to discuss objectives for the children, suggested approaches and activities, and procedures for evaluation. Workshops were held with the participating teachers and classroom educational assistants to teach the use of the camera and techniques for presentation to the children.

WHAT WE DID

Each camera was shared by two children. They took turns using the camera at various times during the school day as designated by the teacher. Each child had use of the camera out of school on alternate weekdays and weekends. Film allotment was two rolls per week per child, for a total of 16 exposures per week. Both black-and-white and color film were provided, and flash cubes were available as needed.

Photographic activities took place daily. Children received individual instruction on how to take and develop photographs. Using a Polaroid camera made it possible for the children to develop their own pictures at once. During the first week all cameras remained on the school premises and picture taking was confined to the general school area. For the remaining three weeks, the children were allowed to take the cameras outside of the school.

The children were allowed to photograph whatever they wished. Teachers encouraged the children to show their photographs to other children, to take their photographs home, and to tell about their photographs using all modes of communication, including talking, signing, writing, and pantomiming. Teachers suggested special activities such as making individual booklets of photographs, mounting photographs, writing stories about them, and arranging an exhibit for parents and other classes.

HOW WE ASSESSED SUCCESS

The extent to which each child achieved the project objectives was assessed by means of the following evaluation instruments:

1. *Teacher report forms* were filled out daily by the teacher to record the child's ability to use the camera, number of photographs taken in and out of school, frequency in showing photographs, and efforts to describe pictures and experiences.

2. *Questionnaires* for teachers, educational assistants, and parents were filled out at the conclusion of the project to provide information from individuals closely involved with the children regarding their perception of the children's interpersonal communication as related to the photography experience.

3. *Structured interviews* with the school's principal, assistant principal, and media specialist were conducted in the two weeks following completion of the project to provide information from observers less closely involved regarding their perceptions of the effectiveness of the photography experience.

Data-gathering procedures, which included the use of anecdotal records, contributed valuable information about the following questions:

- Are there differences in response to the photography project by children who have been identified primarily as presenting behaviors that are withdrawn, hyperactive, or aggressive?

- Are there differences in response to the photography project by children of different age levels?

- Are the photographic activities helpful in increasing the length of time that children are able to spend working at a task?

DID IT MAKE A DIFFERENCE?

Among the 20 children involved in the project, 19 achieved all of the specific behavioral objectives set. All the children learned to operate the camera; 16 children learned in one day; 4 required two days. Most of the children took as many photographs as their film allotment allowed.

All the children regularly showed their photographs to classmates and teachers. Of the 12 mothers interviewed, 8 indicated that taking photographs at home and showing pictures taken at school increased their communication with their child.

Teacher ratings indicated that 18 children showed a significant or outstanding increase in their interaction with peers, expression of feelings, and communication of ideas. These children used varying combinations of speech, manual communication, writing, and pantomime.

In addition, 17 children regularly communicated about their finished photographs either on their own initiative or in response to questioning. The other 3 children communicated about their pictures only with much encouragement from the teacher; but in spite of this reluctance, 1 of the 3 still showed a significant increase in interaction and expression of feelings according to her teacher's rating. The teacher commented, "This girl is rather shy. To get children to pose for her, she had to really make an effort to communicate. It has helped her a great deal. She loves taking pictures."

INCREASE IN SELF-ESTEEM

Teachers and parents described what they perceived as a rise in the self-esteem of many of the children as a result of the project. Mastery of photographic equipment and techniques contributed to a general feeling of competency; for some of the children who had a long history of failure, the project provided success at a task for the first time. Reports of inner-city photography projects have shown similar results and indicate that because photography projects tend to create a chain of successes, they also tend to encourage young people to try new things and to increase their feeling of "being somebody who can do things."[1]

The children were pleased with their new role as photographers and with having others view them in this role. One nine-year-old boy who had in the past avoided any interaction with other children approached a boy on the playground and asked to take his picture. Other children gathered around him and the usually withdrawn boy visibly enjoyed the new experience. Performing an attractive activity in the midst of his peers gave him more social confidence and greater ability to approach unfamiliar situations.

An 11-year-old boy was so excited about taking photographs that he was able to relate to people in ways that were entirely new to him. When his teacher asked him if he wanted to go around the neighborhood with a student teacher to take pictures of whatever he wished, the boy seemed thrilled. He immediately turned to the student teacher (whom he did not know), told her his name, and asked her name. In his enthusiasm he led her on such a run down Twenty-Third Street that she reported she should have been prepared with sneakers and a sweat band. He guided her to a neighborhood park where, abandoning his shyness, he proceeded to position her for the picture he wanted to take. He saw two children with their father, who offered to take his picture, but the boy indicated that he wanted to be the photographer himself. He then took two pictures of the family and gave them to the man, smiling at the family and pleased at the whole event.

OPPORTUNITIES FOR MAKING CHOICES

The children's freedom to decide what photographs they wanted to take and how they wanted to take them played an important part in adding to their feelings of self-worth, personal power, and competence. Most of the time the children did not take shots randomly; rather, they purposefully chose what they wished to photograph and, in many cases, carefully planned the picture. The children had an opportunity to decide, choose, and create—processes that build confidence for any child, but especially for these deaf children who need every opportunity they can get for independent action.

One boy took five pictures during a 45-minute stroll in the neighborhood, apparently snapping whatever appealed to him as he walked along. His pictures were of a car he liked, a construction worker on a scaffold, a lawn mower, a street-cleaning machine, and a man with a McDonald's emblem on his blazer pocket. Another boy deliberated at length about what to photograph. On one occasion, after spending a little while scouting the neighborhood, he picked out a bicycle shop, walked over and asked the proprietor if he could take his picture, and proceeded to do so.

On a class trip one boy decided to take pictures of flowers. The teacher commented on his high degree of concentration to get just what he wanted and his care in making sure the camera was focused properly and adjusted for proper lighting. Several children took many different shots of the new school building being erected next to their school. They watched the construction from their classroom windows and took photographs from the windows and from different angles on the sidewalk outside.

LANGUAGE DEVELOPMENT

Although the primary focus of the project was on helping the children increase interpersonal communication, there were additional positive results. The children enjoyed writing about their photographs, and progress in written language and in reading was observed in all of the classes. One little boy related long stories about his pictures, about what people were doing, and how they were feeling. His teacher helped him write down the stories, which he kept in a little book. Many of the children kept similar personal books of their photographs with written descriptions. They enjoyed reading their own books and showing them to the other children.

The teachers also arranged partially structured photographic activities planned for language development. As part of a unit on which the class was working, one teacher assigned each child to go around the neighborhood with a student teacher and take pictures of various kinds of stores. On a field trip to the Staten Island Zoo, the children took pictures of the ferryboat and the animals. Subsequent discussions and language learning activities centered around the photographs. The children were eager to talk, write, and read about their own pictures and their recollections of the day.

"FAMILY PORTRAIT"

Among the children's parents, two-thirds reported that the photography activities increased their communication with their child. Being able to take photographs at home and then take them back to school helped some children make their life an integrated whole instead of separate school and home compartments with no communication tying them together. One nine-year-old girl with limited language skills had never been able to tell her class anything about her home life. When she was asked about home her comments had been limited and unclear. After she took the camera home she eagerly brought back pictures of her family and her apartment and tried to explain them to the other children. Some children daily carried their pictures back and forth between school and home. One little boy who had almost no verbal language always pasted his pictures on a sheet of paper, wrote a sentence for each picture with the teacher's help, and then carefully put the papers in an envelope to take home.

A BROAD EXPERIENCE

Not the least valuable feature of the photography project was the pleasure and eagerness with which the children participated. A happy experience has reason enough for being, especially for children who have difficulties functioning satisfactorily in a traditional school program. But, in addition, the teachers were able to handle resourcefully the children's high interest in taking photographs and to make the experience pay off in communication and language growth as well as pleasure.

NOTE

1. *Manual for Photo Project Leaders* (Rochester, NY: Eastman Kodak, 1969).

Directed Creativity

by Janice W. Bell

Motivation vs. freedom, direction vs. creativity, freedom vs. direction....
Words spin about and semantics bog one down when the primary purpose of
any art lesson is the individual's involvement in a creatively satisfying experience at the individual's level.

An art lesson at any level starts off with a certain basic amount of insecurity.
The individual is presented with a blank piece of paper on which, in a given
time, s/he is expected to show a personalized statement. Individualism is
encouraged and the prop of imitation is discouraged. It can be a frightening
experience. But "works done according to a wholly preconceived procedure
tend to be essentially alike...yet such a stereotyped work serves a necessary
human purpose: The sharing implied by imitation (being like everyone else
or producing according to an approved or desired standard). . . ."[1]

Recognizing the comforting security of being like everyone else, this
art lesson was planned with the intent of creating a secure environment by
beginning with specific, stereotyped directions for the whole class. From this
directed introduction it was possible to produce very creditable and successfully creative individual results in an art class of seven- and eight-year-old
deaf and brain damaged youngsters.

Verbal motivation is extremely limited with these language impaired
children. Motivation is possible on all other levels, visual, tactile, and kinesthetic, and enthusiam is always easy to generate. But the language limitations
(communication) make it difficult to bridge the gap from the act of motivational teaching to spontaneous creative application with an art media. The
deaf child enjoys and participates in the action and excitement of pantomime
and motivation; but, without sufficient language communication, it is often
confusing for him/her to relate his/her initial activity and excitement to the
blank paper in front of him/her. This is when the security of a directed start
becomes an important means of transferring the exciting motivation to the
process of making a picture. Specific directions provide the child with a secure
springboard toward the act of creative thinking, discovery, and involvement.

Initial, meaningful motivation for this lesson on color took the form of
first observing and discovering colorful plaids and checks in the clothing
material the children and teacher were wearing. Excitement was generated

by the idea that the class would be creating their own plaid or check designs. Next came the specific directed activity. White paper and yellow paint were provided and instructions were demonstrated to be copied by imitation on how to make yellow stripes on the white paper. Stereotyped results gave everyone the security of producing approved and accepted work. Further confidence was inspired by the next set of directed instructions, which was to cross the yellow lines with blue stripes to make a check.

Then began the period of discovery which led to the beginning of satisfying creativity. A new color emerged as the blue paint was dragged across the still wet yellow. Green was suddenly recognized. It was permissible and encouraged at this point to look around at their neighbors' papers to compare and reinforce. This became the "sharing implied by imitation." While excitement was still in the air, magenta paint was added to the pallette with no further instructions or suggestions. From there on, it was no longer necessary to direct, instruct, or motivate. The new color alone started the momentum for individuality of unlimited scope. Personal involvement became so individualized that there was no time nor any need for the crutch of copying. New colors and new patterns continually emerged from experiments and from accidents. For once, the time limit of the art period saved much of the spontaneity of the work from overenthusiastic annihilation.

One exciting discovery in this lesson was the creative satisfaction the brain damaged youngsters in the aphasic classes received from their involvement. Among these children there are perceptual problems and visual-motor difficulties. It is sometimes difficult for them to carry out an intended concept even though there is no motor disability. The abstract element in this lesson freed these children from the necessity of representation. Astonishing creativity can be recognized in the illustration where frames, superimposed circles, and layered paint can be judged as individualism.

Class evaluation came with studying a display of all of the finished papers and discovering that no two papers produced the same design. The children further appreciated the many possible variations starting from a simple striped design. The use of the design was related to clothing by holding the papers against their bodies as a possibility for a shirt, skirt, or even slacks.

A comparison of all twelve illustrations representing both deaf and aphasic children shows no two to be alike. Yet all have a spontaneity, an involvement, and an exuberance that belie their stereotyped beginning.

The objective value of this experience as a lesson on color theory is obvious. The personalized discoveries of green and purple and brown encourage further experimental processes. For the language handicapped child, the concept of such words as *plaid* and *stripe* are reinforced through the visual activity. Recognizing that the creative process is necessary in the production of a commercial product, such as cloth and material, gave these children more identification with the world around them. "There is particular need for self-achievement in children with learning difficulties, as through this they may experience the feeling that they have some control over their environment.''[2]

The simplest, directed instructions to an insecure group give an initial mastery over the blank paper.

Once over the fear of the first marks on the pristine surface, spontaneity and native creativity assert themselves and the child becomes absorbed and involved. Personal satisfaction is the reward for seeing one's own individual and different expression displayed. This lesson, with its directed beginning, left a limitless scope for originality, involvement, and identity.

NOTES

1. Saul Liskinsky, "Rehabilitative Use of Art," *American Journal of Art Therapy* (July 1972).
2. Zaidie Lindsay, *Art and the Handicapped Child* (New York: Van Nostrand Reinhold, 1972).

Using Non-Verbal Films with the Deaf and Language-Impaired

by Salvatore J. Parlato, Jr.

Mainstreaming is one of the current catch-phrases of special education. It represents, as the term itself suggests, the process of educating the deaf, not within the artificial confines of an institution, but within the more natural structure of the public school system. Mainstreaming implies, of course, the participation of specially trained teachers. Its basic premise asserts that, because hearing-impaired students will eventually have to function within a 'normal' world, their assimilation should begin while still within a school setting. Accepting the merits of this argument on the face of it, this same line of reasoning should apply toward the conceptual mainstreaming of deaf people both during and after their school years. By *conceptual* mainstreaming, I mean acquainting deaf students with the ongoing—and upcoming—issues of our society. Such an objective, in itself, presents two barriers; both are big but not insurmountable: (1) the lower language skills of some deaf individuals reduce the advantages of the mass media of newspapers, books, and magazines, while most TV and film fare is too word-oriented to be of much benefit to them; (2) the sheer number of crucial subjects that cry for coverage is bewildering in its multiplicity. In removing—or at least leveling—these barriers, where do we start? Let's start backwards for a change and, to attack problem No. 2 above, I suggest limiting the critical issues of our era to those that relate to the subculture of deafness itself and to other subcultures with which the deaf ought to become familiar, i.e, other minorities with whom deaf Americans may be particularly able to identify. As for the *software* to do the job, I propose the abundant and accessible medium of nonverbal 16 millimeter films.

One risk involved in a compilation like this is that nonverbal films might (if they haven't already) become typecast as being exclusively suited to the needs of people with limited English language skills, such as the deaf. An even greater danger, however, is that film users may come to regard the hard of hearing as the only handicapped people who can benefit from word-free materials. But other viewers who deserve new attention to their media needs are just as likely to benefit from nonnarrated materials: the children of migrant farmers; bilingual urban (mostly Spanish-speaking) families; the elderly with limited hearing and weakened eyesight; American Indians, whether ghettoed within or outside of their reservations; and the poor of Appalachia.

Whichever minority group you're trying to reach, and whatever the intrinsic advantages of picture-based productions, the special strength of word-free materials is their ability to unify—as no other media can—diverse groups of people within a flexible format that neither favors nor hinders any segment of its diverse viewership.

In studying the nonverbals described for you below, keep in mind still another factor: people with aural or language handicaps don't necessarily (if at all) lack comprehension skills on any wider a scale than their hearing peers. In other words, *there's no real correlation between intelligence and the English language*, so don't pick your films as if there were, and don't present them that way, either. With that bit of counsel (hard come by, believe me), here are some relatively recent nonverbal items that should engage the mutual interest of the very same subcultures referred to on film.

By the way, there's a special connotation attached to the terms, *non-narrated* or *nonverbal*. Please interpret those terms to mean, not *silent*, but simply *without reliance on words*. That is to say, a nonverbal film is one that tells its story or conveys its message pictorially, via its visual content. A nonverbal film is not the same thing as a silent film. In fact, most nonverbal films have active and imaginative soundtracks that suggest mood via music or create a feeling of presence via sound effects or snatches of conversation. But even with this audio ambience, the basic function of the nonverbal film is pictorial, not lingual. A few familiar examples of such nonverbal productions are *The Red Balloon, Occurrence at Owl Creek Bridge, Neighbors, Rainshower, American Time Capsule, Solo, Cosmic Zoom, Glass, Pas De Deux, Corral*, and *Skaterdater*. The citations that follow are new at least in the sense that they don't appear in *Films—Too Good for Words* (Bowker, 1973), or they've been released since the 1973 publication of that directory.

The hardest (and possibly the most important) concept for the deaf to understand is—deafness itself. To introduce the subject early in their lives is the purpose of the *Silent World of Jim*, introduced in sign language and speech by actress Nanette Fabray. The rest of this film nonverbally dramatizes, in true-to-life situations, concepts of safety and family relationships of a seven-year-old. On about the same elementary age level (though also useful with adults) is BBC's "Vision On," a series of 12 mime-with-speech-and-music entertainments, all based on subjects of natural interest to children: *Hats, Lights, Paper, Rocks, Balloons, Glass, Water, String, Eggs, Boxes, Holes* and *Spirals and Design*. Further along the same esthetic route of potential interest to deaf adults is *In Praise of Hands*, a world survey of the language of arts and crafts—a form of manual communication shared, not only between the deaf and the hearing, but among diverse nations and societies. Another intercultural bridge is provided by *Ballad of Love*, the Russian-produced story of a contemporary romance between a young man and a deaf ballerina who learn to share each other's lives in spite of apparent obstacles.

Like the rest of us, the deaf should appreciate the fact that romance is not limited to the young. *Flowers* gives a brief insight into expressions of married love between an aged couple, while *Tomorrow Again* provides a seriocomic glimpse at elderly aspirations of love, as seen in the flirtations of a fur-bedecked lady who, though she fails to catch the attention of her male contemporaries, nonetheless resolves to keep trying "tomorrow again." The harsher realities of industrialism's aged castoffs are brought into focus by two mass media releases: *I Think They Called Him John,* about the drab existence of a retired English miner; and *Weekend,* an extension of America's 'throw-away' logic, in which unproductive oldsters are literally let out to pasture. Less symbolic and all the more shocking are two live-action Zagreb productions: *Mortal Body* explores the relative brevity of the life cycle as we know it, whereas *One Day More* is open to more than a few interpretations, so let me volunteer my own. *One Day More,* as a documentation of simple faith in the therapeutic powers of sulphur and baths, seems to be a comment on the extramedical treatments to which the sick will subject themselves when faced with pain or the threat of death. But that's only one person's perception. Any group showing of this film is bound to stimulate a variety of opinions.

New Deal is a little harder to argue about. From WNET's "Bitter Vintage" series, this sardonically titled study exposes the system that condemns so many of its older citizens to latter-day lives of lonely economic desperation. On the brighter side of longevity, however, is *The Joy of Communication,* a mood piece that, though technically not nonverbal because of its musical lyrics, provides a heartwarming picture of the prospective benefits and blessings of old age. To continue and to expand the light and bright side of later life, *For Laughing Out Loud* can be a real nostalgia trip for viewers of advanced enough age to recall the sight gags of Mack Sennett, the Marx Brothers, and W.C. Fields, from whose pantomime comedy this special reissue was compiled.

If a people's music, art, and crafts are important to understanding their heritage, then these next nonverbal titles are worthy of viewing by deaf audiences seeking insights into other subcultures. *Within a Painted Grove* fuses the oil paintings of Louise Cardeiro Boyer and a classical guitar, creating a brief but leisurely impression of the natural beauty of Point Lobos, California. Spanish music also enhances *Trique Weaving,* a demonstration of the taste and skills of the Mexicans of Western Oaxaca. On another esthetic scale, what modern artist is better known than Picasso? And what sport is more Spanish than bullfighting? Both associations are pictorially combined, with minimal narration, in *Picasso: Le Romancero du Picador,* based on that artist's drawings of the life-and-death confrontation between man and beast.

For raising Afro-American consciousness, *The Matter with Me* recreates a pivotal incident in a 12-year-old boy's frustrated life as a Black within an American city that is predominantly White. *Black White Gray* provides a somewhat broader perspective on the same problem, using symbolic animation to outline the history of racial antagonism in the U.S. "Black is beautiful" is obvious in *Jojolo,* a visual essay on a graceful Paris model of Haitian heritage. A soundtrack of American jazz and African rhythms reflect her cosmopolitan biculturalism.

Not just the deaf, but all citizens have a built-in historical interest in Indians, the first and only true Americans. Unfortunately, the mass media have exploited this interest by representing our aboriginals as something just short of humanoid beasts—a distortion that can at least be partly corrected by films like *Winter on a Reservation* and *As Long as the Grass is Green.* Both productions are child-oriented, avoid the usual stereotypes, and replace narration with native music. With older viewers, *Indians and Chiefs* supplies a case study way of introducing the dilemma of American Indian efforts at retaining their ethnic identity on their own terms . . . within a White environment. This cinema-verité document shows how the Los Angeles Indian Center raised funds (and consciousness) by staging a major urban fair, featuring their music, their dancers, their crafts, their sports, and even their own beauty contests. Did this community effort help preserve their culture or commercialize it? That's a good issue for follow-up discussion of this nonnarrated film.

Some Whites are poor, too. And among the very poorest are the people of Appalachia. Although there aren't (to my knowledge) any nonverbal films that directly show their plight, *Tomorrow's People* does show their brightest moments, a blending of Kentucky music and square dancing along with a montage of old-time photographs—all of which may be a better way of enlisting sympathy for their way of life than other more heavy-handed analyses of their predicament.

Departing now from people-oriented topics to problem-oriented ones, here are some nonverbal materials about problems that are more or less common to us all, whether we're deaf, hearing, Black, Brown, White, Red, old, or whatever. Friendship versus property rights is the subject of *What Would You Do?,* in which three possible endings are suggested for discussion by younger viewers. In the area of personal health (mental and physical, respectively), *Drug Boy* is a World Health Organization (WHO) release that employs an animal fable format to spell out the dangers of addiction; *Heart Sweet Heart* is another WHO-sponsored animation on cardiac care for adults. *Family Planning* is still another WHO production that uses a nonverbal cartoon style to reach its multinational audiences.

By contrast, the National Film Board of Canada takes a less oblique approach to related subjects whose titles are just as direct as their content: *About VD; About Puberty and Reproduction;* and *About Conception and*

Contraception. All three films share not only a nonnarration technique but employ no sound at all, only brief captions between sequences. This 'silent treatment' is presumably designed to reflect the seriousness of the subjects being covered, as well as to allow for whatever level of commentary instructors feel is appropriate to their groups. A good four-page study guide is available for each of these animated, nonverbal films.

Has ecology gone out of fashion? No, not according to the amount of interest shown by film makers. Pictures like *Ecology* which, with its fast-paced montages and music, can alert grade school children to the cumulative hazard of air and water pollution. As follow-up material that is similar in tempo and relative wordlessness, *Epilogue* projects the irreversible poisoning our planet will suffer if such abuse of nature is permitted to continue.

"Always leave them laughing " is an old show biz maxim that still makes sense . . . even for film programers. So, turning from the relatively heavy fare of ecology to the lighter functions of the medium, try this American Film Festival winner in the humor category, *Self Service*. It's a Bruno Bozzetto nonverbal animation which, by the clever analogy of mosquitoes feeding on a sleeping human, satirizes man's organized efficiency at greed. You'll roar. Another funny Bozzetto import is *Household Drug,* which is definitely not about medicine cabinets or child-proof aspirin bottle caps. Instead, its live-action story chronicles a timid husband's addiction to the unreal world of round-the-clock TV. When his domineering wife decides to do something about his habit, she's too late—for reasons that will be obvious when you see the film.

Another punch line you'll have to see for yourself is the final scene of the film *The Fur Coat Club*. Two nine-year-olds get their girlhood jollies from comparing the number of stoles and wraps they can furtively touch each day, a thrill they thought they'd never tire of—till circumstances give them more than they bargained for. Their next obsession? It's a little more sophisticated than touching coats but sure to give children and grown-ups either a good laugh or a basis for discussion . . . or both. Since this film, too, is nonverbal, your options are that much more open. Use them.

PART VI

VISUALLY HANDICAPPED AND ORTHOPEDICALLY IMPAIRED

Introductory Comments

Partially seeing and blind children are termed *visually handicapped*. This refers to a visual impairment which, after correction, remains severe enough to adversely affect the child's educational performance. It should be noted that most visually handicapped people have partial vision and that, with training, many can be taught to use their remaining sight more effectively. The development of a number of low-vision aids is also allowing more visually handicapped persons to use printed materials. The term *orthopedically impaired* refers to children having an impairment of the spine, bones, joints, or muscles severe enough to affect the child's educational performance. Some exemplary conditions might be cerebral palsy, amputation, bone tuberculosis, and poliomyelitis.

The first article in this section is directed toward the media specialist facing the problem of providing for children with serious vision problems. In this informative article, "Serving Visually Handicapped Children," John F. Henne offers practical advice on the types of materials needed and their advantages and drawbacks. He has also included a list of suppliers from which to obtain additional information on materials and services.

For the classroom teacher of young, visually handicapped children who respond inappropriately to sound, or do not respond at all, Ruth Silver's article, "Responding to Sound through Toys, the Environment, and Speech," offers a practical approach for beginning auditory training. Sounds made by toys, the environment, and speech are used in a sequentially structured program to teach awareness of sound, localization, and discrimination. Suggestions are also given for expanding the activities to include more advanced aspects of auditory training.

Developing oral language is another critically important aspect of each child's early years. Stimulating language among the visually handicapped child must, in many cases, be accomplished without the benefit of visual materials. Elaine H. Wagener describes a variety of techniques for exploring oral language through kinesthetic experiences in "Language Arts for the Visually Impaired Child." She offers suggestions for sequencing skills and for utilizing one set of materials for several activities as well as for expanding the activities into other areas.

Another curricular area which cannot be taught solely by traditional means to the visually handicapped child is mathematics. The use of inexpensive manipulatives is discussed by Carol Ann Dodd Thornton in her article titled "Multiply Successes When Introducing Basic Multiplication Ideas to Visually Handicapped Children." She also suggests means to aid memorization of basic facts once the concept of multiplication has been grasped.

While a number of aids have been developed for use by the blind in making mathematical computations, they are often cumbersome and time consuming. The development of the Speech-Plus Talking Calculator now provides a compact, accurate tool for computing mathematical problems. In order to determine whether this instrument could be used effectively by children, Richard R. Champion devised a study involving a group of nine blind youngsters in grades three though eight. In "The Talking Calculator Used with Blind Youth," he reports the results of this study. Two forms of the Math Computation and Math Concepts subsections of the Stanford Achievement Test (SAT), in braille, were used with the children. They first took the test using the mathematical aids they were accustomed to using. After one hour of instruction in the use of the talking calculator and three weeks of informal use, the second form of the SAT was taken with each student using only the talking calculator. Large gains were evidenced in both speed and accuracy.

The visually handicapped student can be an active participant in both academic and nonacademic areas of the curriculum. Judith Rubin and Janet Klineman detail the initiation of creative art activities with visually impaired children in "They Opened My Eyes: The Story of an Exploratory Art Program for Visually Impaired, Multiply Handicapped Children." The children depicted in this article are multiply handicapped; blindness is combined with other conditions such as mental retardation, cerebral palsy, hearing and speech handicaps, and emotional disturbance. Although the seven-week art project described was conducted solely with handicapped youngsters, it offers guidance to those individuals who desire to discover the interests and abilities of these complex children and to provide for them. Along with a description of the project, the authors refer to the literature on art with exceptional children and relate it to their own experiences. The project was found to be not only of significant value to the children, but a worthwhile learning process for the teachers.

While art activities obviously offer some difficulties to individuals without sight, creative expression through music is a popular pastime and often a career for many blind persons. Because of the importance of music to this group, "Music for the Blind and Physically Handicapped from the Library of Congress" was included. In this article, Eyler Robert Coates gives detailed explanations of the services and materials available to the beginner as well as to the professional musician. He also discusses borrowing procedures and lists other agencies supplying materials.

The next two articles concern the orthopedically impaired student. "Developmental Restaging: Meeting the Mental Health Needs of Handicapped Students in the Schools," by John D. Swisher, offers a means of dealing with the emotional needs of children with orthopedic handicaps. The elements of several developmental theories are incorporated into a framework which may be used to assist students in gaining self-understanding, developing interpersonal relationships, and creating a role for themselves in school and society. A variety of materials are listed in the bibliography which may be helpful in promoting better mental health for the physically handicapped student.

References to literature dealing with the orthopedically impaired are sparse in selection tools which typically assist librarians and teachers in the choice of books for children. Madeleine Cohen Oakley, in "Juvenile Fiction about the Orthopedically Handicapped," attempts to fill this need by surveying the field of juvenile fiction about the physically handicapped. She discusses the elements to consider when evaluating a book which depicts a handicapped character, and she critically examines a number of fictional works.

The final article, "Garden for the Blind," was included for its uniqueness. While the blind cannot see the contents of a garden, their appreciation of its textures and smells deserves consideration. Joseph Gale describes a garden that was costly and time-consuming; however, the basic idea on a much smaller scale might be feasible as a school or library project, providing both pleasure and practical experience for many individuals, nonhandicapped as well as handicapped.

Serving Visually Handicapped Children

by John F. Henne

While it is difficult to obtain accurate statistics, the American Foundation for the Blind estimates that there are 6.4 million *visually impaired* persons in the United States. Of these, approximately 1.7 million are severely visually impaired. The National Society for the Prevention of Blindness estimates that one of every 500 school-age children is visually impaired. This means chances are that there is a child in your school with serious vision problems. With the implementation of Public Law 94-142, it is virtually certain that you'll meet such children soon in your school, and there are some facts library media specialists should know.

The accepted definition of a visual handicap is based on distance acuity—20/70 in the best eye corrected. If the corrected vision is not better than 20/200 the person is considered legally blind. A person is also considered legally blind if his or her visual field is restricted to no more than 20 degrees. This is called tunnel vision. Children who are legally blind should not automatically be considered blind. Most visually handicapped people retain some usable vision but the degree of the handicap varies. According to Dr. Eleanor Faye of the New York Association for the Blind, "If attention is focused on the visual deficiency, the child is considered a cripple. If attention is focused on the residual vision, the child is considered sighted." Through the use of low-vision aids and visual training, many legally blind children can function as sighted persons.

Many visually handicapped students need large-print books (14-point print or larger). Books not available in large print or braille can be enlarged by several of the vendors who supply these books. A much smaller percentage of visually handicapped children will read braille materials. State education agencies have information about available funding assistance for purchasing materials for the visually impaired.

Perhaps tape recordings are the most common reading mode, especially for older visually handicapped students. Textbooks on cassette or on open reel tapes are less costly, less bulky, and are easier to produce than either books in large print or braille. Volunteers can prepare them at practically no cost, or you may obtain them free of charge from one of the many agencies serving the blind.

Recording for the Blind (RFB), the largest supplier of recorded textbooks, has a catalog with nearly 40,000 titles; approximately 4500 new titles are added annually. On request RFB will record almost any publication required for a student's education. To be eligible for RFB's service, users must be unable to read conventional print (for any of a variety of reasons), and must be registered with RFB. Write to RFB (the address is in the list of suppliers) for specifics on how to go about registering students.

One drawback with using tapes supplied by many of these agencies is that a special machine is required to play them because the cassettes are recorded at 15/16 inches per second (ips); open reel at 1 7/8 ips. Both use a four-track monaural configuration. These machines are available from several of the sources listed here. Again, your state education agency can tell you how to get funding assistance and where to apply for financial assistance in purchasing these machines.

Visually handicapped students will want to, and should, participate in all the library media center activities. Blind children enjoy films when someone describes the action taking place on the screen. Most visually impaired children will be able to see much of the action without assistance if they are allowed to sit close enough to the screen. (Rear projection of the film is ideal because it allows children to get as close as necessary without blocking out the image.) You'll find that children will find the right viewing/reading distance and position for their personal needs and comfort.

Using reference books can create problems for visually handicapped students because many reference books, especially dictionaries, are printed in very small type. Those printed in large type or braille present a storage problem. For example, *Webster's New World Dictionary of the American Language* in 18-point type is printed in 24 volumes at a cost of $399; in braille, the same dictionary at $526 consists of 72 volumes and requires 16 feet of shelf space.

One possible solution to the storage problem is a closed circuit TV system, which takes up no more space than a study carrel. Most systems consist of a camera with a zoom lens, a monitor, and a platform for the book that can be moved back and forth under the lens. The cost of these systems is over $2,000.

For readers who use braille there is an excellent aid known as an Optacon, a portable device about the size of a cassette recorder that converts letters into tactual images when a small probe is passed over a line of print. The drawback here is that quite a bit of training is required for readers to gain proficiency with the Optacon, and the cost of the machine is quite high. However, the US Bureau of Education of the Handicapped does fund Optacon training programs and will assist in obtaining a machine for students who complete the training programs.

Even with aids and electronic devices, librarians must provide a great deal of assistance to visually handicapped students. They need personal attention and guidance in performing most library routines from consulting a card catalog—a frustrating chore for the visually impaired—to learning how to make the best use of library materials purchased for their use.

SUPPLIERS

American Foundation for the Blind
15 West 16th St.
New York, NY 10011
Publications, aids and appliances,
  films

American Printing House for
  the Blind, Inc.
1839 Frankfort Ave., P.O. Box 6085
Louisville, KY 40206
Instructional materials; braille,
  large-print and recorded
  textbooks; aids and appliances

Christian Record Braille
  Foundation, Inc.
4444 So. 52nd St.
Lincoln, NE 68506
Braille reading materials,
  transcriptions

Dakota Microfilm Co.
501 N. Dale St.
St. Paul, MN 55103
In-stock and custom large-print
  books

G. K. Hall and Co.
70 Lincoln St.
Boston, MA 02111
Large-print books

Howe Press of Perkins School for
  the Blind
175 No. Beacon St.
Watertown, MA 02172
Reading materials, aids and
  appliances

Johanna Bureau
22 W. Madison St., Suite 540
Chicago, IL 60602
Braille, large-print and recorded
  materials

Library of Congress
Div. for the Blind and Physically
  Handicapped
1291 Taylor Street, N.W.
Washington, DC 20542
Talking book service, braille books

Microfilm Co. of California
1977 So. Los Angeles St.
Los Angeles, CA 90011
In-stock and custom large-print books

National Braille Assn.
Braille Book Bank
85 Goodwin Ave.
Midland Park, NJ 07432
Braille textbooks, reading materials,
  custom transcriptions

National Braille Press, Inc.
88 St. Stephen St.
Boston, MA 02115
Braille textbooks, reading materials;
  custom transcriptions

Pelco Sales Inc.
351 E. Alondra Blvd.
Gardena, CA 90248
Closed circuit TV systems

Recording for the Blind, Inc.
215 East 58th St.
New York, NY 10022
In-stock and custom recorded
  textbooks

SFB Products
221 Rock Hill Rd.
Bala-Cynwyd, PA 19004
Special and adapted instruments
  and materials

Southern Microfilm Corp.
900 W. 34th St., Box 1824
Houston, TX 77018
In-stock and custom large print

Telesensory Systems, Inc.
1889 Page Mill Rd.
Palo Alto, CA 94304
Optacon, Speech + talking
  calculator, electronic devices

Visualtek
1610 26th St.
Santa Monica, CA 90404
Closed circuit TV and microfiche
  reader

Volunteer Services for the Blind,
  Inc.
919 Walnut St.
Philadelphia, PA 19107
Braille reading materials and custom
  transcriptions

Volunteer Transcribing Services
205 E. Third Ave., Suite 201
San Mateo, CA 94401
In-stock and custom large-print books

Xavier Society for the Blind
154 East 23rd St.
New York, NY 10010
Braille, large-print and recorded
  textbooks and reading materials

Responding to Sound through Toys, the Environment, and Speech

by Ruth Silver

The classroom teacher who has multiply handicapped, visually impaired children many times has children who do not respond to sound, or respond inappropriately. Certain activities have proven successful with these students and can become a part of your classes' repertoire of work.

Quite often visually impaired children have other disabilities. Because the disabilities can be many, varied, and subtle, it is imperative that every child be thoroughly examined. Included should be a hearing evaluation by an audiologist, although teacher evaluations can be made over a period of time. Such long-term evaluations together with all available background information should be helpful in ascertaining whether the child has a hearing loss or whether his/her inadequate responses are the result of some other disability.

Those visually handicapped children who prove to have a severe hearing loss would most likely benefit from procedures designed specifically for the deaf blind, not by the procedures outlined in this article. Those visually handicapped children having mild hearing losses, as well as those having central nervous system dysfunction, retardation, or emotional disturbance which is not too debilitating, might benefit from some of the following suggestions. Those with a mild hearing loss, of course, might not hear all sounds and could not be expected to localize if they did not have similar hearing in both ears. Visually handicapped children with no additional disabilities might benefit from some of the less structured suggestions. Ideally, training should begin at the preschool level.

CONSIDERING A TRIUMVIRATE OF SOUNDS

Three kinds of sounds will be considered: sounds made by toys, environmental sounds, and speech. The various examples presented here are intended for the classroom, and others can easily be devised. The suggestions for teaching outlined in each section contain some structured procedures and some which are less so. The more structured procedures are for the most unresponsive children, and it should be remembered that not every child will need them. The teacher will have to evaluate each child to determine which sounds or aspects of sounds are most troublesome for him/her, and then select from the following suggestions the ones which would be most helpful. The teacher may wish to modify or revise some of the other suggestions. Time should not be spent on needless drill. As soon as the child indicates that s/he can respond, the teacher should move on.

Auditory training should take place in a controlled environment. Selected sounds should be presented in an environment as free from all other sounds as possible. This will help the child focus his/her complete attention on the desired sounds. Periods of auditory training should be followed by activities using little, if any, sound.

In a few cases the visual as well as the auditory environment may have to be controlled. A child with residual sight who is preoccupied with visual stimuli or continually distracted by them would find it difficult to attend to sound. The teacher can reduce or eliminate distracting visual stimuli by using a small bare room or a secluded corner of a larger one, darken a room, or, if necessary, cover the child's eyes for a brief period of time. Control of auditory or visual environment can gradually be relaxed as the child becomes more aware and attentive to auditory stimuli.

Sounds Made by Toys

Sound toys can be used to capture the interest of those children who do not respond to sound or do not respond appropriately. These sounds can be produced easily. Training with sound toys may make the child more aware of sound and better able to localize and discriminate. Finally, sound toys may help foster good listening habits which could carry over into other areas of auditory training.

Examples of sound toys include horn, rattle, triangle, maraca, bell, clacker, sand blocks, wood blocks, drum, tambourine, toy accordion, squeeze toys, xylophone, toy guitar, whistle, windup toys, friction car, bouncing ball, and homemade sound toys.

Teaching Awareness

The teacher can help the child become aware of a sound toy by first enabling him/her to use all senses, then isolating the auditory component, and finally returning to the use of all senses.

1. *Using all senses*. Present a toy. Let the child examine it using all senses—looking, listening, touching—even smelling and licking. Give him/her time to experience it in whatever way is meaningful to him/her. If the child shows no interest in the toy or its sound, the teacher should place his/her hands gently over the child's and manipulate the toy with him/her. If the child is not only disinterested, but even reluctant to touch the toy, the teacher should play with it in such a way as to capture his/her interest.

2. *Isolating the auditory component*. Sound the toy outside of the child's visual range only after ample multisensory exposure. If s/he reacts to the sound, let him/her play with the toy. If s/he does not react, sound the toy again and place his/her hand on it. Let him/her play with it.

3. *Returning to the use of all senses*. End the lesson as it was begun, using all senses. In this way, the child will experience the sound toy in as complete and normal a way as is possible for him/her.

Detecting the Presence and Absence of Sound

A procedure for detecting the presence and absence of sound can be used with children who continue to be unresponsive after repeated efforts to make them aware of toys and their sounds. This procedure can also be used to condition a child for an audiometric test when nonverbal responses will have to be relied upon.

1. *Choosing a mode of response*. Choose a motor response or a simple activity which the child has mastered, such as raising his/her hand, tapping the table, dropping a block in a box, or removing a ring from a peg.

2. *Choosing a sound toy*. Almost any sound toy can be used to teach the presence and absence of sound. If the procedure is being used to prepare a child for a hearing test, select a toy such as a whistle whose sound approximates that of the pure tone audiometer.

3. *Listening and responding*. Sound a toy. The child should indicate that s/he hears the sound by performing the appropriate motor response. For example, place a peg with rings on it in front of the child. Show him/her that the teacher has a whistle and sound it. The child should remove a ring from the peg each time s/he hears the whistle. S/He may need to have his/her hand guided many times to remove the ring at the exact moment the whistle is sounded in order to establish the response.

Sound toys can be used in a meaningful way to signal activities. The child can be encouraged to listen by having the same toy sounded each day at the onset of a specific activity. The teacher, for example, could ring a bell when it is time for recess, blow a whistle when it is time to come to the table and work, or sound a friction car or some other favorite toy when it is time to come to the area for free play.

Teaching Localization

The child can be taught at first to locate nearby sounds and later to respond to more distant sounds.

1. *Locating sounds near the child.* Sound a toy immediately to the left or right of the child. If s/he locates it, let him/her play with it; if s/he does not, sound the toy again and direct his/her hand toward it. Let him/her play with it. Vary the direction of the sound. Once the child locates sound to the left or right, present sound in front of him/her, behind, close to the floor, above, and at points in between. Avoid the midline since sound presented equidistant between the two ears is more difficult to localize.

2. *Increasing the distance.* As the child is able to locate sounds near him/her, increase the distance of the sound from him/her. S/He may eventually cross a room to locate it. Some children may respond better at first if the sound is continuous rather than intermittent. Remember to vary the direction of the sound. Occasionally a child may respond to distant sounds before those nearby.

Hide and seek is an enjoyable activity which can offer experience in localizing. The teacher sounds a favorite toy. One or more children seek it. The one who finds the toy hides with it and sounds it while the teacher or another child seeks it.

Teaching Discrimination

Discrimination of sound toys is concerned with the sounds made by the toys, not the names of the toys. A child must be aware of and responsive to individual sounds before s/he can be expected to discriminate between them.

A procedure preliminary to discrimination is presented in order to evaluate the child's awareness of sound and at the same time familiarize him/her with the mode of response to be used in discrimination.

1. Give the child a sound toy such as a drum. Let him/her examine and sound it. Have him/her place it on the table.

2. Show him/her that the teacher has a drum exactly like his/hers.

3. The child is to listen for the teacher's drum. S/He is not to sound his/her drum until s/he hears the other one.

4. Other sound toys can be used. Do not repeat the preliminary procedure so often, however, that the child becomes bored and unresponsive. As soon as s/he is ready, move on to discrimination.

A discrimination procedure using duplicate sets of sound toys, one for the child and one for the teacher, includes three steps.

1. *Presenting two sets of dissimilar sound toys.* Give the child one toy like a bell. Let the child examine and sound it. Have him/her place it on the table. Present a second toy like a drum. Let the child examine and sound it. Have him/her place it on the table. Show the child that the teacher has a set exactly like his/hers.

2. *Selecting the correct sound.* The teacher sounds one of his/her toys outside of the child's visual range. The child selects from his/her own set the one s/he thinks s/he heard and sounds it. Initially the child may need to have his/her hand guided to the correct sound toy. After that, give him/her enough time to respond, helping him/her only if s/he needs help.

3. *Using finer discrimination.* Increase the number and similarity of sound toys when the child is ready. For example, once a child can discriminate between a bell and a drum, a horn and a maraca, a rattle and wood blocks, add a squeeze toy to one of these sets. Later present sets of similar sounding toys, such as a maraca and a rattle, a large bell, a small bell, and a triangle.

A single set of sound toys can be used if a duplicate set is not available. After the child has examined and placed each toy on the table, the teacher can take one, sound it, and replace it on the table. The child then selects the one s/he has heard. A padded surface is recommended so the child does not merely localize the placement of the toy on the table.

Environmental Sounds

Many multiply handicapped, visually impaired children are puzzled or even frightened by sounds around them. Sounds we hear and take for granted may be upsetting to them. A knowledge of sound and its source should help the child understand what is happening around him/her. It should reduce his/her fears and encourage him/her to venture out into his/her environment.

Some children are not puzzled or frightened by sounds around them. In fact, they may be unresponsive to these sounds. Because certain environmental objects are of high interest to some of these children, auditory training with the sounds made by these objects can motivate listening. In fact, some children may be more responsive to the sounds of real objects than those made by toys.

Examples of environmental sounds include several categories:

1. *General:* A knock at the door, door opening, closing, slamming, sliding; light switch on, off; chair moving, scraping; water running, dripping, flushing; liquid pouring; food rattling in packages or containers; objects being collected for the lesson; objects dropped on the floor, table, or desk; telephone ringing; keys jingling or turning in the lock; money jingling; hair being brushed; coin purse being opened and shut; lotion being squeezed from a bottle.

2. *Weather:* rain, hail, wind, leaves rustling.

3. *Human sounds:* coughing, clearing throat, sneezing, laughing, crying, whistling, yawning; running, walking, tiptoeing, stumbling, slipping, tripping, slapping, clapping, rubbing, tapping, scratching.

4. *Animal sounds:* dog barking, cat meowing, and any others the child may have an opportunity to hear.

Teaching Sounds which Puzzle or Frighten

Incidental training and planned training can be used to help children identify sounds and their sources. Incidental sounds are those which occur in natural everyday situations. They are not planned by the teacher. When a sound occurs which puzzles or frightens the child, stop whatever activity is in progress. Point out what is producing the sound, then return to the original activity.

In planned training, observe and evaluate the child's reaction to environmental sounds. Note those sounds which upset him/her, such as a door slamming, or which s/he does not seem to comprehend, such as the scraping of a chair. Select one to be worked on. Identify the sound and its source, repeating if necessary. Let the child produce the sound if possible, again repeating as often as needed.

Teaching Awareness

Certain real objects, such as money in a bank or a plastic bottle of lotion, as well as certain snack foods, such as M&M's, cheese curls, or dry cereal, are of high interest to some children. The sounds of these objects being handled or snack foods being shaken in a dish or package can motivate the child to listen.

Present a favorite object or snack food in the same manner as that used to present a sound toy, permitting the child first to use all senses, then isolating the auditory component, and finally returning to the use of all senses. Remember to let the child handle the object or sample the food when s/he reacts to its sound.

Take advantage of opportunities throughout the day to make the child aware of environmental sounds. For example, take the child with you to answer a knock at the door or a ring of the telephone, to water running, a child crying, a key turning in a lock, or a cupboard being opened.

Teaching Localization

Localization of favorite objects or snack foods should also be taught in the same manner as that used with sound toys. Begin with a sound near the child, varying the direction and increasing the distance when s/he is ready.

Remember to let him/her handle the object or sample the food when s/he locates it.

Localization of environmental sounds should be incorporated into all activities throughout the day as in the following examples. Place the objects for the lesson on the table rather than in the child's hands. Have him/her listen and locate them by sound. Place a cup of juice and a cracker on the table. Have the child listen and locate them by sound. If the child drops an object, have him/her listen and find it. If s/he is to wash his/her hands, have him/her listen to the running water and find the sink. If the child is to join others for an activity, have him/her listen and locate them by sound.

Teaching Discrimination

If the teacher feels that the child might enjoy or benefit from discrimination exercises with environmental sounds, s/he can use the same procedures as those outlined with sound toys.

Speech

Some multiply handicapped, visually impaired children seem to have difficulty attending to speech. Some of these children are talked to infrequently while others are bombarded by talk. A certain number, regardless of the amount of exposure, seem to hear words only as meaningless sounds.

Since this article deals with auditory training, the emphasis will be on speech reception. Structured procedures are provided to present speech in tolerable doses and in a manner which illuminates meaning. As the child learns to listen and understand, structured presentations can be gradually decreased and replaced by more natural speech. This is the ultimate goal of auditory training.

The following procedures for dealing with input will be of little value if they are carried on without close attention to the child's responses. The teacher must expect and encourage the child to respond. The child must be given time to react, even if it means waiting a minute or more. To make the child feel that his/her responses are important, the teacher should convey his/her approval with a favorite treat, a hug, a pat, a word of praise, or a combination of these.

Helping the Child Attend to Speech

The teacher can help the child focus his/her attention on speech by controlling the auditory environment, regulating speech exposure, and using headphones.

The importance of controlling the auditory environment during auditory training was noted in the introduction to this article. Keeping the environment free from all background sound seems to be especially important in the case of speech reception. The child with difficulty in speech reception must learn to attend to words before s/he can be expected to separate them from background sounds. Control of the auditory environment can be relaxed as soon as the child indicates that s/he can tolerate interfering sounds and is able to separate them from the words s/he hears.

The visually handicapped child with problems in attending to speech will find it difficult to focus on long streams of words. S/He may be more likely to attend if words are meaningful and limited in number. This holds true with words used during activities throughout the day as well as those used during specific training periods in speech reception.

Since specific training periods can be demanding, they should be followed by an activity requiring few, if any, words on the part of the teacher. In some cases, a rest period providing total quiet might be advisable.

A child does not have to have a hearing loss to benefit from headphones. Headphones plugged into an auditory trainer, a tape recorder, or other equipment can channel sound directly to the ear. Such channeling might help a child who has difficulty attending to speech even though s/he has adequate hearing.

Before the teacher introduces the headphones to the child, s/he should make certain that they are turned on and operating properly and that the intensity is not too loud. Intensity is an individual matter. However, intensity slightly above normal is generally effective.

The child's first experience in using headphones should be pleasurable. S/He should be permitted to hold and examine the headphones before formal training begins. With the teacher's hands over the child's, they should place the headphones over the teacher's ears while s/he expresses pleasure. With his/her hands still over the child's, they then should place the headphones over the child's ears. It is important that the visually handicapped child have his/her hands on the headphones when they are guided to his/her ears so that s/he is aware of their placement and is not suddenly startled. The teacher should avoid the use of bells and other toys whose sounds may be irritating and even painful when intensified and channelled directly. S/He could hum, sing, name a favorite object held by the child, or engage in vocal interplay by imitating his/her sounds. This and every subsequent session must be brief and pleasurable.

Helping the Child Attend to Words and Short Sentences

The teacher can encourage the child to listen to simple speech by the appropriate selection and presentation of single words and short sentences.

1. *Selection of words*. Select words naming things of interest and relevance to the child. Initially, present concrete rather than abstract words. Use

parts of the body; clothing; toys; favorite foods; actions such as jump, march, clap; and directions such as up and down.

2. *Simultaneous presentation of a single word with the object or action.* Use single words with the unresponsive child or one who seems confused by more than one word. Say the appropriate word at the exact moment the child touches an object or performs an action. For example, say "ball" the moment the child's hand touches the ball, or "jump" the moment the child jumps or is helped to jump.

If the child continues to be unresponsive to this simultaneous presentation, try the following conditioning procedure. In this procedure the child cannot have the desired object until it is named. Initially the child may be responding merely to the teacher's voice and only later realize that s/he is naming the item. Place an M&M candy in a dish. Make certain that the child knows it is there. The child is to take the candy when s/he hears the teacher say "M&M." If s/he does not, repeat the word and place his/her hand on the candy. Let him/her eat it. If the child reaches for the M&M before the teacher speaks, gently but firmly remove his/her hand from the dish without saying anything. No other sounds or words should be made during the lesson in order to emphasize the desired word. Repeat as often as is necessary. Other favorite snack foods, objects, or actions may be used instead of M&M's to condition the child. The child, for example, holds a ball but is not permitted to bounce or to throw it until s/he hears the word "ball."

3. *Presentation of short sentences emphasizing the key word.* Use short sentences as soon as the child is ready. The rate of the teacher's speech will depend upon the individual child. Some are able to respond to normal rate, while others respond better if the rate is slow. Emphasize the key word in a sentence by repeating it. The amount of repetition will depend upon the child's response. For example, place the child's hand on his/her shoe and say, "shoe." Pause. Say, "Take off your shoe" while the child removes the shoe or is helped to remove it. Pause. Repeat the word "shoe" after the child has removed the shoe and is holding it.

Helping the Child Attend to His/Her Own Vocalization

The teacher can encourage a child to attend to his/her own vocalizations by reinforcing positively, attaching meaning to his/her vocalizations, and tape recording them. Since this article deals with reception rather than expression, no specific procedures will be given for teaching speech. A few suggestions will be offered to encourage the child to attend to any vocalization s/he may make.

1. *Using reinforcement.* Encourage the child to pay attention to his/her vocalizations by reinforcing him/her positively. If the child is extremely nonvocal, it may be helpful to reward any sound s/he makes. If the child

makes sounds but does not pay attention to them, it might be effective to reward one particular sound that could later be shaped into a word. In any case, make certain the reinforcer is something the child especially enjoys.

2. *Attaching meaning to the child's vocalization.* Select a sound the child makes frequently and imitate it. Use it in a word naming something the child especially enjoys and would consider a reward. In this way, the teacher can attach meaning to the child's vocalizations. For example, the child says *k*. Repeat the sound immediately after the child. Use the sound in the word, "cookie," and give the child a cookie at the exact moment the word is said. If the child says the word, or makes an approximation of it, or even merely repeats the *k* sound, respond approvingly and give him/her another cookie. Be on the alert for a delayed response during the lesson or even after it. Reinforce it whenever possible.

3. *Using the tape recorder.* A child may enjoy listening to himself/herself on tape and be encouraged to attend and vocalize even more. When the child first makes and listens to a tape recording of himself/herself and the teacher, s/he should be permitted to place one hand on the side of the tape recorder and the other hand on the face of the speaker—either his/her own or his/her teacher's. In this way, s/he will become acquainted with the source of the sound. The teacher may wish to keep some of the tapes in order to have a permanent record of the child's progress.

Teaching Speech Discrimination

Some multiply handicapped, visually impaired children with severe language limitations find it difficult, if not impossible, to identify pairs of sounds, syllables, or words as sounding the same or different. The concept of sameness is abstract and difficult even for some children who are less limited. It would be simpler and more meaningful for a child to listen and select from two or more objects the one s/he hears named.

There are some multiply handicapped, visually impaired children who may not respond even to the simplest and most realistic speech discrimination procedures. To insure that every effort is made to reach even the most severely handicapped, the teacher should keep the following recommendations in mind throughout all speech discrimination exercises.

1. Present words naming things of special interest to the child.

2. Make certain the child has had experience with each of the items separately before s/he is expected to discriminate among them.

3. Plan to present some discrimination exercises just before or even during an activity in which the words would normally be used. For example, work on the words *mitten* and *cap* just before it is time to go outdoors; *cup* and *napkin* just before snack time; or *juice* and *cracker* during juice and cracker period.

4. Give the child adequate time to respond.

5. Permit the child to briefly play with the toy or handle the object which s/he has correctly selected. There is no reason for a child to listen and select something if it is immediately taken away from him/her.

6. Use a stronger reinforcement if the child does not consider playing with the toy or handling the object as enough of a reward. An M&M candy, a sip of a drink, rubbing the back of his/her neck, or anything else the child especially enjoys can be used to reward a correct response.

7. Do not repeat an exercise so often that the child becomes bored and unresponsive.

The teacher can help the child to discriminate words and short sentences by progressing from simple to more complex exercises.

1. *Presenting words of varying length*. Work on the names of two toys or objects the child has experienced and especially enjoys. Initially, present two words of varying length such as *balloon* and *top,* or a single word and a two- or three-word utterance such as *comb* or *lotion bottle*. The child may be helped to discriminate at first on the basis that one sounds long and the other short. For example, place the balloon on the table. Name it and have the child find and play with it. After a few seconds put it aside. Then place the top on the table. Name it and have the child find and play with it. After a few seconds put it aside.

Place both the balloon and the top on the table, letting the child touch each as it is named and placed. Name one and have the child find and play with it briefly. The contrast in length can be further accentuated by saying the long word more slowly. Repeat, sometimes naming one and sometimes the other. Give the child time to respond, helping him/her only if s/he needs help. Reward him/her by letting him/her play briefly with the correctly selected toy. If playing with the balloon or top is not rewarding enough, and there are no other toys or objects the child prefers more, give him/her an M&M or some other strong reinforcement for a correct response.

The following list of long and short words or utterances are merely suggestions: *candy dish, box* (place a treat in the one named); *telephone, ball; music box, drum; lotion bottle, comb; wash cloth, soap; napkin, cup; cracker, juice; mitten, cap; jacket, boot;* and *pull the wagon, stop.*

2. *Presenting words of similar length but contrasting sound*. When the child is ready, present words of similar length that do not sound alike, especially initially, such as *ball, drum; mittens, jacket; cup, spoon.*

3. *Using finer discrimination*. Once the child can discriminate between words of similar length that do not sound alike, present words that do. For example: *cap, cup; can, fan; bell, ball, bowl.*

Incorporate words the child has learned to discriminate into sentences such as, bounce the *ball,* spin the *top,* open the *box,* open the *can.* As the child begins to respond to these discrimination exercises, give him/her the opportunity to use this ability in more natural and complex situations.

MOVING FORWARD AND EXPANDING ACTIVITIES

Mastery of these procedures does not signal the end of auditory training. As soon as the child is ready, the teacher can enlarge upon auditory aspects listed in this article or proceed to others. For example, once the child can discriminate between the sounds made by toys, s/he may be taught to discriminate volume, pitch, and rhythm by first using sound toys and later, music. As the child demonstrates increased proficiency in discrimination, s/he may be introduced to sequencing. This auditory aspect requires the ability to remember and identify the exact order in which sounds are presented. Memory, another auditory aspect, is not only an integral part of sequencing, but also of discrimination and of localization of intermittent sounds. Difficulty in any of these areas may be the result of deficiencies in memory. The teacher can work on memory by increasing the time lapse between the presentation of the auditory stimuli and the child's response. These are only some suggestions as to the direction auditory training can take.

To develop a specific program for any one child, close observation and regular evaluation of him/her in every possible situation will provide insights which will guide the teacher in his/her planning. Individualized planning will require a great deal of ingenuity and creativity, but it is the most effective method of helping the multiply handicapped, visually impaired child develop his/her auditory sense to its fullest.

Language Arts for the Visually Impaired Child

by Elaine H. Wagener

The limitation of stimuli which occurs in visually impaired children can be partially ameliorated by strengthening other sense modalities. A strong language arts program can facilitate this process.

The sense of touch obviously becomes an avenue of increased significance in the visually impaired. It is, however, the *combination* of many opportunities for tactile exploration *and* exposure to language concepts involved which will allow for maximum cognitive growth. The child moves from the manipulative or concrete operational stage to a more abstract form of thinking, promoting his/her cognitive flexibility.

The range of possibilities for exploring oral language through kinesthetic experiences is endless. Use of various concrete objects can develop discrimination power as well as descriptive skills. With text and photographs, *Aids for Teaching Basic Concepts of Sensory Development*[1] describes materials which can be prepared for teaching concepts of up, down, thick, thin, over, under, top, bottom, alike, different, large, small, hard, soft, in front of, and behind. It also discusses ways of using special materials to teach, shape, number, texture, and sound.

Another suggestion which could be teacher-made is a *cloth box*. It consists of a collection of various types of fabrics either glued to poster board or cut in swatches for the child to manipulate more easily. As children handle the materials they develop concepts of soft, stiff, smooth, rough, silky, sticky, furry, thick, thin, hairy, and bumpy. They could then be asked to find pieces that are exactly alike. Another task is to compare two pieces of different materials and decide which is softer, thicker, furrier, or any other one-to-one comparison of texture. A more difficult task is to allow the child to attempt putting three or more pieces of fabric into a sequential order from soft to stiff or thick to thin. A discussion based on characteristics of certain fabrics which would make them suitable for certain purposes such as pajamas, dresses, coats, raincoats, place mats, blankets, or overalls is then appropriate.

Other similar boxes include rocks, shells, wood (including driftwood, various kinds of paneling, and highly sanded pieces), sandpaper (with different grades of roughness), art objects (marble, wood, metal, glass sculpture) and building materials (brick, foam, plastic, sheetrock, rubber, metal pipes, wiring).

Directions in braille would allow the child self-exploration with oral language following. Cassette tape recorders may be available for the child to record responses.

Other objects used in oral language development are tools of various trades—carpentry, auto mechanics, gardening, electrical, architectural, baking, and so forth. Conversations based on shape, size, texture, and usage expand basic concepts and vocabulary.

SAMPLE DIRECTION CARD

Directions

The shells in this box are numbered.
You will find the names of the shells on cards with matching numbers on the back.
Match the name cards with the shells using the numbers.
Now try to match the shells and names without using the numbers on the back.
Some shells have no numbers. They are almost exactly like some of the numbered ones.
Can you match the shells that are alike?
Ask your teacher if you are right.
Play Tape #4a if you would like to hear some poems people have written about shells.
If you like, tape your own poem at the end of Amy Lowell's "The Sea Shell"
  or write your own story about a day in the life of a shell on a braille writer.
Read the information card on shells in this box or listen to Tape #4b.
You may plan a report to the class describing shells you have chosen from the shell box.

Games in which the child has an object in a bag and tries to describe it so another can guess what it is enlarge descriptive powers. Word strips in braille could be available on what Roach Van Allen[2] refers to as a "word wall," a wall covered with lists of form class words: shape words, color words, size words, taste words, sound words, action words. The word strips grow as children expand their verbal skills.

Dramatizations with objects can occur when the child's imagination is stirred. "What do you suppose this egg might say to the frying pan as it sizzles there?" "What would the pan reply?" "How would the potato describe life underground to a shoe?" "If a hammer could talk, what might it tell of the day's adventures?"

Oral language stimulated by these tactile experiences is a natural base for creative writing. In fact, if one imagines the creative writing process as that of composing independent of the process of getting the thoughts in written form, then creative composition should offer no special problem to the visually handicapped child. The child dictates, the teacher or aide transcribes; or the child dictates into a tape recorder. When the story has been brailled by an older child or another adult, it becomes a vital piece of reading material both to the creator and others. Reading becomes very personal and individualized when the child is reading his/her own writing or that of a peer. Other language-experience stories based on events in the school day, happenings at home, feelings about themselves or others, or responses to radio or television are valuable instruments to composition and eventually to reading instruction. It is important to remember that creative writing does not usually flourish in a stagnant, bleak atmosphere. Rich sensory input, lively interchange with ideas and people, and a variety of engaging experiences are important to the flow of words and ideas.

The sense of touch widens the child's world and helps open the language world. The sense of hearing is equally important in growth as a human being, producer and receiver of ideas and feelings.

Reading aloud to children is one of the most rewarding experiences which builds listening skills. This is doubly true with the visually impaired child. Not only is a child's literary world enlarged by the warmth of sharing a good book with teacher and friends sitting together in a cozy atmosphere, but hearing a story with strong emotional appeal can assist children in sensing emotion within themselves and the literary characters involved and perhaps in time aid in expressing those feelings either orally or in writing on a braille writer.

Charlotte's Web, *The Biggest Bear*, *Year of the Raccoon*, *Benji*, *Pavo and the Princess*, *Tales of a Fourth Grade Nothing*, *William's Doll*, *The Jazz Man*, *The Pine Tree*, *The Wave*, and *J.T.* are all examples of books with strong emotional elements. Commercially prepared records are available in which famous actors read aloud children's books. Carol Channing reading "Madeline" stories (Caedmon), Hans Conreid reading highlights from *Treasure Island* (Literary Records), *Grimms' Fairy Tales* by Danny Kaye (Golden Records), or the Winnie the Pooh series by Sterling Holloway (Disneyland Records) are but a few of those available. Many children's picture books have been recorded by Columbia Records—*Make Way for Ducklings*, *Andy and the Lion*, *The Biggest Bear*, *Lentil*, *Drummer Hoff*, *Harold and the Purple Crayon*, *Mike Mulligan and His Steam Shovel*, and *Custard the Dragon*.

A rich listening-literature program builds readiness and motivation for reading which is sometimes neglected in the home. Brailling the simple stories available on record or tape can provide an additional learning experience with the child following the text as the tape plays.

Listening can be a means for building skills in memory, information retrieval, and simple recall. Science Research Associates (SRA) has produced Listening Skill Builders as a part of their SRA Reading Labs in which the teacher reads a passage and the children choose the correct answer to a series of questions asked at the end of the exercise.

However, although listening for simple recall type responses is important, it is certainly not the only skill to encourage. Listening can be used to develop skills in making inferences, making comparisons, following directions, discerning sequence, recognizing cause and effect, and identifying emotions. A set of cassette tapes on these skills, developed by Dorothy Bracken, is also available through SRA.

Discrimination in hearing sounds can be developed by using records of common sounds or taping your own set of sounds. Commercial recordings of sounds have been prepared by Elektra Records (*Authentic Sound Effects*) and Audio-Fidelity (*Sound Effects*). Common animal, weather, and situational sounds have been recorded as well as more unusual sounds. *Sounds of My City* by Tony Schwartz (Folkways Records), which depicts New York City in story, music, and sound, allows identification by the city child and can be an adventure in discovery for the child with few city experiences.

A xylophone or other musical instrument is useful in discriminating high and low sounds. Seed boxes or other sound boxes can be used to match sounds that are alike or to sequence sounds from high to low or from loud to soft.

Systems of tactile, auditory, and concept expansion used in a language arts program such as this are time-consuming, but well worth the efforts of the teacher or aides to visually impaired children. The children themselves might become interested in preparing activity boxes or tapes at home with the help of parents or siblings. The end result of these efforts—the expansion of the visually impaired child's world—is limited only by the ingenuity, imagination, and energy of the teachers involved.

NOTES

1. Natalie Barraga, Barbara Dorward, and Peggy Ford, *Aids for Teaching Basic Concepts of Sensory Development* (Louisville, KY: American Printing House for the Blind, 1973).
2. Roach Van Allen, "A Learning Environment Where Everyone Reads" (Paper delivered at the Texas Association for the Improvement of Reading Conference, Beaumont, Texas, June, 1972).

Multiply Successes When Introducing Basic Multiplication Ideas to Visually Handicapped Children

by Carol Ann Dodd Thornton

The teaching of basic multiplication ideas first focuses on the concept of multiplication—the joining of equivalent sets—and then extends to encourage mastery of the multiplication facts. Careful planning, coupled with attention to thinking strategies and the creative use of inexpensive manipulatives, can make these early experiences in multiplication both profitable and enjoyable for the visually handicapped child.

TECHNIQUES FOR INITIAL DEVELOPMENT OF IDEAS

The development of initial concepts in multiplication frequently utilizes the array as a *thinking model*. The array, a rectangular arrangement of objects or symbols, can first be presented to the visually handicapped child through familiar objects. Milk cartons, eggs, soft drink bottles, buttons, crayons, even some candies and cookies are cartoned or packed in rows, with the same number in each row.

The child cues in on the thinking model by feeling and describing what is before him/her. Using egg cartons (or the flats used to store larger quantities of eggs), children can form and then describe their own arrays. The print reader can use objects such as beads or buttons to fill the egg cups (see Figure 1). The braille reader may prefer to turn the carton or flat upside down, feel the bumps, and outline an array of his/her choosing with a narrow strip of modeling clay or yarn. If, for example, three rows of five are outlined (filled), the key question should be asked: "How many rows of five did you make?" The child should note that s/he has a row of five, three times. Devices such as the bead frame (ten rows of ten beads), unifix cubes (or large pop beads), and grooved Stern blocks can be used by children to identify and describe arrays.

Tapping games appeal to both braille and print readers and should not be overlooked. Listening carefully, children identify how many times they hear a set of four taps, of two taps, and so on.

Throughout the initial development of multiplication ideas, problems applying simple multiplication ideas which relate to the child's experiences should be raised. If peanut butter cups cost 2¢ and s/he wants three of them, how much will they cost? These and similar problems can help make mathematics more realistic for children.

THINKING STRATEGIES

Once the basic concept of multiplication is grasped, children begin to memorize the basic facts. Several logical thinking strategies can be gainfully employed to help children remember the basic combinations.

1. The realization that, for example, three fours are as much as four threes. (The product is not changed when the order of the factors is interchanged.) Turning an egg carton array 90 degrees illustrates this fact.

2. The use of multiplication as *repeated addition* to go from known to unknown facts. If a child knows that four threes are 12, then five threes are three more: 15. Rows of buttons or bottle caps glued to tagboard can be used to illustrate the repeated addition idea. A second piece of tagboard can be slid down over the rows to help the child skip count. The Cranmer abacus could be used to find more difficult facts by adding on to easier known products.

3. The use of doubles, which seems to come easily to children. If a child knows that two sixes are 12, then four sixes are twice as much—four sixes are 24. The button array in Figure 2 illustrates this latter strategy. The tagboard is folded in half, then unfolded when one factor is doubled.

FIGURE 1   **FIGURE 2**

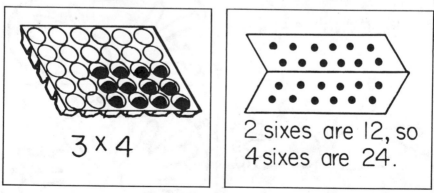

3 × 4

2 sixes are 12, so 4 sixes are 24.

MASTERY OF FACTS

Activities, games, and devices which reinforce the recall (drill) of basic facts enter as a last stage in the learning of multiplication combinations. Card games based on Old Maid rules can be used and adapted to the needs of individual children. 3 × 8 and 24, for example, make a pair. For the print reader the numerals should be printed with a wide felt-tip marker. For the braille reader the numerals can be typed with a braille writer—then cut out and pasted on the cards.

Multiplication records which provide for a sing-along rehearsal of facts are available commercially, and these can be tuned into via earphones. Large homemade die, with braille or large-print numerals on the faces, can also be used to reinforce the recall of troublesome facts. A pair of die should be thrown into a shallow box. The child can then find the product of the two numbers which fall face up, and check his/her memory (if necessary) by referring to a key which you provide.

The nines are usually the most difficult multiplication facts for children. Experience has verified that a simple technique, sometimes called *finger magic*, becomes a ready cure-all for learning the nines table.

Figure 3 shows how the child numbers his/her fingers from left to right. Then, placing his/her hands on a table surface, s/he multiplies 3 × 9 folding his/her third finger under and "reading" the product from his/her fingers: two tens, seven ones, or 27. The child can push his/her fingers against the table to tell how many are on either side of the folded finger. Simply, to multiply 7 × 9, s/he folds his/her seventh finger under and reads the product: six tens, three ones, or 63.

FIGURE 3

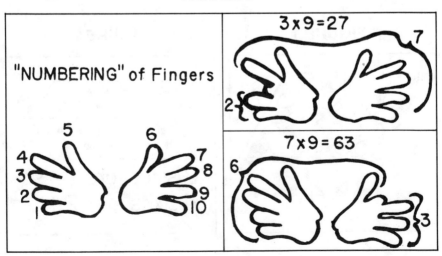

Other more troublesome facts, such as 7 × 8 and 8.× 6 can be reinforced using the disguised practice of *matching boards* or *multiblocks*. Both devices are homemade.

Matching boards, cut from heavy tagboard, are shaped to fit together as a two-piece puzzle (see Figure 4). String or carpet thread can be used to keep the two pieces from falling more than several inches apart. Number facts are printed on both sides of the cards. The *match* then becomes self-checking. When pieces match, so do factors with products on both sides of the card.

Multiblocks, made either of Styrofoam or wood, can be used with braille readers to reinforce both multiplication and corresponding division facts. The cubes have numerals epoxied to only three sides. These correspond to the two factors and the product of a multiplication sentence. When a child draws a cube (multiblock) from a shoebox, his/her task is to pause when s/he has located two of the numbers and identify the multiplication or division sentence which corresponds to those two numbers. If a child locates seven and eight, s/he can suggest either the multiplication sentence 7 × 8 = 56 or 8 × 7 = 56. If 56 and 8 are the first numbers located, then 56 ÷ 8 = 7 or 56 ÷ 7 = 8 would be appropriate number sentences. The child can check his/her thinking by locating the third number on the multiblock. For more capable children, the game is made more difficult by placing two sets of number combinations on the same cube. For example, the numerals 7, 7, 49, 8, 5, and 40 might appear on the same multiblock. In this case the child would attempt to correctly identify at least two number sentences before checking his/her answers against a key.

A variation of the multiblocks game is appropriate for both print and braille readers. For this game, numerals are printed on or epoxied to all sides of the cubes; but, for any single multiblock, only three numerals "go together" to form a true number sentence. For instance, the numerals 6, 8, 48, 56, 5, 9, 3, and 2 may all be found on one block. But only three of them—6, 8, and 48— match to make a true multiplication (or division) sentence. Games with multiblocks can be played with pairs of children. While one child plays the game, the other child can check answers using a chart or booklet which contains possible correct responses.

FIGURE 4

Many variations of familiar games can be adapted for the visually handicapped child. Figure 5 shows a number square game which uses the tic-tac-toe idea. Numerals (large print or brailled) are cut out and glued to a grooved playing board. A tic-tac-toe can be made either diagonally, vertically, or horizontally by finding three number combinations with the same product. (This idea can be adapted for addition, subtraction, or mixed combinations as well.) The child's task would be to discover how many tic-tac-toe's are possible on any one playing board and to identify the number(s) of the square. In this case 36 and 24 are the two tic-tac-toe numbers.

FIGURE 5

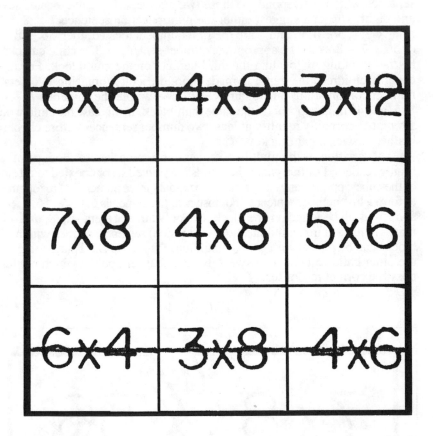

The Talking Calculator Used with Blind Youth

by Richard R. Champion

Mathematics computation has long been one of the more difficult tasks for blind children. Various aids have been developed over the years to make computation less difficult for the blind student: the Taylor slate, the abacus, the cube board, and, of course, the braille writer using Nemeth Code. While each of these methods is accurate, they are both cumbersome and slow. Observing a blind child laboriously solving a problem using one of the above aids gives cause to wonder if we are not doing the blind child a disservice by not affording him/her the use of the most efficient, accurate, and compact method available for computing mathematical problems.

The recent development and marketing of calculators with auditory output has opened a new door for the blind. Competency in mathematics, a difficult task at best for the blind, may now be within the grasp of a large number of blind individuals.

PURPOSE

A study was undertaken to determine whether blind elementary school children are able to compute mathematical formulas with ease, speed, and accuracy using the Speech-Plus talking calculator as a computational aid. (This calculator—developed, manufactured and distributed by Telesensory Systems, Inc.—was selected for this study because of its availability and price and does not reflect the investigator's bias.)

SUBJECTS

A group of nine blind children was selected from elementary and intermediate school grades. Subjects were selected according to the following criteria:

1. Subjects were in the normal range of intelligence.
2. Subjects were blind.
3. Subjects used braille as their primary reading mode.
4. Subjects were in grades three through eight.

PROCEDURE

Each subject was given the Stanford Achievement Test, Math Computation and Math Concepts subsections (Form A). The battery appropriate for age and grade was used with each subject. The American Printing House Braille Adaptation of the Stanford Achievement Test was used. Subjects were encouraged to use the mathematical aid(s) they were accustomed to using. A record was kept of:

1. Raw score achieved.
2. Time to complete tests.

Following the pretest, each subject was given instruction in the use of the talking calculator. Instruction was limited to orientation to the calculator, the operation of the calculator, and functions of the calculator. The instruction was given individually in one hour-long session.

The classroom teachers were asked to allow the subjects to use the calculator to do their curricular mathematics if appropriate, use the calculator to check their work, and/or review their mathematics. No additional instruction was given. After having access to the calculator for three weeks on a demonstrated competency,[1] subjects were post-tested with the Stanford Achievement Test, Math Computation and Math Concept (Form B). The talking calculator was available to the subjects while they were taking the post-test. A record was kept of:

1. Raw score achieved.
2. Time to complete tests.

RESULTS

This project began March 1, 1976, and was completed by May 31, 1976. Upon completion, a comparison was made of the raw scores achieved on the pretest and post-test and the time needed for completion of the pretest and post-test.

All nine of the subjects were able to master the operation of the Speech-Plus after a one-hour orientation-instruction session and informal exposure over a three-week period. The subjects learned the operation more readily than was anticipated. Two factors may have contributed to this ease in learning:

1. The Speech-Plus keyboard has the same configuration as that of the touch-tone telephone, and most of the students have had previous experience with the touch-tone telephone.

2. In the speech mode the calculator gives immediate feedback to the users.

These two factors, coupled with the novelty of the calculator and high motivation, may have contributed to the ease with which the subjects learned the operation of the calculator.

The mean computation raw score for the pretest, using the computational aid they were accustomed to, was 22.66. The mean computation raw score for the post-test using the Speech-Plus calculator was 29.22; a raw score gain of 6.56 or a 28.95% gain. The mean concepts raw score for the pretest, using the computational aid they were accustomed to, was 14. The mean concepts raw score using the Speech-Plus calculator was 16.88, a raw score gain of 2.88 or a 20.57% gain (see Table 1).

TABLE 1 Raw Scores Achieved

Subject	Grade	Pre		Post	
		Computation	Concepts	Computation	Concepts
1	6	28	19	31	18
2	5	18	15	20	16
3	4	28	21	29	18
4	3	15	10	30	20
5	3	15	8	23	17
6	3	26	13	27	15
7	7	28	14	35	16
8	8	20	12	35	13
9	3	26	15	33	31

TABLE 2 Time for Completion

Subject	Grade	Pre		Post	
		Computation	Concepts	Computation	Concepts
1	6	47	25	23	28
2	5	40	33	30	20
3	4	40	35	33	27
4	3	45	30	32	25
5	3	43	35	23	20
6	3	25	35	35	22
7	7	40	33	13	20
8	8	45	32	35	30
9	3	25	15	20	21

The mean time of completion for the computation subsection on the pretest was 39 minutes. The mean time for completion of the computation subsection on the post-test was 27 minutes; a mean time difference of 12 minutes or 30.77% less time. The mean time for completion of the math concepts subsection pretest was 30.33 minutes. The mean time for completion of the math concepts subsection post-test was 23 minutes; a time difference of 7.33 minutes or 24.16% less time (see Table 2.)

OBSERVATIONS

In the process of conducting this study, there were several things observed that are of interest:

1. *Hand Use*. Teachers of the blind usually attempt to get children to use both hands while reading braille. One hand, however, becomes dominant. When using the calculator for auditory dictation, subjects used their dominant hand to manipulate the calculator; the other hand was used for location and place holding. They soon discovered that, unlike the braille writer, they could do their calculations with one hand on the book and the other on the calculator. When taking mathematics problems from a book, the subjects used their dominant hand on the book and the other hand on the calculator.

The importance of this becomes apparent as one designs a method of teaching the use of the calculator to the blind. The method and its effectiveness will vary according to the source of the material.

2. *The Decimal Point*. The auditory output always gives a decimal point as part of its answer. This is somewhat confusing to young children who have not previously encountered decimals. Division problems having remainders in the quotient are given in a decimal fraction. In the early grades children are usually taught to find the quotient and give the remainder as whole numbers. This must either be explained or avoided.

3. *The Division Sign*. When the sign for divide is depressed, the auditory output is "Over." This, at first, is confusing, but with very little explanation the subjects were able to make the transition readily.

4. *Finger Position*. Most subjects devised a system for locating and depressing the keys. They favored the use of the first three fingers across the top row of digit keys. From this position they moved to and depressed other keys, then returned to those keys before continuing. The raised dot on the five was helpful for some, but was not established as the main reference point as is usually the case on business machines for the sighted. There seemed to be little advantage in using the raised dot for orientation. Several factors may have an influence on this:

a. Hand size. From the position of the middle finger on the five, it is often difficult to reach the other keys comfortably.
b. Blind children tend to rely less on information received by the little finger and thumb than on their other fingers.
c. The keyboard on this and most other calculators is designed for a right-handed user. When doing math problems from a book, the subjects used their left hand on the calculator even though their dominant hand was the right hand.

5. *The Younger Child*. In the sample there were four subjects at the third grade level. The mean raw score gain of these four was higher than the mean raw score gain for the group of nine. These four third graders were able to use the Speech-Plus as efficiently as the remainder of the group.

SUMMARY

It is difficult to make generalizations about the school-age blind as a result of a study involving nine subjects. The results reported here reflect how these nine subjects performed on the Speech-Plus. The following are statements of the performance of those nine:

1. Subjects were able to learn the operation of the Speech-Plus calculator with only one hour-long instruction session and three weeks of informal use of the calculator.

2. Raw score gains indicate that the use of the Speech-Plus helped the subjects achieve higher scores on a standardized test.

3. Time records reveal that subjects were able to complete comparable work in much less time.

4. The gains on the computation subtest were higher than on the concept subtest.

CONCLUSIONS

These subjects could benefit from the aid of a talking calculator in their curricular mathematics when there is need for a fast, accurate, and highly portable aid to mathematics computation.

Observation of subjects using their nondominant hand seems to suggest to manufacturers the possibility of repositioning the function keys to accommodate the majority of users.

Since these blind children were able to use the calculator with ease using their nondominant and presumably their less sensitive hand, there may be a large population with decreased tactual sensitivity that could benefit from the use of the calculator.

The ease with which the subjects learned the use of the calculator seems to contraindicate the development of special materials to teach blind youth to use the calculator. Instruction can be kept at a minimum, with a greater emphasis on exploration, experimentation, and practice. Perhaps there would be cause for a more formalized approach if there were a vocational objective requiring speed as the goal.

NOTE

1. Competency: A subject was considered competent with the Speech-Plus when s/he was able to perform the following with 100 percent accuracy:
- Turn the calculator on and set volume.
- Set calculator for speech or no speech mode.
- Locate and depress the four basic signs of operations keys.
- Locate and depress the ten digit keys.
- Compute without auditory/feedback in the four basic functions of math.

They Opened Our Eyes: The Story of an Exploratory Art Program for Visually Impaired, Multiply Handicapped Children

by Judith Rubin
and Janet Klineman

In a search for modes of communication with and for complex children, an art program grew out of a partnership between the authors.[1] Involved in the art program were 16 multiply handicapped children, ages five to thirteen, who were participants in a federal project conducted during the 1969-70 school year.[2] Our experiences with these youngsters, who "opened our eyes" to their creative abilities, have also been recorded on film.[3]

These children were like those described by Wolf[4] and by Moor[5] in *No Place to Go* (1961) and *No Time to Lose* (1968). All were legally blind, half with useful residual vision. In addition to retardation (mean IQ 65), they had to cope with other disabilities like cerebral palsy, hearing losses, speech handicaps, and emotional disturbances. Twelve had been attending the Western Pennsylvania School for Blind Children but, unable to learn with their peers, had been placed in a classroom for 'slow learners'. One had spent five years in a custodial institution for the retarded, another had been considered for expulsion because of disruptive behavior, and five could not previously have been accepted at the school because of their unusual management problems.

The withdrawn child who spent most of his time with his head nested on his chest, the ten-year-old with a vocabulary of a few words, the hyperactive boy who screamed, bit, or scratched when he couldn't have his way . . . such children created problems for their teachers and houseparents, as well as for the 'normal blind children' in the school. Many staff members were skeptical about what such youngsters could learn, and the difficulties of working with them often made previously confident professionals feel inadequate.

Understanding the staff's negative feelings toward these children was important, but it was equally vital to try new approaches to assess objectively what abilities they might have in order to determine what help might be provided for them.[6] While in the process of assessing the children's achievement levels and creating educational environments for them, the arts seemed an appropriate avenue to explore.

THE EXPLORATORY ART PROGRAM

Because so little is known about the artistic capacities of such complicated children, the program was indeed a voyage into uncharted territory. We began with individual interviews,[7] evaluating each child's responses to different media, such as fingerpaints, clay, paints, wood scraps, and drawing materials. The children were offered a free choice of creative materials and were also asked to respond in an open-ended way to such tactile stimuli as rabbit fur, foam rubber, smooth wood, and sandpaper; and to auditory stimuli like rattling objects in a can, a slide whistle, and a bell. These interviews were taped, recorded, and rated by pairs of graduate student and staff observers. They used a nine-point, 24-item scale, which included such dimensions as: independence/dependence, flexibility/rigidity, relaxation/tension, and involvement/distractibility.

On the basis of each child's degree of vision, intellectual level, and behavior in these interviews, we arranged small homogeneous groups of two to five children who met weekly for one-half hour for a seven-week period. We hoped to explore the children's potential for creative growth, given a free choice of materials within a planned learning environment. An experienced teacher of art to blind youngsters, however, predicted chaos, saying that these multiply handicapped children would have clay on the ceiling and a mess on the floor without step-by-step instructions.

Indeed, the literature on art for the retarded reveals "a definite attitude that the retarded child [is] not capable of developing creative and imaginative concepts.[8] Despite the positive and successful free approaches of a few,[9-16] the more common assumption has been that retarded children require "highly organized . . . step-by-step procedures,"[17] that "only one activity at a time is desirable," that they "have to be constantly supervised to see that they do not misuse materials and supplies," and that "retarded children generally lack imagination."[18]

Similarly condescending attitudes are frequent in the limited literature on art for the blind: "negative sentiment exists concerning the creative aspects of the blind child and feasible art activities . . . with the result that the child's handwork time has been consistently devoted to learning repetitious movements which evolve a craft skill ."[19] Again, despite many reports of successful creative art teaching experiences,[20-29] there remains a strong feeling that "repetitive skill work . . . should not be underestimated or discredited."[30]

Nevertheless, the exploratory art project truly opened our eyes, while it opened the children's worlds. It made us aware of their creative potential, and of their unexpected capacity for growth. Not only did they not mess as feared; they responded enthusiastically and constructively. We saw children, some in their first contact with new materials, creating artwork of sometimes surprising beauty.

While at first uncomfortable with freedom of choice, the children soon understood that we really expected them to make their own decisions about medium, theme, and place of work. They then exercised the newly acquired privilege (or is it a right?) with gusto. Our experiences, like those of Lowenfeld, contradicted the "frequent arguments . . . that handicapped persons need the security and confidence which results from mere imitative occupation, such as copying or tracing."[31] Instead, we learned, like Charlotte Haupt, the need for the worker "to have faith in the inner potential of her students so that she will trust them when they wish to explore on their own."[32]

Often, the children opened our eyes to previously hidden capacities. Jimmy's meaningful responses to color, for example, initiated his individualized visual stimulation program. Carl's skill and interest in wood scrap constructions resulted in a successful after-school woodworking club. All of them revealed a surprising ability to function independently in a setting which allowed freedom of choice. Impressed by this, the staff subsequently created 'free learning environments' and 'open classrooms' (at a time when these were new for the sighted, even more so for the blind).

In yet another way, the art program revealed to us the values, the uniqueness, the beauty in their different ways of perceiving and knowing. Although in our society "handicaps are not recognized as differences or unique aspects of self, but [are] seen as inadequacies,"[33] the children with whom we worked enabled us to revise our perception of *handicap* from primarily *defect* to primarily *difference*. It was difficult to deny the existence of their disabilities or the many painful feelings they cause. One could not, in candor, say that their perceiving and creating in art was the same as the sighted, as has been suggested.[34] What we did find, however, was "that blindness may become the basis of a specific and unique creativeness,"[35] and that "sighted individuals may be missing great riches by the lack of kinesthetic awareness."[36]

As we opened ourselves to their unique ways of being, we learned to value their otherness, to treasure the ways in which they sensitized us. The children expanded our sensory awareness by referring to "clay that smells like candy," "ether markers," or "soft paper." They tuned us in to sounds, like Billy, who took intense pleasure in "a marker that squeaks a whole lot . . . that makes a whole lotta noise." Although one would not have chosen a felt-tip marker as the most appropriate tool for a boy with no vision, Billy taught us not to allow our own preconceptions to interfere with what media we might offer a handicapped child. Indeed, rather than finding a 'best' medium for these blind children, we discovered that almost every one selected his/her own preferred material from those available (clay, wood, wire, paint, chalk, markers, crayons, etc.).[37]

Through their sensitive use of their hands, those who could see nothing taught us about a kind of *free-floating tactile attention* in their approach to shape and form and texture. They seemed to know where to position their wood scraps, suggesting a *tactile aesthetic* different from the visual one. Indeed, when we put blindfolds on our eyes, we found that their sculptures felt quite different to us than they looked.[38] We wondered if there could be a kind of *tactile thinking* analogous perhaps to *visual thinking*.[39] Similarly, those with limited vision sensitized us to the excitement and impact for them of new visual experiences. Peter, for example, responded with a kind of *color shock* to the intense tempera paint hues. And Terry literally jumped for joy, after accidentally discovering that wet clay pressed on white paper made a visible mark.

Their use of materials was often quite free and inventive, perhaps in part because of a genuine naiveté and openness. David made, with foam tubes and pipe cleaners, a delightful "sweeper," and then zoomed around the room with it, making "sweeper noises." Greg used wood scraps and glue for his sculpture, "The Office of Peace and Quiet," with bright "lights" made of pipe cleaners. There was poetry in Peter's painting titles, like "A Mountain Hilltop 'Way out West," and "A Coyote Howling in the Night, with a Full Moon." And there was charm in his animistic description of "The Memorial Toll Bridge," which "lets the people walk across it, and it lets cars through it." Perhaps because of their developmental immaturity, they were less self-critical than most children their age. Thus, Peter could say of his creation with unself-conscious pride, "It's a pretty good sculpture!"

The art program also opened our eyes to their need and capacity for joy. For in the course of a short time, these children, who at first seemed lifeless and depressed, who were characterized by an observer in the first session as "compliant and docile,"[40] came alive. They began to smile, to move and laugh and speak more freely, and to show real pleasure in both process and product. Many have suggested that the need to play may be as fundamental as the need to love,[41] that we have an innate "exploratory urge,"[42] that "the opposite of interplay is deadness,"[43] or that "playfulness makes life worth living."[44]

The intensity of the children's sensory-motor pleasure in the art experience was inescapable. The paintings of David, for example, who often pretended that his brush strokes represented cars careening down roads and around curves, were "muscular equivalents of total experiencing."[45] The notion of expressive art activities as a tension-release is often found in the literature on art for the handicapped, and the vigorous pounding of clay and rhythmic zooming of arms and hands with brush or paint was eloquent testimony to that need. Because they must often inhibit and control their motoric responses in order to be safe, it seems especially important for blind children to have opportunities for free movement. As Burlingham has noted: "As soon as conditions of absolute safety are provided, the blind child too will hop and jump eagerly."[46]

Several authors who have taught art to the visually and orthopedically handicapped have noted the helpfulness of providing physical outlines or boundaries within which the children could work comfortably.[47, 48] We too found that bowls and trays were helpful containers, not only because they reduced the chance of mishap, but because they enabled the regressive and potentially 'naughty' or disorganizing behavior to remain 'contained' psychologically as well. Messy media like clay and fingerpaint initially stimulated anxiety in many, but such physical boundaries eventually helped them to master the discomfort.

The children not only 'let go' physically, but psychologically as well. Even in the initial evaluation sessions, strong feelings poured forth as if a dam had been opened. Staff observers were at first surprised, shocked, and uncomfortable at the many expressions of anger and distress. Then, as the program progressed, they saw a disruptive child happily doing constructive work and a quiet, withdrawn girl laughing and painting. The children thus opened our eyes to the intensity of their feelings, and their need to express them. From these complex children, the staff learned the need for emphasizing expressive arts and mental health learning opportunities (affective education) in the regular school curriculum.

One major value of art for these blind children was that they could be the active ones who did something to and with the materials, since so often they are passively led, dressed, doctored, etc. In another way, they were able to achieve active mastery through dramatic play with the art media. In reliving traumatic situations, the children often assumed the stronger and more controlling role rather than the original weaker and often helpless one. Thus Kay, a victim of child abuse, played the role of an angry, punitive, withholding mother to her clay "babies," screaming "You go to bed! You don't get no more food. You don't get nothin' to eat today!" They expressed many feelings in and through their art, safely relieving inner pressures while creating aesthetic forms.

FACILITATING CONDITIONS

From the children we learned the importance of flexibility and imagination in adapting the art learning situation to their needs. We saw too that it was essential to arrange a consistent, predictable, and physically negotiable environment within which blind children could have maximum independence.

We found that it was helpful to have available a variety of sturdy, good-quality materials which the children could truly control themselves. Each week we set out, in the same places on a table, the following materials: crayons (which made a mark that could be felt), felt-tip markers, chalk, fingerpaints, paper and fabric scraps, glue, scissors, clay, clay tools, and paper of different sizes, colors, and textures. Double easels with tempera paint and a choice of brushes were also available. Each child was encouraged to find and choose what s/he wanted to use in a location (table, floor, or easel) that was comfortable for him/her. If a child needed help in finding, choosing, or using materials, an adult was available as a facilitator.

We soon realized the importance of "a secure framework for the free activities."[49] For a blind child that might be a tray in which s/he can comfortably smear with fingerpaint, a chair which helps him/her stay focused on his/her easel painting, or the vocal and physical presence of a supportive, empathic adult.[50] For these children, who found it difficult to express freely their feelings, it was extremely helpful to have the symbolic safety of an art form. It was also essential to have as a listener an adult who did not fear the 'Pandora's box' of feeling in all of us.[51] Like all children, the blind have within them powerful negative feelings often denied by adults,[52] and many fewer ways of expressing and understanding them. Just as we saw the need to accept what the children could create independently, so we saw the need to accept (nonjudgmentally) all of their feelings and fantasies. There could be no right or wrong in art or inner thought.

We learned that these children stirred up in us many strong and uncomfortable feelings, and that we needed to be aware of our own responses to their disabilities. There was a natural inclination, a need to do things for them, perhaps in order to compensate for their handicaps. We had to constantly guard against making and keeping the children too dependent upon us. Conversely, fearful of too great an attachment, we found ourselves on occasion denying them a necessary degree of dependency. At times our expectations were too low, and we inadvertently interfered with their progress by premature interventions or excessive restrictions. At other times, we were tempted to pressure or seduce the children to work in a way that we knew would impress sighted adults. Although to some their crude creations might have seemed inartistic or ugly, we firmly agreed with Lowenfeld that "the most primitive creative work born in the mind of a blind person and produced with his own hands is of greater value than the most effective imitation."[53] Still, there were times when, despite our enthusiasm, we found it frustrating that progress was so slow as to be "almost imperceptible in some."[54]

These multiply handicapped children were not easy to work with, but the rewards were great. They did need more help, not in being told what to do or how to do it, but in becoming aware of what was available and in articulating their own creative schemes. We found a greater need, especially at first, for adult intervention and motivation, often to "simplify the learning situation for each individual child,"[55] or to help him get started, as in Lowenfeld's "closure" technique.[56] We found that we often needed to join into their play[57] because, like disadvantaged children who do not know how to play spontaneously, "the apparatus . . . is potential but requires nutriment—a feeding from without—for that particular apparatus to be nourished."[58, 59] Our facilitating role in the program was similar to Wills' suggestion that a young blind child's mother should function "as the child's auxiliary ego helping him to . . . organize his world without the aid of sight."[60]

CONCLUSION

It seemed, indeed, that the children in the art program grew perceptibly in the formal quality of their work, in the controlled freedom of their working process, and in their good feelings about themselves. The individual art interviews administered initially were repeated immediately following the seven weeks of half-hour group sessions. Of the 16 children actively involved, 13 were present for pre- and post-program evaluations. Ratings by pairs of observers indicated a gain for all children in all dimensions of the 24-item scale, especially striking in the areas of independence, flexibility, relaxation, involvement, and originality.

It was as if, in the process of creating their increasingly complex and personalized products, the children were also discovering and defining (and perhaps actualizing) themselves as unique individuals. And paradoxically, they were, in the process, teaching us—in spite of their blindness, they 'opened our eyes.' We learned that "eventual levels of attainment may be curtailed not only by whatever inherent limitations may be present in the children themselves, but also by the restrictions imposed upon them by adults."[61] We learned, too, that "the only meaningful readiness . . . is a flexibility and a willingness to meet the child as he is, and a belief in him as a whole person of immeasurable potential."[62]

NOTES

1. Consultation and education are offered to those concerned with promoting mental health through the clinic's Department of Community Services. The work described herein was conducted under its auspices and with the supervision of its first Director, Marvin I. Shapiro, MD, now in Burlingame, CA. We are also grateful to June Mullins, PhD, of the Department of Special Education and Rehabilitation of the University of Pittsburgh, who initially brought us together and whose support was helpful throughout the art program.

2. This program, part of Project No. 48-7022-02-959-01 (Phase II), was conducted pursuant to funds allocated through the Commonwealth of Pennsylvania under Title I of the Elementary and Secondary Education Act, Public Law 89-313 amendment.

3. "We'll Show You What We're Gonna Do!" (Art for Multiply Handicapped Blind Children) is a 27-minute, 16-millimeter sound film in black and white and color. It is available for purchase or rental from ACI Films, Inc., 35 W. 45th Street, New York, NY 10036.

4. J.M. Wolf, *The Blind Child with Concomitant Disabilities* (New York: American Foundation for the Blind Research Services, 1967), no. 16.

5. P. Moor, *No Place to Go* (New York: American Foundation for the Blind, 1961); idem, *No Time to Lose* (New York: American Foundation for the Blind, 1968).

6. A detailed description of the objective educational assessments is available [J. Klineman, *An Objective and Systematic Procedure for Developing an Educational Program for Young Visually Impaired Children with Concomitant Disabilities* (Ann Arbor, MI: University Microfilms, 1971), no. 71-26, 183].

7. J.A. Rubin, "A Diagnostic Art Interview," *Art Psychotherapy* 1 (1973): 31-43.

8. R.J. Saunders, *Art for the Mentally Retarded in Connecticut* (Hartford, CT: State Department of Education, 1967), p. 4.

9. B. Baumgartner and J.B. Schultz, *Reaching the Retarded through Art* (Johnstown, PA: Mafex, 1969).

10. J.W. Crawford, "Art for the Mentally Retarded," *Bulletin of Art Therapy* 2 (1962): 67-72.

11. C.D. Gaitskell and M.R. Gaitskell, *Art Education for Slow Learners* (Peoria, IL: Chas. A. Bennett, 1953).

12. Z. Lindsay, *Art Is for All: Arts and Crafts for Less Able Children* (New York: Taplinger, 1968).

13. V. Lowenfeld, *Creative and Mental Growth*, 3d ed. (New York: Macmillan, 1957), ch. 12.

14. Saunders, *Art for the Mentally Retarded in Connecticut*.

15. M. Site, "Art and the Slow Learner," *Bulletin of Art Therapy* 4 (1964): 3-19.

16. D.M. Uhlin, *Art for Exceptional Children* (Dubuque, IA: Wm. C. Brown, 1972).

17. W.C. McNeice and K.R. Benson, *Crafts for Retarded* (Bloomington, IL: McKnight and McKnight, 1964), p. 14.

18. A.C. Schmidt, *Craft Projects for Slow Learners* (New York: John Day, 1968), pp. 3-4.

19. R.J. Decker, "Creative Art Experience for Blind Children," *International Journal for the Education of the Blind* 9 (1960): 105.

20. M. Bains, "Art and Blind Children," *School Arts* 63 (January 1964): 3-9.

21. M.E. Freel, "Art for Visually Impaired Children," *Education of the Visually Handicapped* 1 (1969): 44-6.

22. S. Fukurai, *How Can I Make What I Cannot See?* (New York: Van Nostrand Reinhold, 1974).

23. C. Haupt, "Self-Realization—But Not through Painting," *New Outlook for the Blind* 60 (1966): 43-6.

24. C. Haupt, "Creative Expression through Art," *Education of the Visually Handicapped* 1 (1969): 41-3.

25. J. Kewell, *Sculpture by Blind Children* (New York: American Foundation for the Blind, 1955).

26. E. Kramer, *Art as Therapy with Children* (New York: Schocken Books, 1972).

27. Y. Lisenco, *Art Not by Eye* (New York: American Foundation for the Blind, 1971).

28. V. Lowenfeld, *The Nature of Creative Activity,* 2d ed. (London: Routledge and Kegan Paul, 1952).

29. Lowenfeld, *Creative and Mental Growth.*

30. V.H. Coombs, "Guidelines for Teaching Arts and Crafts to Blind Children in the Elementary Grades," *International Journal for the Education of the Blind* (March 1967): 79-83.

31. Lowenfeld, *Creative and Mental Growth,* p. 431.

32. Haupt, "Creative Expression through Art," p. 43.

33. C. Moustakas, *Psychotherapy with Children* (New York: Ballantine, 1968), p. 247.

34. C. Freund, "Teaching Art to the Blind Child Integrated with Sighted Children," *New Outlook for the Blind* 63 (1969): 205-10.

35. Lowenfeld, *Creative and Mental Growth,* p. 446.

36. Haupt, "Creative Expression through Art," p. 42.

37. While there is no question that Haupt (1966) and Lisenco (1971) are correct in stressing the need for a blind artist to have a responsive and meaningful three-dimensional medium; it seemed that for some of these multiply handicapped youngsters who were still in an exploratory, nonfigurative stage, sensory exploration of the media through sound and smell and kinesthesis were also valid.

38. Haupt, "Creative Expression through Art," p. 42.

39. R. Arnheim, *Visual Thinking* (Berkeley: University of California Press, 1969).

40. D. Burlingham, *Psychoanalytic Studies of the Sighted and the Blind* (New York: International Universities Press, 1972).

41. N.E. Curry, "Consideration of Current Basic Issues on Play," in *Play: The Child Strives toward Self-Realization* (Washington, DC: National Assoc. for the Education of Young Children, 1971), pp. 51-61.

42. D. Morris, *The Naked Ape* (New York: Ballantine, 1968), ch. 4.

43. E.H. Erikson, "Play and Vision," *Harvard Today* (May 1972): 13.

44. B. Sutton-Smith, "The Playful Modes of Knowing," in *Play: The Child Strives toward Self-Realization* (Washington, DC: National Assoc. for the Education of Young Children, 1971), p. 21.

45. T. Pasto, *The Space-Frame Experience in Art* (New York: A.S. Barnes, 1964), p. 67.

46. Burlingham, *Psychoanalytic Studies of the Sighted and the Blind*, p. 239.

47. Z. Lindsay, *Art and the Handicapped Child* (New York: Van Nostrand Reinhold, 1972), p. 15.

48. R.A. McVay, "A Crafts Program for Blind Children," *New Outlook for the Blind* 60 (1966): 243.

49. M. Milner, *On Not Being Able to Paint*, rev. ed. (New York: International Universities Press, 1957), p. 105.

50. J.A. Rubin, "Framework for Freedom," *The Arts in Education International Seminar Series* (Lancaster, MA: Doctor Franklin Perkins School, 1973).

51. B.S. Bloom et al., *Taxonomy of Educational Objectives, Handbook II: Affective Domain* (New York: David McKay, 1964), p. 91.

52. D. Baruch, "Little Mocking Bird," in *Existential Child Therapy*, ed. C. Moustakas (New York, Basic Books, 1966), pp. 30-44.

53. Lowenfeld, *Creative and Mental Growth*, p. 446.

54. Lindsay, *Art and the Handicapped Child*, p. 139.

55. Ibid.

56. Lowenfeld, *Creative and Mental Growth*, p. 435.

57. Moustakas, *Psychotherapy with Children*, ch. 6.

58. This statement was made by Rex Speers, MD, panel moderator at a conference on children's play.

59. Curry, "Consideration of Current Basic Issues on Play," p. 53.

60. D.M. Wills, "Some Observations on Blind Nursery School Children's Understanding of Their World," *Psychoanalytic Study of the Child* (1965): 363.

61. B.B. Weiner, "Arts and Crafts for the Mentally Retarded: Some Hypotheses," in *Expressive Arts for the Mentally Retarded*, ed. D. Ginglend (New York: National Assoc. for Retarded Children, 1967), p. 7.

62. Moustakas, *Psychotherapy with Children*, pp. 217-8.

Music for the Blind and Physically Handicapped from the Library of Congress

by Eyler Robert Coates

While the blind musician usually experiences some difficulty acquiring the music information s/he needs for playing or singing, blindness itself presents no real obstacles to the actual performance of music. With access to appropriate materials for training and practice, blind people are able to participate fully in music; many visually impaired people, in fact, select music as a career.

The opportunities for blind students to study music and to have ready access to music materials do not seem to exist in proportion to the need. Sighted musicians generally have more extensive and more readily accessible library resources than have blind musicians. The dearth of materials, of course, is inherent in the nature of the problem. Having braille music transcribed can be very expensive and can make the acquiring of a large personal library of materials impossible. This situation tends to make the blind musician more dependent than the sighted musician upon the resources of a publicly supported library program. Since blind people are scattered throughout the nation, any library serving blind musicians would need to cover a very wide geographic area, thereby preventing the immediate service that a sighted person might have from a library in his own community. Nevertheless, compensating for these problems is possible and poses a great challenge to those who work in this area.

Recognizing the importance of music to blind people, Congress in 1962 established the Library of Congress program of music for the blind. Later, when the scope of services performed by the Division for the Blind was enlarged to include the physically handicapped, music services were similarly extended. The Music Section of the National Library Service for the Blind and Physically Handicapped (NLS) is first a library, but it is also much more than a library. It not only "develops, maintains, and promotes the use of the national collection of musical scores and instructional texts," it is also charged with encouraging "the development of new techniques and materials for teaching." (Library of Congress Regulations, 213-4.2) This last responsibility—developing new techniques and materials—goes far beyond the traditional role of a music library.

Except for music, the NLS program is administered through a network of cooperating regional and subregional libraries located in almost every state. Although authorized to create regional deposits of music material, the Library has opted to have one music collection located in Washington, DC, to serve the entire nation. This decision makes very good economical and practical sense. It is possible to serve the music needs of blind musicians at a centralized location with only a fraction of the number that would be necessary in order to deposit even one or two with each network library.

With the collection located in Washington, DC, however, certain very real problems arise. Personal contact and promotion of music services at the local level is considerably more difficult. Many blind musicians and most music teachers are not even aware of the existence of the service. With circulation handled almost entirely through the mails, visits to the premises are rare, and it is difficult for those who use the services to understand the scope of the collection. Being unaware of the materials available for the occasional blind student s/he may have the opportunity to teach, the teacher without experience in teaching the blind is often reluctant to accept blind students, and this necessarily leads to lessened educational opportunities for blind musicians.

The remainder of this article describes the Library's collection in sufficient detail that a teacher with a blind student might have some concept of the range of available materials and services. The information might also suggest undeveloped areas that an experienced teacher might wish to pursue as a special project. The Library has always been open to such suggestions, and has, on several occasions, contracted with individuals to develop new techniques and materials in furtherance of the musical education of blind and physically handicapped students.

The National Library Service for the Blind and Physically Handicapped provides braille music scores and braille books about music; music instruction on cassettes and on records; music books on records and on magnetic tape; large-print music books and scores; music periodicals in braille, large print, on records, and cassettes; reference services in all areas of music; and training of volunteer music transcribers. The scope and emphasis in each of these areas vary. Users of large-print music scores, for example, have needs and interests quite different from users of braille.

THE COLLECTION

Braille Music

This is the largest segment of the collection, consisting of more than 25,000 items. Because of the effort required in learning to read braille music, it is a medium used primarily by students and professional musicians. The braille collection tends to reflect this more serious interest. It includes some popular music, but chief emphasis is on the classics. The level of difficulty for voice and the instruments most frequently played by blind individuals extends from method books for beginners through materials used by undergraduates in college music programs. The collection is quite extensive in piano and organ, somewhat less so in voice and violin and considerably less so in other instruments.

Any blind music student interested in becoming a professional musician would be well advised to learn braille music. The learning of braille music usually occurs under the instruction of a teacher, and NLS has several books to aid the blind student in this study. Bettye Krolick's *How to Read Braille Music,* available in both braille and print, can help the student who knows literary braille and wishes to acquire a basic knowledge of music braille on his/her own. It can also be used by a teacher who does not read braille music to guide the blind student in learning braille music.

Mrs. Krolick is also author of the Library of Congress publication, *Dictionary of Braille Music Signs.* This comprehensive reference work identifies and defines both standard and obsolete braille music signs used since 1888. It also provides supplementary information that explains the many facets of the braille music system.

Braille Books about Music

Music books available from Music Section—as distinct from those distributed through the network libraries—are specialized music texts. Many of these are texts that a student might need as a music major in college. All the usual college-level courses are covered including music history, harmony and theory, sightsinging, orchestration, form and analysis, and counterpoint.

Tape and Disc Recordings

Books on tape available from the Music Section are complete with music examples performed as scored in the text. There is also a collection of instructional tapes that include an analysis of performance problems along with an actual performance of certain compositions for the piano—the sole instrument for which these are available at present. The works are played slowly and explained where necessary so that the student can learn the correct notes to play by listening and through the oral directions. Many blind musicians develop their musical ear to such an extent that they can learn music more quickly this way than by any other means.

Instructional discs from Music Section, recorded at 33⅓ rpm, deal with various music subjects. Although many are available through normal commercial channels, they are provided by Music Section because they are especially useful to blind individuals, and they are not readily available through local sources. Some self-instructional methods for piano and guitar (described below under "Cassettes") are also available on disc. NLS attempts to locate and acquire all commercial discs that are instructional in nature and not dependent on accompanying printed materials. A large number of private individuals and nonprofit associations produce instructional discs that receive little notice or publicity. Recommendations from teachers and students for additions are always welcome.

Large-Print Music

This collection is for the partially sighted and emphasizes beginning methods, easy pieces for playing, and songs for recreational singing. The majority of users are young beginners with limited vision and older persons who have lost part of their sight. Therefore, there is an emphasis on method books and easy pieces for playing and singing. Advanced students are usually able to learn and memorize music with regular print editions and magnifying aids. Nevertheless, advanced pieces are gradually being added to the collection for the use of those who prefer to work with the printed score. The largest part of the collection is for piano and voice, but most other instruments are also represented.

When first produced for the NLS collection, large-print music was laboriously copied by hand on extra-large sheets of staff paper. Today, this music is produced by photoenlargement of the standard print edition. This process, developed by the Music Section, results in pages of manageable dimensions but with the notation four times its original size. *Large-Print Music: An Instruction Manual* was written by the Music Section for use by volunteers in preparing large-print music.

Cassettes

The most popular items in this collection are the beginning instructional courses, especially those for piano, organ, and guitar. Several other instructional courses are available, and beginning courses for recorder and accordion are nearing completion. These elementary methods are most useful to the student with a more casual interest in music, s/he may, for example, wish to learn to strum a few chords on the guitar in order to accompany his/her own singing. The courses do not require that the student learn to read either braille or large-print music. Nevertheless, they are based on solid musical fundamentals, and a student could later study music more seriously if s/he chose.

NLS also makes available a collection of instructional cassettes containing discussions, demonstrations, and rehearsals of music and interviews with well-known musicians.

Periodicals

The *Musical Mainstream* is an NLS publication, issued bimonthly in braille, cassette, and large-print formats. It includes a sampler of articles from national magazines as well as occasional original articles related to the study, performance, and teaching of the classics. It also contains a special column about music braille notation or other topics of interest and lists new NLS music titles in all formats.

Contemporary Sound Track: A Review of Pop, Jazz, Rock, and Country is an NLS bimonthly publication for those interested in the popular scene. It is available only on 15/16 ips cassette and includes articles selected from a large number of national magazines in this area.

Several other music magazines are available through the national library network. These include *Overtones* (bimonthly), a braille sampler similar to the *Musical Mainstream; Braille Musical Magazine* (monthly), a British publication; *Braille Piano Tuners' Journal* (bimonthly), for the piano tuner and repairman; and *Music Journal* (10 issues a year) and *Stereo Review* (monthly) on 8 rpm disc.

The *Musical Article Guide* is a well-known quarterly index of significant articles appearing in a large number of US magazines. NLS makes it available in braille and on cassette, and enables the reader to order recorded or brailled copies of the articles. This service opens to blind and physically handicapped readers a large portion of the periodical literature in music.

Popular Music Lead Sheets is an irregular braille publication of NLS. It contains popular songs of the past and present with the melody, chord symbols, and words to all verses.

All of the above periodical publications are available on free subscription to eligible individuals and institutions serving blind music students.

BORROWING PROCEDURES

Any blind or physically handicapped individual who is unable to use conventionally printed material is eligible for services. Readers must file an application form with either the Music Section or their regional library. All music materials except those distributed through the network libraries are circulated directly to readers free from the Music Section, National Library Service for the Blind and Physically Handicapped, Library of Congress, Washington, DC 20542. Requests for music materials received by a network library are forwarded to the Music Section, but patrons are encouraged to send their requests directly to the Music Section for speedier service.

Materials are loaned for two months and renewable for an indefinite number of two-month periods thereafter as long as they are being used. Materials requested, but not available because in circulation, can be placed on reserve.

A complete catalog of all materials in the music collection is nearing completion. Under the series title *Music and Musicians*, catalogs of material in every format will be available in large print and the format that is the subject of the list. Catalogs have been issued thus far for large-print scores and books, instructional disc recordings, with separate catalogs for piano, organ, voice, and choral music in braille. Catalogs of instrumental braille music, talking books about music, and braille books about music are planned for the near future and will complete the series.

A packet of brochures and other descriptive material will be sent to any teacher or blind music student on request, together with any catalogs that may also be of interest.

WATS Telephone Service

Patrons may use the NLS IN-WATS telephone number (800/424-8567) provided the call is related only to music services and materials and concerns matters requiring quick action or involving problems that should be discussed with the Music Section staff. Patrons with routine requests are encouraged to send their requests to the Music Section by mail.

ADDITIONAL SERVICES

Reference Services

The Music Section has a print reference collection and will perform reference services for blind or physically handicapped music patrons. Inquiries that go beyond the scope of this collection can be relayed by Music Section to the Music Division of the Library, one of the world's great music libraries with outstanding resources in all areas of music.

Music Enlarging and Transcribing

The Music Section does not produce materials as a service to individuals. It will, however, consider all requests and have material transcribed if an item would make a suitable addition to the collection. Persons wishing material transcribed for their own use, i.e., material that would not be appropriate for general circulation, should attempt to have the material produced by a volunteer agency or individual transcriber. The directory, "Volunteers Who Produce Books," lists agencies in each state that do volunteer copying and transcribing. If a blind person is unable to locate a suitable agency, the Music Section can help in locating an individual volunteer or paid transcriber.

Other Agencies that Supply Materials

Recording for the Blind, 215 East 58th Street, New York, NY 10022, has a large number of music texts on tape in its collection. These are available on free loan to blind and physically handicapped persons. RFB will also record books on request. Their holdings are listed in their "Catalog of Recorded Books." NLS does not sell any of the materials in its collection, but some braille music may be purchased from the American Printing House for the Blind in Louisville, Kentucky; National Braille Press in Boston, Massachusetts; National Braille Association Braille Book Bank in Rochester, New York; and the Royal National Institute for the Blind in London, England. The National Braille Book Bank can provide thermoform copies (duplicates made on a plasticized paper by a heat process) of braille masters in the NLS collection. Large-print scores produced by the Music Section are not available for purchase from any source.

The Music Section responds to requests for specific compositions or works of music by conducting a thorough search of the resources of other agencies, as well as its own collections. Referrals to other sources are made, as appropriate.

SERVICES TO THE PHYSICALLY HANDICAPPED

Service to the physically handicapped is limited by law to those who cannot use or handle conventionally printed material. Since most physically handicapped people who can play an instrument or sing can also use conventionally printed music scores, the Music Section is limited to furnishing music books and texts to those who are unable to hold a book or turn pages.

NLS music library services are constantly growing and moving into new areas. In the immediate future efforts will be concentrated on developing additional instructional material in recorded form, so that eventually courses for all popular instruments will be available. Other areas of activity include testing the concept of dictated music notation in cassette form as an alternative to braille in some circumstances; utilizing international exchange and interlibrary loan to expand resources; and encouraging increased use of the reference services of the Music Section by students, teachers, and professionals. NLS welcomes the participation of service users and interested music specialists in the development of the program. Suggestions for new projects and services are always welcome.

Developmental Restaging: Meeting the Mental Health Needs of Handicapped Students in the Schools

by John D. Swisher

INTRODUCTION

Mental disability may not be physical whereas physical disability usually has some degree of mental disability.[1] Fletcher's view from 25 years ago remains an important realization in counseling for the positive mental health of disabled students. Physically disabled students are not also emotionally disturbed, but rather these students experience significant readjustment problems as one phase of their total (re)habilitation. This article attempts to describe the major areas of adjustment faced by physically handicapped students and suggests implications for a developmental restaging program in the schools.

DEVELOPMENTAL PERSPECTIVE

In considering the normal development and/or positive mental health of physically disabled students, it is important to recognize two basic developmental principles.

1. Normal development of congenitally disabled students is frequently impeded in its course. The term *impeded* as used in this context implies that the normal progression of the student through stages of developmental and/or mental health has been negatively influenced by the student's environment. This slowing may occur, first, through a loving family that tends to help too much and consequently greatly prolongs the individual's ability to become independent. Human nature propels individuals toward independence, but a genuine fear by a family for the disabled person's physical and/or psychological safety typically results in fewer opportunities for independence. Parents of these individuals need a great deal of support from the school team. One

recommendation would be for the school to play a role in the development of parent groups for parents of handicapped children that would allow parents to vent their frustrations and share ideas, common problems, and general emotional support.

Other environmental factors which also impede development are the physical barriers (e.g., steps) which bar access to many otherwise normal social experiences and opportunities. Each school should survey the barriers it creates which are not under the purview of the building code but are all part of the impeding process. For example, even when ramps are provided, it is important to consider whether they are conveniently located or do they require extra effort to use?

One's peers and teachers in their well-intended efforts can also create dependency rather than independency. The quality of helping should be guided by the criterion of independence.

When congenitally disabled students enter the school environment either as new students or as transfer students, they should be given the opportunity to review and enhance their developmental progress.

2. Normal development may need to be recycled when the onset of disability occurs at a later stage of maturation.

An individual born with a physical disability has a somewhat different set of consequences than an individual who experiences the sudden onset of a physical change. Depending on the particular age/stage of development during which the individual contracts a disease (e.g., juvenile arthritis) or experiences an accident and suffers some physical consequence (e.g., paralysis), the individual should be provided with the opportunity to systematically recycle through the preceding stages of development. The obvious reason for this need is that the individual has a new physique and must redefine himself/ herself in terms of self-concept, interpersonal relations, and a role in the school as a social institution.

The concept of recycling through stages of physical development is frequently employed in certain forms of physical therapy and a similar concept and process needs to be developed for physically handicapped students in order to create the most promising climate for positive mental health. While no such program exists for the schools today, there are excellent materials available in the field which could be adapted for the development of a comprehensive program (see References at the end of this article).

DEVELOPMENTAL DIMENSIONS

Regardless of the onset of a physical problem, it is important to consider the major stages of development and some of their specific implications for the mental health of disabled students.

There are several megatheories of normal development[2] as well as emerging microtheories.[3] Vicary[4] and Swisher[5] have attempted to synthesize the common elements or stages that occur frequently in many developmental stage theories. Based on their work, the following three stages of development appear to be common to many developmental schemes.

1. *Intrapersonal*. This is the earliest phase of development and it involves defining one's self-concept, understanding one's strengths and weaknesses, clarifying one's values, and defining one's goals and aspirations. These tasks, skills, and processes tend to occur in childhood, and success in this stage influences the extent of success in subsequent stages.

2. *Interpersonal*. Early in life, a host of complex relationships must be established with others in one's environment. These relationships provide opportunities for expressing one's identity and for refining as well as redefining one's self. Furthermore, the quality of these relationships form the basis for much of one's daily living and existence. The ability to enter into sharing and caring relationships with others contributes to very positive mental health. Skills in this domain include effective and reflective listening, assertiveness, coping with peer influence, parenting, etc.

3. *Extrapersonal*. As one matures, the focus of one's energy shifts to a concern for the well-being of society and its institutions. The skills necessary for coping with this stage of development (e.g., Erikson's Generativity) include *coping* with situations that cannot be changed, *contributing* to those institutions that reflect one's values (political, religious), and *changing* those situations that can be changed. The wisdom to know the difference notwithstanding, this phase of development greatly affects a person's level of learning and vocational expression.

IMPLEMENTING DEVELOPMENTAL RESTAGING

For well-being and general mental health, it behooves the schools to provide opportunities for handicapped individuals to discover and define themselves, develop interpersonal skills, and create a role for themselves in society. One way of creating such a program would be to involve small groups of handicapped students in a series of group meetings and discuss each of these topics or stages of development. It would be particularly important to ask these individuals what they have experienced in each stage, how they have resolved problems, and what they would recommend to their peers that might be helpful as a means of reworking their developmental process. Another important task for this group would be to review the various programs for psychological and/or affective education. Their adaptations and insights would be extremely useful in selecting materials for a program for the disabled student.

TABLE 1 Selected Developmental Education Materials for Review and Adaptation to Developmental Restaging

Stages of Development	ELEMENTARY (K–6)	JUNIOR HIGH (7–9)	SENIOR HIGH (10–12)
Intrapersonal	*Developing Understanding of Self and Others* (Dinkmeyer, 1970) *Dimensions of Personality* (Limbacher, 1970) *I Am Loveable and Capable* (Simon, 1973)	*Alternatives to Drug Abuse* (Cohen, 1973) *Getting It Together* (Mattox, 1975) *Meeting Yourself Halfway* (Simon, 1974) *The Centering Book* (Hendricks and Wells, 1975)	*Taking Charge of Your Life* (Howe, 1977) *Values Clarification: Handbook of Practical Strategies for Teachers and Students* (Simon, Howe, and Kirschenbaum, 1972)
Interpersonal	*Life Skills for Mental Health* (Dixon, Frye, Tetel, Vicary and Wiggins, 1977) *Magic Circle* (Human Development Institute, 1970) *Super Me Super You* (Krughoff and Zerkin, 1974)	*Explorations in Social and Peer Influence* (Shute, 1977) *Learning Together and Alone* (Johnson and Johnson, 1975) *Health Games Students Play* (Engs. Barnes, and Wantz, 1975)	*Peer Program for Youth* (Hebersen, 1973) *Values in Sexuality* (Marrison and Price, 1975) *Reaching Out* (Johnson, 1972)
Extrapersonal	*100 Ways to Enhance Self-Concept in the Classroom* (Canfield and Wells, 1976) *Role Play in the Elementary School* (Furness, 1976) *The New Games Book* (Fluegelman, 1974)	*Clarifying Values through Subject Matter* (Harwin, Simon, and Kirschenbaum, 1973) *Classroom Climate* (Withall, 1962) *Life Career Game* (Boocock, 1968)	*Getting It Together: Moral Dilemmas for the Class Room* (Maddox, 1975) "*Field Theory and Differential Press: Implications for Counseling*" (Herr, 1965) *Dynamic Consumer Decision Making* (J.C. Penney, 1972) "*Voluntary Simplicity*" (Elgin and Mitchell, 1977)

MATERIALS FOR DEVELOPMENTAL RESTAGING

Most of the materials in the references are available through the National Humanistic Education Center, 110 Spring Street, Saratoga Springs, NY 12866, or the Philadelphia Humanistic Education Center, 8504 Germantown Avenue, Philadelphia, PA 19118, or directly from the publishers. The total cost for the selected materials would be approximately $300.

Materials were selected from an almost infinite number of possibilities. In order to narrow down the list, the guidelines below were followed in the final selection.

1. Recency.
2. Critical topic.
3. Research support.
4. Health related.
5. Activity oriented.

The materials have been categorized according to the most appropriate developmental theme and age level (see Table 1). Not all of the materials meet all of the criteria, and there are many other possibilities. Regardless of what materials are used, of ultimate importance are the reactions and suggestions of handicapped students in the process of creating a developmental restaging program. The process of designing such a program would also be of considerable developmental benefit to the handicapped students involved.

NOTES

1. F. Fletcher, "The Role of Counseling in Rehabilitation," *Journal of Counseling Psychology* 4 (1954): 240-3.

2. E.H. Erikson, *Childhood and Society* (New York: Norton, 1950).

3. L. Kohlberg, "The Cognitive-Developmental Approach to Moral Education," *Phi Delta Kappan* 10 (1975): 670-7.

4. J.R. Vicary, "Toward an Adaptive Developmental Education," in *The Disciplines, Current Movements and Instructional Methodology,* ed. L. Rubin (Boston: Allyn and Bacon, 1977).

5. J.D. Swisher, "Mental Health—The Core of Preventative Health Education," *Journal of School Health* 46 (1976): 386-91.

REFERENCES

Boocock, S. *Life Career Game*. New York: Western, 1968.

Canfield, J. and Wells, H. *100 Ways to Enhance Self Concept in the Classroom*. Englewood Cliffs, NJ: Prentice-Hall, 1976.

Cohen, A. Y. *Alternatives to Drug Abuse: Steps toward Prevention*. Washington, DC: National Clearinghouse for Drug Abuse Information, US Government Printing Office, 1973.

Dinkmeyer, D. *Developing Understanding of Self and Others*. Circle Pines, MN: American Guidance Services, 1970.

Dixon, B.; Frye, B.; Tetel, J.,eds. *Life Skills for Mental Health: A Guide for Trainers*. Atlanta, GA: Prevention Unit, Georgia Department of Human Resources, 1977.

Elgin, D. and Mitchell, A. "Voluntary Simplicity." *The Futurist* 21 (1977): 200-62.

Engs, R.; Barnes, S.; Wantz, Y. *Health Games Students Play*. Dubuque, IA: Kendall/Hunt, 1975.

Fluegelman, A. *The New Games Book*. Garden City, NY: Doubleday, 1974.

Furness, P. *Role-Play in the Elementary School: A Handbook for Teachers*. New York: Hart, 1976.

Gelatt, H. et al. *Decisions and Outcomes*. Princeton, NJ: College Entrance Examination Board, 1973.

Harmin, M.; Kirschenbaum, H.; Simon, S. *Clarifying Values through Subject Matter*. Minneapolis, MN: Winston Press, 1973.

Hebeisen, A. *Peer Program for Youth*. Minneapolis, MN: Augsburg, 1973.

Hendricks, G. and Wills, R. *The Centering Book: Awareness Activities for Children, Parents and Teachers*. Newark, NJ: Prentice Hall, 1975.

Herr, E. "Field Theory and Differential Press: Implications for Counseling." *Personnel and Guidance Journal* 43 (1965): 586-90.

Howe, L. W. *Taking Charge of Your Life*. Niles, IL: Argus Communications, 1977.

Human Development Institute. *Magic Circle: An Overview of the Human Development Program*. La Mesa, CA: Human Development Institute, 1970.

J.C. Penney Company. *Dynamic Consumer Decision Making*. New York: Educational and Consumer Relations Department, J.C. Penney, 1972.

Johnson, D. and Johnson, R. *Learning Together and Alone: Cooperation, Competition, and Individualization*. Englewood Cliffs, NJ: Prentice Hall, 1975.

Johnson, D. *Reaching Out—Interpersonal Effectiveness and Self-Actualization*. Newark, NJ: Prentice-Hall, 1972.

Krughoff, G. and Zerkin, E. *Super Me. Super You*. Washington, DC: National Coordinating Council for Drug Education, 1973.

Limbacher, W. *Dimensions of Personality Series*. Dayton, OH: Pflaum/Standard, 1970.

Matton, A. *Getting It Together*. San Diego, CA: Pennant, 1975.

Morrison, E. and Price, M. *Values in Sexuality: A New Approach to Sex Education*. New York: Hart, 1974.

Shute, R. *Explorations in Social and Peer Influence: A Resource Manual for Teachers—Grades Seven Through Ten*. University Park, PA: Pennsylvania Addictions Prevention Laboratory, Pennsylvania State University, 1977.

Simon, S.; Howe, L.; Kirschenbaum, H. *Values Clarification: A Handbook of Practical Strategies for Teachers and Students* (Teacher's Guide). New York: Hart, 1972.

Simon, S. *I am Loveable and Capable*. Niles, IL: Argus Communications, 1977.

————. *Meeting Yourself Halfway*. Niles, IL: Argus Communications, 1974.

Smith, M.F. *The Valuing Approach to Career Education*. Waco, TX: Education Achievement Corporation, 1973-74.

Withall, J. "A Symposium on Conceptual Frameworks for Analysis of Classroom Interaction." *Journal of Experimental Education* (1962): 307-8.

Juvenile Fiction about the Orthopedically Handicapped

by Madeleine Cohen Oakley

Within the past few years, heretofore "forgotten children"—the blind, the deaf, the retarded, the emotionally disturbed, the brain-damaged, and, of course, the racial minorities—have all received a great deal of attention in education and librarianship, but those affected by a motor, that is, orthopedic handicap have not been the object of similar concern.[1] Although there is actually a significant body of work for children on this theme, one finds practically no indication of it in the professional literature, the bibliographies, or the other secondary material. The subject is almost ignored and, when treated at all, is most often handled poorly and inadequately. There are numerous articles, booklets, etc., describing reading aids and library services for the handicapped, but little critical material about or compilations of the related literature itself.

Charlotte Huck and Doris Young, for example, in their standard text, *Children's Literature in the Elementary School,* start a discussion of "Learning to Live with Physical Handicaps" with the example of Jerrold Beim's *Freckle Face,* the story of a girl whose so-called handicap is that of having freckles—"a minor problem, it may be serious if perceived by the child as a barrier to self-realization."[2] While it is true that having freckles may be disturbing to a child, and that this is a legitimate theme for a book, for Huck and Young to consider freckles a physical handicap is practically an insult to people who have to cope with major physical problems which are barriers in fact, not merely perceived as such. Surely a book about the problem of having freckles is not a proper introduction to a serious discussion of physical handicaps such as cerebral palsy, blindness, and polio.

May Hill Arbuthnot's literary consideration of the physically handicapped is no better. In fact, her well-known text, *Children and Books,* contains no section on the topic at all, and it is nowhere to be found in the index. All Ms. Arbuthnot has to offer on the subject are brief phrases in the midst of other discussions. When speaking for example of Marguerite De Angeli's

The Door in the Wall, Arbuthnot comments, "The book is of great interest to all children, and brings special comfort to the handicapped."[3] We might hope for something more than "comfort." The New York Public Library's Central Children's Room, to give one example of a failure in acquisitions policy or in assigning subject headings, had only three catalog cards with the heading, "Handicapped—Stories."

The literature itself is actually quite sizable, and within it one can find examples of both the best and worst in children's books. The importance of good books about the handicapped is dual; it is, of course, desirable for handicapped youngsters to find within some books that with which they can identify, but it is equally important for physically normal children to learn intelligent understanding of the handicapped. In other words, such books are valuable in helping children towards understanding both of self and of others. There are many sound values in much of the juvenile fictional literature concerning handicapped individuals, values important to communicate to all children. This article will present a survey of the field of juvenile fiction about the physically handicapped, and attempt to demonstrate its importance.

In assessing the relative merits of the books discussed, I have considered factors related to the subject of the handicapped in addition to the standard literary considerations of plot, characterization, and dialogue. Such factors include the accuracy of the description of the handicapped involved and its effect on the individual, and the degree of realism with which other characters relating to the handicapped central character are portrayed. Equally important are the honesty of the advice offered the handicapped character about his/her condition and future possibilities, and the soundness of the author's underlying philosophy.

Perhaps it would be useful to discuss first an example of the wrong kind of book—I have purposely not used the word *literature* here. This genre manages to combine the worst features of teenage romance, career novel, and inspirational tract when it appears as fiction about the handicapped, and unfortunately it is this type of book which may first come to mind when considering the field. *Sally, Star Patient,* by Alice Ross Colver, is a star offender, and in fact is unequivocally one of the worst books I have ever come across in any field. It does not even have the excuse of being old-fashioned, since it was published in 1968.

Supposedly about Sally, a high school senior who has cerebral palsy, the book is actually more about her unofficial physical therapist (PT), Janet. Speaking from personal experience as a former PT, I have never met a therapist like Janet, presented here as a mindless, melodramatic piece of cardboard. Upon meeting Sally, Janet says, "You're wonderful . . . you're special"— one does not talk this way to a new acquaintance. Ms. Colver's characters are always murmuring things: " 'Oh tragic!' Janet murmured" (when told that Sally has cerebral palsy). *Sally, Star Patient* is one long cliché: it is a compendium of simple-minded, improbable dialogue, out of touch with the modern world. The constant use of italicized words is irritating, and the syntax is often awkward; "so complete," for example, or, "sorority club."

The antifeminism of the book is also disturbing. Ms. Colver is constantly preoccupied with an artificial conflict between being a physical therapist and a wife-and-mother. Her impassioned rhetoric about motherhood and being fair to one's husband make it hard to believe that this book was written during the past decade. The business world, she tells us, is where one deals with the "realities of life"; this from someone who is working with a cerebral palsy victim—how much more real could one get? Her young-marrieds details are too cute, and the expressions of love and jealousy are juvenile in conception. Janet, looking at her husband while he is driving, "feels sorry for all the girls who don't have one" (a husband, that is).

Especially since Sally is presented as only mildly handicapped, it is simply not believable for a therapist to assume that Sally could not marry, should she so desire, and to want to discourage her accordingly. When Sally does in fact meet a man whom she eventually marries, Ms. Colver has her say: "I'm a cripple, and Howard isn't; I must never forget that."[4] What a terrible viewpoint to present from or about a handicapped person.

There are one or two good points in *Sally, Star Patient*. The fact of Sally's learning how to drive is useful for readers to know, her anxiety about going to college is legitimately expressed, and there is an excerpt of one passage spoken by Sally toward the end of the book which is worth noting: "What I'm trying to say is that I don't feel any longer that I have to handle a cup and saucer as well as everyone else does. If I can manage it like *myself*—in my own way—that'll be enough. . . ."[5]

I have discussed *Sally, Star Patient* at such length to make clear all the things that books in this field should not be. *Triumph Clear*, by Lorraine Beim, is another example of nonliterature about the handicapped, although it is not an offensive book and does have some merit. Dated (it was written in 1946), and, as one could imagine from the title, oversentimental, *Triumph Clear* is concerned with the treatment of polio. Ms. Beim does present some realistic situations and personality problems, and discusses some issues of consequence. These include the importance of not pitying the handicapped (the problem of self-pity is also discussed), and the need to see handicapped persons for what they are as individuals, not as *stereotyped cripples*.

One of the oldest juvenile fictions about a handicapped child is also one of the best. Dinah Maria Mulock's *The Little Lame Prince*, although a fairy tale, is actually a very sound and realistic story as well. Within the framework of a moving, charming tale, it offers valuable advice to the lame boy: "You are a prince, and you must behave as such—let us see what we can do; how much I can do for you, or *show you how to do for yourself*"[6] [italics added]. In this instance, as throughout the book, Ms. Mulock recognizes the fundamental importance of teaching, helping, enabling the handicapped individual to become as independent as possible: "[he came to] almost forget his lameness—which was never cured. However, the cruel things which had been once foreboded of him did not happen . . . with the help of a [wonderful pair of crutches], though he never walked easily or gracefully, he did manage to walk so as to be quite independent and such was the love his people bore him that they never heard the sound of his crutches on the marble palace floors without a leap of the heart, for they knew that good was coming to them whenever he approached them."[7] The writer can vouch for this last reaction: a close friend and colleague is physically handicapped; when we hear her crutches and braces, we know Ruth is coming and we are glad.

Ms. Mulock's observations are consistently astute: "The sense of the *inevitable,* as grown-up people call it—that we cannot have things as we want them to be, but as they are, and that we must learn to bear them and make the best of them—this lesson, which everybody has to learn soon or late—came, alas! sadly soon, to the poor boy. He fought against it for awhile, and then, quite overcome, turned and sobbed bitterly on his godmother's arm. She comforted him—I do not know how, except that love always comforts. . . ."[8] Or, "When we see people suffering or uncomfortable, we feel very sorry for them; but when we see them bravely bearing their sufferings, and making the best of their misfortunes, it is quite a different feeling. We respect, we admire them. One can respect and admire even a little child.[9]

Perhaps most important, the author gets into the mind of the handicapped child. " 'You're no good to me,' he said, patting [his feeble, useless legs] mournfully. 'You never will be any good to me. I wonder why I had you at all; I wonder why I was born at all, since I was not to grow up like other little boys. *Why* not?' "[10] Ms. Mulock respects the child, and answers him intelligibly and honestly: "even if he had put [the question] to his mother, she could only have answered it, as we have to answer many as difficult things, by simply saying 'I don't know.' There is much we do not know, and can not understand. . . ."

Similar in spirit to *The Little Lame Prince* is Marguerite De Angeli's *The Door in the Wall,* a Newbery winner. Beautifully illustrated by the author, well-researched, and carefully written, *The Door in the Wall* is good historical fiction; its medieval setting lends special interest. The book is accurately described on the jacket blurb as "A dramatic story of Robin, crippled son of a great lord, who proves his courage and wins his king's recognition—set against a background of thirteenth-century England." The theme, as indicated by the title, is that "Thou hast only to follow the wall far enough and there will be a door in it," and it is carried through the book.[11] "Whether thou'lt walk soon I know not. This I know. We must teach thy hands to be skillful in many ways, and we must teach thy mind to go about whether thy legs will carry thee or no. For reading is another door in the wall. . . .''[12] Or, "Remember, even thy crutches can be a door in the wall,"[13] and, "Each of us has his place in the world . . . If we cannot serve in one way, there is always another. If we do what we are able, a door always opens to something else."[14] Ms. De Angeli emphasizes dignity, common sense, and honesty. " 'Sir,' he addressed his father, 'mind you not that I must go thus, bent over, and with these crutches to help me walk?' . . . Gravely Sir John answered, 'The courage you have shown, the craftsmanship proven by the harp, and the spirit in your singing all make so bright a light that I cannot see whether or no your legs are misshappen.' ''[15]

In the book's most beautiful and important passage, the author has captured the essence of the situation: " 'What think you, Brother Luke, shall I ever straighten?' 'I know not what to think about that.' Brother Luke sighed. Then he lifted his head and said firmly, 'God alone knows whether thou'lt straighten or no. I know not. But this I tell thee. A fine and beautiful life lies before thee, because thou hast a lively mind and a good wit. Thine arms are very strong and sturdy. Swimming hath helped to make them so, but only because thou hast had the will to do it. Fret not, my son, none of us is perfect. It is better to have crooked legs than a crooked spirit. We can only do the best we can with what we have. That after all, is the measure of success! what we do with what we have.' ''[16]

Esther Forbes' *Johnny Tremain,* also a Newbery winner, is another distinguished book of historical fiction whose protagonist is handicapped. Set in Boston of the American Revolution, the book tells the story of its fictional title character, whose crippled hand, injured in the silver shop where he was an apprentice, is an important aspect of his life. There is realistic treatment of others' remarks and reactions, ranging from " 'That's quite a recent burn'—It was the first intelligent remark any man, woman, or child had made about Johnny's hand . . .''[17] to "Don't touch me! Don't touch me with that dreadful hand!''[18] Johnny's actions and reactions are realistic, too; his initial desire for revenge, which eventually disappears, his ultraself-consciousness—at first "unconsciously trying to impress others with the injury morbidly," which also decreases, and his having to change his plans and life's work.[19] Johnny comes across as a multidimensional, real person.

The historical portrait is informative and absorbingly interesting. There are occasional instances of unlikely foreknowledge, and it is too bad that the author chose a melodramatic profighting ending; she had kept a good balance between the pressures for and against war and fighting until then.

Within the past decade or so, a number of good books about the handi-capped have been published for children. *Mine for Keeps,* by Jean Little, is set in Ontario, and is the story of a cerebral palsied little girl returning to live at home with her family after a long stay in a residential school for CPs. A complete story, peopled with real characters and dealing with problems besides that of Sal's cerebral palsy, *Mine for Keeps* is a realistic portrayal of Sal, her family, and friends. Jean Little gives good, simple explanations of cerebral palsy, and exercises common sense; she recognizes the dramatic or overdramatic for what it is.

The illustrations by Lewis Parker are pleasant and informative, as are the details in the story—specially designed clothing for Sal, for example, and modifications of furniture. The book, to its credit, mentions problems concerning the toileting needs of handicapped children. Sal's family is depicted with good humor and realism; her parents are very understanding, but believable; her older sister tends to overprotect Sal and to try to live her life for her (sometimes more out of her own needs than to protect Sal), and is herself able to grow; Sal is able to help one of her new friends with an important family problem of her own. *Mine for Keeps* is a thoroughly enjoyable book.

Wheels for Ginny's Chariot, by Eulene W. Luis and Barbara F. Millar, tells of a high school girl who is paralyzed from the waist down as a result of an automobile accident and is now confined to a wheelchair. We meet her as she is about to begin attendance at a special public school for the handicapped in Florida. This is a generally realistic and interesting story, including useful details for the nonhandicapped reader and good descriptions of Ginny's feelings of frustration and being different. Her friends' initial reactions of awkwardness and discomfort are presented well, too. There are accurate depictions of strangers' as well as friends' reactions. Some are oversympathetic and effusive in feeling sorry for Ginny; some are impatient; others are crude; and many people thoughtlessly do not bother to notice or pay attention at all, and are thus unable to be of help.

The book demonstrates an important point: once Ginny is able to accept herself and her situation, as well as other handicapped persons, she is then able to interact again with her old, nonhandicapped friends. The importance of a lack of pity and sentimentality in working with handicapped children is appropriately stressed—they are children first, handicapped children second. Descriptions of the special school, its variously handicapped students, school trips, therapy, etc., are generally accurate, although there are one or two inaccuracies or omissions; Ginny is surprised about her going swimming— this probably would have been mentioned to her earlier; the obvious and enormously important problems of sex and bathroom activities are totally absent from the book; and it would certainly be nice if all school-bus drivers of hydraulic lift buses for the handicapped were as unfailingly courteous, helpful, understanding, cooperative, and full of good cheer as those portrayed here!

Ivan Southall has written an unusual and very interesting book, *Let the Balloon Go,* which takes place in Australia. A very well-written account of a boy with mild cerebral palsy involvement, *Let the Balloon Go* is an excellent portrayal of some of the possible personality problems and frustrations of such a child. Many of John's problems stem from his mother's problems regarding him and from other children's attitudes towards him. This book shows effectively that a handicapped child must be allowed to grow; to take chances and risk accidents just as a normal child does. Southall gets into the child's imagination and describes superbly how John hears and perceives things. He is less accurate and helpful in medical details, however, and in his descriptions of the visible effects of the child's condition.

Another interesting setting is provided in *Other Sandals*, by Sally Watson, a story of life in Israel and, more specifically, of Eytan, a boy with a leg injury and limp resulting from an automobile accident. Thoroughly researched, *Other Sandals* vividly describes Israeli life, both on a *kibbutz* (communal farm) and in the city. It smoothly incorporates many non-English words—Hebrew, Arabic, and even French, and provides Hebrew and Arabic glossaries. Although the book is politically slanted toward Israel, the Arab-Israeli conflict is handled well in personal terms—Israeli and Arab characters form an integral part of the story, and Arab culture is treated with interest and respect.

Ms. Watson's presentation becomes awkward at one point, when she has explanations of kibbutz life spoken among the kibbutz children and from parent to child—one would be unlikely to suddenly explain one's life-style and circumstances to others who live within it. Also, the surprise element of the ending is somewhat unrealistic as it is presented. These are only minor flaws, however, in an otherwise excellent novel which is highly informative and enlightening about another way of life as well as about handicaps and handicapped individuals.

The characterization is excellent throughout *Other Sandals;* one really gets to know and like all the featured protagonists. Ms. Watson treats her characters and situations with a sense of perspective and a good sense of humor. She presents a graphic picture of Eytan's initial resentment and fear, and describes clearly and realistically how the adults and the other, well-intentioned children react and try to help, and how Eytan works all this out in his own mind. The story contains an effective, low-keyed example of a handicapped adult character who has suffered a leg amputation and is living a full, enjoyable life. The author understands some of the bitterness that a handicapped individual may develop: ''It hurts not in his leg, but in his heart and mind . . . Often a person will have something that is not a real handicap, but only affects the appearance, like . . . scars or buck teeth or being the wrong size or shape. These things are perhaps unfortunate, but they are nothing to be ashamed of. And yet sometimes a person so takes it to heart that he lets it sting and rankle in his mind, and poison his nature so that he becomes bitter and sour and disagreeable. Such a person needs very much to know that other people don't judge him by his looks or whether he limps, but only what sort of person he is. . . .''[20]

Besides Eytan, *Other Sandals* includes Devra, who stutters badly. Sensibly and appropriately, this fact is commented on only once—and briefly, by Devra herself. An atmosphere of common sense, acceptance, confidence, and lack of pressure is created by the adults around her. There is also, realistically enough, a somewhat slow-witted boy in the group, but he too is treated with thoughtfulness and acceptance by the children as well as the adults. One of the most important aspects of the book is its story of how Devra overcomes a different kind of handicap—that of prejudice (in this case, towards Arabs). There are many worthwhile lessons in *Other Sandals,* but they all flow naturally from its varied and colorful story elements. They can all be summed up as learning to put oneself into someone else's shoes (or sandals, as in the title).

There are a number of good books which deal with an individual who has had polio. In *Tall and Proud,* Vian Smith has created a generally well-written and interesting story of a girl who develops polio as a teenager. Gail and her parents are well-characterized, and their various reactions, emotions, and interrelationships strongly and realistically presented—Gail's resentment, her mother's overprotection, the doctor's determination for her. The author graphically depicts the onset, course, and aftermath of polio. Horse-story lovers will enjoy *Tall and Proud,* as Gail's father uses her love of horses to motivate her. There is also a pleasant boy-next-door element. The suspense ending is perhaps overdramatic, and a bit careless—Gail's residual paralysis is forgotten during the climatic scene as she "darts" to the passageway "without making a sound."

Five against the Odds, by C. H. Frick, depicts a high school basketball star in the Midwest who contracts polio and is left using crutches and wearing a brace on one leg. The author has obviously investigated the appropriate details, and uses informative orthopedic and therapy terminology. He presents a generally realistic picture of polio's effect on Tim's life, his feelings, future plans, effect on others, etc., and incorporates an interesting mystery story into the book. The writing is uneven, however; the author is sometimes guilty of oversimplification, and needlessly throws in clichés, having already said the same thing in a noncliché. "Tim felt warm and complete. This was what a man needed: a feeling of pride in himself. Now he could hold up his head again, knowing that powerful legs were not the only means to achievement, not the end-all of being."[21]

Alberta Armer has written a good story in *Screwball.* Filled with home-made racers, junk, and sports-lore, this story is about one twin who had polio as a young child and is now mildly handicapped. His right side is weak, he is unable to compete at sports (at which his twin excels), and he has trouble with handwriting, too. Most important is his concomitant lack of self-confidence, and *Screwball* tells of how he gains it. This book is important because it deals effectively with the problems of the minimally handicapped—at least people know that something is wrong if one is wearing a brace or using crutches and may make allowances accordingly. The author expresses this well: "I'm glad only one of us had it. But why did it have to be me? And if it was going to cripple me, why didn't it do a real good job instead of just twisting the muscles of my right arm and leg? Other kids all tho\~ght I was just naturally awkward—'crazy' they said sometimes, or 'screwball.' "[22]

Finally, there are a number of books that might be mentioned which deal incidentally with handicapped individuals. Despite its inclusion in most bibliographies that have anything on orthopedic handicaps, Valenti Angelo's *Hill of Little Miracles* is only peripherally concerned with Ricco's handicap (a shortening of one leg). The book has a strong religious (Roman Catholic) orientation, and is colorfully set in the Italian-Irish neighborhoods of San Francisco during World War II. In *The Jazz Man,* a beautiful and moving book by Mary Hays Weik with outstanding woodcuts by Ann Grifalconi, a young black boy limps because one leg is shorter than the other. The children tease him, so he stays upstairs and watches life from his window.

Chuck, by Evelyn Elkins, subtitled *A Story of the Florida Pinelands,* makes good use of dialect and regional flavor, and Chuck's love for animals is well described. The literary treatment of his polio is simplistic, however; it is considered only a bit of stiffness that needs to be worked out. Giving Chuck a goal to work for is, of course, sound therapy, but the minor degree of his polio is not one on which to base a story. Howard Pyle's *Otto of the Silver Hand* barely touches on the subject of Otto's amputated hand. And, of course, there is Johanna Spyri's *Heidi,* and, similarly beloved, *The Secret Garden,* by Frances Hodgson Burnett, where the invalids (the exact nature of their conditions vague) are rehabilitated by fresh air and the loving and secretive ministrations of friends.

We see, then, that there exists a sizable and important body of juvenile literature about the handicapped. It is a growing body as well. Among a number of recent additions to the field is Rosemary Sutcliff's new book, *The Witch's Brat,* which tells the story of a crippled boy in twelfth-century England. Included in the American Library Association (ALA) list of 1970 Notable Children's Books, *The Witch's Brat* is a historical fiction about the founding of St. Bartholomew's Hospital in London, and is similar in type, style, and setting to Marguerite De Angeli's *The Door in the Wall.* It is a realistic story, written with careful attention to historical detail, and graced by Richard Lebenson's fine black and white sketches.

Young Lovel, like Robin in *The Door in the Wall,* learns that his strength of character and the opportunites he finds to use his unique skills and personality can overcome his physical deformity—a humped shoulder and twisted leg. *The Witch's Brat* is marred only by a surprisingly weak ending and by occasional overexplicit point-making; for example, "he was puzzling at the back of his mind over the surprising fact that Rahere had called him 'the brat' and it hadn't brought the sound of stones whistling round his ears. He hadn't minded at all. *Perhaps it did not matter what names people called you by, only what they meant behind them.''*[23] [italics added.]

In closing, I think that May Lamberton Becker's introduction to an edition of *The Little Lame Prince* serves to characterize not it alone, but rather all the good literature for children about the physically handicapped: ''It is a fairy tale which lives because it is true . . . There are many [children] today who have had to escape from the prison tower of paralysis and pain without a magic carpet or a fairy godmother. The magic they had was in their courage, their making the best of things, their good will, all the qualities you will find in this story. . . .''[24]

NOTES

1. Orthopedic or physical handicaps, as used in this article, include cerebral palsy; polio; amputations; paralyzing accidents; and other nerve, muscle, and bone disorders.

2. Charlotte A. Huck and Doris A. Young, *Children's Literature in the Elementary School* (New York: Holt, Rinehart and Winston, 1961), p.253.

3. May Hill Arbuthnot, *Children and Books,* 3d ed. (Chicago: Scott, Foresman, 1964), p. 496.

4. Alice Ross Colver, *Sally, Star Patient,* p. 179.

5. Ibid., p. 118.

6. Dinah Maria Mulock, *The Little Lame Prince* (Cleveland, OH: Collins-World, 1975), p. 62-3.

7. Ibid., pp. 152-3.

8. Ibid., p. 65.

9. Ibid., p. 75.

10. Ibid., pp. 109-10.

11. Marguerite De Angeli, *The Door in the Wall* (New York: Doubleday, 1949), p. 16.

12. Ibid., p. 29.

13. Ibid., p. 38.

14. Ibid., p. 71.

15. Ibid., p. 120.

16. Ibid., p. 76.

17. Ester Forbes, *Johnny Tremain* (Boston: Houghton Mifflin, 1943), pp. 47-8.

18. Ibid., p. 62.

19. Ibid., p. 192.

20. Sally Watson, *Other Sandals* (New York: Holt, Rinehart and Winston, 1966), p. 103.

21. C. H. Frick, *Five against the Odds* (New York: Harcourt Brace, 1955), p. 141.

22. Alberta Armer, *Screwball,* p. 12.

23. Rosemary Sutcliff, *The Witch's Brat* (New York: Henry Z. Walck, 1970), p. 41.

24. May Lamberton Becker, "Introduction," in Dinah Maria Mulock, *The Little Lame Prince* (New York: World, 1948), pp. vii-ix.

REFERENCES

Angelo, Valenti. *The Hill of Little Miracles.* New York: Viking Press, 1942. 200 p.

Arbuthnot, May Hill. *Children and Books.* 3d ed. Chicago: Scott, Foresman, 1964, 688 p.

Armer, Alberta. *Screwball.* Cleveland: World Publishing, 1963. 202 p.

Bailey, Matilda. "Therapeutic Reading: Revised Bibliography." *ABC Language Arts Bulletin* 1, no. 6, 1948.

Becker, May Lamberton. "Introduction," in Dinah Maria Mulock. *The Little Lame Prince,* pp. vii-ix. New York: World, 1948.

Beim, Lorraine. *Triumph Clear.* New York: Harcourt, Brace, 1946. 199 p.

Burnett, Frances Hodgson. *The Secret Garden.* New York: Lippincott, 1962. 256 p.

Colver, Alice Ross. *Sally, Star Patient.* New York: Dodd, Mead, 1968. 181 p.

De Angeli, Marguerite. *The Door in the Wall;* illus. by the author. New York: Doubleday, 1949, 121 p.

Elkins, Evelyn. *Chuck.* Philadelphia: Lippincott, 1948. 211 p.

Forbes, Esther. *Johnny Tremain.* Boston: Houghton Mifflin, 1943. 256 p.

Frick, C. H. *Five against the Odds.* New York: Harcourt Brace, 1955, 210 p.

Huck, Charlotte A., and Young, Doris A. *Children's Literature in the Elementary School.* New York: Holt, Rinehart and Winston, 1961. 522 p.

Kircher, Clara J., comp. *Behavior Patterns in Children's Books: a Bibliography.* Washington: Catholic University of America, 1966. 132 p.

Little, Jean. *Mine for Keeps;* illus. by Lewis Parker. New York: Little, Brown, 1962. 186 p.

Luis, Eulene W. and Millar, Barbara F. *Wheels for Ginny's Chariot.* New York: Dodd, Mead, 1966. 205 p.

Mulock, Dinah Maria. *The Little Lame Prince.* Cleveland, OH: Collins-World, 1975.

Pyle, Howard. *Otto of the Silver Hand.* New York: Scribner's, 1957. 136 p.

Smith, Vian. *Tall and Proud.* New York: Doubleday, 1966. 159 p.

Southall, Ivan. *Let the Balloon Go.* New York: St. Martin's Press, 1968. 142 p.

Spyri, Johanna. *Heidi;* trans. by Helen B. Dale. New York: Grosset and Dunlap, 1927. 324 p.

Sutcliff, Rosemary. *The Witch's Brat;* illus. by Richard Lebenson. New York: Henry Z. Walck, 1970. 145 p.

Watson, Sally. *Other Sandals.* New York: Holt, Rinehart and Winston. 1966. 223 p.

Weik, Mary Hays. *The Jazz Man;* illus. by Ann Grifalconi. New York: Atheneum, 1966. 42 p.

Garden for the Blind

by Joseph Gale

Flowers not only are for seeing. They are for smelling and feeling as well. The Woodbridge Garden Club and the Iselin Lions Club (New Jersey) hold to that, and recently they completed construction of a Garden for the Blind and Handicapped at the Iselin branch of the Woodbridge Public Library. The unusual facility is open annually from April 1 to October 1.

Philip Anderson, a florist and secretary of the Lions Club, and Martha Morrow, chair of the garden club's environmental improvement program, were mainly responsible for the planning. They believe the garden may be unique in this country.

Through a family connection, Anderson introduced the idea to the Spokane (Washington) Lions Club. As a result, a similar garden was planned to be built there on Expo grounds after the fair closed in September. The Lions Clubs in both places have named Spokane and Woodbridge "sister cities," and a Spokane planting of indigenous lilacs, daphne, and alyssum is now growing in Woodbridge.

The 20-foot-wide and 200-foot-long garden is topped by the Morrow Circle of Senses, a brick rotunda three feet high and 18 feet in diameter. Handicapped people can negotiate the long strip and the circle on foot or in wheelchairs and easily read the large-print identifications of the 43 flowers, plants, and shrubs.

At the head of the column, the Circle of Senses has its own entrance. Twenty-six varieties of touch-and-smell plantings are set out in a clockwise pattern along the top of the brick. The blind and partially sighted may finger a circular metal rail until they come to a "bead" in the metal that tells them that an identification in braille and in large print lies just above. The rest is all touching and smelling.

Inside, the library maintains visual aids, talking books, tapes, and large-print magazines and books for persons with sight problems. Those who wish the plantings explained may borrow tape-cassette playbacks that deliver casual, precisely paced garden talks.

The garden was more than a year in development and required the assistance of innumerable citizens and municipal and service organizations.

Its $8,000 cost was raised largely through gifts and such fund-raising ideas as issuing first-day covers to philatelists commemorating the Garden of the Blind and Handicapped. The money paid, in part, for bringing in the garden's own water line from the street and for two vandal-proof hydrants.

The plantings are arranged with a touch of subtlety. They begin with spring flowers and proceed into the fall. The rose garden has specimens with names of particular meaning, such as Aquarius (''for our youth'') and Bob Hope (''for our older youth''), and in the center of the display, a Peace Rose.

PART VII

PREVOCATIONAL/ VOCATIONAL PROGRAMING

Introductory Comments

According to the regulations of PL 94-142, *vocational education* means educational programing which is directly related to preparing an individual for employment or a career which does not require a college degree. For background information on this provision of the Education for All Handicapped Children Act as well as other recent legislation pertaining to vocational education and their far-reaching implications, the reader is referred to "Federal Mandates for the Handicapped: Vocational Education Opportunity and Employment" in the first section of this book.

Since vocational education is specifically mentioned in PL 94-142 as part of a free appropriate education, individualized education programs (IEP) for many students at the secondary level will, no doubt, include prevocational and vocational objectives. Patricia T. Cegelka and Misha W. Phillips Gover in "Individualized Education Programing at the Secondary Level" point out that, for the mildly and moderately handicapped, the least restrictive setting for vocational training would mean integration into regular vocational programs. Cooperation between special educators and vocational educators, therefore, will be essential in designing programs which meet individual needs. The problems of developing, implementing, and monitoring the IEP as a cooperative effort is given deserved consideration by the authors.

In the article by Cegelka and Gover, reference is made to a competency-based curricular approach by D.E. Brolin, who specifies competencies and subcompetencies needed by mildly handicapped individuals. Allen Mori utilized Brolin's major competency areas when selecting materials to be listed in his "Annotated Bibliography of Prevocational and Vocationally Oriented Materials for Secondary Educable Mentally Handicapped Pupils." The commercial materials included are designed to aid teachers working with secondary level EMR students in teaching daily living skills, personal social skills, and occupational guidance and preparation.

The remaining articles in this section address one or more specific handicapping conditions and describe either an actual program or a model for providing vocational opportunities to special students. The first of these articles, "Handicapped Students Learn a Helping Way of Life," details a health careers program for neurologically impaired and physically handicapped students. Designed to provide paramedical skills training to prepare students for employment in hospitals and nursing homes, the three-year program offers classroom, laboratory, and on-site training.

The more severe the handicapping condition, the more difficult the challenge for educators attempting to provide prevocational and vocational programs which will adequately prepare the handicapped individual for as independent a life as possible. In "A Prevocational Program for Secondary TMR Students: The Canby Project," Thomas J. Lombard and Laird Schultz emphasize the necessity of instructing the trainable mentally retarded student in certain skills and work attitudes prior to his/her entrance into a program of specific vocational training. Many details of the program are not included in the article but may be obtained from its authors. The relevance of the prevocational training program centered around altering the classroom environment to that of a work environment by inclusion of such features as a time clock, schedules, specific tasks, coffee breaks, and pay. The resulting changes in the behavior and enthusiasm of the students involved were encouraging.

A more comprehensive approach to vocational education for the handicapped than that of the Canby Project is employed in Fairfax County, Virginia. Louis Godla outlines the approach in "Program Changes to Accommodate Handicapped Students." The main thrust of the article is that vocational training must be accomplished in a realistic job environment. The county's building trades program is used as an example of how handicapped students are integrated into the regular vocational program and receive on-the-job training by actually constructing residential and commercial-type buildings. According to the article, all but the most severely handicapped are eligible for the program and receive skill development training at the job site before being gradually assimilated into the work activities. In addition, English, social studies, and reading are offered in portable classrooms at each construction site.

One of the most neglected groups of handicapped youngsters at the secondary level, according to Richard L. McDowell and Gweneth Blacklock-Brown, is the emotionally disturbed. In "The Emotionally Disturbed Adolescent: Development of Program Alternatives in Secondary Education," the authors give a careful overview of the issues pertaining to emotionally or behaviorally disordered adolescents and the problems in assessing, defining, and providing education for this population. Typical placement options are described along with their concern that the major factor to be considered is the effect of placement upon the individual child. As an alternative to traditional programs, the authors propose a model for offering vocational and occupational experiences which will provide the student with competencies needed for entering the world of work. The rationale, objectives, personnel required, and plans for implementing such a program are included.

Individualized Education Programing at the Secondary Level

by Patricia T. Cegelka
and Misha W. Phillips Gover

During the past several years, increased attention has been focused on the vocational preparation of handicapped children and youth. In 1972, the US Office of Education predicted that the future of 77 percent of the handicapped children leaving school programs over the next few years would be unemployment, underemployment, or total dependency. As one step toward rectifying this situation, the Bureau of Education for the Handicapped (BEH) declared career education as a priority program area for exceptional children. . . . BEH emphasized that every exceptional child leaving school should have, at minimum, entry level job skills. At the same time, increased concern and support has been expressed regarding the issue of training the handicapped for qualitative levels of employment. The mere fact of employment, regardless of job attributes or their match to the individual, is no longer acceptable for the handicapped any more than it is for the nonhandicapped. The following summarizes current thinking:

> We have, for far too long, seemed to act as though a handicapped person should be both pleased with and grateful for any kind of work society provides. Unlike other persons, we seem to assume that, if a person is handicapped, boredom on a job is impossible. Worse, much of society has seemed to assume that, while most persons should seek work compatible with their interests and aptitudes, such considerations are not necessary when seeking to find employment for handicapped persons. If any job in the world of paid employment can be found for the handicapped person, we seem far too often to be personally relieved and surprised when the handicapped person is anything less than effusively grateful. [1]

VOCATIONAL EDUCATION LEGISLATION

An increased emphasis on vocational education programing for the handicapped has been one approach to preparing this population for more suitable employment opportunities. The passage of various federal legislation has underscored the increasingly important role that vocational education must play in the education of handicapped children. The 1963 Vocational Education Act specifically extended vocational education services to both handicapped and disadvantaged populations. When expansion in program effort did not follow, the 1968 Amendments to that law required each state to spend a set proportion of the federal vocational education monies to provide vocational education to handicapped students not otherwise being served. Even then, the required federal monies frequently were not spent. When they were, they were usually allocated to the development and support of special segregated vocational education programs. A scathing Government Accounting Office report[2] criticized this approach as both educationally unsound and economically inefficient. The report suggested that larger numbers of handicapped youth could receive more meaningful and appropriate training through integration into existing programs.

That the educational neglect and mismanagement of the past will no longer be tolerated is clearly indicated by the provisions of the 1976 Amendments to the Vocational Education Act and by Public Law 94-142. The 1976 Amendments specifically mandated that handicapped children must be included in regular vocational education programs whenever possible. In addition, Public Law 94-142 requires that appropriate programs be provided for handicapped children in the least restrictive environment possible. It specifically alludes to vocational education and, in fact, its provisions supersede those of the Vocational Education Act and its amendments. Consequently, it can be expected that the individualized education programs developed for most high incidence, mildly or moderately handicapped children will specify vocational education training as appropriate and regular vocational education classes will be determined to be the least restrictive environment in which the requisite training can be provided. Cooperation between vocational education and special education is no longer a matter of choice; it is fast becoming a matter of compliance. By virtue of the provisions of the Vocational Rehabilitation Act of 1973, vocational rehabilitation counselors will also become increasingly involved in the delivery of services to school-aged handicapped youth.

SPECIAL EDUCATOR/VOCATIONAL EDUCATOR COOPERATION

Despite federal mandates to the contrary, cooperative efforts toward providing improved career preparation opportunities to the handicapped are not yet a widely prevalent practice. Several factors appear to account for this.

First, the historical orientation and training of both special educators and vocational educators has not been toward programing for the adolescent handicapped person. Vocational educators have developed programs for nonimpaired youth while special educators have concentrated most of their efforts on programing for young children. Consequently, few professionals in either discipline have been trained to meet the unique needs of the adolescent handicapped individual. Neither the skills nor the attitudes required for such an orientation have been developed. Finally, neither group has been particularly motivated to venture into this new arena. We have found it easier, as well as more comfortable and secure, to do those things with which we have previously experienced some success.[3]

Attempts to remedy these situations have been made at national conferences for teacher educators from both the special and vocational education disciplines, as well as through the development of in-service and preservice programs for public-school personnel.

THE IEP PROCESS

All professional personnel concerned must be prepared to demonstrate the needed competencies in assessing the student's skills, planning an individualized program, determining the program placement, specifying the instructional components, and evaluating the total program. This article focuses on the development of the individualized education plan as the structure for the delivery of services. Vocational educators in cooperation with special educators, other teachers, parents, administrators, and when appropriate, other individuals, must share in the process of developing, implementing, and monitoring the educational programs for handicapped adolescents. The following discussion deals with some basic considerations inherent in this process.

Assessment

Assessment should be viewed as a two-stage process: assessment occurring prior to the initial development of the IEP and the program placement; and ongoing assessment of abilities and interests that occurs as the student participates in a developmental sequence of academic and career preparation experiences. Brolin's[4] text provides an excellent review of a wide variety of interests and aptitude tests that are potentially useful for both the academic and vocational assessment of the adolescent handicapped student. The academic skills of the student can best be assessed through a combination of standardized tests, informal assessment procedures, and behavioral observation techniques.

These assessments will provide a basis for decision making regarding the identification of the child as exceptional, the appropriateness of placing the child in selected mainstream classes, and the prescription of necessary remedial procedures. The assessment of the student's skills will suggest a general direction for the career preparation components of the program.

Additional tests and techniques, such as work-sample systems, provide the evaluator with data that delineate or further support the identified skill aptitudes of the student as well as with observational data on a wide range of behavioral characteristics. Data such as these are the basis from which tentative long-term career objectives are developed and program experiences planned.

As a function of his/her career development experiences, the student should develop new skills that will facilitate exploration and clarification of individual occupational interests. Through ongoing assessment with the student, areas of strengths and weaknesses and career interests will continually be scrutinized and, where indicated, appropriate alterations in the education program as initially written can be modified to include these as reflected in the IEP.

Placement

It has been stated that the initial labeling of an individual as handicapped will probably be the most significant event in that person's life. Another event with similar significance is the development of the education plan that culminates in a special education placement for that individual. Decision making that leads to initial special education placement usually occurs at the elementary level. However, of no less importance are those decisions that are required as the student's program is reviewed and revised throughout his/her educational experience. At the secondary level these program decisions have a direct and foreseeable impact on the quality of adult adjustment that the individual is able to attain. Programs can no longer be designed primarily in terms of their relationship to future academic programing, as often is the case during the elementary years. The imminence of the secondary student's adulthood requires that the quality of his/her total life adjustment be of paramount concern to those persons involved in developing the IEP and designing the educational experiences.

If it is determined that placement in a special education program continues to be the appropriate placement for the handicapped student, a wide range of program alternatives—from self-contained special education programs to almost totally mainstreamed programs—are available. While there are many positive benefits to be gained from the integration of a student into the regular school program, it should not be assumed that this programing alternative will be appropriate for all handicapped students. Some may not have the skills necessary to succeed in regular academic or vocational programs, even with the provision of additional support services. Further, the focus of the regular program may not be compatible with the needs of the individual handicapped student.

One recommendation regarding mainstreaming that has a great deal of merit includes the prescriptive placement of students into those classrooms that offer the best means of obtaining specified competencies, with students remaining in these classrooms only as long as required to achieve the competency or competencies. This suggests that some students may be placed in vocational education programs for the entire vocational training sequence while others will receive only that training necessary for them to attain the minimum entry level skills for the jobs of a particular occupational cluster.

Curriculum

Each program alternative available to meet the needs of any handicapped student must be considered in light of the curriculum design. An excellent framework for the development of the curriculum of the secondary program is found in Brolin's [5] competency based approach which specifies 22 competencies and 102 subcompetencies that mildly handicapped individuals should attain. The provision of Public Law 94-142 for the extension of secondary programs until age 21 should mean that ample time is available for this competency attainment. In this system, academic skills play a supportive role, being viewed primarily as a means to attaining occupational, daily living, and personal-social competencies. This approach has significant implications for the curriculum experiences specified in the IEP.

The career education model also has important implications for the achievement of skill levels of students entering secondary programs. During the career awareness stage in the elementary years and the career orientation and exploration phase of junior high school, students can be expected to develop the essential attitudes and skills prerequisite to the more specific occupational orientation of the secondary level career preparation experiences. This should simplify the task of vocational education teachers, as they can then concentrate all of their efforts on skill development training. Nonetheless, the special education program components at the secondary level should continue to emphasize the acquisition of those personal characteristics and attitudes necessary for successful employment.

Research has indicated that it is frequently deficiencies in these areas that account for employment failures among the handicapped. The vocational education teacher may find it necessary to alter instructional methods (such as substituting oral directions for written ones), to adapt machines and tools, and to differentiate instructional goals for the handicapped student. The IEP may specify that the student complete the entire vocational training sequence or only a portion of it. Even though an initial IEP may call for only a limited level of vocational skill training, the ongoing assessment of student progress and abilities may indicate that these objectives should be revised to include more sophisticated skill training.

Two sets of curriculum materials that should be of particular value to vocational educators wishing to provide competency based programing are the Learning Activity Packages (LAPs) developed by the Interstate Distributive Education Curriculum Consortium and the Competency Based Vocational Education Modules developed at the University of Kentucky. Both of these programs afford individualized, competency based instruction across a wide range of occupational skills. One of them, a combination, or neither might be determined to be the most appropriate approach to the curriculum design. The critical consideration is that the program be developed or modified to follow a logical skills sequence leading to the student's achievement of long-term goals and objectives of his/her IEP.

Program Management

The development of the IEP is the initial step in appropriate programing for the handicapped student. However, equally important is the task of monitoring the implementation of this plan. If it is determined that the student's instructional needs can best be met through placement in special education classes for a portion of the day, the special education teacher would be responsible for the implementation of that portion of the plan. However, if the student can perform successfully for the remainder of the specified academic subjects in regular classrooms, it would be the responsibility of those teachers to manage those portions of the educational program. A third alternative is the placement of the student in a vocational education program under the guidance of either a regular or a special needs vocational teacher. This teacher is then responsible for programing for these goals and objectives.

All of these teachers share collectively in the responsibility for monitoring the student's progress toward the goals and objectives of the total program. Public Law 94-142 requires that the placement committee, which now includes those persons who originally developed the IEP as well as those individuals designated as responsible for portions of the prescribed program, meet at least annually to review the student's progress and determine what program extensions or expansions should be written into the IEP. A key person to the success of this endeavor is the committee manager or chairperson. The manner in which this role is fulfilled can be critical both to compliance with the law and to the achievement level ultimately attained by the handicapped student.

The following conceptualization outlines some of the major responsibilities of the program manager.

1. *Monitoring timelines*. The program manager, through consultation with the responsible teachers, must determine that the goals and objectives targeted in the IEP are being met by the specified dates.

2. *Contacting committee members*. Committee members must have time prior to the committee meetings to summarize the required data on student progress toward goals and objectives and to prepare statements of alternative suggestions as necessary.

3. *Scheduling placement committee meetings*. This must be accomplished in advance of the dates targeted for the attainment of the short-term instructional objectives.

4. *Maintaining records*. Records must be maintained on current data provided by the teachers and from any additional assessments. Relevant information relating to the committee meetings must be disseminated to appropriate persons (e.g., the parents, should they fail to attend a review meeting).

5. *Chair the meeting*. A task orientation must be maintained and the unique professional competencies of the staff utilized in an effective and efficient manner.

Evaluation

The evaluation component is the key to insuring the student's successful progression through his/her individualized education program. Evaluation is initially structured by the writing of short-term instructional objectives. The objectives include statements of each terminal behavior, expected conditions under which the behavior is to occur, and the criteria for evaluation of the student's performance level. Monitoring and evaluating the student's progress is further indicated by the projection of dates for the initiation of a task and the anticipated duration of that task. A review, to be held at least annually, is required by Public Law 94-142. However, in order to monitor the IEP effectively for the student's maximum success, the review should occur as often as necessary to coincide with the objectives. In this way, an appropriate decision can be made as to whether the student should remain in the same program for an extended but specified period of time, whether the program should be redirected, or whether additional components should be added to the initially planned and completed program.

SUMMARY

This article has reviewed the implications for secondary level students of legislative mandates requiring individualized education programing for handicapped children. It is clear that these youngsters must be included, where appropriate, in vocational education programs as well as other mainstream programs. The development and implementation of the IEP was discussed as the structure for the delivery of these educational services. Five basic considerations for the development, implementation, and monitoring of the IEP were discussed: assessment, placement, curriculum, program management, and evaluation. It was emphasized that the role of the program manager is one that is essential to comply with both the letter and intent of the law.

NOTES

1. K.B. Hoyt, "Career Education and the Handicapped Person," (US Office of Education, 1975), pp. 6-7.

2. *Training Educators for the Handicapped: A Need to Redirect Federal Programs* (Washington, DC: US General Accounting, 1976).

3. G.B. Gover, Personal communication.

4. D.E. Brolin, *Vocational Preparation of Handicapped Youth and Adults* (Columbus, OH: Charles E. Merrill, 1976).

5. D.E. Brolin, ed., *Life Centered Career Education: A Competency Based Approach* (Reston, VA: The Council for Exceptional Children, 1978).

Annotated Bibliography of Prevocational and Vocationally Oriented Materials for Secondary Educable Mentally Handicapped Pupils

by Allen Mori

With the passage of Public Law 94-142, teachers of secondary educable mentally handicapped (EMH) pupils will be required to provide greater emphasis on the introduction of prevocational and vocationally-relevant information into the school curriculum. To provide adequate educational experiences for the high school-aged EMH student, curricular approaches will need to become more process oriented and competency based. A process-oriented approach would relate the curriculum to the outside world and focus upon the development of skills which are critical to effective and independent functioning. With the process orientation, content for the curriculum is selected for its usefulness in developing those skills (competencies) with less emphasis placed upon acquiring knowledge and information. Emphasis should be placed on skill development, with the acquisition of competencies which would make the EMH student more functionally adequate as a citizen, learner, worker, etc.[1]

Brolin suggested that the curriculum for secondary level EMH students emphasize three primary areas and one support area. The three primary areas include: (1) daily living skills, (2) occupational guidance and preparation, and (3) personal-social skills. The fourth area, considered as supportive to the other three, would be academic skills.

A variety of research studies support the importance of personal-social and daily living skills as important determiners of the vocational success of the EMH student.[2-5] Further, Brolin has noted 22 major competencies in the three primary curriculum areas that the EMH student should acquire prior to leaving a secondary program. The competencies and curriculum areas are as follows:[6]

Daily Living Skills

1. Managing family finances.
2. Caring for and repairing home furnishings and equipment.
3. Taking care of personal needs.
4. Raising children and family living.
5. Buying, planning, and preparing food.
6. Selecting, buying, and making clothing.
7. Engaging in civic activities.
8. Utilizing recreation and leisure time.
9. Mobility (getting around the community).

Personal-Social Skills

10. Attaining a sufficient understanding of oneself (self-awareness and appraisal).
11. Obtaining a positive self-confidence, self-concept.
12. Desiring and achieving socially responsive behavior.
13. Choosing, developing, and maintaining appropriate interpersonal relationships.
14. Achieving independent functioning.
15. Making good decisions, problem-solving.
16. Communicating appropriately with others.

Occupational Guidance and Preparation

17. Knowing about and exploring job possibilities.
18. Selecting and planning the most appropriate occupational choice(s).
19. Exhibiting the necessary work habits required in the competitive labor market.
20. Developing the necessary manual skills and physical tolerances required in the competitive labor market.
21. Obtaining a specific and salable entry level occupational skill.
22. Seeking, securing, and maintaining jobs appropriate to level of abilities, interests, and needs.

To adequately plan for and implement a curriculum to provide for the acquisition of these 22 competencies, teachers will need to become far more knowledgeable about the most current and effective instructional materials.

Unfortunately, demands upon teacher time and the rapidly expanding market of instructional materials prohibit many teachers from keeping abreast with current and effective materials.[7]

ORGANIZATION OF THE ANNOTATED LISTING

To aid teachers of secondary EMH students in the selection and use of relevant materials for the three primary areas, a selected annotated list of pertinent materials will be presented. The organization of the listing will be according to the primary areas suggested by Brolin. The list will include information on the title or name of the material, a brief description of the nature and purpose of the material, and the source from which it can be obtained.

The reader should note that there are certain qualifying statements that must be made regarding this list:

1. The inclusion of any material does not necessarily constitute an endorsement or evaluation by this author.

2. The annotated comments are not conclusive or inclusive, but rather should be viewed as descriptive.

3. The listing is not complete but rather includes only selected materials used by the author or classroom teachers who have taken university courses taught by the author.

4. Accurate and detailed information regarding specific materials may be obtained by writing directly to the source.

SELECTED MATERIALS FOR DEVELOPING DAILY LIVING SKILLS

Accent/Consumer Education
> This series of six booklets present financial principles applied to daily situations, and is designed to aid the student in handling money and other assets wisely. Suggested reading levels: 5-7. Follett Educational Corp., 1010 W. Washington Blvd., Chicago, IL 60607.

Accent/Family Finances
> This series of booklets examines situations relevant to family budgeting and permits students to use basic math skills to analyze financial situations in family life. Topical areas include interest charges, budgets, income taxes, sales taxes, charge accounts, and medical bills. Suggested reading levels: 5-6. Follett Educational Corp., 1010 W. Washington Blvd., Chicago, IL 60607.

Arithmetic Skill Text for Daily Living
> Series with consumable workbooks containing practical math problems depicted in newspapers and magazines. Includes both problems and exercises. Special Service Supply, Box 705, Huntington, NY 11743.

Arithmetic that We Need
A consumable worktext includes a variety of exercises from simple measurement up through temperature. Frank E. Richards Publishing Co., 324 First St., Liverpool, NY 13088.

Be Informed Series
A package of high-interest, low-vocabulary materials with exercises in writing, listening, word study, and comprehension. Topics covered include credit, buying a car, owning a car, renting a house, taxes, banking. New Readers Press, P.O. Box 131, Syracuse, NY 13210.

Better Buymanship Series
A series of four texts covering home economics and consumer guidance. Scholastic Book Services, 904 Sylvan Ave., Englewood Cliffs, NJ 07632.

Building a Strong Body
Designed for use as a one-semester health science text for high school-aged slow learners. Covers activities of daily life including sleep, recreation, care of teeth, etc. Burgess Publishing Co., 426 S. 6th St., Minneapolis, MN 55415.

Color Me American
A consumable worktext with units on the US Constitution, Bill of Rights, etc. Tests and activities included. Gary Lawson Co., 9488 Sara St., Elk Grove, CA 95624.

Driver Education, Drive Right Program
A program designed to aid students in developing proper attitudes for driving and for understanding defensive driving. Scott, Foresman and Co., 99 Bauer Dr., Oakland, NJ 07436.

Everyday Business
Consumable worktext with units on banking, budgeting, buying, etc. Includes true and false tests on each unit. Gary Lawson Co., 9488 Sara St., Elk Grove, CA 95624.

Facts about Sex: A Basic Guide
An illustrated text, written on a sixth-grade level, which presents the facts of life in frank language, including slang terms. John Day Co., 257 Park Avenue South, New York, NY 10010.

Family Financial Management
Vocational practice materials which simulate money management problems faced during a three-month period by a family of four. Typical business papers such as payments and a checkbook are included. Pages in teacher's manual may be used for making transparencies. South-Western Publishing, 512 North Ave., New Rochelle, NY 10802.

Family Life
   Stories about a young couple, their problems, and how they solved
   them. Topics include marriage plans, finding an apartment, budgeting, etc. Consumable workbook accompanies text. Frank E. Richards
   Publishing Co., 324 First St., Liverpool, NY 13088.

Finding Ourselves
   A consumable workbook providing instruction in map reading skills in
   a town, city, county, and state. Reading level: 3-4. Frank E. Richards
   Publishing Co., 324 First St., Liverpool, NY 13088.

Fundamental Forms Skilltext
   A text containing a variety of forms compiled from different sections
   of the country. Some of the forms include: loan applications, credit card
   forms, social security forms, etc. Special Service Supply, Box 705,
   Huntington, NY 11743.

Getting Ready for Payday
   Three illustrated workbooks, written at the third-grade level, contain
   practical suggestions and exercises for the EMH student preparing for
   employment. Frank E. Richards Publishing Co., 324 First St.,
   Liverpool, NY 13088.

Modern Consumer Education
   A multi-media, basic consumer education course for classes in home
   economics, business education, social studies, math, English, and
   industrial arts. The kit includes 39 teaching units made up of 27
   programed texts, 13 cassettes, 2 filmstrips, 180 student record books,
   answer keys, and wall charts. The six areas include: food; clothing; cars;
   furniture and appliances; family health and security; you and the law;
   ways to handle money; and ways to shop. Prerequisite skills in reading
   and math: sixth grade and below. Grolier Educational Corp., 575
   Lexington Ave., New York, NY 10022.

My Country
   A high-interest, low-vocabulary worktext with exercises and activities
   presenting information about our country and government. Suggested
   reading level: 3-4. Steck-Vaughn Co., P.O. Box 2028, Austin, TX
   78767.

New Fabrics, New Clothes, and You
   A book describing methods of determining the content of fabrics and
   ways of selecting and caring for clothes. Suggested reading level: 5-6.
   Steck-Vaughn Co., P.O. Box 2028, Austin, TX 78767.

Newspaper Reading
A consumable workbook designed to motivate students to read the newspaper. Units cover various sections of a typical newspaper. Tests and activities are included. Gary Lawson Co., 9488 Sara St., Elk Grove, CA 95624.

Our United States
A high-interest, low-vocabulary text covering the history, geography, and industry of each of the 50 states. Suggested reading level: 3-4. New Readers Press, P.O. Box 131, Syracuse, NY 13210.

Plans for Living: Your Guide to Health and Safety
An illustrated, consumable workbook with topics including: body growth, personal cleanliness, good grooming, exercise and rest, illness, etc. Suggesting reading level: 2.5-3.0. Fearon Publishers, 2165 Park Blvd., Palo Alto, CA 94306.

Programmed Math for Daily Living
Sequentially arranged math workbooks suggested for EMH students from ages 13 to 18. Everyday transactions used as examples. Materials can be used independently or with class. Topics covered include grocery bills, paychecks, checking accounts, bills, time cards, credit cards, etc. TQ Publishers, 3912 Ramsey, Corpus Christi, TX 78415.

Safe and Sound
A consumable workbook with topics including planned parenthood, prenatal care, baby care, accident prevention, and first aid. Includes tests and activities. Gary Lawson Co., 9488 Sara St., Elk Grove, CA 95624.

Sue Learns about the Measurements in Cooking
A self-paced workbook designed to teach homemaking and cooking measurements for the EMH student. Frank E. Richards Publishing Co., 324 First St., Liverpool, NY 13088.

Supermarket—Arithmetic Worktext
Simple everyday problems in grocery buying, making change, check writing, can size, weight, ounces, pounds, and dozen. Fern Tripp, 2035 East Sierra Way, Dinuba, CA 93618.

Training Fun with Activities of Daily Living Series
An activities workbook program covering experiences in personal care, social adjustment, occupational maturity, etc. Mafex Associates, Inc., P.O. Box 519, Johnstown, PA 15907.

Understanding the Automobile

Worktext in which the nine systems of the auto are discussed on both general and detailed basis. Illustrated overview gives full picture of auto operation. Suggested reading level: 5-6. Follett Educational Corp., 1010 W. Washington Blvd., Chicago, IL 60607.

Young Homemakers to Work

A series of workbooks designed to provide instruction in basic homemaking tasks. Tasks are analyzed and arranged sequentially. Suggested reading level: 2-5. Fearon Publishers, 2165 Park Blvd., Palo Alto, CA 94306.

SELECTED MATERIALS FOR DEVELOPING OCCUPATIONAL SKILLS

Accent/Jobs and Job Models

Booklets presenting five-part stories about the common work experiences of young adults. Designed to show how mathematical, social, and communication skills are used in job situations. Suggested reading level: 5-6. Follett Educational Corp., 1010 W. Washington Blvd., Chicago, IL 60602.

Accent/World of Work

The booklets deal with social skills related to the work world. Content includes interviews, salaries, promotions, employment applications, personal records, qualifications, and job choices. Suggested reading level: 3-4. Follett Educational Corp., 1010 W. Washington Blvd., Chicago, IL 60602.

Campus Work Experience (In high school)

Consumable workbook includes chapters on a variety of school, helper-type jobs. Different kinds of student activities follow the units. Allen Co., 4200 Arbitus Court, Hayward, CA 94542.

Choosing Your Career

A linear programed booklet designed to assist students in job guidance in grades 10-12. Contents include personal appraisal of strengths and weaknesses, job requirements, and the impact of automation on the labor market. Coronet Learning Programs, 65 East South Water St., Chicago, IL 60601.

Finding Your Job

A series of occupational monographs which give pertinent information on a wide variety of helper-type jobs. Series includes six units, with five volumes in each unit, and 12 job descriptions in each volume. Student workbook accompanies the series. Finney Co., 3350 Gorham Ave., Minneapolis, MN 55426.

Follett Vocational Reading Series

Series of six worktexts developed for junior and senior high students reading below grade level. Stories provide introduction to various occupations. Teacher's guide and answer sheets included. Suggested reading level: 4-6. Follett Educational Corp., 1010 W. Washington Blvd., Chicago, IL 60607.

Getting a Job

Consumable, illustrated workbook includes kinds of jobs, how to read and use help wanted ads, job applications, interviews, forms, government programs, wages, taxes, social security, work laws, etc. Teacher's manual included. Suggested reading level: 3-6. Fearon Publishers, 2165 Park Blvd., Palo Alto, CA 94306.

Getting and Holding a Job

Consumable worktext developed for young adults getting ready to enter the business world. Includes information on pertinent employment practices. Book is designed to be retained by the student for later reference. Suggested reading level: approximately 4. Frank S. Richards Publishing Co., 324 First St., Liverpool, NY 13088.

Help Yourself to a Job

Part I: Consumable worktext covering job hunting, using newspaper ads, applying for a job, filling out applications, the interview, etc. *Part II:* Explains difference in skilled, semi-skilled, and unskilled jobs, salary deductions, fringe benefits, unions, etc. Suggested reading level: 3-4. Finney Co., 3350 Gorham Ave., Minneapolis, MN 55426.

How to Find a Job

Illustrated booklet written for work-oriented study groups of upper level students. Material covers finding the right job, applying, common questions and answers about jobs, etc. Suggested reading level: 3-4. New Readers Press, P.O. Box 131, Syracuse, NY 13210.

How to Get a Job and Keep It

A workbook providing basic information on how to find a job, make an application for the job, and complete the job interview. Suggested reading level: 5-6. Steck-Vaughn, P.O. Box 2028, Austin, TX 78767.

How to Hold Your Job

Teacher's book and accompanying student workbook, composed of 12 units of daily curriculum material for use with EMH students reading on a second grade level. Includes lesson plans for school year. John Day Co., 257 Park Ave. South, New York, NY 10010.

Jerry Works in a Service Station

Illustrated high-interest, low-vocabulary reader presenting realistic situations, intended to help students to develop academically, socially, and vocationally. Includes exercises in reading and prevocational skills related to general occupations but with emphasis on service station employment. Suggested reading level: 2-3. Fearon Publishers, 2165 Park Blvd., Palo Alto, CA 94306.

Job Application Skilltext

Consumable worktext includes variety of actual job applications used in business and industry. Special Service Supply, Box 705, Huntington, NY 11743.

Jobs A to Z

Illustrated consumable worktext designed to familiarize students with wide variety of occupations while developing reading comprehension skills. Suggested reading level: 3. Frank E. Richards Publishing Co., 324 First St., Liverpool, NY 13088.

Occupational Education Fact Finding Series

Consumable workbooks developed to offer practice in looking up everyday information in newspapers, magazines, and brochures. Suggested reading level: 3-4.

Part 1: want ads, building supplies, home furnishings, sporting goods, and map mileage.

Part 2: telephone books, train schedules, and used car sales.

Part 3: real estate, trucks, business opportunities, and tools.

Special Service Supply, Box 705, Huntington, NY 11743.

Pre-Vocational Series

Soft-cover, programed booklets developed for special occupational training programs—designed for self-instruction. Subject matter organized into small sequential steps with questions after each step.

Start in the Right Direction
Finding and Holding a Job
Finding a Job through the Newspaper
Choosing Your Job
Air Conditioning/Refrigeration Repairman
Automobile Mechanic

> *Building Maintenance Worker*
> *Electronics Technician*
> *Food Service Worker*
> *Heating Technician*
> *Household Appliance Repairman*
> *Office Machine Repairman*
> *Office Occupations*

Del Mar Publishing Co., P.O. Box 5087, Mountainview Ave., Albany, NY 12205.

Teen-Agers at Work

Consumable workbook containing activities in English, arithmetic, and social studies for use in work-study programs. Contents: school cafeteria, gas station attendant, bakery work, supermarket helper, shipping clerk, hospital aide, and worker's holidays. Suggested reading level: 4. Frank E. Richards Publishing Co., 324 First St., Liverpool, NY 13088.

Teen-Agers Prepare for Work

Consumable workbook designed for use with a work-study program with EMH junior/senior high students. Includes chapters on types of occupations, qualifications, work forms, and a personal evaluation. Suggested reading level: 4. Allen Co., 4200 Arbitus Court, Hayward, CA 94542.

Turner Career Guidance Series

Consumable workbook dealing with major concerns of occupational and career experience. Suggested reading level: 5.

> *Wanting a Job*
> *Training for a Job*
> *Looking for a Job*
> *Holding a Job*
> *Changing a Job*

Follett Educational Corp., 1010 W. Washington Blvd., Chicago, IL 60602.

Turner-Livingston Reading Series

Series of workbooks which contain basic elements of language arts, social studies, math, guidance, and world of work. Suggested reading level: 5.

> *The Person You Are*
> *The Money You Spend*
> *The Family You Belong To*
> *The Jobs You Get*
> *The Friends You Make*

The Town You Live In

Follett Educational Corp., 1010 W. Washington Blvd., Chicago, IL 60602.

Unemployed Uglies

Set of 20 different, consumable cartoon pads designed to stimulate discussions with EMH pupils. Bottom part of each sheet is blank for writing, drawing, or other activities. Good grooming, safety, etc. emphasized. Teaching guide included. Frank E. Richards Publishing Co., 324 First St., Liverpool, NY 13088.

Unemployment is No-Cents

Consumable worktext written for EMH students in junior-senior high. Units cover choosing the correct job, job interviews, job forms, and how to keep a job. Tests and suggested activities included. Suggested reading level: 3-4. Gary Lawson Co., 9488 Sara St., Elk Grove, CA 95624.

World of Work

Illustrated worktext for EMH students seeking jobs. Covers where to find jobs, job applications, interviews, work habits, and job training programs. Suggested reading level: 4-5. New Readers Press, P.O. Box 131, Syracuse, NY 13210.

SELECTED MATERIALS FOR DEVELOPING PERSONAL-SOCIAL SKILLS

Accent/Personality

A series of booklets designed to teach social skills and encourage the development of positive social attitudes. Booklets contain exercises in reading and speaking as well as suggestions for group discussions. Suggested reading levels: 3-4. Follett Educational Corp., 1010 W. Washington Blvd., Chicago, IL 60607.

American Girl Book of Teen-Age Questions

Actual questions from teenagers on problems concerning family, friends, school, career, personal life, etc. Includes author's answers to the questions. Random House/Singer, 201 E. 50th St., New York, NY 10022.

Better Living

A consumable workbook with units presented as short stories. Topics include morals, virtues, marriage, etc. Gary Lawson Co., 9488 Sara St., Elk Grove, CA 95624.

English on the Job Series
A basic English text series designed to offer fundamentals of English usage and clear, correct expression in oral and written contexts. Globe Book Co., 175 Fifth Ave., New York, NY 10010.

Facing Life
A book for teenagers concerning psychosocial development. Designed to enhance development for facing adult problems. Mafex Associates, Inc., P.O. Box 519, Johnstown, PA 15907.

Life Today (II)
See description above.

Manners
A workbook with contents including social adjustment, good manners, and consideration for others. Frank E. Richards Publishing Co., 324 First St., Liverpool, NY 13088.

Spring Board
A consumable workbook including 40 discussion essays with questions relevant to problems associated with students entering the world of work. Suggested reading level: approximately 4. Special Service Supply, Box 705, Huntington, NY 11743.

Target Series
A series for EMH students designed to provide experiences in family and everyday life, social skills, etc. Suggested reading level: 4. Mafex Associates Inc., P.O. Box 519, Johnstown, PA 15907.

Target Series—Social Adjustments
A series of five booklets presenting problems in story form. Problems include self-pity, self-deception, hostility, feelings of inadequacy, and antisocial behavior. Suggested reading level: 4. Mafex Associates Inc., P.O. Box 519, Johnstown, PA 15907.

Turner-Livingston Communication Series
Series of workbooks with emphasis on world of work but includes units on English, social studies, and personal problems. Teacher's guide includes teaching suggestions. Suggested reading level: 5.

> *The Television You Watch*
> *The Language You Speak*
> *The Phone Calls You Make*
> *The Newspapers You Read*
> *The Movies You See*
> *The Letters You Write*

Follett Educational Corp., 1010 W. Washington Blvd., Chicago, IL 60607.

You
> An illustrated text and workbook designed to aid teenagers to increase self-understanding and self-control, as well as to help them improve their social skills and attitudes. Frank E. Richards Publishing Co., 324 First St., Liverpool, NY 13088.

NOTES

1. D.E. Brolin, *Vocational Preparation of Retarded Citizens* (Columbus, OH: Charles E. Merrill, 1976).

2. O.P. Kolstoe, "An Examination of Some Characteristics which Discriminate between Employed and Non-Employed Mentally Retarded Males," *American Journal of Mental Deficiency* 66 (1961): 472-82.

3. J.R. Peck, "The Work-Study Program—A Critical Phase of Preparation," *Education and Training of the Mentally Retarded* 2 (1966): 68-73.

4. E.M. Goodman, "Vocational Education for the Handicapped: A Cooperative Approach," *Rehabilitative Literature* 30 (1969): 199-202.

5. G.E. Ayers and A.R. Duguay, "Critical Variables in Counseling the Mentally Retarded," *Rehabilitative Literature* 30 (1969): 40-2, 50.

6. Brolin, *Vocational Preparation of Retarded Citizens*, pp. 194-200.

7. A.A. Mori, "The Development and Utilization of an Evaluation Device for Instructional Materials Completed by Subscribers to the Western Pennsylvania Special Education Regional Resource Center" (PhD diss., University of Pittsburgh, 1975).

Handicapped Students Learn a Helping Way of Life

by Joel Beller

Teaching science to the neurologically impaired child calls for an extra measure of attention, patience, and creativity. Many such children are hyperactive, so they tend to fidget and have short concentration spans. Too, their motor skills are often poor, requiring extra safety considerations.

Unique problems arise, however, in teaching science to *any* child, handicapped or not; and, as Public Law 94-142 suggests, there is no reason why such impediments in the handicapped child should necessarily constitute a roadblock to learning.

In fact, we at Francis Lewis High School (Flushing, New York) have initiated a three-year program in paramedical skills training which clearly demonstrates the learning potential of the neurologically impaired and the physically handicapped. . . . (three-year funding was provided by the Vocational Educational Administration of the US Office of Education, HEW.

The Health Careers Program, as it is called, seeks primarily to teach students entry skills necessary for employment in selected health-support occupations. The program does so by a concentrated round of science laboratory sessions (two periods per day), nonscience classes in office skills and patient care (one period per day), *plus* on-site training at local hospitals and other medical facilities. As the program title implies, another major ongoing facet is that of career guidance.

Last year's program involved 127 students—95 of whom were neurologically impaired and 32 physically handicapped. We make no attempt to group the students in the program by grade level. A student may, for example, be in an eleventh-grade hematology class, but tenth-grade chemistry. We are fortunate to have 11 staff members (not all full-time) on hand—three science teachers, three teachers of nursing, three special education teachers, a teacher coordinator, and a laboratory specialist.

BARRIER-FREE LEARNING

The first step in implementing our program was to bring our facilities up to par. We decided to hold the Health Careers classes adjacent to our regular science rooms. (Gas, water, and waste lines were already installed in that wing of the building, and an elevator was also accessible for students.) In addition, we equipped two student rest rooms for the handicapped.

We butted against the real world, however, when it came to redesigning laboratory furniture. Our grant covered only personnel, equipment, and supplies—not furniture. (We await funds for this purpose from the New York City Board of Education; in the meantime, we have had to improvise.)

We would have preferred "U"-shaped laboratory tables (which allow wheelchairs to slide under), island service areas, and ample wheelchair access between all furniture. While our present makeshift setup doesn't give the efficiency we would like, it still affords a workable program. Our saving grace has been a number of mobile laboratory tables, each with self-contained water and waste facilities, and acid-resistant tops, which are ideal for letting students perform routine laboratory tests and prepare stock solutions. We had extra electrical outlets installed to service the autoclaves, plus pH meters, refrigerators, microscope lamps, and so on. We also installed gas jets, so that we could use Bunsen burners rather than alcohol lamps. Finally, we equipped a special safety cabinet and located it conveniently near a door leading to the hall.

EIGHT SKILL PATHS

Numerous conferences with hospital directors, laboratory technicians, and hospital-supply personnel revealed at least eight basic skill areas important in paramedical training. Our laboratory exercises thus center on the following techniques:

- Sterilization;
- Preparing hematological and bacteriological specimens;
- Operating autoclaves, centrifuges, incubators, and bacteria colony counters;
- Timed incubations;
- Preparation of molar and normal solutions;
- Column fraction collection;
- Staining techniques; and
- Facility with the metric system.

In-class laboratory training is augmented by weekly visits to local hospitals, medical laboratories, and nursing homes. At first, these visits are purely for observation. As each student becomes proficient in a particular skill or technique, however, s/he is given the opportunity to assist qualified hospital professionals with diagnostic procedures. (Senior students are allowed to participate in these on-site training sessions on a daily basis. Juniors and sophomores spend one or two days a week in such training, depending upon their school schedule and performance at the hospital.) At each site, one of our teachers assists the professional staff with training and administrative details such as attendance and grading.

Back at school, another major aspect of our program is that of office skills and patient care. Two words kept popping up in our initial talks with hospital personnel: *automation* and *computerization*. Clearly, no health careers course could realistically ignore computers. We decided, therefore, to purchase two machines: the Hewlett Packard 9820A and the more complicated Digital PDP/8E. Students learn how to set up a simple program using programmable calculators. They also observe operating computers at various health facilities.

In the patient-care modules, students learn how to feed, groom, and transport patients and take their vital signs. They also do messenger duty and learn admitting and discharging procedures.

TEACHING FOR REINFORCEMENT

Teaching techniques are adapted to fit the special needs and abilities of our students. To assure mastery of content as well as classroom safety, a science teacher (who acts as the leader) and a special education teacher supervise each laboratory session. They may also be assisted by our laboratory specialist—whose primary job, however, is to set up and maintain classroom demonstrations and supplies. Teachers for the office-skills and patient-care components include teachers of nursing.

We rely heavily on teacher-prepared worksheets, containing review questions and homework items. Outstanding student work is regularly displayed on bulletin boards. Three other techniques that we have used deserve mention. Each emphasizes the handicapped child's need for extra reinforcement, both in terms of varied approaches to learning and promoting self-confidence.

The first is a *Skills Achievement Chart*. The charts, which adorn each classroom, record student progress in a variety of skills. When a youngster demonstrates competency in a particular technique, the appropriate box on the chart is colored.

The second device we call the *Talking Chart*. Talking Charts originally evolved to help handicapped students catch up after absences; they also provide review for the child who is having difficulty in a certain area. Each Talking Chart corresponds to a specific assignment—such as "How to examine urine under the microscope" or "How to use a pH meter." The chart—on cardboard sheets—typically contains a written script, plus appropriate line drawings and illustrations. In addition to the chart, the student is given a tape recorder and cassette, containing the identical script as that on the chart. Usually the voice on the cassette is that of a student who has mastered the equipment or technique in question. This requires the child who is recording to articulate exactly what s/he has performed; also, to the student listening, the voice of a fellow student may be less intimidating than that of a teacher. Furthermore, use of cassettes in tandem with script helps to reinforce students' reading ability. Some children find it necessary to replay portions of the tape over and over.

A third teaching device is that of *peer training*. Competent students are asked to help those who are having difficulty. We have found no peer ridicule based on a child's failure to learn quickly. *Helping one another is a way of life for the handicapped.*

In terms of career guidance, we use many strategies to help our students select potential future jobs in keeping with their desires and abilities. Speakers are invited from numerous medical-support occupations. Films, pamphlets, brochures and so on also supplement our efforts. Several of our first graduates have been hired by local hospitals and nursing homes.

Future plans call for increasing the number and types of on-site training centers. Particular emphasis will be given to canvasing local physicians in need of assistance.

Certainly anything we can do to impart the excitement of learning science, and thereby help to separate a child from his/her disability, may eventually enable that child to think in larger terms about building a satisfying life.

A Prevocational Program for Secondary TMR Students: The Canby Project

by Thomas J. Lombard
and Laird Schultz

In many states there has been substantial improvement in public school programing for mentally handicapped students. There has been an emphasis on *normalization,* largely achieved through mainstreaming and various program changes. Many public school districts can display examples of mentally retarded students who have achieved comparatively normal social adaptation with varying degrees of self-sufficiency. This is easier to accomplish with educable mentally retarded students (EMR), but it remains a difficult and largely unaccomplished task for those students who are lower functioning (the trainable level of mental retardation, or TMR). TMR students typically become dependent on home or institutional management, seldom achieving any degree of self-support and maintenance. Although sheltered workshops provide some opportunities for employment and personal accomplishment, it is often too little or too late for this exceptional group.

Educators in the Canby, Minnesota, School District have designed a simplified and economical alternative to meet this pressing need for its secondary level TMR students. A program was developed with two basic goals: to teach the students adaptive personal living skills, and to provide opportunities to facilitate vocational adjustment. The purpose of this article is to describe the Canby Project in a way which might be applicable to other school districts that must serve the needs of TMR students at the secondary level. Specific curricular activities will not be described in detail but can be obtained through personal correspondence with one of the authors. What will be discussed here is the design and methodology used in this program, which is predicated on certain ideas regarding the needs of this exceptional group of students. It is necessary to present these ideas in order to understand what the project was designed to accomplish.

RATIONALE

Psychological principles and observations which are relevant to normal persons are often relevant as well to the mentally subnormal, including the low functioning or trainable level. One such observation is the stability and purposefulness one achieves from being a productive, useful citizen. For most people this is largely accomplished through gainful employment, which is usually unavailable for low functioning mentally retarded persons. Whether a person has an IQ of 50 or 150, feeling productive and useful with observable results of one's efforts promotes mental health in the following ways:

1. It fosters harmony in family and peer relationships;
2. It leads to positive psychological attitudes related to self-image and self-esteem;
3. It results in better job performance; and
4. It increases motivation to perceive and participate in self-enhancement opportunities.

For mentally subnormal persons, successful opportunities to feel productive and useful promote personal independence and self-sufficiency as well as mental health. Educators have the responsibility to respond to these needs.

We have observed that secondary and post-school mentally retarded persons achieve the greatest degree of family and social acceptance when they are successfully employed. However, vocational adjustment is especially difficult for the TMR student to achieve, and a proper orientation should be taught prior to actual training. The Canby Project was designed to provide such a vocational orientation and to prepare its secondary TMR students for more specific training.

THE CANBY PROJECT

Perhaps the most difficult concept for TMR students to learn is to be responsible for finishing a task by a certain time and within a certain standard of performance. Learning this concept prior to the actual job training greatly improves the efficiency and success of the training. Recognizing this need to reinforce successful task completion, educators made a concentrated effort to teach the secondary TMR students: (1) to increase their awareness of their vocational potential as working persons; and (2) to learn that they must perform an expected task at a specific time for which they receive certain compensation.

The daily classroom environment was made relevant to the role and responsibilities of a working person. This taught the students that they are in a daily work situation in school, and consequently they must learn certain things which enable them to complete work assignments. They were given opportunities and encouragement to see the relevance of learning certain skills needed to complete an assigned job.

In Canby, the program is based in a house owned by the school district. There, the students take most of their classes. There are nine secondary TMR students—five males and four females—with an age range of 14 to 23 years. All the students function in the moderate to severe range of mental retardation. There are three with Down's syndrome, and the others show various conditions of brain injury, central nervous system dysfunction, birth trauma, and unexplained causes for their retardation. Except when working on assigned jobs, the students are kept together as a class. This provides opportunities to use peer recognition as a form of positive reinforcement, since it is the most efficient means to maintain attention and cooperation with this particular group. While the teacher or aide is present at all times, students are frequently delegated the role of 'teacher', 'boss', or 'assistant' to demonstrate and lead an activity. This has proved to be a prized form of recognition which the students will work hard to achieve.

Early in the school year the procedure for teaching vocational preparation was designed. Maintenance on the house was divided into specific jobs, which were carefully task-analyzed and taught as one phase of a work training program. The school day was organized into a precisely timed schedule including arrival, physical education, some academic instruction, lunch and coffee breaks, and more specific work training units. In addition to teaching the students how to perform the jobs, they were taught how to use a time clock and stick to the daily schedule. They had to punch in and out when assigned a job, reinforcing the concept that the job must be completed within a specified time period indicated by a bell timer. Whether they wanted to do it or not, they learned that the job must be done according to certain standards. Successful job performance was determined by a 'boss' or 'foreman' (usually the teacher), and the students were held accountable to finish the job correctly. It was felt to be an important goal for the students to work without constant supervision, and to rely on their own judgment of acceptable job performance before receiving the 'foreman's' evaluation. This procedure met with fair success, but it was evident that something more was needed to simulate a real work situation with its inherent reinforcements.

The students had difficulty conceptualizing that eventually they would work for monetary compensation, and that it would provide a means for them to spend money for consumer purposes. The obvious solution was to pay the students for their maintenance work on the house, thus providing a completely realistic work environment. While the solution was obvious, the means to accomplish it was not until it was discovered that the students were eligible for financial support from a government-funded agency. This agency was authorized to financially support eligible persons for work training, including municipal employment. Maintenance on a public school building was considered "municipal employment," and permission was obtained to use the hourly wages these students could receive as a general fund for their work in the TMR program. This provided a source of money to use as wages for the students, compensating them for successful job performance on work training assignments. The end result was a completely modified educational program to provide a vocational orientation, along with practical work experience, in an environment closely simulating a real employment situation.

OBSERVABLE RESULTS

The students responded with apparent enthusiasm and intrinsic motivation to learn what was necessary to accomplish their jobs. Perhaps the most important result was the realization that it was necessary for them to learn certain job skills. They realized they had the capabilities, provided the skills were task-analyzed and taught in a manner from which they could realistically learn.

It was necessary to prepare curricular units to teach certain skills relevant to the work training program. Time concepts were taught with the use of schedules, a time clock for punching in and out, a bell timer for designating work periods, as well as the wall clock and wrist watches. Acceptable personal appearance was considered an important unit and included cleanliness, dental hygiene, cleaning eyeglasses, toileting, and using deodorant. The unit on money covered counting, making change, saving, and spending money for store purchase and vending machine operation. Functional reading was taught for survival words and job-related performance.

This program has been highly successful in teaching a vocational orientation to TMR students. The students became aware of their vocational potential and the material compensation they could achieve. While their self-concept and personal satisfaction were difficult to quantify for measurement purposes, there were several observable changes which indicated positive results. The students showed a vigor and enthusiasm which they did not show previously. Attendance was better and they genuinely seemed happier about coming to school. They seemed busier and their activity was purposeful and goal-oriented. They were reluctant to idly sit around. This is seen as an important change since there was more conversation, spontaneous social interaction, smiling, and laughing (this is based on subjective assessment by the staff, which also smiled and laughed more).

The amount of participation varied with individual students and circumstantial factors, but all the students seemed positively affected to a noticeable degree. All the students adjusted to the program change with no resulting management problems, and in some cases previous management problems dramatically improved. Other results which have yet to be determined and need to be studied further are the students' success in specific vocational training, eventual work adjustment, and the attitudes of 'normal' persons toward this form of *normalization* with low functioning mentally retarded persons. Families, teachers, work associates, and other involved persons should be surveyed for their reactions on this approach to normalized vocational preparation.

CONCLUDING REMARKS

While this project is a small attempt to improve the future outlook for a group of nine exceptional children, it provides some understanding of vocational preparation as a necessary emphasis for TMR programs in conventional public school settings. Through gainful employment with observable results, low functioning mentally retarded persons can look forward to some degree of self-support and personal productivity. It is just as necessary for these persons to achieve this as it is for the professional persons who read this report. Realistically, there is a difference in how this can be accomplished for persons with mental deficiency, and it requires parents, educators, and other professionals to take the initiative to develop vocationally oriented alternatives. While this project shows how nine students received an opportunity to realize previously unrecognized personal potential, it regrettably points out that this potential goes ignored in thousands of similar persons. What the future holds for them are variations of family and institutional maintenance, in many cases a euphemistic form of vegetative dependency. These people have a potential for some degree of self-support and personal productivity which will be unavailable without some effort made to provide appropriate opportunites. Increasing their self-support and personal productivity reduces the progressively prohibitive maintenance costs, and at the same time fosters mental health. Public schools have to be involved in preparing low functioning mentally retarded persons for improved vocational futures. The program described here is one way educators can contribute toward this end through a simplified, economical program applicable to a conventional school setting.

REFERENCES

Bellamy, C.T.; Peterson, L.; and Close, D. "Habilitation of the Severely and Profoundly Retarded: Illustrations of Competence." *Education and Training of the Mentally Retarded*, vol. 10, no. 3 (1975): 174-86.

Cromwell, R.L. "A Social Learning Approach to Mental Retardation." In *Handbook of Mental Deficiency*. Edited by N.R. Ellis. New York: McGraw Hill, 1963.

Edgerton, R.B. and Bercovici, S.M. "The Cloak of Competence: Years Later." *American Journal of Mental Deficiency*, vol. 8, no. 5 (1975): 485-97.

Flores, C.N. "An Experiment in the Preoccupational Education of Mentally Retarded Students on the Junior High School Level." *Education and Training of the Mentally Retarded*, vol. 10, no. 1 (1975): 26-9.

Justen, J.E. and Cronis, T.K. "Teaching Work Attitudes at the Elementary Level." *Teaching Exceptional Children* (Spring 1975): 103-5.

Lawrence, E.A. and Winschel, J.F. "Self-Concept and the Retarded: Research and Issues." *Exceptional Children*, vol. 39, no. 4 (1973): 310-9.

Meyen, E.L. and Altman, R. "Public School Programming for the Severely/Profoundly Handicapped: Some Researchable Problems." *Education and Training of the Mentally Retarded*, vol. 11, no. 1 (1976): 40-5.

Philips, I. and Williams, N. "Psychopathology of Mental Retardation: A Study of 100 Mentally Retarded Children: 1. Psychopathology." *American Journal of Psychiatry*, vol. 132, no. 12 (1975): 1265-71.

Taylor, J. and Achenback, T.E. "Moral and Cognitive Development in Retarded and Nonretarded Children." *American Journal of Mental Deficiency*, vol. 80, no. 1 (1975): 43-50.

Walls, R.T.; Tseng, M.S.; and Zarin, H.N. "Time and Money for Vocational Rehabilitation of Clients with Mild, Moderate, and Severe Mental Retardation." *American Journal of Mental Deficiency*, vol. 80, no. 6 (1976): 595-601.

Ziegler, E. "Motivational Determinants in the Performance of Retarded Children."*American Journal of Orthopsychiatry* 36 (1966): 848-56.

Zisfein, L. and Rosen, M."Self-Concept and Mental Retardation: Theory, Measurement, and Clinical Utility." *Mental Retardation*, vol. 12, no. 4 (1974): 15-9.

Program Changes to Accommodate Handicapped Students

by Louis Godla

For years vocational educators have complained about guidance personnel sending less than the best students to their classes, and over the years, they have developed many techniques and methods for selecting and rejecting students. As pure logic, all other considerations aside, this was not bad reasoning. Vocational education is evaluated on its delivery system, and in order to control output, vocational educators had to have some method of controlling input.

Employers judge vocational education by performance of students after they are on the job. They have no way of knowing what the students' ability level was when they entered training or how that training improved the students' potential. Vocational education output is judged solely on the performance of recent graduates as compared with the accomplishments of skilled workers.

A supervisor in any industrial plant or business is evaluated in terms of the production for which s/he is responsible. The supervisor will strive for and probably insist that s/he be given the best possible workers. This fact was brought home emphatically by a top personnel official of one of the largest utility companies during a recent tour of industries in Fairfax County, Virginia. He said that a high school diploma was mandatory even for the least skilled jobs and that his company was upgrading its requirements for all positions.

CASUAL TRAINING IS OUT

The utility official's statement reflects the dilemma faced by vocational educators. The day of selectivity is past, but training will still be measured mostly in terms of initial and sustained employment.

Superficial training can no longer do the job for any student, and certainly not for the handicapped. Sheltered workshops, simulation, mobility training, and other approaches including regular vocational programs have been found lacking simply because they do not always train students in realistic job environments. Lack of experience in an actual job setting is particularly traumatic for the handicapped student when s/he is thrust into a totally strange work environment.

Program goals and objectives must be rewritten for handicapped students in terms of individual capabilities. Occupations must be broken down into tasks that handicapped students can handle, and the students must be trained for job groups where those tasks are performed. Above all, occupational training for the handicapped must duplicate actual working conditions as closely as possible. This may require a completely new approach to training.

In Fairfax County, where training programs for handicapped students have been in existence since 1960, the current approach is heavy emphasis on on-the-job training in a community-based endeavor. Handicapped students are getting this kind of exposure now in the county's building trades program; and, when implementation of current plans is complete, an increased number will get on-the-job training in cooperative education programs tailored to meet their needs.

The reasoning in Fairfax County is that revision of the school curriculum to accommodate handicapped students should be approached through changes in philosophy and curriculum rather than equipment and facilities. The belief is that the vast majority of handicapped students, mental or physical, can be trained on equipment and in facilities used for the regular vocational programs—assuming that the school is equipped to match working conditions in the employment world.

At the moment, the best example of this concept in Fairfax County is found in the building trades program which has been in operation since 1971. In this program students actually construct residential and commercial-type buildings.

All but the most severely handicapped students are eligible for participation in the program. Students identified as mildly retarded, learning disabled, and emotionally disturbed are working at construction sites now.

The main objective of the program, for all students including the handicapped, is to provide occupational training in the building trades under the same working conditions that exist in the construction industry. Construction projects underway, which have a combined value of approximately 1.5 million dollars, include a large rowing center (storage for crew shells) and a nine-building environmental studies center.

In addition to these ongoing projects, which will last for several more years, two ten-house subdivisions are due to start soon—one for the school year 1978-79 and the other for 1979-80. The first of these subdivisions will house an off-campus occupational training park for the county's 22 high schools and four vocational centers.

Not only does the construction program provide training under actual working conditions, but it uses the same equipment and building materials on the job sites that students will encounter later in the construction industry. Students become 'construction wise' and the transition from school to work is less traumatic.

ALTERNATIVE EDUCATION

The building trades program in Fairfax County is, in effect, an alternative high school. Most of the students in the program are assigned to the job sites for the entire day. English and social studies are offered in portable classrooms at each construction site. A reading specialist is also available at each site, principally to help the handicapped students, although some of the regular students are assigned to reading classes.

Handicapped students have been assimilated into all phases of the projects—academic as well as vocational. Students may enroll at any time during the school year, which means that individual instruction is used throughout the program. On the construction sites, there is one teacher for every 15 students.

Even students who have not had basic skill training at a vocational center are allowed to enroll and are given basic skill development at the job site before being assigned to actual construction tasks. After basic training they are gradually assimilated into the flow of activities. Handicapped students follow the same procedures as other students and, after a certain period of time, many perform on an equal basis with regular students. For the most part, regular students are unaware of the handicapping conditions of these students and, as a result, accept them as fellow workers.

Because Fairfax County is a metropolitan area, workers are usually hired on the strength of specialized skills. Thus each trade is taught as a specialized occupation, although some students transfer from one trade to another.

PARK OPENED

The occupational training park which is part of this building trades program has been in operation since the fall of 1979, even while some of the facilities were still under construction. It offers training in landscaping and horticulture, small gasoline engine repair, welding, plumbing, and wood products manufacturing, with other courses added as the demand grows. These courses are available to all students, including the handicapped. Again, the objective is to provide training that has an on-the-job component and to duplicate as closely as possible the working conditions the students will experience later as employed adults.

In addition to on-the-job training, the curriculum offers opportunities for individual assessment, counseling, and basic training. Job placement and follow-up are also a part of the program.

The assessment process, counseling, and training allow students to move from one occupational area to another so that individual interests and aptitudes can be accommodated. Students are helped to find employment that is to their best advantage, which means that some students may be placed on jobs during the school year.

Transportation is provided from each of the 22 feeder schools and four vocational centers, and is available for both half- and full-time students. When handicapped students are placed on a job, they may travel to and from the job by school transportation. Fairfax County already operates a bus system for transporting many of its handicapped students to special centers.

Some buildings on the park site will be renovations of existing facilities; for example, a dwelling on the site is being renovated now for use as administrative offices and classrooms. Others will be built from the foundation up, but in both cases students will do the construction work. All facilities, whether renovations or new buildings, will be designed to accommodate the physically handicapped. The equipment will be the same as that used in the occupations, although some modifications may be necessary.

Items in the wood manufacturing shop will be manufactured on a speculative basis or on requests from local residents. This arrangement will give students basic carpentry skills in the use of hand and power tools usually found at construction sites as well as skills in operating the heavy equipment used in a production shop.

Students enrolled in landscaping and horticulture participate in welding and small engine repair classes during inclement weather. A walk-in repair shop for small engines and equipment is open to local residents. Thus a side benefit of this program is to give students the opportunity to interact with the general public.

TAILORING THE CO-OP PROGRAM

Some handicapped students in Fairfax County are already enrolled in the regular distributive business, and T&I cooperative programs, but a systematic expansion of these opportunities for the handicapped is planned.

This is one area where separate programs for the handicapped can be recommended, primarily because on-the-job training for these students should be under the direction of a teacher-coordinator who has the knowledge and expertise to work with students who have handicapping conditions.

Full-time coordinators with this kind of expertise will know the limitations of the students, how best to train them for designated tasks, and how to orient the immediate job supervisor to the students' handicapping conditions. The student literally becomes the charge of the teacher-coordinator.

It is recommended also that a board consisting of the coordinator, a personnel analyst, and the job supervisor be established to periodically review the student's record of progress in order to prevent or correct any problems that might erupt in a dismissal.

DEVELOPMENTAL PERIOD

As a first step in the expansion of on-the-job training experiences in Fairfax County, separate teacher-coordinators will be assigned to work full time placing and training students with the county government and county school system. In Fairfax County these two agencies are large enough to readily participate in on-the-job training programs for the handicapped. This is not to suggest that smaller schools and government units are incapable of providing training stations for these students. Even in small communities, the school system and local government should set the example.

In Fairfax County, teacher-coordinators will be expected to work as job developers. They will evaluate most job openings and break the jobs down into separate tasks for which one or more handicapped students can qualify. After placement, the teacher-coordinator will be responsible for developing a long-range training program for each student and also for helping the student maintain employment after s/he leaves school.

A set of guidelines and operating procedures will be developed while working with the two public agencies before expanding on a mass scale with business and industry. This developmental period, which is expected to take one school year, will also allow for revision of the ongoing vocational programs to accommodate all students.

Before embarking on a venture of this kind, it is essential to get the support and commitment of the chief executive of your city or county government and the superintendent of your school district. Their commitments should be made known to all educators and employees.

That Fairfax County has this kind of commitment from its top officials is made clear in the following statements. They are quoted here partly because they can serve as an example of the kind of commitment vocational educators should strive for.

County Executive Leonard Whorton made this statement in the *County Courier,* a house organ that goes to all county employees:

> Let me begin by saying that I support the concept wholeheartedly. Equal employment not only is the law; it is also a basic human right. But it is a right which often has been denied women, blacks, Hispanics, Asians, American Indians, the handicapped, and many other classes of persons.
>
> Affirmative action, then, begins with, and totally rests upon, positive attitudes toward the rights of others. It does not mean giving up our own rights, but it does mean sharing them. Specifically, it means not just admitting but positively supporting the idea that the right to fair consideration in the job market—particularly when the job is in a public agency—belongs to all kinds of applicants.
>
> It is critical that honest, more than ordinary effort be made to eliminate bias in hiring and to hire qualified members of the groups which have been discriminated against in the past.

Superintendent of Schools S. John Davis stated his views publicly in a speech given to the 1977 fall meeting of the Women's Committee, a standing committee of the President's Committee on Employment of the Handicapped. His statement was in the form of advice to a "new super-intendent."

> I would suggest you begin with commitment— your personal commit-ment — and proceed to gain the commitment of others.
>
> If your objectives are to provide limited maintenance services to meet the letter of the law, then I suggest you are about to waste everybody's time, including yours. The handicapped person, given an opportunity, can become a productive citizen, and to ensure this we must guarantee not only a 'free and appropriate education' but also a 'free and appropriate vocational education.' If we do not, we will find handicapped persons at age 22 returning to the attics and closets, returning to the lonely hours of watching television, nullifying years of effort on the part of the handicapped people as well as of special educators.
>
> Begin with your own organization. Train handicapped students, on the job, for employment within the school system. Then survey industry and business organizations to assess their needs and begin job training with the handicapped individual as soon as possible—first in the classroom, next in a simulated job situation, and finally on the job with supervision. These first efforts are crucial.

SELF-ASSESSMENT VEHICLE

Fairfax County's oldest program for handicapped students is the Maintenance and Repair Program which was established originally to accommodate disadvantaged and handicapped students but currently is available to all students. In existence since 1960, it could be called by a dozen other names.

Its main objective is to allow students to experience success in one or more vocational areas. Students may use the program as an assessment vehicle to determine if they have the interest or aptitude necessary for a career in any one of several occupational areas. After they have completed the program, students may enroll in one of the many trade courses at a vocational center, or after next fall, in the occupational training park. Or they may stay in the course and specialize in one or more occupational areas.

The facility for this program—and there is one in each of the county's 22 high schools—is a general vocational shop containing equipment for many occupations: welding, small gasoline engine repair, auto mechanics, auto body, bricklaying, carpentry, woodworking, plumbing, and machine shop.

Some vocational teachers may claim they cannot do justice to teaching all of these areas, but it has been proved during the past 16 years that it can be done. Admittedly, it requires a lot of in-service workshops in skill development.

ADVICE FOR VOCATIONAL TEACHERS

Teachers in regular vocational programs may feel apprehensive when asked to train students they are accustomed to thinking of as unable to 'cut the mustard.' This apprehension is likely to be more pronounced in programs where the program objectives override concern for the individual.

As most educators already know, there is no pat procedure for training the handicapped. It is possible, however, to suggest some guidelines. It is worth noting also that in schools where competency based vocational education has been implemented as an approach to training the handicapped, apprehensions are minimized.

The best advice to teachers might be in the form of the following summary:

- Develop a personal commitment to training the handicapped and see that there is an occupation or job subgroup for which most handicapped students can be trained. In masonry, for example, a job subgroup might be the tasks involved in laying brick to a line. Few handicapped students can aspire to the skills of a journeyman bricklayer, but many can be taught to lay bricks to a line and perform all tasks up to that skill level.
- Break down occupations into subgroups for which there are employment opportunities. Train students to achieve entry level skills relating to these

occupational subgroups. The student's progress should not be determined by length of time but by demonstrated competency.

- Be patient! Do not allow students to move from a simple to a more complex task until complete mastery is indicated.
- To minimize problems that arise in the transition from school to work, duplicate as closely as possible the working conditions and job skills your student will find after employment.
- Whenever possible, place students in on-the-job training programs after they have achieved basic skills.
- Seek advice from experts in special education to learn how to deal with the handicapping conditions of the students you will be teaching.
- To accommodate various handicaps, devise modifications in equipment and furniture. Improvise. Use your ingenuity. (Some adaptive equipment is already on the market.)
- If you are teaching in a co-op program, orient the students' supervisors to the problems of the handicapped.
- Find out what you can about competency based vocational education and how you might apply it to teaching your handicapped students.

The Emotionally Disturbed Adolescent: Development of Program Alternatives in Secondary Education

by Richard L. McDowell
and Gweneth Blacklock-Brown

A major dilemma confronting public education today is how to provide an appropriate education for adolescents who exhibit a variety of behavior disorders. The Education for All Handicapped Children Act (Public Law 94-142) has the potential to dramatically change the educational prospects of this previously neglected secondary level group. University personnel, state directors of special education, public school administrators, and teachers have begun to direct attention toward discovering and developing educational procedures that will be effective with disturbed and troubled youth. The time when these youth can be rejected by or expelled from the public schools is passing.

Although the law states that all children must be served by the public schools, the *how to's* of an appropriate education for secondary age handicapped youth are in the beginning stages of development and, in all likelihood, will take many more years to evolve. In the meantime, educators charged with the responsibility of developing and establishing programs for adolescents with behavior disorders need to take stock of where the field has been and what is currently known. Until more relevant research is forthcoming, the sharing of information pertaining to successful programing strategies is critical if the full potential of the law is to be realized.

Throughout most of history, individuals with physical or behavioral differences were systematically abused, neglected, and excluded from important segments of society. Efforts to provide services for what we now term *exceptional* or *handicapped* persons began in Europe approximately 150 years ago. The first real efforts in the United States to educate exceptional persons occurred in the latter half of the nineteenth century with the establishment of residential schools. A majority of these schools, however, did not address the needs of emotionally or behaviorally disordered children.

By the late 1960s and early 1970s, public educational services for select categories and age groups of handicapped children were provided in most local community schools but, unfortunately, children and youth with emotional and behavioral disorders all too frequently were still neglected by the schools. Expulsion was the most commonly used practice in dealing with the emotionally or behaviorally disordered child — especially youth at the secondary school level. As late as 1976, the National Advisory Committee for the Handicapped estimated that 81 percent of the nation's emotionally disturbed children were not being served by the nation's public schools. Of those served, most fell in the mild to moderate range, and almost all were of elementary age.

With so few schools providing adequate educational programs for emotionally or behaviorally disordered youth, college and university special educational personnel interested in children with behavior disorders began to focus their attention and energies on the mild to moderately disturbed elementary age child. Nelson and Kauffman[1] found a paucity of published information on the secondary level student. Similarly, in a review of the Bureau of Education for the Handicapped's personnel preparation programs in emotional disturbance, Brown and Palmer[2] found that only 10 of the 118 projects, in their request for funds, demonstrated an attempt to provide teachers with the skills and competencies necessary for working with the secondary level student. Even among the 10 projects providing some experiences at the secondary level, most focused on the elementary child and paid only limited attention to the secondary level.

In their review, Brown and Palmer state that

> of all the age groups, the education of the secondary level emotionally disturbed child appears to be the most neglected by special education. Programs focused on the skills and competencies necessary for setting up quality educational programs at the secondary level simply do not exist in most areas of the country.[3]

It is no wonder, then, that with so little published information available and with so few teachers having received educational experiences related to teaching this population, school administrators find it difficult to locate and hire teachers with the skills and *know how* to appropriately educate the disordered secondary level student. Until systematic programing and research efforts can be conducted at the secondary level, much of what gets implemented will be adapted from techniques found to be successful with students at the elementary level.

POPULATION

Identification and Classification

Teachers, when given the task of identifying emotional or behavioral disorders in children, can think immediately of some child they have taught whom they believed to have been behaviorally disordered. If pressed to elaborate on what caused them to believe that a child was behaviorally disordered, many would identify aggressive behavior, others might indicate the child's inappropriate verbalization, and still others might point to withdrawing behavior. The point is that emotional or behavioral disorders come in many forms. Attempts to classify or categorize emotional or behaviorial disorders have been of little value in developing educational programs. Classification has implied that there is a preferred or prescribed method of treatment for specific categories — but this has not been the case. Those who have worked with disordered children know from experience that each case must be studied individually and that a treatment plan must be designed to meet the child's specific needs without regard to the assigned classification. Classification, however, does allow us to make generalizations with regard to the similarities found in certain groupings, as well as to provide us with a rather standardized method of communication.

Some professionals believe that some type of homogeneous grouping is necessary when designing educational programs; others advocate some type of heterogeneous grouping so that, for example, you don't end up with eight highly aggressive, acting out boys in one classroom. There are pros and cons for each view. Before accepting either position, three questions should be considered:

1. How will such placement affect the child?
2. How will the behavior of the identified child affect the other children in the program?
3. How will the behavior of this child affect the teacher's interactions with all the children in the program?

These three factors are listed in order of priority. The major concern always should be the effect upon the individual child being considered for placement. Placement in a special program should be made with the primary purpose of benefiting the individual child — not simply to provide convenience for the teacher or the school system.

Definitions and Descriptions

Defining the emotionally or behaviorally disordered child is a difficult task that becomes even more difficult and complex when applied to an adolescent population. The problem of definition is compounded by normal deviations in behavior during the period referred to as adolescence. Typical crises, for example, might be the stress that occurs when the adolescent attempts to establish autonomy or when relationships with the opposite sex are redefined. These crises are experienced by everyone. How they are handled determines the comfort or stress the individual feels when confronted with situations that require resolution of the issues involved.

Some individuals handle adolescent crises easily and are able to resolve such issues with limited effort. For these individuals, adolescence is largely an enjoyable experience. For others, who have more difficulty in dealing with and finding solutions to their crises situations, adolescence is a time of stress and pain. The behavior they exhibit in their attempt to resolve issues often exceeds the limits society has established for behavior variability. Depending upon the extent to which the behavior exceeds the limits, the behavior may be excused as being normal adolescent behavior or punished, if it infringes upon adult society. *Any definition of behavior disorders that is to be applied to an adolescent population must approach the fine line separating accepted behavior variance and behavior viewed as being deviant.*

Definitions presently in use by educators were written with the elementary age child in mind. The easiest of these definitions to adapt to the secondary age child is the classical list of characteristics developed by Bower[4] for use in identifying the emotionally disturbed child. Bower believed that to be considered emotionally disturbed a child had to exhibit one or more of the following characteristics, either to a marked extent or over a period of time.

1. An inability to learn which cannot be explained by intellectual, sensory, or health factors.
2. An inability to build or maintain satisfactory interpersonal relationships with peers and teachers.
3. Inappropriate types of behavior or feelings under normal conditions.
4. A general, pervasive mood of unhappiness or depression.
5. A tendency to develop physical symptoms, pains or fears associated with personal or school problems.[5]

Another definition that begins to recognize not only degrees of severity but differences in educational programing was developed by Kauffman.[6] It was written for educators, and apparently with the elementary age child in mind. With a little effort, however, the reader should be able to adjust it for an adolescent population.

Children with behavior disorders are those who chronically and markedly respond to their environment in socially unacceptable and/or personally unsatisfying ways but who can be taught more socially acceptable and personally gratifying behavior. Children with mild and moderate behavior disorders can be taught effectively with their normal peers (if their teachers receive appropriate consultive help) or in special resource or self-contained classes with reasonable hope of quiet reintegration with their normal peers. Children with severe and profound behavior disorders require intensive and prolonged intervention and must be taught at home or in special classes, special schools, or residential institutions.[7]

The commonalities between Bower's definition and Kauffman's, as well as those of others,[8-10] seem to rest on two major points: (1) the inability to establish appropriate satisfying relationships with others; and (2) demonstration of behavior which either fails to meet or exceeds the expectations of those with whom the individual comes in contact.

Given the earlier statement pertaining to normal adolescent crises, great care must be taken in determining whether the behavior being considered is within a normal development pattern and is progressing toward a satisfying solution, or whether it is a behavior pattern resulting in conflict and stress and is making little or no progress toward more acceptable and rewarding ways of behaving. If, in fact, definitions do establish the parameter for conducting identification, screening, and diagnostic procedures, care must be taken, on an individual basis, to assure that special services are indeed a necessary step in assisting the adolescent's development. Then, if such a program is warranted, the public schools have a responsibility to provide it.

Continuum of Behavior Disorders

Kauffman,[11] in his definition of behaviorally disordered children, suggests a continuum of behavior disorders ranging from mild to profound. He appears to divide this continuum into two major segments—mild-to-moderate and severe-to-profound. Admittedly, to separate mild disorders from moderate disorders and severe disorders from profound disorders is often difficult. For program purposes, however, more of a distinction can be made between mild and moderate. The child or adolescent with a mild disorder can in all likelihood be provided assistance and remain within the regular educational program. Mild disorders tend to be more transient in nature than do the other levels of the continuum.

Moderate disorders tend to last longer and usually require some type of special placement. Length of placement, however, tends to reflect school policy rather than the condition of the child.[12] Schools have a tendency to think in terms of school year with regard to placement. In fact, within a majority of public school programs, the appraisal and review procedure is designed to function within that time framework. It appears to be an accepted belief and practice that movement of a child from one program to another is easier on the child and everyone else concerned if that movement takes place at the end of the nine-month term. In reality, of course, behavior disorder is not designed around the school year. With appropriate intervention, and many times without any intervention, the behavior may change or improve in a much shorter time period, such as in the case of an acute situational stress. The child or adolescent may need only to be shown an alternative method or behavior for dealing with the stress even though at the time the stress was introduced, the individual's behavior was disturbed to the extent that special services were required.

The distinction between moderate disorders and severe disorders usually is made on the basis of the amount of contact with reality maintained by the individual. Children or adolescents in the moderate category tend to have problem behaviors but retain relatively intact contact with reality and, with the exception of the specific problem area, are able to function fairly well. (We, of course, recognize that behavior problems can generalize and interfere to a great extent with the individual's ability to function in many aspects of living.) The moderately disordered individual usually will require some type of special intervention program. To date, these individuals have been served through either the resource room or the self-contained classroom.

The severely disordered child or adolescent, because of the exaggerated state of his/her behavior, has required a special self-contained class. A majority of these children have yet to be served by the public schools. Instead, they are found in residential schools, institutions, or at home. A distinction is not made here between the severely disordered and the profoundly disordered in that both require essentially the same type of placement and services. To many professionals in the field, the two terms are used interchangeably, although a case can be made for separating the two groups. Present technology, however, does not make it expedient to do so.

Juvenile Offenders

Another type of behavior disorder overlaps to a certain extent with the previously described continuum but, at the same time, is treated as if it were a separate entity. The label given to this problem is *juvenile delinquency* or a *juvenile offender*. Since such labels are attached through a legal process rather than through a diagnostic process, educators have attempted to ignore this problem, for the most part. If the individual so labeled creates problems for the school, s/he usually is passed back to the juvenile justice system to resolve the problem.

In a majority of these cases, the school problem is truancy—a situation many schools choose to ignore. The typical comment pertaining to such a situation is that to do anything other than ignore it would be more trouble than it's worth. Schools are having to face the fact, nevertheless, that state laws dictate the age at which students can terminate their school experience. Also, the juvenile justice system is emphasizing, as part of its conditions for probation or parole, that youth return to school. This gives the school another population of students who, because of their behavior, have been identified as being "different" and, as such, may require special attention and/or special programs.

Children and adolescents from each of the described categories exist and can be found in every school district. Public Law 94-142 has mandated that appropriate educational programs be provided for them. Each state education agency is responsible for developing programs at the local level to provide for these needs.

THE ROLE OF EDUCATION

The role of secondary education in America today is somewhat unclear because of the generalized expectations placed upon it by the community. Secondary education is expected to produce graduates who, in addition to becoming responsible members of society, are capable of entering the world of work or of continuing their education at a higher level. Limitations as to how this is to be accomplished have been imposed under the guise of economic prudence; and the result of such a stance has been the development of large high schools which appear incapable of keeping track of their students on a daily basis, much less on a period-to-period basis. An agency or system that is unable to determine where its clients are at a given time is not able to enforce effective management procedures or provide effective leadership.

An increase in student population decreases the probability that its members will have a feeling of involvement with the program. If experience has taught us anything, it is that for optimal learning to occur, the student must have a feeling of belonging and involvement. Without these conditions, pride and accomplishment are lacking. Many of the students who are experiencing this lack merely go through the motions of learning. The relevancy of the available curriculum also may contribute to this lack of involvement. A curriculum presented in a format that does not allow for generalization to the students' everyday environment runs the risk of being perceived as not relevant and not worthy of the time or investment of self on the part of students to acquire that particular piece of knowledge. Certain areas within a curriculum do not lend themselves to immediate application to the individual student's environment but, hopefully, a majority of students are able to experience relevancy in most of what they study and to develop self-control that allows them to handle nonrelevant material in an appropriate manner.

For a growing percentage of the student population, the traditional curriculum does not appear to be relevant or even appropriate. For years, America's secondary education was geared to produce graduates who were expected to enter college. This emphasis led to development of the college preparatory curriculum to the point that it became almost the only way a student could earn a high school diploma. Educators closed their eyes to alternatives to the college preparatory curriculum. Anything less was looked upon as having little value. This was a time when the high school diploma was viewed as a prerequisite for a successful career.Next, it was the college degree. Today, even the college degree does not guarantee its holder a job, much less any success. Is the next step or basic requirement a graduate degree? Such a proposal would not be realistically possible nor even reasonable.

The obvious alternative to the questions posed here is reassessment of the secondary curriculum to determine alternative routes a student may choose to reach graduation. Because of court rulings pertaining to the tracking of secondary students, it would be necessary to devise a mechanism whereby students would be able to shift from one route to another should they change their mind with regard to the desired outcome. The point of entry into an alternative would have to be established. Core areas common to all alternatives would need to be identified. Desired competencies for each alternative also would need to be identified, along with establishment of criteria for determining attainment of those competencies. This would be a massive undertaking, not only in redesigning the curriculum but in convincing many educators and a large segment of the general population that such an endeavor would be worthwhile and beneficial. The flexibility that such a program could allow, nevertheless, would permit the development of individualized educational planning. Such planning is necessary if we are to provide for the individual needs of students. Only through such flexibility can we approach the concept of an "appropriate education" as proposed in Public Law 94-142.

In the past, special education programs for the emotionally or behaviorally disordered adolescent have been tied to the traditional curriculum. Educators didn't necessarily want to prepare this student for college, but if the student was to earn a high school diploma rather than a certificate of attendance, s/he must do it in the traditional manner. That meant accumulating an established number of units of credit in varioius academic areas. Some educators operated from the position that these units could be earned only in the regular classroom—which had the effect of excluding the special education student who for any reason was unable to function in the regular classroom, regardless of whether or not s/he could demonstrate the competencies being taught. Other educators interpreted the regulations pertaining to these units of credit to mean that if the student could demonstrate the required competencies of an academic area, whether in the special classroom or in the regular classroom, the student earned the credit toward graduation and the high school diploma. This matter of administrative interpretation is an issue that should be resolved. A resolution supporting the concept of competency demonstration would not cheapen the high school diploma but, rather, could serve to strengthen it for all students. The diploma would represent acquired skills rather than attendance and minimal performance.

Acquiring a high school diploma may not be an appropriate goal for some adolescents with emotional or behavioral disorders. Goals or objectives may need to be varied depending upon the severity of the disorder and the way in which it manifests itself. Students with mild disorders probably would be able to complete the requirements for an academic diploma in the regular program if that were the direction or alternative they chose to pursue. Decisions pertaining to terminal outcomes or goals should be made on a case-by-case basis and should be flexible enough that, should the adolescent's disorder improve or deteriorate, the individual plan could be revised so as to be appropriate.

Alternatives available to the educator for working with the emotionally or behaviorally disordered adolescent should range from (1) a self-help program that might include motor training, language training, social skills, and survival skills, to (2) a vocational program that might include training in survival academics as they apply to vocational areas, social skills, vocational skills, on-the-job training and work-study activities, to (3) an academic program. Program alternatives should not operate in isolation from each other but should serve to support each other, each an integral part of the total education program.

PROGRAM DEVELOPMENT

Successful implementation of any new program is contingent upon the thoroughness with which its designers develop the total plan for operation. Such planning should begin with establishment of a number of statements or principles that reflect the population to be served, the purpose of the program, and the philosophical base upon which the program is to be built. A secondary public school program for emotionally or behaviorally disordered adolescents has the purpose of assisting students in their academic and social growth in a way that will allow them to function successfully within their environment. This statement encompasses the belief that every child or adolescent, regardless of the severity of any disorder, is capable of learning something; and that, through learning, positive change can occur within the individual. Also included in this statement is the belief that each student should have the opportunity to develop his/her potentials to the best ability.

Given appropriate curriculum alternatives, the development of an individual educational plan provides the student the best chance to accomplish this. Here, the educational environment is seen as supportive to the adolescent. Success on assigned tasks assists in developing a positive self-concept. Disordered behavior is viewed as the result of faulty learning experiences. The educational environment is structured so as to support the introduction of order and consistency into the student's daily life. Through the use of order and consistency, the student learns what to expect from the environment and to develop self-control. The ability to appropriately exercise self-control is a major goal of this program.

Program planners should recognize the importance of administrative support in the operation of any project. Administrative support for a program should be obtained prior to introducing the program within the system. Too many special educators have learned the hard way that special classes cannot be operated in the manner in which they were designed if the administrator of the facility in which they are located is not supportive of the program. Further, such a program can be damaged even if the administrator does not take a position with regard to it; simply by allowing it to exist with no active involvement either way is perceived by many as lack of support. The administrator does set the model which a majority of employees will follow. An informed administrator is usually a supportive administrator— this should be taken as a cue to involve the selected building administrator in early stages of planning. If the administrator is unable to take an active role in the planning process, s/he should be kept informed of its progress, preferably through direct communication. If this is not possible, his/her appointed representative should be included, with periodic direct contacts to help determine if the administrator is receiving the correct information.

At the appropriate time, the entire building staff should be included in the planning process. The more staff members know about a program and what it is trying to accomplish, the greater the likelihood that they will become actively involved in it. Carefully planned in-service meetings pertaining to the special program can facilitate establishment of cooperative arrangements between regular programs and the special program. Once a special program has been implemented, some type of continuing dialogue should be established with the regular program. One method of doing this is through formation of an advisory committee to the program. One of the functions of the program advisory committee should be to involve the community and maintain contact. In many instances, state and community resources can be called upon to provide some program funding, as well as to provide outside expertise pertaining to various aspects of the program.

Environmental Arrangement

The educational environment is designed to provide support to the students as they work with assigned tasks. The amount of structure is determined, for the most part, by the severity of the student's disorder. One way of conceptualizing this is to consider the student and his/her relationship to these three dimensions (see Figure 1).

The first dimension is the extent of *environmental structure* required to provide the optimum learning environment. For moderately and severely disordered students, this represents a high degree of structure. The educational environment may be regarded as a prosthetic environment in that it contains controls not usually found in the classroom. As the student gains in self-control, the prosthetic environment is gradually faded so that the classroom structure approximates that found in the regular classroom.

The second dimension pertains to acquisition of desired *competencies*. Basic skills in a given area may need to be taught before entering other areas. As the student progresses, s/he moves closer and closer to the terminating competencies established.

The third dimension is *time*. As the student moves from the prosthetic environment and gains in the successful acquisition of competencies, time in the program becomes a factor. Time represents the interval necessary for the student to acquire the ability to function within the real environment and, at the same time, to move toward the acquisition of terminating competencies. These two processes are not separated for treatment purposes. They work in harmony, but not necessarily at the same rate.

FIGURE 1   The Relationship between Environmental Structure and the Acquisition of Competencies Across Time

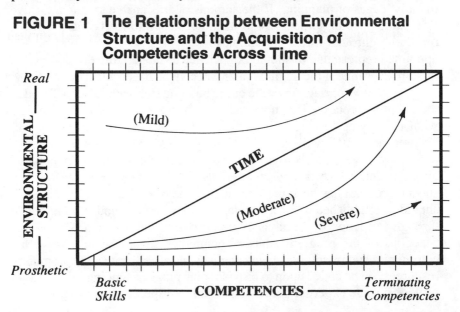

The lines in Figure 1 marked "mild," "moderate," and "severe" are approximations of how each of those categories might be represented as the student progresses across the three dimensions. These dimensions serve as the underlying organization of educational environment.

At least four environmental arrangements are appropriate for use in secondary level programs within the school. Selection of program for placement purposes usually is determined by severity of the disorder.

1. *Regular Class Placement.* This option is used when the disorder is considered to be mild and when the regular class teacher is provided supportive assistance in working with the child's problem. Multiple teachers at the secondary level can create some problems with this approach. The strong point in favor of this option is that the student remains with his/her peers.

2. *Resource Room Model.* In this option the student goes to the resource room or teacher for limited periods each day. The rest of the school day is spent in regular classes. This approach is recommended primarily for students with mild behavior disorders and has the advantage, like the first option, of integrating the student with peers.

3. *Special Class Placement.* This option is usually a self-contained classroom where the student may remain with one teacher for most, if not all, of the school day. An advantage with this type of arrangement is that it allows the teacher to control the amount of structure necessary for each student. This is the traditional type of program that has been used extensively in the past. It has been used primarily with students who are in the moderate to severe categories. Students in this program are integrated into the regular program whenever such a move is deemed feasible and desirable; unfortunately, though, such integration has met with only limited support from regular class teachers. A major limitation to this type of arrangement at the secondary level is that it inhibits certain types of movement on the part of the students. Movement from one classroom to another between periods is the normal state of affairs in secondary programs, and lack of this type of movement many times is seen by the special student as something that makes him/her different from the rest of the student body. If possible, some form of comparable movement should be built into the special student's daily schedule.

4. *Special Program.* This option is being used to only a limited extent at the present time. Nevertheless, it is a model that appears to be most appropriate for use at the secondary level. The program consists of multiple classes organized into an integrated unit to provide students with as near a normal type of program as possible. It is located within the regular school facility, allowing close proximity to regular classes, which facilitates integration of special students whenever possible. The special student may

spend a majority of the day within the special program. Since the program consists of multiple classes, the student may change classes each period, allowing movement similar to that of the regular program. When used in the public school setting, this type of arrangement seems to best serve the moderate to mildly disordered student. It also works quite well with the adjudicated student. It does not segregate him/her from the student body or mark the student as different in the same way the self-contained class does, yet it provides an educational environment that offers an opportunity to be successful with learning.

Selection of a particular environmental arrangement for use in a secondary program may be determined by factors including the availability of space, program funds, and trained staff. A comprehensive approach to working with the emotionally or behaviorally disordered student at the secondary level would include all four options described. Such a continuum would provide services for all levels of severity.

Behavior Management

Behavior management is just as important at the secondary level as at any other level. The teacher's ability to manage the behavior of students determines the smoothness of flow through the daily schedule. The secondary teacher is in a somewhat different position than his/her elementary counterpart. The secondary teacher is not as naturally reinforcing, and teacher praise may work just the opposite from what is expected.

Peer reinforcement has a larger role among adolescents. Educators need to learn or develop effective ways of using the peer group to reinforce desired behaviors in students. One effective technique of behavior management with secondary students uses the Premack Principle in the form of contingency contracting.[13] This procedure allows for student participation in selecting reinforcers and establishing procedures or criteria to be met before receiving reinforcement. Essentially, it is represented by a written agreement between student and teacher that spells out what the student is expected to do, what the teacher is expected to do, and the consequences for meeting the agreed upon expectations.

Long and Newman,[14] in their article on managing surface behavior, described several techniques that can be used to influence ongoing classroom behavior. These range from "planned ignoring" to physical restraint. Most of these techniques would be appropriate for use at the secondary level. Caution should be used with regard to physical restraint; most of us have found this technique to be an unsatisfactory alternative with secondary students. Most adolescents have sufficient language skills to allow the teacher to use words as a means of defusing conflict situations that have the potential of developing into physical aggression. A teacher should learn to talk with students and watch for clues of student frustration that might result in a conflict situation. One of the best skills a teacher can develop in regard to behavior management is the ability to plan ahead for behaviors that might occur and the resulting consequences for the individual student.

Sound behavior management is based on four major components:

1. Planning.
2. Arranging the classroom to be conducive to the desired activities.
3. Selecting appropriate educational tasks.
4. Selecting appropriate consequences to behavior.

If these four components are taken into consideration and the teacher remembers to place the major emphasis on positive behavior, a solid foundation will be established from which to manage the student's behavior in the classroom.

Curriculum

The curriculum serving the secondary level emotionally or behaviorally disordered student should be multifaceted to encompass needs identified at various degrees of severity. For a number of these students, adaptation of the traditional curriculum is sufficient. For others, the traditional curriculum has been inefficient in assisting them to gain basic skills. Remedial teaching based on a watered down version of this curriculum also has shown itself to be an ineffective technique. The time for traditional remediation has passed. Curriculum at the secondary level needs to be made relevant to the student. A curriculum should be allowed to evolve from functional life skills, and it should be organized in a manner that allows the student to utilize his/her life experiences. The curriculum must be relevant to the student's everyday needs. Basic concepts should be taught through the use of such topics as money management, job applications, bus schedules, obtaining a driver's license, home management, etc.

A teacher must be realistic in assessing the student's assets and deficits and understand that some of these students have been in special classes most of their school career. They probably have been exposed to many of the remedial techniques such as math programs that use the standard gimmicks of blocks, rods, chips, or money to teach number concepts. At this point, it may be more important that the student be taught to use a pocket calculator to carry out mathematical functions correctly. The teacher maybe should be more concerned with survival reading than with pleasure reading. A quick assessment should let the teacher know if the student can best use a phonetic approach to reading or a sight-say method. The format of any material used with adolescents should be geared to their age level. Reading and language skills might be approached by using newspapers, magazines, or high interest material like a driver's instruction manual.

Secondary curricula breaks down functionally into five general training areas: (1) Social Curriculum; (2) Academic Curriculum; (3) Vocational Curriculum; (4) Vocational Training; and (5) Work-study Experiences. The social curriculum's purpose is to assist the student in developing skills necessary for successful and appropriate interaction with others. A major component of this area is helping the student learn self-control. Many approaches are available to help the student achieve this, two of which will be mentioned here. . . . Goldstein [15] has developed a social learning curriculum for use at the elementary level; the kit contains many helpful ideas and activities sequenced for the user. The secondary version [provides] the secondary teacher with an organized program for approaching the area of self-control. The second technique is the "Class Meeting," as described by Glasser. [16] The Class Meeting gives students an opportunity to learn problem-solving skills through group interaction.

The academic curriculum may involve both the regular school curriculum and the special class curriculum. Students who are capable of handling the regular program should be encouraged to do so and supported in their efforts. Students who are unable to function successfully with the regular curriculum should receive an individual educational plan, devised to incorporate methods and techniques of special education to present academic areas in which the student is capable of being successful.

The vocational curriculum includes prevocational training as well as assessment of vocational aptitudes. Its purpose is to provide the student with the basic skills necessary to function successfully in a vocational training program. The vocational curriculum must be modernized to reflect the changes in the job market if it is to provide a meaningful experience for the student. The vocational training area is concerned with developing competencies in a particular job area.

The work-study area is a continuation of vocational training, with the student receiving on-the-job experience and, in most cases, a salary for this work. While participating in the work-study program, the student may return to the school for a portion of the day to complete additional training or to earn additional credits toward graduation.

Each of the five areas described above interacts with the others. They are mutually supportive as the student moves toward independence.

Parent Involvement

Parent participation in programs for the secondary level emotionally or behaviorally disordered student is a positive addition to the program. Too many parents of adolescent students have given up on trying to effect positive change in their child's behavior. They have tried every technique they know and some that others have suggested, with the hope of getting their child to behave in a manner acceptable to them. If these efforts have failed, by the time the child reaches high school they probably are ready to throw up their hands and usually make some comment like, "He's yours now! I've tried everything I know and it hasn't helped a bit." Actions and remarks like these illustrate the frustrations parents feel in raising a child, particularly a child with behavior problems.

Kroth[17] emphasizes the importance of establishing clear and direct lines of communication with parents. Such communication opens the door to a real team approach for working with behavior problems. Communication permits a sharing of ideas for working with behavior, as well as a supportive system for both the parent and the teacher. Parents who are knowledgeable about their child's program and who feel comfortable talking with the teacher tend to be supportive of the program. When questions arise, they feel free to contact the teacher and seek some type of resolution.

In-person conferences should be held between teacher and parents prior to a child's entering a special program. These initial meetings usually are of an informative nature. Regularly scheduled meetings, or even parent group meetings, should be established once the student has entered the program. These meetings serve to continue to provide information about the student's progress, to provide instruction on alternative techniques of working with the student, and to help in the problem-solving process. Educators need to place more emphasis on developing new procedures for interacting with parents. Parents can be a formidable foe, but they also can be a strong ally. At this stage in the development of secondary programs, school personnel are well advised to seek parent support and find ways to maintain it.

PROPOSED PROGRAM ALTERNATIVE

Following is a brief description of one type of program alternative. It includes basic rationale, staff considerations, program objectives, and plans for implementation. It does not represent the only alternative but is a logical starting point based on the needs of secondary students in programs for the emotionally and behaviorally disordered.

Career and vocational education provide an alternative to the traditional (college preparatory) curriculum.[18] This alternative is logical when one considers that the major purpose of formal education is to prepare the student to become a productive member of society. Employability has become the primary factor by which this goal is measured. Then, our high schools have a responsibility to provide students with an appropriate program that assists in attaining skills necessary to successfully enter the job market.

Career and vocational programs for the regular student are not new.[19] Such programs to serve handicapped students within the public schools, however, are relatively new. Special education programs at the secondary level have given limited assistance in prevocational training and work-study experiences. Although these programs have helped to revise existing curricula to make subject matter more usable and have introduced a broader use of individualized instruction, they have been limited in their ability to develop extensive training models for career and vocational education.

Program Description

This model, for vocational/occupational experiences for handicapped students, relies upon full cooperation of the school administration, the state department of education, and the parents of students participating in the program. All must agree that career and vocational education is a suitable and realistic alternative to the standard curriculum. Through joint agreement of these parties, successful completion of the program should result in high school graduation and a diploma. A solid commitment of facilities, personnel, equipment, and materials is a must. This commitment is necessary to guarantee continuation of the program and to protect the students participating in the program. Further, the model presented here is not meant to stand in isolation but is to be an integral part of the total educational program. It provides tasks and activities specific to the handicapped student and integrates where feasible with the regular program.

The vocational program model requires a minimum of three self-contained classroom areas in close proximity. These accommodations should be part of the regular physical plant to assist in integration of the special students into appropriate components of the regular program. Two of the classrooms are used for academic activities; one is defined as the *math room*, and the other is the *language arts room*. The third classroom should be twice the size of a standard classroom; this room is used for *vocational preparation activities*.

Personnel for the program include a program director to administer the program, one math teacher, one language arts teacher, one industrial arts teacher, one home economics teacher, one work-study coordinator, and two teacher aides. All teachers are to be certified in their identified area of speciality and in special education (preferably, in either behavioral disorders, learning disabilities, or mental retardation).

The program director's responsibilities include: (1) writing and evaluating objectives, (2) scheduling, (3) communications and coordination, (4) assisting the other teachers when necessary, (5) keeping records on student progress, (6) consulting with counselors, vocational teachers, regular staff, and appropriate district specialists, and (7) organizing and conducting in-service training. The program director is responsible to the building principal and the director of special education.

The math teachers and language arts teachers are responsible for their respective fields. The industrial arts teacher and the home economics teacher work together in the vocational preparation room and are assisted by two teacher aides. The work-study coordinator is responsible to the program director. S/He works closely with the business community to arrange student job placements and to provide for supervision and evaluation of on-the-job performance.

The program's overall objective is to assist the student in attaining identified competencies which will provide a firm foundation for entering the world of work. The specific program objectives are:

1. To provide for social, vocational, and academic skill development that will aid students in formulating the basic competencies for employment and entrance into society.

2. To continually evaluate the students' skill performance and attitude, to determine the areas of skill strengths and weaknesses, and to provide occupational guidance based upon interest and areas of vocational strength.

3. To assist in the development and practice of good safety habits necessary in a working environment.

4. To assist students in developing positive feelings toward self and task performance.

5. To perform satisfactorily the assigned vocational tasks and to make related social attitude adjustments.

6. To present an occupational orientation related to relevant community employment.

7. To reduce the dropout rate of handicapped students.

8. To develop an awareness of the responsibilities of being productive, self-supporting citizens.

Most of these objectives are written as general statements and, as such, need to be broken into component parts and rewritten in behavioral terms to allow for clearer measurement and evaluation.

Prior to entering the program, the student and parents meet with the program director. A questionnaire designed around the vocational areas available in the program is completed by the student and parents with assistance by the program director. The purpose of this questionnaire is to identify hobbies, areas of interest, and aptitudes a student may have for given vocational areas. This information is used in assigning the student to a vocational task area. Students perform better when their initial experience in a new program involves a familiar task at which they can be successful. High interest, coupled with a task that is within the student's range of abilities, is a strong motivator.

The program itself is composed of two phases. An entering student is placed in Phase 1, where s/he receives a general orientation to the program and is administered a battery of interest and aptitude tests.[20] Test results are used in planning the areas of vocational consideration. Programs of study are individualized for the students; they are geared toward the student's areas of identified potential.

During Phase 1, the student enters both the general education sequence and the vocational preparation area. The general education sequence contains the math program, the language arts program (reading, writing, and spelling), and the social economics program. The student's present level of functioning in each of these areas is determined by testing conducted by the teacher. The individual educational plan for each student begins at a level where there is a high probability of success.[21]

In the vocational preparation area, the student is assigned to one of the 25 available task work areas—an area identified as having a high success probability for the student. The vocational preparation area is located in the largest of the three rooms and is supervised by the two vocational teachers assisted by the two aides. The room is arranged so that each vocational task area is located in a work station. In addition, an open crafts area and a closed storage area are provided. Instructional units in the work stations include:

1. Tool Usage	14. Window Repair
2. Soldering	15. Pipe Fitting
3. Lawnmover Repair	16. Adding Machine
4. Electrical Wiring	17. Cash Register
5. Gear Assembly	18. Filing
6. Automotive	19. Typing
7. Engraving	20. Sewing
8. Jewelry	21. Baby Care
9. Leather Crafts	22. Ironing
10. Book Binding	23. Mail Sorting
11. Upholstery	24. Telephone
12. Dexterity	25. Appliance Repair
13. Bicycle Repair	

FIGURE 2 Secondary Vocational Program for Handicapped Adolescents

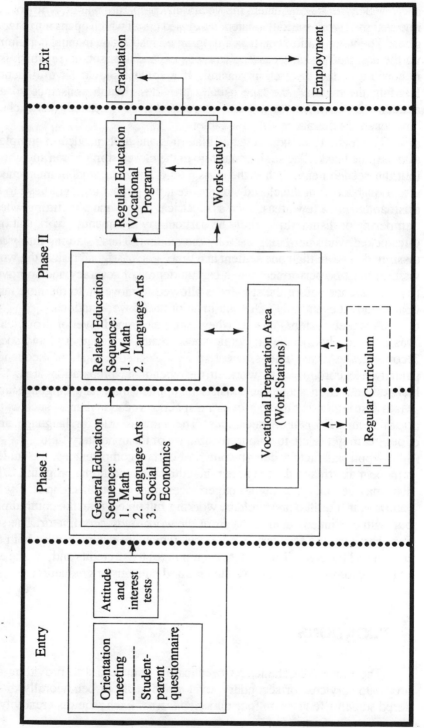

When the student enters the vocational preparation area, s/he goes to the assigned work station, located in a closed carrel which opens into a work area. The work station contains a programed instruction manual pertaining to the assigned tasks, a cassette tape player, and a cassette tape which is a recording of the instruction manual. If a student should have difficulty reading the manual, the tape usually provides enough assistance so the student can continue the work. If more assistance is needed, the teachers and teacher aides are readily available.

The manual includes a list of materials and tools needed to complete the assigned task. The student must go to the closed storage area and check out the needed items. When the class period ends, the student must check the tools back in at the closed storage area; the project does not have to be dismantled. In a few areas, such as electrical wiring and pipe fitting where tampering or dismantling would be particularly detrimental, work stations are locked when not being used by the student. These stations rarely are assigned to more than one student at a time. Each assigned task at the work station must be performed with a certain degree of accuracy and approved by the teacher before the student is allowed to move on to the next task. Each student eventually will work in all of the 25 work stations.

A student enters Phase II when a predetermined level of proficiency has been reached in the academic areas (math, language arts, and social economics). At this time, s/he enters the "Related Education" sequence, meanwhile continuing to work in the vocational preparation area. The related education sequence consists of applied math and language arts. Math instruction is directed toward a specific vocational area, such as the math required for auto mechanics. The same is true for language arts. Spelling might relate to unique vocabulary of the upholstery field.

Upon satisfactory demonstration of certain competencies, the student may be mainstreamed into the regular education vocational program. S/He also may be placed in a work experience either on or off campus. By the senior year, the student should be working full time within the community, but with continued supervision from the work-study coordinator. The student earns credits for work experiences which are recognized by both the school and the state. The student accumulates these credits and, by the end of the senior year, should have the required number for graduation.

IMPLICATIONS

The immediate challenge to educators with regard to providing appropriate services for secondary level emotionally or behaviorally disordered students focuses on four major concerns. Each requires creativity in thinking and planning, not only to reassess the importance or value of present practices, but to design innovative programs to realistically meet the needs of students as they prepare to enter adult society.

1. Reevaluate the purpose and goals of secondary education for the emotionally or behaviorally disordered student. The curriculum needs to be clarified and expanded to provide alternatives for reaching those goals.

2. Identify and evaluate community resources to determine the ways in which they may be utilized appropriately.

3. Develop an organized and systematic approach to train teachers for these secondary level programs. Most states already provide guidelines for certification, but specific training to work with disordered students at the secondary level is lacking. Decisions need to be made regarding the appropriateness of preservice training, in-service training, and graduate training, as well as content to be included in the preferred model.

4. Identify or develop sources of funding sufficient for programs to operate in the manner in which they were designed. Funding also needs to be made available at the university level to support training programs.

The requirement for developing individualized education programs (IEPs) for students to meet the intent of an "appropriate education" dictates that regular education and special education work in close harmony. Service delivery systems for the emotionally or behaviorally disordered student must be designed, implemented, and evaluated to determine their effectiveness in providing a relevant education. This is a task that cannot be assigned to tomorrow; it is one that should have been completed yesterday. Today is the time for action.

NOTES

1. C.M. Nelson and J.M. Kauffman, "Educational Programming for Secondary School Age Delinquent and Maladjusted Pupils," *Behavior Disorders*, vol. 2, no. 2 (1977): 102-13.

2. G.D. Brown and D.J. Palmer, "A Review of BEH Funded Personnel Preparation Programs in Emotional Disturbance," *Exceptional Children*, vol. 44, no. 3 (1977): 168-74.

3. Ibid., p. 173.

4. E.M. Bower, *Early Identification of Emotionally Handicapped Children in School* (Springfield, IL: Charles C. Thomas, 1960).

5. Ibid., p. 9-10.

6. J.M. Kauffman, *Characteristics of Children's Behavior Disorders* (Columbus, OH: Charles E. Merrill, 1977).

7. Ibid., p. 23.

8. J.E. Pate, "Emotionally Disturbed and Socially Maladjusted Children," in *Exceptional Children in the Schools*, ed. L.M. Dunn (New York: Holt, Rinehart & Winston, 1963).

9. F.M. Hewett, *The Emotionally Disturbed Child in the Classroom* (Boston: Allyn & Bacon, 1968).

10. R.L. McDowell, *Program Designs for Teachers of the Behaviorally Disordered* (Santa Fe, NM: State Department of Education, Division of Special Education, 1975).

11. Kauffman, p. 23.

12. R.L. McDowell, "An Evaluation of a Residential Treatment Program for Adolescents as Measured by Post-Hospital Adjustment: A Follow-up Study" (PhD diss, University of Kansas/Lawrence, 1969).

13. L. Homme, A. Csanyi, M. Gonzales, and J. Rechs, *How to Use Contingency Contracting in the Classroom* (Champaign, IL: Research Press, 1969).

14. N.J. Long and R.G. Newman, "Managing Surface Behavior of Children in School," in *Conflict in the Classroom*, eds. N.J. Long, W.C. Morse, and R.G. Newman, 3d ed. (Belmont, CA: Wadsworth, 1976), pp. 308-16.

15. H. Goldstein, *The Social Learning Curriculum* (Columbus, OH: Charles E. Merrill, 1974).

16. W. Glasser, *Schools without Failure* (New York: Harper & Row, 1969).

17. R.L. Kroth, *Communicating with Parents of Exceptional Children* (Denver: Love, 1975).

18. D.E. Brolin, *Vocational Preparation of Retarded Citizens* (Columbus, OH: Charles E. Merrill, 1976).

19. Ibid.

20. O.P. Kolstoe and R. Frey, *A High School Work-Study Program for Mentally Subnormal Youth* (Carbondale, IL: Southern Illinois Press, 1965).

21. J. Vogel, "Learning and Self-Esteem: You Can't Have One without the Other," *Learning*, vol. 2, no. 7 (March 1974): 68-9.

BIBLIOGRAPHY

Bibliography

The following selective bibliography includes print and nonprint materials appropriate for either developing programs for special students or expanding collections of materials which speak to the needs of this population. For the most part, the annotations are descripive and not evaluative. If the reader is interested in purchasing a particular item, then s/he should contact the publisher or distributor regarding cost and availability. (Note: OP at the end of a bibliographic entry indicates that the book is currently out of print.)

Adams, R. C.; Daniel, A.; and Rullmar, L. *Games, Sports and Exercise for the Physically Handicapped*. Philadelphia: Lea and Febiger, 1975.

Detailed descriptions and examples are given for prevalent physical defects along with the incidence, treatment, implications for physical activity programs, and exercises. A number of sports, games, and activities are given with instructions as to how they may be adapted for the physically handicapped. Another major section of the book is devoted to low organization games; games which require fewer rules and less equipment adaptation. Appendix material offers information on therapeutic exercises for various parts of the body, body building, crutches, balance beam exercises, calisthenics, and organizations concerned with the physically handicapped.

"Adapted Equipment for Physical Activities." *Practical Pointers* 1 (October 1977): 7 p. Washington, DC: American Alliance for Health, Physical Education and Recreation, 1977. ERIC Document No. ED 154 548.

Equipment and devices which may enable handicapped individuals to participate in physical activities are described. Categories of equipment included are: aquatic devices, bicycling equipment, devices for ball activities, bowling aids, assistive devices for young children, and other adapted equipment ideas.

"Aids and Appliances for the Blind and Visually Impaired." American Foundation for the Blind, 15 West 16th Street, New York, NY 10011.

The catalog describes aids and appliances available from the American Federation of the Blind. Included are watches, clocks and timers, canes, household appliances, recreational materials, tools, writing materials, mathematical aids, and medical devices. Prices are given.

Alvin, J. *Music for the Handicapped Child*. London: Oxford University Press, 1965.

The book includes a wide variety of song activities specifically for use with handicapped children.

Andresen, Tish, comp. *Books for Storytelling to Young Deaf Children*. Idaho: Sandy Point Publications, 1977. OP

The picture books chosen for this list were selected for their high quality, simple story lines, and limited vocabulary. They are intended to be used with young deaf children by individuals who have some but limited skill in signed language.

Baskin, Barbara Holland, and Harris, Karen H. *Notes from a Different Drummer: A Guide to Juvenile Fiction Portraying the Handicapped*. New York: Bowker, 1977.

Most of the book is an annotated bibliography of 311 books of juvenile fiction depicting handicapped characters and published between 1940 and 1975. Along with each description are the suggested reading level and the type of disability depicted. Additional chapters are included on the role of the handicapped person in society, the treatment of the disabled in literature, and the selection and utilization of books.

————, eds. *The Special Child in the Library*. Chicago: American Library Association, 1976.

The Special Child in the Library is a book of readings designed to provide librarians with resources for working with children having serious sensory, intellectual, emotional, and physical problems. The book is divided into six sections, each dealing with a different aspect of service to handicapped children. Articles in the section on "Structure, Design, and Ambience" offer practical ideas for the design of libraries and media centers as well as for modifying existing library facilities to accommodate handicapped patrons. Other sections cover criteria to be used in the selection of materials as well as ways of adapting existing materials, successful activities conducted by librarians with certain groups of exceptional children, and the use of reading guidance and bibliotherapeutic techniques to clarify problem areas and explore methods of resolving conflicts. The final portion of the book is devoted to a compendium of agencies providing assistance to the handicapped.

Bennett, Janet M. "Films on Handicaps." *Sightlines* 10 (Winter 76/77): 4-9.

Annotated films on handicaps are discussed in four categories: institutions and communities, techniques and approaches, handicapped individuals, and causes.

Books for Mentally Retarded Children. Cincinnati, OH: Public Library of Cincinnati and Hamilton County, 1977.

Books which have been successfully utilized with mentally retarded children in the Cincinnati public schools are listed. The books are classified according to their appropriateness for EMR children, aged 6 to 9, 10 to 12, 12 to 15, and TMR children.

Brolin, D. E. *Vocational Preparation of Retarded Citizens*. Columbus, OH: Charles E. Merrill, 1976.

The author describes the process of vocational training for retarded individuals. Specific programs are discussed and evaluative criteria are set forth for each.

Cawthorne, Edythe, and Wolfson, Barbara. "Library Kits for the Deaf." *School Library Journal* 20 (October 1973): 98-9.

In order to better serve deaf children, the librarians at Prince George's County Memorial Library developed kits of educational materials for circulation to families with preschool age, hearing impaired children. The contents of the kits are described.

Dattner, Richard. "Play Without Barriers." *American School and University* 50 (September 1977): 60-1, 63-6.

Drawing from his own experiences with designing play facilities for handicapped children, Mr. Dattner discusses the general elements a good playground should provide its users. Consideration is given to problems involved in designing play facilities for the physically handicapped, emotionally disturbed, and retarded; and suggestions are offered for providing each with a rich variety of experiences.

Dequin, Henry C. "Sources of Information about the Handicapped." *School Library Journal* 26 (November 1979), 38-41.

The author surveys a number of bibliographic sources to aid the librarian in the selection of appropriate materials to use with handicapped students. Retrieval systems usage is examined, and the addresses of the databases are listed. Criteria to be considered in the selection process are also mentioned.

"Developmental Purposes of Commercial Games." *Practical Pointers* 1 (August 1977): 20 p. Washington, DC: American Alliance for Health, Physical Education and Recreation, 1977. ERIC Document No. ED 154 546.

Commercial games are listed under the categories of table, target, manipulative, active, and creative games. The address of the distributor, the price, and a description of the item are given for each game listed. Brief comments are also included on how each item could contribute to the user's growth and development.

Dorward, Barbara, and Barraga, Natalie. *Teaching Aids for Blind and Visually Limited Children*. New York: American Foundation for the Blind, 1968.

The 29 educational aids described in this book are designed to be constructed by parents or teachers and used under their guidance. A photograph of each aid is included along with a materials list and categories. Each separate category begins with an explanation of the purposes of the aids contained in that section.

Finger Spelling. Nine super 8 mm films in a series. Captioned. A few minutes each. US Bureau of Education for the Handicapped. 1972.

Nine super-eight films in cartridge form introduce finger spelling and basic word signs. Rental and loan information is available from National Audiovisual Center, National Archives and Record Service, General Services Administration, Order Section DA, Washington, DC 20409.

Fusco, Carol B. "Individually Prescribed Program of Instruction for Pupils Who Are Orthopedically Handicapped." Columbia, SC: South Carolina State Department of Education, 1977. 451 p. ERIC Document No. ED 140 558.

This document is designed to aid teachers of the orthopedically impaired to implement individualized educational programs. Definitions, levels of orthopedic handicaps, and program goals are outlined in the beginning chapters. Later sections are devoted to activities divided according to academic and social areas. Among the information given for each activity are the developmental level, degree of physical handicap, behavioral objective, enabling activities, facilities, materials, and equipment. Task analysis, communication boards, assessment, and teaching aids are also covered. A bibliography is included.

Gearheart, Bill, and Weishahn, Mel. *The Handicapped Child in the Regular Classroom*. Saint Louis, MO: C. V. Mosby, 1976.

A resource for individuals who find themselves working with handicapped children, this book suggests strategies for teaching children who are hearing impaired, visually impaired, crippled or other health impaired, learning disabled, mentally retarded, or who have speech or behavior problems. The appendices contain information on sources of materials and services, national organizations for the handicapped, and an annotated bibliography of books about handicapped individuals.

Good, Margaret. "Stories about Handicapped Children: A Select List." *School Librarian* 25 (June 1977): 110-6.

A synopsis of the story is given for each of a total of 41 books under the headings of physically handicapped, blind, deaf, dumb, mentally handicapped, and autistic. The books included are suitable for children age ten and above.

Hanley, Robert J., Jr. "The Special Student: Selected Media for Special Education." *Previews* 7 (1979): 2-6.

Robert Hanley reviews media which may assist educators in complying with the

Education for All Handicapped Children Act and suggests instructional materials for working with special children.

Haring, Norris G., ed. *Behavior of Exceptional Children*. 2d ed. Columbus, OH: Charles E. Merrill, 1978.

The second edition is a revised and expanded survey of the field of special education which includes chapters on the mentally retarded, behavior disordered, learning disabled, severely handicapped, profoundly handicapped, language and communication disorders, hearing handicapped, visually handicapped, physical and multiple disorders, and gifted. In addition, introductory chapters give an overview of the field, examine key issues including the major provisions of Public Law 94-142, and discuss early childhood special education. Also included are annotated lists of commonly used tests and diagnostic instruments, major journals and other publications on exceptional children, and a glossary.

Hunt, A.C., comp. "Annotated Bibliography of Books Depicting the Handicapped." In *Now Upon a Time: A Contemporary View of Children's Literature,* by Myra Pollack Sadker and David Miller Sadker. New York: Harper & Row, 1977.

Over 170 books are included in this annotated list of books depicting the handicapped. A suggested age range for each book is given.

"Ideas and Help, Too." The State Library of Ohio, 65 South Front Street, Columbus, OH 43215.

Librarians from various libraries in Ohio have submitted short narratives of programs that they have used with handicapped children.

I'm Just like You: Mainstreaming the Handicapped. Two sound filmstrips. Sunburst Communications, 1977.

The benefits of mainstreaming for the handicapped as well as the nonhandicapped are depicted in this set of two filmstrips centered around the experiences of three handicapped children. The children, their parents, teachers, and therapists discuss their attitudes and concerns. Recommended in *Booklist* as being suitable for children in grades four through eight and for adults.

Integration of Children with Special Needs in a Regular Classroom. Ten videocassettes, with discussion leader's/teacher's guide for each. Agency for Instructional Television, Box A, Bloomington, IN 47401.

This material is designed to aid teachers in recognizing and providing for individual differences. Program titles include: *Diagnosis and Educational Planning, Early Assessment, After Assessment, Every Child Can Learn, Together They Learn, Correcting Handwriting Problems, Mastering Math Skills, Developing Children's Languages, Reading and Learning Styles,* and *Every Student Is Different: The High School.*

Karnes, Merle B. *Creative Games for Learning: Games for Parents and Teachers to Make*. Reston, VA: Council for Exceptional Children, 1977.

The 50 games described in this book were chosen from several hundred for their ease of construction, ability to foster learning in young children, and adaptability for use with handicapped children. For each game are listed objectives, materials, directions for making the game and playing the game, vocabulary, variations of the basic game, and storage instructions. Detailed illustrations accompany each description.

Kirchner, Suzie Linton. *Play It by Sign, Games in Sign Language*. Northridge, CA: Joyce Media, 1974.

Games involving finger spelling and sign language are contained in a binder with removable pages. Objectives, level of instruction, materials needed, and directions are given for each of the 26 games.

————. *Signs for All Seasons: More Sign Language Games*. Northridge, CA: Joyce Media, 1977.

More than 50 games that are designed or adapted to be played in sign language have been compiled by the author. A number of *finger plays* are also included.

Lansdowne, Stephen C. *The Handicap Primer: An Introduction to Working with Young Handicapped Children*. Austin, TX: Austin Independent School District, 1978. 66 p.

Basic information about types of handicaps and teaching strategies to use with exceptional children is given. Various types of exceptionalities are described such as physical disorders, communication disorders, learning deviations, and behavior disorders. There are additional sections on working with the handicapped and what it is like to be disabled. The appendix includes a list of developmental schedules, developmental assessment checklists, and a glossary pertaining to exceptional children.

Like You/Like Me. Ten 16 mm films, 6 mins. each. Encyclopedia Britannica Educational Corporation, 425 North Michigan Avenue, Dept. 10A, Chicago, IL 60611.

This series of ten animated 16 mm color films of six minutes each is designed to aid teachers in preparing children in the early grades for the integration of handicapped with nonhandicapped children in the classroom. A comprehensive Teacher's Guide accompanies the series.

Lindsay, Zaidie. *Art and the Handicapped Child*. New York: Van Nostrand Reinhold, 1972. OP

Art and the Handicapped Child presents guidelines for providing creative art experiences for children with visual or auditory handicaps, autism, brain damage, and mental retardation. The major portion of the book describes techniques for drawing, painting, modeling, carving, printing, and puppet making and gives examples of artwork by handicapped pupils.

McCarr, Dorothy, and Wisser, Mary W., comps. *Curriculum Materials Useful for the Hearing Impaired*. Beaverton, OR: Dormac, 1979.

The commercially available materials selected for inclusion in this annotated bibliography are listed according to the following subject areas: career education, driver education, family life and health, language, mathematics, reading—high interest, reading—skills, resource materials, science, social studies, speech-auditory training, and total communication. Materials are for all levels from preschool through secondary, and each listing contains the title of the material, name and address of the publisher, approximate reading level, interest level, approximate cost, and a description of the contents.

"Media Review." 343 Manville Road, Pleasantville, NY 10570.

Formerly "Media Index," this reviewing tool is to aid librarians in making media purchases. Monthly supplements offer program summaries and evaluations, new media ideas, current funding information, and reviews of professional books. One section of the index is devoted to "Mainstreaming."

Miles, Dorothy. *Gestures; Poetry [in Sign Language]*. Northridge, CA: Joyce Media, 1976.

Thirty-nine poems, many of which were composed expressly to be performed in sign language, are included in this collection. The poems are arranged under the headings of nature poems, animal poems, poems of love and womanhood, and poems of experience.

Mullins, June, and Wolfe, Suzanne. *Special People behind the Eight-Ball*. Johnstown, PA: Mafex, 1975.

One-sentence annotations are given for children's books, autobiographies, biographies, books by parents and for parents, and fiction which relate to handicapped individuals. The books are listed and cross-referenced according to common medical categories.

People. . . Just like You. About Handicaps and Handicapped People (An Activity Guide). Washington, DC: President's Committee on Employment of the Handicapped, 1978.

Six separate activities with variations for four age levels are described. Their purpose is to improve the understanding and attitudes of school-aged children toward handicapped persons. Appendix material includes children's books with handicapped characters, films, and organizations from which resources may be obtained.

People You'd Like to Know. Ten live action 16 mm films, ten mins. each. Encyclopaedia Britannica Educational Corporation, 425 North Michigan Avenue, Dept. 10A, Chicago, IL 60611.

Live action film portraits of handicapped youngsters are shown in this series of ten, ten-minute color films. The series is designed to aid teachers in preparing non-handicapped children in the middle and upper grades for integration with handicapped children in the classroom. A comprehensive Teacher's Guide accompanies the series.

Pokorni, Judith, and Wujcik, Ann. *Audiovisual Guide for Services to Handicapped*. 1977. ERIC Document No. ED 145 616.

Approximately 110 audiovisual materials related to young handicapped children are presented in this annotated list. Films, filmstrips, and slides are categorized according to the following subject areas: child abuse, child development, exceptional children—general, screening and assessment, and specific handicapping conditions. Along with a brief description, each entry contains information on title, length, color, date, and availability as well as the names and addresses of the producers and distributors.

Pool, Jane. *Library Services for the Blind and Physically Handicapped: A Bibliography 1968-1978*. Washington, DC: Library of Congress, 1979.

The citations included in this bibliography were compiled from standard indexes covering the years 1968 through August 1979. The first listing of entries concerns services in the United States, the second is for services in other countries.

Additional titles that may be requested from the Library of Congress, National Library Service for the Blind and Physically Handicapped, include: *Subject Guide to Spoken Word Recordings; Magazines in Special Media; Closed Circuit Television Reading Devices for the Visually Handicapped; Architectural Barriers; Reading Machines for the Blind; Reading Materials in Large Type;* and *Reading, Writing, and Other Communication Aids for Visually and Physically Handicapped Persons*. These are periodically updated.

Physical Education for Blind Children. 16 mm film. Color. 18 mins. Campbell Films. Cory Hill. Saxtons River, VT 05154.

The movie shows ways in which the visually handicapped child may be integrated into the physical education program of the public school. Each scene in the film depicts visually impaired students and sighted students engaged in various physical activities. Some of the activities require modifications to accommodate the handicapped, others do not. Specific techniques are shown for including the visually impaired in team sports.

The Retarded Child. Two filmstrips, two cassettes, one script book, one question/answer book. Western Psychological Services, Educational Materials Division, 12031 Wilshire Blvd., Los Angeles, CA 90025.

Designed primarily for teachers and parents, this program offers an introduction to the intellectual and social needs of the moderately retarded. The accompanying booklet contains information on the profoundly and severely retarded.

Robertson, Mary L. "Materials, Program Suggestions for Hearing-Impaired Children." *School Media Quarterly* 4 (Spring 1976): 263-8.

This list of books and materials was selected for use by teachers, librarians, and parents. Included are books on educating the deaf child, as well as books with words and pictures, simple tales, picture storybooks, and wordless books for use with hearing-impaired children. Sources for obtaining books in signed English are also given.

Rosenthal, Judy S., ed. *Ideas for Kids: A Multi-Arts Approach to Fostering Creativity*. New Haven, CT: Area Cooperative Educational Services, 1978.

Over 50 activities for handicapped and nonhandicapped are presented. This book of ideas is centered around the areas of self-expression/communication, sensory awareness, skill development, originality, and creative thinking exercises in four art forms: music, movement, visual arts, and drama.

Rubin, Rhea Joyce. *Using Bibliotherapy: A Guide to Theory and Practice*. Phoenix, AZ: Oryx, 1978.

Although this book deals mainly with the philosophy behind bibliotherapy and the training of professional bibliotherapists, it contains information which would be useful to teachers and librarians. Procedures for using bibliotherapy with children are discussed along with books in which the characters depicted have language and hearing problems, obesity, diseases, mental retardation, eyesight problems, and other disabilities.

Silver, Ruth. *Listening and Responding to Sounds and Language*. Multimedia kit with three sound recordings and manual. Kimbo Educational, P.O. Box 477, Long Branch, NJ 07740.

Structured teaching materials designed to aid auditory training and language comprehension are presented in this multimedia kit. Body identification, body movement, recognition of name, following simple directions, auditory discrimination, and auditory memory are taught via songs and activities. This material is for use with severely handicapped children functioning at low developmental levels.

Smith, Shirley C., ed. *Clarification of P.L. 94-142 for the Classroom Teacher*. Philadelphia: Research for Better Schools, 1978.

An overview of the Education for All Handicapped Children Act is presented and its implications for the regular classroom teacher are discussed. One section of the text is devoted to activities designed to help teachers and students better understand the needs of the handicapped. Also included are selected annotated references pertinent to classroom teachers.

Special Children: Blind, Deaf and Physically Handicapped. 16 mm film. 11 mins. Educational Communications, 2814 Virginia, Houston, TX 77098.

This film was designed to promote a better understanding of special children by their normal peers. Handicapped children are depicted in a variety of classroom activities.

Special People, Special Needs, Special Services. Athens, GA: University of Georgia, 1978.

This 78-page handbook by the Department of Educational Media and Librarianship reviews the regulations concerning handicapped children in the schools and lists national and state agencies concerned with exceptional children. A bibliography of titles is included on serving the special student in the school media center, modifying facilities and equipment for the handicapped, and bibliotherapy. Selection sources and titles recommended for purchase are given.

Sports and Games for Handicapped Persons. Washington, DC: Library of Congress, 1979.

The first section lists organizations and companies that offer sports activities, equipment, and information about specific sports for handicapped individuals. The second section lists sources for purchasing table games that have been adapted to facilitate their use by the handicapped. The final two sections give addresses for information centers and clearinghouses and list periodicals concerned with sports and recreation for the handicapped.

Storytelling. 16 mm film. 17 mins. US Bureau for Education of the Handicapped. n.d.

Storytelling with hearing-impaired children is demonstrated in this film. Techniques for introducing storylines prior to reading to the group and converting stories into plays are shown. Rental and loan information is available from National Audiovisual Center, National Archives and Record Service, General Services Administration, Order Section DA, Washington, DC 20409.

Strom, Maryalls G., ed. *Library Services to the Blind and Physically Handicapped.* Metuchen, NJ: Scarecrow, 1977.

The first series of articles in this compilation describes the services provided through the Library of Congress National Library Service (formerly Division) for the Blind and Physically Handicapped and lists regional and subregional libraries in this network. Other sections offer articles on various types of handicapped individuals and the ways in which libraries can best meet their needs, and material selection and accessibility. The final portion of the book covers programs in which libraries are providing services to individuals who are confined to their place of residence.

Toomey, Deborah A., comp. *Toys, Games and Gift Ideas for the Blind and Handicapped*. Daytona Beach, FL: Florida Regional Library for the Blind and Physically Handicapped, 1976.

This annotated list of toys and games designed or adapted for the handicapped also supplies the price, order number, and address of the agency from which the materials may be purchased. The categories of materials are card games and accessories, puzzles, sports accessories, and toys and games. A revised compilation is currently under way.

We Did It...So Can You! Mainstreaming Special Needs Children. Five filmstrips. Five cassettes. Selective Educational Equipment, 3 Bridge Street, Newton, MA 02195.

The series has been designed for viewing by adults. It depicts several handicapped youngsters being educated in regular classrooms. Some specific classroom techniques are shown and suggestions are offered for easing the transition to mainstreaming.

What Is a Handicap? Four filmstrips. Four cassettes or records. One teaching guide. Set of masters. BFA Educational Media, 2211 Michigan Avenue, Santa Monica, CA 90404.

Each filmstrip depicts a handicapped child interacting with family, friends, classmates, and teachers. The programs are aimed at upper elementary-aged students and each includes a teaching guide, bibliographies, and activities to extend the filmstrip content.

Why Am I Different? Four filmstrips. Four cassettes. Teacher's guide. Library cards. Barr Films, P.O. Box 5667, Pasadena, CA 91107.

This filmstrip program is designed to aid nonhandicapped upper elementary-aged students to better understand handicapped individuals. Titles included are: *I Am Different, I Am Blind, I Am Deaf,* and *I Can't Run.* A teacher's guide offers suggestions for effective use of the filmstrips and for additional activities.

Workshop: Creating Instructional Materials for Handicapped Learners. Multimedia kit. Produced by the former Northwest Special Education Instructional Materials Center. University of Oregon, 1974. Reissued by National Center on Educational Media and Materials for the Handicapped, National Audio Visual Center, General Services Administration, Order Section DA, Washington, DC 20409. 1975. #009688.

Two color filmstrips and three cassettes cover ways to adapt and improve instructional materials for handicapped students. Suggestions for evaluating the teaching tools are also given.

Wright, Kieth C. *Library and Information Services for Handicapped Individuals*. Littleton, CO: Libraries Unlimited, 1979.

This text is designed to assist the librarian or library school student in planning services for the major groups of handicapped individuals. An overview of the blind and visually impaired, deaf and hard of hearing, mentally handicapped, aging, and physically handicapped is given along with methods of meeting their unique needs. Laws pertaining to the handicapped are reviewed, and their implications for library services are discussed. Additional information includes a glossary of acronyms, a list of selected organizations providing services to the handicapped, and a directory of selected sources for materials and information.

Yearbook of Special Education. 4th ed. Chicago: Marquis Academic Media, 1979.

In addition to information on innovations in the education of persons with special needs, the fourth edition of the yearbook includes a chapter on mainstreaming. Other topics covered are rights and litigations, teacher preparation, and gifted and talented students; and separate chapters are devoted to various handicaps such as physically handicapped and speech and hearing impaired.

Zajac, Mary. "Learning Is for Everyone." *Reference Quarterly* 18 (Spring 1979): 248-50.

This article is written from the point of view of a public librarian who shows how mainstreaming of the mentally retarded should be supported and encouraged by the entire community. The objectives of the program are set forth along with selection criteria for materials and the basis for programing for this population. Ms. Zajac, along with Anne Forer, has compiled a detailed description of the program in *Library Services to the Mentally Retarded*, available through the State Library of Pennsylvania, US Office of Education, Box 1601, Harrisburg, PA 17126.

APPENDICES

APPENDICES

Appendix I
Selection of Materials

If administrators, teachers, and school library media specialists are to select and evaluate materials suitable for meeting the needs of the special student, then they must be aware of and use a standard procedure for building and developing the collection. Karen H. Harris in "Selecting Library Materials for Exceptional Children" examines three special categories—physically handicapped, mentally retarded and emotionally disturbed—and the materials suitable for each. She then focuses on the need for selection of materials for developing the social skills of these children and for locating materials suitable for the nonimpaired to learn about the handicapped. Throughout her discussion, the author points to numerous examples of books which should or should not be used and justifies each title evaluated.

The National Center on Educational Media and Materials for the Handicapped (NCEMMH) in cooperation with the national system of learning resource centers, professional associations, various other public and private agencies, and interested individuals provided a comprehensive program of activities to facilitate the use of new educational technology in instructional programs for handicapped persons.NCEMMH provided leadership and service in the development, design, and dissemination of learning resources that are effective for the handicapped.

The Center was funded under Contract OEC-300-72-4478 by the Bureau of Education for the Handicapped, US Office of Education, Department of Health, Education and Welfare. The contract was administered through the College of Education and the Research Foundation of the Ohio State University.

The document, "Standard Criteria for the Selection and Evaluation of Instructional Materials," was prepared pursuant to a contract with the US Office of Education, Department of Health, Education, and Welfare, Bureau of Education for the Handicapped. Contractors undertaking such projects under government sponsorship are encouraged to express their judgment freely in professional and technical matters. Points of view or opinions do not, therefore, necessarily represent official Office of Education position or policy. Duplication of the criteria, as distributed by NCEMMH, is permitted.

NISCEM at the University of Southern California has now taken over the function of NCEMMH.

Selecting Library Materials for Exceptional Children

by Karen H. Harris

I would like to begin with a story. A friend of mine was the parent of a second grader. A new teacher, a male, was assigned to the second grade. He was the first male teacher assigned to the school. The mother was rather pleased about her son's having a male teacher. The teacher had a very good reputation and related well to the children. The mother thought that having a male model for her son was going to be very good.

While I was visiting the family about the second week of school, I asked the boy about school. "I hear that you have a new teacher," I said. "Tell me, is this teacher really good?" Very indignantly he put his fists on his hips and said, "I don't know. I haven't met her yet. She keeps sending her husband."

Just as we have sex-role stereotypes, we also have disability-role stereotypes. And despite the really impressive achievements of many disabled persons, these stereotypes persist. They are so very persuasive that even young children have internalized them.

Who are the blind? The blind are people who run concession stands in state and federal office buildings. Who are the physically handicapped? They are the people who work at Goodwill. We all know that. And what about the retarded? The retarded are those people who are a burden to their families and to society and who are going to be dependent all of their lives.

None of these things needs to be true. The library has a role in not making them true. We really have two things to do. We have a role in developing the kinds of competencies and skills that give people who are handicapped the options they should have for functioning in society and we also have the job of disproving those stereotypes that are rampant.

Where do we begin? We probably begin where most things begin in a library—with selection. In this presentation I should like to examine selection for three categories of handicapped—the physically handicapped, the mentally retarded, and the emotionally disturbed. Also I would like to discuss three categories of selection. The first is selection for cognitive growth, which is developing the knowledge, the skills, and the competencies that are going to yield good academic achievement. The second category is selection for social development, which involves the learning of social skills and the achievement of developmental growth. The third category is selection for promoting understanding by nonimpaired children of those who are about to be mainstreamed.

PHYSICALLY HANDICAPPED

The first problem that the librarian encounters in dealing with the physically handicapped is getting them into the library. Once we remove the architectural barriers, and the physically handicapped actually come into the library, the problems of selection are not so complex. The overriding principle in selection is to deal with interests and abilities. And what are their interests? They include everything from aardvark to zeppelin. What are their abilities? They include everything from low retarded to genius.

We ought to be able to challenge them in the areas in which they are interested and at whatever levels they are functioning. There are some particular problems with selection of materials for the physically handicapped that relate to format and content. When we talk about children who are disabled, we are talking about a wide range of disability. Not all generalizations can be applied to every child.

Many of the physically handicapped children will have lower energy levels than their peers. They will fatigue more easily, especially during periods of hospitalization or trauma. Many of these children regress to lower levels of functioning. For instance, even though we know that a particular child can operate at a sixth-grade level, s/he might regress at times of trauma to a fourth-grade or third-grade level. At that time, we certainly ought to respond to the child's needs, which means that we have to provide the child with materials on a lower level than s/he would normally require.

Depending upon the impairment, physically handicapped children may be eligible for talking books. Once talking books were available only to the blind, but now they are available to anyone who cannot handle standard print. Therefore, many of our physically handicapped children who are not blind are eligible for talking books and should be given the opportunity to use them.

Many of these children have poor muscle development, and, therefore, they lack good muscle control. Thus, we ought to think in terms of formats that are more highly automated. For example, cassette tapes may be a better choice than reel-to-reel tapes because of the difficulty a physically handicapped person may encounter with the manual threading of a tape recorder.

Things that do not seem significant to us may be significant to children with various physical disabilities. The weight of a book may be important to a child with a muscle development problem. A hardcover book and its paperback edition have different weights. While the weight difference might not be significant to a person with no problems, it might make the difference between whether it can or cannot be handled by a handicapped child.

Librarians need to be concerned about the format of the materials that are selected and the placement of the materials. The materials should be placed where the handicapped child can reach them without calling for assistance. We need to be concerned about the development of independence within a child.

The content of the materials is another important consideration. My first example is *Howie Helps Himself* by Joan Fassler. From the pictures, one can see that Howie is in a wheelchair waiting for an adapted school bus to pick him up while the other children are picked up by a regular bus. The question is, ''Do children in wheelchairs need a book about Howie?'' The story about Howie is really how he tries and tries and finally learns how to manage his wheelchair.

The story of Howie was read to a group of physically handicapped children, all of whom happened to be in wheelchairs. After the story was read, we asked how the children liked it. Their response was negative. The problem was that the author didn't tell the reader how really hard it is to learn to use the wheelchair. In this and in many other instances, the handicapped are more knowledgeable from firsthand experience about the situations that are being described than the authors themselves.

When I criticize these books in terms of the special child, I certainly do not mean to imply that this is a general criticism of the books. In other words, such books may be very useful with nonimpaired children, but the child who has the handicap does not usually need a book about a child who is similarly handicapped.

Librarians often make that mistake. We say to the child, ''Here is a book about a little boy just like you.'' What we have done when we make such a recommendation is to say that we identify the child on the basis, not of his/her strengths, but of his/her disability. I do not think that we can make such a statement to a child, for children have multifaceted personalities to which we should be relating. Generally, then, books about the disabled are not for the disabled.

What about books that deal with activities from which physically handicapped children are obviously excluded? Does Howie need a book called *Great Heroes of the NFL?* Yes, he does. The one thing that a book does best is to take readers out of the limitations that reality has imposed upon them. Books introduce us to the kinds of experiences that we can never have. These children may be in wheelchairs and braces, but there is no reason why they cannot leap with Baryshnikov and Kareem Abdul-Jabbar. These are the kind of books the physically handicapped children want and need for themselves.

MENTALLY RETARDED CHILDREN

Once again, the overriding principle in selecting books for the mentally retarded is to work through the interests and abilities of the children. Abilities do vary among these children. When working through the interests of the children, librarians will also discover that the abilities of the children are higher than the scores recorded in the files. Don't be restricted by the scores recorded on permanent records. We think of children who are retarded as being limited, and that is not necessarily true.

Long before 1975, when all of the laws regarding handicapped were adopted, I was in a school where a child with Down's syndrome had been mainstreamed into the second-grade class. While I was observing, the child said to me, "I need help. The word on the board is a funny word." I asked him what was funny about the word, which was spelled C-I-R-C-U-S. He replied, "It's got two letters that are both the same, but they sound different." Yet, this child was labeled "Down's syndrome." We cannot limit a child by a label. Many times mentally retarded children will delight and surprise us by what they are able to master.

In selecting books for mentally retarded children, we ought to be prepared to move from the familiar to the less well known. We should use pictures whenever possible to aid in communicating the message. Mentally retarded children have a shorter attention span than their peers. In other words, seven books of 30 pages are better than one book of 200 pages.

Books used by the mentally retarded should have a simple structure and should have simple sentences. The vocabulary should be within the reach of the children. It is important to emphasize reach as opposed to emphasizing range. We need to introduce new words, but they ought to be accessible to these children. There should be no complex structure, time manipulations, flashbacks, etc. The changing of narrators within a story is equally inappropriate. Mentally retarded children tend to be very literal and devices such as irony tend to be inappropriate.

The concepts that are being introduced to the children should be logically developed. There should be no gaps. Mentally retarded children often have surprising gaps in their knowledge; thus, every step ought to be complete and sequential. Redundancy is very desirable. The children need the message told, they need it told again, and they need the message retold.

There are many books that are useful in working with mentally retarded children. Among them is *Davy's Day*. Davy gets up in the morning; he brushes his teeth; he gets dressed; he has breakfast; he goes out to play; he comes in; he has lunch; he goes out to play again; he takes a nap; he has dinner; and he goes to bed. It is not high drama, but it is a familiar experience to every child. It is very easy to involve the children as the story is read, and the involvement is very important.

Such stories as *Davy's Day* are successful with mentally retarded children because they accommodate the limited attention span of these children and because the children can be actively involved with the story. The involvement with the story enables the children to develop their vocabularies and their way of talking about events that occur daily within their lives. These stories are very useful.

Another story that seems to involve the children is *Caps for Sale* by Esphyr Slobodkina, which is the story of a peddler who finds and sells caps. The caps are stolen by a tree-full of monkeys, and the children within a group can be involved in looking for the caps. Such a story creates a situation of high expectancy. After the first few repetitions, the children are going to know what is expected of them and are going to anticipate the questions and to participate in the story.

The use of repetitions or a refrain is commonly identified with folktales. They have a definite pattern or cycle. The child can come into a story on the refrain and anticipate what is going to happen. No matter whom Henny-Penny meets, the news is going to be "The sky is falling!".

Another excellent book to use with the children is *Curious George* by H. A. Rey, of which every special education teacher should have a copy. It has an excellent vocabulary and sentence structure. It is a fairly simple story that is absolutely fascinating. *Curious George* has humor. The humor is obvious, and the children are able to understand it. This is important because mentally retarded children are quite often characterized as not having a sense of humor.

Many times there don't seem to be materials available to which the children can relate. What is our option? Our option is to make the materials. We need to use children's interest, their current reasons for excitement, etc., to develop materials for them. Materials prepared especially for them will enable them to deal with words and concepts beyond what their tests say they are able to do.

At the secondary level, popular magazines are very important to use in working with the mentally retarded for a number of reasons. One of the most important reasons is that magazines serve to camouflage the problem. Everybody reads magazines. The reading of a magazine carries no special label with it. It is not obviously easy material. The structure of magazines is very suitable, and the pictures carry a large part of the message. Often, it is possible to get the sense of the article or story through the pictures alone. The sentences tend to be simple, the articles short, and the vocabulary, except for technical terms for which there are contextual clues, simple. Remember, mentally retarded children who have difficulty in reading all kinds of materials can often read technical terms in the areas in which they are interested. If mentally retarded children are going to develop a lifelong habit of reading, it is going to grow out of reading popular magazines.

EMOTIONALLY DISTURBED

There are several points to remember in selecting materials for the emotionally disturbed or emotionally dysfunctional child. Not all generalizations will apply equally, but there are characteristics that are typical of a large number of children. Their emotional problems may interfere with their academic achievement. That the emotionally disturbed child may operate on a lower level than his/her innate abilities would indicate is possible. Among emotionally dysfunctional children there is a very wide range of abilities from low retarded to genius.

These children often have difficulty attending to tasks, often have short attention spans, and often are easily distracted. Such characteristics have implications for the kinds of materials the librarian is going to select for them. They have a high need for success, and it is important for librarians and teachers to have them work particularly and initially with materials that will be minimally frustrating.

In terms of themes, relevant books have been limited to young adult literature but now they are a part of literature at all levels. Some of these books are available on topics that are highly charged and to children with severe emotional problems, potentially threatening. These are now available to very young children. The topics treated include abandonment, child abuse, alcoholism, drug abuse, gangs, violence, death, etc.

While books on these topics may have usefulness for other categories of children, the librarian needs to be cautious in using them with children or young adults who have emotional problems. *Don't Hurt Laurie; Bang, Bang, You're Dead; The Beast of Monsieur Racine; Are You in the House Alone?* are a few examples of the kinds of books that I would avoid using with the emotionally dysfunctional.

Books for the emotionally dysfunctional should provide nonthreatening situations showing models of acceptable and coping behavior. Books that show social problems, familial problems, and interpersonal relationships of all kinds are good choices, but the books should show a resolution of differences and disputes. Books that are open-ended and contain unresolved situations are not the kind of books that we need for children who like and need certainty and closure.

Many times these children have difficulty in accepting themselves. They need stories dealing with coming to terms with their own limitations and accepting and enjoying one another's strengths.

SELECTION FOR SOCIAL SKILLS DEVELOPMENT

An important area of selection is selection for the purposes of developing social skills and accomplishing developmental tasks. Many children, not just those with special problems, have difficulties within these areas. They have concerns about making and keeping friends, having fun while keeping out of trouble, and working with peers, parents, teachers, and others in authority.

Exceptional children are especially subject to having difficulties in these areas. The physically handicapped experience difficulty because they often have been more isolated and have had less opportunity for social interchange than their peers. Depending upon the nature of the disability and the family's response to it, the child may have assumed habits of dependency that are not productive in social situations.

Mentally retarded children have trouble in this area because of an inability to read the dynamics of a situation and to respond appropriately. The emotionally disturbed have special problems because of the pressures that may render them insensitive to the situation or may call forth inappropriate responses. Books can help the children here, also.

We need to introduce exceptional children to situations that have the potentiality of being traumatic. Some books provide the opportunity to discuss with children the kinds of behavior that are appropriate. In *Will I Have a Friend?* by Miriam Cohen there are opportunities to discuss friendship—what it is, how to find a friend, how to be a good friend. Parents send children to school to learn how to read and write. Children want to know what to expect.

What about feelings? Norma Simon's book *How Do I Feel?* helps children to deal with feelings that are difficult to articulate. It allows them to talk about their feelings—all kinds of feelings. They need to learn how to deal with disappointment and how to deal with happiness and success. *How Do I Feel?* enables the children to explore their feelings openly.

Sam, written by A. H. Scott, deals with interpersonal relationships. Sam wants attention, but everybody is too busy. Every child has experienced this situation but really doesn't know how to articulate it. *Sam* looks at a situation within the family and the needs of a child. The book talks about those needs in terms of identifying them and responding to the needs of others.

Judith Viorst has written a number of books about victims. *Alexander, Who Used to be Rich Last Sunday* is the story of the youngest child who is the butt of everybody's jokes. He is readily duped. Children can easily identify with the situation. She has also written *Alexander and the Terrible, Horrible, No-Good, Very Bad Day*. This book, too, is very useful.

Sunflowers for Tina, written by Anne N. Baldwin, looks at family relationships and a particular need of Tina. Many times the text specifically calls attention to how Tina feels. This book enables the child to look at the needs of others and, in particular, at personal needs. It is extremely useful for a child to look at personal needs.

SELECTION FOR NONIMPAIRED

Librarians have a major responsibility in selecting materials for the non-impaired that promote understanding of the handicapped. Sarah Bonnet Stein's *About Handicaps* tells the story of Matthew and his concern about his neighbor who has cerebral palsy. The book is an important book because it helps to interpret handicaps to children; it deals with the superstitions; and it deals with unreasonable fears of the handicapped. The book enables children who may be afraid to ask questions to raise their questions and to articulate their fears.

In *Deenie,* Judy Blume portrays an adolescent girl with idiopathic scoliosis who has to deal with her aspirations, with wearing a brace, and with labeling. The book contains many excellent scenes. Deenie's contact with a young girl who has been severely injured brings Deenie to a realization of herself as a regular child.

Winning, by Robin Brancato, is the story of a football player who is severely injured and becomes a paraplegic. The novel deals with the self-doubts, perplexing questions, and, most important, avoidance by friends. *Winning* is an excellent examination of the responses to disabilities.

E. L. Konigsburg's *Father's Arcane Daughter* is one of the most subtle and sophisticated treatments of response to disability. The young girl in the story, Heidi, is deaf and also has an undefined physical problem that might be cerebral palsy. The mother deals with the problem by denying it and the father spends a great deal of time away from home. Heidi becomes her brother's responsibility and he responds to her with very mixed feelings. Eventually, another sister returns home and through her efforts Heidi is tested and, despite many demands on her, Heidi begins to enter the mainstream of life.

Racecourse for Andy by Patricia Wrightson is one of the best treatments of retardation. Andy is retarded and he is not able to handle subtleties. Through a game he becomes convinced that he actually owns a race course. Everyone goes along with his misconceptions until some of his friends become concerned about the consequences. The book is very good in its portrayal of Andy's relationship with his nonimpaired friends.

Hey, Dummy by Kin Platt is one of the few attempts to deal with severe retardation and the world as seen through the eyes of a severely retarded child. The book is interesting and tragic. In *The Hayburners* a retarded adult works on a farm and, through love and care, turns a steer that had been labeled a loser, a hayburner, into a prize winner.

Books for emotionally dysfunctional children are difficult to find. *Lisa, Bright and Dark* is probably one of the most popular. It is flawed in a number of ways. For example, all the adults are bad. The adults tend to be drawn in rather extreme forms. But there is one aspect of the novel that is highly interesting, and that is the relationship of Lisa's friends to her. As her behavior becomes more inexplicable, more grotesque, more bizarre, they remain her friends. They never lose sight of their responsibility to Lisa in spite of their inadequacies. This novel has an important message, particularly in terms of people whose behavior seems unacceptable.

A new book by Florence Heide, *Secret Dreamer, Secret Dreams,* attempts to do for the severely dysfunctional child what *Hey, Dummy* did for the retarded child. This book describes the world through the eyes of an emotionally dysfunctional person. This is an extremely sensitizing book.

I would like to close with this thought. Children who are labeled *special* typically function poorly in either academic, social, or recreational endeavors. The library is one place in school that combines these three areas of functioning in a nonjudgmental environment. Therefore, I think that we librarians have a particular role to play in helping disabled children develop skills in those areas and take their rightful place in the mainstream of society and school.

REFERENCES

Baldwin, Anne N. *Sunflowers for Tina*. Englewood Cliffs, NJ: Scholastic, 1970.

Blume, Judy. *Deenie*. New York: Bradbury, 1973.

Brancato, Robin. *Winning*. New York: Knopf, 1977.

Cohen, Miriam. *Will I Have a Friend?* Macmillan, 1967.

Fassler, Joan. *Howie Helps Himself*. Chicago: Albert Whitman, 1975.

Fitzhugh, Louise, and Scoppettone, Sandra. *Bang, Bang, You're Dead*. New York: Harper & Row, 1969.

Heide, Florence P. *Secret Dreamer, Secret Dreams*. New York: Lippincott, 1978.

Konigsburg, E. L. *Father's Arcane Daughter*. New York: Atheneum, 1976.

Lenski, Lois. *Davy's Day*. New York: Walck, 1943.

Neufeld, John. *Lisa, Bright and Dark*. New York: S. G. Phillips, 1969.

Peck, Richard. *Are You in the House Alone?* New York: Viking, 1976.

Platt, Kin. *Hey, Dummy*. Radnor, PA: Chilton, 1971.

Rey, H. A. *Curious George*. New York: Houghton, 1941.

Roberts, Willo D. *Don't Hurt Laurie*. New York: Atheneum, 1977.

Scott, A. H. *Sam*. New York: McGraw-Hill, 1967.

Simon, Norma. *How Do I Feel?* Chicago: Albert Whitman, 1970.

Slobodkina, Esphyr. *Caps for Sale*. New York: A & W, 1947.

Smith, Gene. *The Hayburners*. New York: Delacorte, 1974.

Stein, Sarah Bonnet. *About Handicaps*. New York: Walker, 1974.

Ungerer, Tomi. *The Beast of Monsieur Racine*. New York: Farrar, 1971.

Viorst, Judith. *Alexander and the Terrible, Horrible, No-Good, Very Bad Day*. New York: Atheneum, 1976.

_____. *Alexander, Who Used to Be Rich Last Sunday*. New York: Atheneum, 1978.

Wrightson, Patricia. *Racecourse for Andy*. New York: Harcourt, 1968.

Standard Criteria for the Selection and Evaluation of Instructional Material*

TEACHER LEVEL

I. IDENTIFICATION OF NEEDS

The outcome of stage I will be: a definition of the target learner and the learning environment prior to any selection of suitable instructional materials.

A. Learner Characteristics

(The following outline is intended to serve as a guideline to the selector of instructional materials in identifying the characteristics and educational requirements of the specific learner for whom material is being sought.)

1. Has an assessment of the learner occurred, and does the resulting data specify:

   a. demographic information about the learner, including:

Yes No NA

____ ____ ____   (1) age

____ ____ ____   (2) sex

____ ____ ____   (3) instructional/developmental level

____ ____ ____   (4) language development or preference

____ ____ ____   (5) interest level

____ ____ ____   b. limiting conditions (medical/physical factors, etc.)

____ ____ ____   c. behavioral/affective characteristics

____ ____ ____   d. preferred modalities

____ ____ ____   e. strength areas

____ ____ ____   f. deficit areas

2. Has an educational plan been developed, based on learner assessment data, which specifies:

____ ____ ____   a. needed skill area

____ ____ ____   b. short and long-term instructional objectives

  c. instructional strategies, including:

____ ____ ____   (1) sequencing

____ ____ ____   (2) reinforcement

*Prepared by the ALRC/SO/NCEMMH Program. Distributed by NCEMMH, Ohio State University, Columbus, OH 43210.

Yes No NA

   —— —— ——   (3) modalities (input/output)

   —— —— ——   (4) monitoring

                 d. recommendations for:

   —— —— ——   (1) general instructional areas

   —— —— ——   (2) specific materials

   —— —— ——   (3) related activities

B. Program Characteristics

(The following outline is intended to serve as a guideline to the selector of instructional materials in identifying the overall program considerations with the specific learner(s) and learning requirements in mind.)

                 1. Have provisions been made for integration of the individual educational plan into the total instructional program:

   —— —— ——   a. content

   —— —— ——   b. curricular compatibility

   —— —— ——   c. format/alternatives

                 2. Would implementation of the educational plan be affected by any of the following environmental constraints:

   —— —— ——   a. time/cost/physical considerations

   —— —— ——   b. grouping

   —— —— ——   c. equipment

   —— —— ——   d. personnel

   —— —— ——   e. teacher skill

II. INITIAL SELECTION

The outcome of stage II will be: the identification of at least two pieces of instructional material which, on first screening, appear compatible with learner requirements and which will be considered for further review. Identification of alternative materials for examination will facilitate final selection decisions on a comparative basis.

A. Search

(The items listed below outline the most common information resources available to the selector of instructional materials. The intent of this section is to encourage the user to investigate various potential materials information sources.)

         1. Have you located resources which might provide information about materials:

   ——   a. colleagues

   ——   b. commercial

   ——   c. materials bibliographies

_____   d. journals
_____   e. curriculum libraries and centers (colleges, schools for handi-
         capped, learning resource centers)
_____   f. professional organizations
_____   g. governmental agencies (national network, audiovisual center,
         etc.)
_____   h. information systems (NIMIS, EPIE, ERIC, etc.)

   2. As a result of the above process, have you identified at least two
   instructional materials which appear to address the learner's needs?

B. Screen

(Under optimal conditions, a written product abstract or review will provide information pertaining to all of the items listed below, so that actual inspection of the product is not necessary. In the absence of thorough and accurate material descriptions, however, scrutiny of the material itself will be required. A secondary intent of this selection is to educate both material users and material abstractors [including commercial publishers] about desirable elements to be included in product reviews.)

Yes   No   NA

   1. Does the material information resource provide information about the identified instructional product(s), such as:

_____ _____ _____   a. instructional level
_____ _____ _____   b. language level
_____ _____ _____   c. interest level
_____ _____ _____   d. sensory input and output modalities
_____ _____ _____   e. educational subject/skill content
_____ _____ _____   f. format
_____ _____ _____   g. cost
_____ _____ _____   h. grouping requirement(s)
_____ _____ _____   i. required equipment

   2. On the basis of the available information, does the
   identified instructional material appear compatible with:
   a. learner characteristics
_____ _____ _____   (1) the learner assessment
_____ _____ _____   (2) the learner educational plan
   b. program characteristics
_____ _____ _____   (1) the total instructional program considerations
_____ _____ _____   (2) the identified environmental constraints

III. REVIEW

The outcome of stage III will be: an in-depth analysis of an instructional material in order to define the material's characteristics and match these characteristics to previously defined learner requirements. Implementation of this stage necessitates actual examination of the instructional material.

A. Analysis of Material

(This section includes recommended questions for determining the intrinsic qualities of the material[s] independent of specific learner characteristics and program requirements.)

Yes   No   NA

_____ _____ _____ 1. Are objectives in behavioral terms (specifying what the student task is, under what conditions, and level of performance expected)?

_____ _____ _____ 2. Are techniques of instruction for each lesson either clearly specified or self-evident?

_____ _____ _____ 3. Are facts, concepts, and principles ordered in a logical manner (e.g., chronologically, easy to difficult, etc.)?

_____ _____ _____ 4. Does the material contain appropriate supplementary or alternative activities that contribute to or extend proposed learning?

_____ _____ _____ 5. Is repetition and review of content material systematic and appropriately spaced?

_____ _____ _____ 6. Does the content appear accurate?

_____ _____ _____ 7. Does the material avoid content which betrays prejudice, perpetuates stereotypes, or neglects the talents, contributions, or aspirations of any segment of the population?

_____ _____ _____ 8. Can the material be readily adapted to meet individual learner differences in abilities and interests?

_____ _____ _____ 9. Can pacing of the material be adapted to variations in learner rate of mastery?

_____ _____ _____ 10. Is provision made for adapting, altering, or combining input and response modalities according to learner variations?

_____ _____ _____ 11. Does the material incorporate evaluation items and procedures which are compatible with program objectives?

_____ _____ _____ 12. Are there sufficient evaluative items to accurately assess student progress?

_____ _____ _____ 13. Is performance assessed frequently enough to allow accurate assessment of student progress and continuous feedback to learner?

_____ _____ _____ 14. Is the format uncluttered, grammatically correct, and free of typographical errors?

Yes No NA

___ ___ ___   15. Are illustrations and photographs clear, attractive, and appropriate to content?

___ ___ ___   16. Are auditory components of adequate clarity and amplification?

___ ___ ___   17. Are all necessary components either provided with the material or readily and inexpensively available?

___ ___ ___   18. Can consumable portions of material be easily and inexpensively replaced or legally reproduced?

___ ___ ___   19. Is cost reasonable in comparison with similar commercial materials or homemade alternatives?

___ ___ ___   20. Does the publisher clearly state the rationale for selection of program elements, content, and methodology (e.g., choice may be based on tradition, survey of other materials, logic of subject matter, experimental evidence, unvalidated theory)?

___ ___ ___   21. Are testimonials, research, and publisher claims clearly differentiated?

___ ___ ___   22. Are reinforcement procedures and schedules clearly indicated?

___ ___ ___   23. Is a variety of cuing and prompting techniques used?

B. Matching Material to Learner

(This section involves the integration of the identified learner needs with the analyzed material characteristics to determine compatibility for instructional purposes.)

___ ___ ___   1. Are stated objectives and scope of the material compatible with learner's need?

___ ___ ___   2. Are prerequisite student skills/abilities needed to work comfortably and successfully with the material specified and compatible with the learner's characteristics?

___ ___ ___   3. Are the skills and abilities needed by the instructor to work effectively with the material specified and compatible with the instructor's expertise?

___ ___ ___   4. Are levels of interest, abstraction, vocabulary, and sentence structure compatible with characteristics of the learner?

___ ___ ___   5. Is the degree of required teacher involvement (constant interaction, supportive or monitoring role, largely student directed, variable) compatible with teacher resources and learner characteristics?

Yes   No   NA

——— ——— ———   6. Does the material incorporate motivational devices to sustain student interests which are appropriate to the learner's characteristics?

——— ——— ———   7. Are input and output modalities (visual, auditory, motor, tactile) compatible with learner characteristics?

——— ——— ———   8. Is the demonstration of task mastery (e.g., written test, performance test, oral test) compatible with or adaptable to intended learner's characteristics?

——— ——— ———   9. Is the format of the material (e.g., game, book, filmstrip, etc.) compatible with the learner's mental and physical abilities?

——— ——— ———   10. Is the durability and safety of the material adequate for the learner?

——— ——— ———   11. Is information provided indicating (successful) field testing of the material with students similar in learning characteristics and interests to those of the learner?

IV. DECISION MAKING

The outcome of stage IV will be: a final determination of material suitability for use in a specific learning situation. Individualization of the decision making, based on items of priority concern, is implicit in this process.

A. As a result of the review process, which questions have you identified as (most) critical to you in deciding to utilize the material with the learner?

B. On the basis of those critical priority concerns, is the material appropriate for specified learning requirements?
  ___ Yes (implies accept)
  ___ No (implies reject)
  ___ Unsure (requires more analysis)

C. If unsure of appropriateness, are there other less critical questions which could be considered in making the decision to utilize the material?

D. On the basis of those additional considerations, is the material now deemed appropriate for specified learning requirements?
  ___ Yes
  ___ Unsure

E. If still unsure of appropriateness of the material, will comparison with other previewed material(s), in relation to critical questions, help identify the material which most closely approximates the specified learning requirements?

F. If still unsure of the appropriateness of the material, would modifications
    of the material render it usable?
    1. Do you have access to resources for required modification?
G. If no:
    1. Return to search process. Reexamine sources of material identifi-
        cation and information in locating other potential materials.
    2. Review learner characteristics in an effort to modify requirements
        for material.

NATIONAL LEVEL

I.   IDENTIFICATION OF NEEDS

The outcome of stage I will be: identification of the availability and
adequacy of sources of need information prior to any selection of suitable
instructional materials.

A.   Sources

_____ 1. The National Needs Assessment sponsored by the Bureau of
          Education for the Handicapped
_____ 2. Consumers who are currently working with handicapped children
_____ 3. Analysis of curriculums and instructional priorities at
          Learner Level
_____ 4. Analysis of learner characteristics
_____ 5. Availability of appropriate materials for curricular areas
_____ 6. Availability of effective materials for learners

II. INITIAL SELECTION

The outcome of stage II will be: the identification of at least ten pieces
of instructional material which, on first screening, appear compatible with
learner requirements and which will be considered for further review. Identification of alternate materials for examination will facilitate final selection
decisions on a comparative basis.

A.   Search

(The items listed below encourage the user to investigate various potential
materials information sources and to consider essential points when gathering
information about materials.)

Yes   No   NA

____ ____ ____   1. Have you identified resources for materials which
                     have potential use with the handicapped?
____ ____ ____   2. Have materials been identified which may be appro-
                     priate for the learner characteristics of the handicapped?
____ ____ ____   3. Have materials been identified which may be appro-
                     priate for the curricular needs of the handicapped?

B.   Screen

(Under optimal conditions, a written product abstract or review will provide information pertaining to all of the items listed below, so that actual inspection of the product is not necessary. In the absence of thorough and accurate material descriptions, however, scrutiny of the material itself will be required.)

Yes   No   NA

____ ____ ____   1. Is it a learner-use material?

____ ____ ____   2. Is it an instructor-use material?

____ ____ ____   3. Are all components of the material available?

____ ____ ____   4. Does the material have potential for use with the handicapped?

____ ____ ____   5. Is the material designed for use by the handicapped?

____ ____ ____   6. Does the material appear to be practical to use with the handicapped?

____ ____ ____   7. Does the material appear to be easily usable by the handicapped?

____ ____ ____   8. Is the format of the material appropriate for the target handicapped audience?

____ ____ ____   9. Is the material of acceptable technical quality?

____ ____ ____   10. Does the material have instructional objectives?

____ ____ ____   11. Does the material appear to meet the curricular needs of the handicapped target population?

____ ____ ____   12. How does the cost of the material affect the accessibility to the material?

____ ____ ____   13. Does the material appear to present any physical danger to the target handicapped audience?

III.   REVIEW

The outcome of stage III will be: an in-depth analysis of an instructional material in order to match (section D) the material for use with a specific student based on section A, Learner Characteristics, section B, Teacher Requirements, and section C, Materials Characteristics. Implementation of this stage necessitates actual examination of the instructional material.

A.   Learner Characteristics

(The following outline is intended to serve as a guideline to the selector of instructional materials in identifying the characteristics and educational requirements of the specific learner for whom material is being sought.)

1. What are the possible modes of input?

____ auditory

____ visual

____ tactile

_____ kinesthetic
2. What are the preferred modes of input?
    _____ auditory
    _____ visual
    _____ tactile
    _____ kinesthetic
    _____ multisensory
3. What are the possible modes of response?
    _____ verbal
    _____ written
    _____ gesture
4. _____ What is the learner's instructional level?
5. _____ What is the learner's interest level?
6. _____ What is the learner's reading level?
7. _____ What are the learner's interest areas?
8. What are the learner's interest/motivation requirements?
    a. _____ use of game-type format
    b. _____ use of humor
    c. _____ use of variety of stimuli
    d. _____ use of suspense
    e. _____ use of novelty
    f. _____ use of an interaction system of instantaneous feedback
    g. _____ use of cartoon format
    h. _____ use of puppets
    i. _____ use of characters
9. _____ What are the learner's entry level skills?
10. _____ What are the learner's reinforcement requirements?

B. Teacher Requirements

(The following outline is intended to serve as a guideline to the selector of instructional materials in identifying the requirements to allow a teacher/instructor to effectively use the material.)
1. _____ Are a teacher's manual and/or instructions provided?
2. If a teacher's manual and/or instructions are provided, does it include:
    a. _____ philosophy and rationale
    b. _____ statement of objectives
    c. _____ statement of instructional and interest levels
    d. _____ statement of reading level
    e. _____ statement of prerequisite skills
    f. _____ listing of material/program elements
    g. _____ listing of required materials and equipment
    h. _____ suggestions for teacher/instructor use
    i. _____ suggestions for student/learner use

    j. _____ suggestions for instructional alternatives
    k. _____ suggestions for evaluation
    l. _____ suggestions for additional resources
3. Instructor time requirements:
    a. _____ training
    b. _____ preparation
    c. _____ use
    d. _____ cleanup
4. What is the degree of instructor involvement?
    a. _____ full-time teacher involvement is required during instructional period
    b. _____ part-time teacher involvement required
    c. _____ no teacher involvement required
    d. _____ full-time aide involvement required
    e. _____ part-time aide involvement required
    f. _____ no aide involvement required
    g. _____ full-time parent involvement required
    h. _____ part-time parent involvement required
    i. _____ no parent involvement required
    j. _____ full-time peer involvement required
    k. _____ part-time peer involvement required
    l. _____ no peer involvement required
    m. _____ materials can be used independently by learners
5. Is the material practical?

Yes No NA

_____ _____ _____ a. maneuverability
_____ _____ _____ b. ease of storage
_____ _____ _____ c. number of parts
_____ _____ _____ d. identification of parts
_____ _____ _____ e. size of parts
_____ _____ _____ f. storage/organization of parts
_____ _____ _____ g. durability of product and packaging
_____ _____ _____ h. replaceability of consumable and nonconsumable parts
_____ _____ _____ i. requires use of specialized equipment

6. Is the total cost reasonable?

_____ _____ _____ a. in-service training
_____ _____ _____ b. initial cost
_____ _____ _____ c. per use cost (replacement of consumables)
_____ _____ _____ d. required supplementary materials cost
_____ _____ _____ e. replacement cost (replacement of nonconsumables)

7. _____ _____ _____ Is the material appropriate for the curriculum?
8. _____ _____ _____ Has this material been field tested?
9. _____ _____ _____ If so, has it been found to be effective?

C. Materials Characteristics

(The following outline is intended to serve as a guideline to the selector of instructional materials in identifying specific characteristics a material requires to allow for communication with a learner.)

1. Technical quality

    a. Quality of auditory presentation: Acceptable Unacceptable

        (1) clarity (easily understood, recording quality good) _____   _____

        (2) amplification _____   _____

        (3) voice level _____   _____

        (4) dialect/accent _____   _____

        (5) voice speed _____   _____

        (6) voice quality _____   _____

        (7) sequence _____   _____

        (8) quality of narration (reader style) _____   _____

        (9) music/sound/voice mixing _____   _____

    b. Quality of visual presentation:

        (1) sharpness _____   _____

        (2) color _____   _____

        (3) distracting elements _____   _____

        (4) complexity _____   _____

        (5) size relationships _____   _____

        (6) sequence _____   _____

        (7) subjective angle (learner point of view) _____   _____

        (8) objective angle (observer point of view) _____   _____

        (9) composition (visual format, visual arrangement) _____   _____

        (10) figure-ground definition _____   _____

    c. Quality of print and graphic presentation:

        (1) legibility (style and size) _____   _____

        (2) captioning (location and pacing) _____   _____

        (3) clarity of print (contrast) _____   _____

        (4) accuracy _____   _____

    d. Quality of tactile presentation:

        (1) Braille (clear and easily discriminable) _____   _____

        (2) tactile drawings (clear and easily discriminable) _____   _____

        (3) texture (clear and easily discriminable) _____   _____

        (4) composition (physical format, physical arrangement) _____   _____

        (5) manipulables (discriminable, dimension, shape, mass) _____   _____

2. Instructional quality

Yes   No   NA

_____ _____ _____   a. Does the selection of subject matter facts adequately represent the content area?

_____ _____ _____   b. Is the content presented in the material accurate?

_____ _____ _____   c. Is the content logically sequenced?

_____ _____ _____   d. Is the content organized for ease of study?

_____ _____ _____   e. Are various points of view, including treatment of minorities, handicapped, ideologies, personal and social values, sex roles, etc., objectively represented?

_____ _____ _____   f. Are the objectives of the material clearly stated?

_____ _____ _____   g. Is the content of the material consistent with the objectives?

_____ _____ _____   h. Are the prerequisite skills for use of the materials stated?

_____ _____ _____   i. Are essential sub-skills required included in the instructional sequence?

_____ _____ _____   j. Is the reading level of the material stated?

_____ _____ _____   k. Is the vocabulary systematically introduced?

_____ _____ _____   l. Is the vocabulary consistent with the stated reading level?

_____ _____ _____   m. Is the instructional level stated?

_____ _____ _____   n. Is the interest level stated?

_____ _____ _____   o. Is the material self-pacing?

_____ _____ _____   p. Does the material provide for frequent reinforcement of major concepts?

_____ _____ _____   q. Does the material summarize and review major points?

_____ _____ _____   r. Does the material provide frequent opportunities for active student involvement and response?

_____ _____ _____   s. Does the material provide for evaluation of user performance?

_____ _____ _____   t. Does the material provide criterion-referenced assessment?

_____ _____ _____   u. Are all of the supplementary materials needed for instruction included in the materials package?

D. Matching Material to Learner

(The following questions require a synthesis of information gained from stage III, Review. The synthesis is essential before proceeding to stage IV, Decision.)

_____ _____ _____   1. Are the characteristics of the material compatible with perceived learner characteristics?

Yes No NA

——— ——— ——— 2. Are the characteristics of the material compatible with perceived teacher characteristics?

——— ——— ——— 3. Have you checked the list of criteria in the TEACHER LEVEL, stage III, Review, section B, Matching Material to Learner?

IV. DECISIONS

The outcome of stage IV will be: a final determination of material suitability for use in a specific learning situation. Individualization of the decision making, based on items of priority concern, is implicit in this process.

After this review process, it was found that the material was:

——— ——— ——— needed by the learner
——— ——— ——— usable with the learner
——— ——— ——— usable by the instructor
——— ——— ——— effective

Decisions to: **A. Use** . **B. Adapt**   **C. Field Test**

can be made by identifying from the review data responsiveness of the material to learner need, usability with the learner, usability by the instructor, and effectiveness.

Directions: For each criterion met, place a "+" in the appropriate box. For each criterion not met, place a "−" in the appropriate box. If no information is available, place an "NI" in the appropriate box.

Needed	Usable with Learner	Usable by Teacher	Effective

Match your review summary with the decision matrix below:

D. Recommendations

N	UL	UT	E	Recommended for:
+	+	+	+	U=Use/make available for use/information dissemination
+	+	+	−	A=Adapt
+	+	+	NI	U/FT=Use/Field Test
+	+	−	+	R/A/D=Reject/Adapt/Develop
+	+	−	−	R/A/D=Reject/Adapt/Develop
+	−	−	−	R/A/D=Reject/Adapt/Develop
+	−	+	−	R/A/D=Reject/Adapt/Develop
+	−	+	+	R/A/D=Reject/Adapt/Develop
+	−	+	NI	R/A/D=Reject/Adapt/Develop
−	+	+	+	R=Reject/Not Acceptable
−	−	+	+	R=Reject/Not Acceptable
−	−	−	+	R=Reject/Not Acceptable
−	−	−	−	R=Reject/Not Acceptable
−	−	−	NI	R=Reject/Not Acceptable

V. EVALUATION

The outcome of stage V will be: a final judgment, either positive, negative, or inconclusive, as to the usefulness and effectiveness of the material with the learner in a given learning situation.

Yes   No   NA

—— —— ——   1. Does this material meet the requirements of the teacher? (see teacher requirement section in review instrument)

—— —— ——   2. Does this material meet the requirements of the learner? (see learner characteristics section in review instrument)

—— —— ——   3. Does this material lead to the attainment of the specified objectives? (see instructional quality section in the review instrument)

—— —— ——   4. Does the technical quality of the material meet the specified objectives? (see instructional quality section in the review instrument)

—— —— ——   5. Do the instructional qualities of the material meet the requirements of the learner? (see instructional quality section of review instrument)

Appendix II
Producers of Materials for
Exceptional Children*

In day-to-day teaching situations, special education teachers—and others who work with handicapped children—need answers to questions about instructional materials. The National Information Center for Special Education Materials (NICSEM), University of Southern California, University Park (RAN), Los Angeles, CA 90007 provides information about commercially produced instructional materials.

Abbey Rents
600 S. Normandie
Los Angeles, CA 90005

ABC School Supply, Inc.
437 Armour Circle
Atlanta, GA 30324

ACI Media, Inc.
35 West 45th Street
New York, NY 10036

Acropolis Books Ltd.
2400 17th Street NW
Washington, DC 20009

Adapt Press, Inc.
808 West Ave. North
Sioux Falls, SD 57104

Addison-Wesley Publishing Co.
2725 Sand Hill Road
Menlo Park, CA 94025

Alfred Publishing Co., Inc.
75 Channel Drive
Port Washington, NY 11050

Allied Educational Council
P.O. Box 78
Galien, MI 49113

Allyn and Bacon, Inc.
470 Atlantic Avenue
Boston, MA 02210

Alpha II, Inc.
2425 Alamo Avenue SE
Albuquerque, NM 87106

American Art Clay Co., Inc.
4717 W. Sixteenth Street
Indianapolis, IN 46222

•American Foundation for the Blind°
215 East 58th Street
New York, NY 10022

American Guidance Service, Inc.
Publishers' Building
Circle Pines, MN 55014

American Handicrafts
3 Tandy Center
Ft. Worth, TX 76102

---

*Teacher 94 (May/June 1977): 119-22.
•Added by editors.

°Supplier of talking books.
**Supplier of large-print materials.

American Printing House for the Blind
1839 Frankfort Avenue
Louisville, KY 40206

The American University
Washington, DC 20016

Paul S. Amidon & Associates, Inc.
1966 Benson Avenue
St. Paul, MN 55116

Ann Arbor Publishers, Inc.
P.O. Box 388
Worthington, OH 43088

Barnell Loft & Dexter Westbrook
  Publications
958 Church Street
Baldwin, NY 11510

Clarence L. Barnhart, Inc.
P.O. Box 250
Bronxville, NY 10708

Beckley Grady Co.
1900 No. Narragansett Avenue
Chicago, IL 60639

Bell & Howell Co.
7100 McCormick Road
Chicago, IL 60645

Alexander Graham Bell Institute
  for the Deaf
1537 35th St. NW
Washington, DC 20007

*Bell & Howell Company**
Micro Photo Division
Old Mansfield Road
Wooster, OH 44691

Bel-Tronics Corp.
344 Interstate Rd.
Addison, IL 60101

Bemiss-Jason Corporation
1100 W. Cermak Road
Chicago, IL 60608

Benchmark Films
145 Scarborough Road
Briarcliff Manor, NY 10510

BFA Educational Media
P.O. Box 1795
Santa Monica, CA 90406

Binney & Smith, Inc.
1100 Church Lane
Easton, PA 18042

Dick Blick Co.
Box 1267
Galesburg, IL 61401

Book-Lab, Inc.
1449 37th Street
Brooklyn, NY 11218

Borg-Warner Educational Systems
600 West University Drive
Arlington Heights, IL 60004

*R. R. Bowker & Company**
1180 Avenue of the Americas
New York, NY 10036

Bowmar Publishing Corporation
4563 Colorado Boulevard
Los Angeles, CA 90039

Brodhead-Garret Co.
4560 East 71 Street
Cleveland, OH 44105

The Brown Schools
P.O. Box 4008
Austin, TX 78765

Bureau of Education for the
  Handicapped
400 Maryland Ave. SW
Washington, DC 20202

*Caedmon Records °
505 Eighth Avenue
New York, NY 10018

*Captioned Films and
   Telecommunications Branch
Division of Media Services
Bureau of Education for the
   Handicapped
Room 4819
400 Maryland Avenue SW
Donahue Building
Washington, DC 20202

Cebco/Standard Publishing
9 Kulick Road
Fairfield, NJ 07006

Centron Educational Films
1621 W. 9th Street
Lawrence, KS 66044

Centurion Industries, Inc.
2549 Middlefield Road
Redwood City, CA 94063

Changing Times Education Service
1729 H Street NW
Washington, DC 20006

Childcraft Education Corp.
20 Kilmer Rd.
Edison, NJ 08817

The Children's Company
11715 Administration Drive
St. Louis, MO 63141

Children's Press
1224 W. Van Buren Street
Chicago, IL 60607

Chileda Institute
Box 520
Stevens Point, WI 54481

Church & Dwight
Two Penn Plaza
New York, NY 10001

Classroom World Publications
14 Glenwood Avenue
Raleigh, NC 27602

Clearvue, Inc.
6666 N. Oliphant
Chicago, IL 60631

Columbus Educational Products
P.O. Box 4736
Columbus, OH 43202

The Combined Book Exhibit, Inc.
Route 9
Briarcliff Manor, NY 10510

Communication Skill Builders, Inc.
817 E. Broadway
Tucson, AZ 85719

Constructive Playthings
1040 East 85th
Kansas City, MO 64131

Consulting Psychologists Press
577 College Avenue
Palo Alto, CA 94306

The Continental Press, Inc.
520 East Bainbridge Street
Elizabethtown, PA 17022

Ken Cook Co.
9929 West Silver Spring Rd.
Milwaukee, WI 53225

Coronet Instructional Media
65 E. South Water Street
Chicago, IL 60601

Council for Exceptional Children
1920 Association Drive
Reston, VA 22091

Craig Education
921 W. Artesia Boulevard
Compton, CA 90220

Cran Barry, Inc.
2 Lincoln Avenue
Marblehead, MA 01945

Creative Playthings
Edinburg Road
Cranbury, NJ 08512

Creative Publications, Inc.
P.O. Box 10328
Palo Alto, CA 94303

Creative Teaching Press
1900 Tyler
South El Monte, CA 91733

CTB/McGraw-Hill
Del Monte Research Park
Monterey, CA 93940

Cuisenaire Company of America, Inc.
12 Church Street
New Rochelle, NY 10805

Curriculum Associates, Inc.
6 Henshaw Street
Woburn, MA 01801

A. Daigger & Co.
159 West Kinzie Avenue
Chicago, IL 60610

Davidson Films, Inc.
3701 Buchanan Street
San Francisco, CA 94123

John Day Co.
666 Fifth Avenue
New York, NY 10019

DCA Educational Products
424 Valley Road
Warrington, PA 18976

T.S. Denison
9601 Newton Avenue South
Minneapolis, MN 55431

Designs for Learning
P.O. Box 417
Hinsdale, IL 60521

Developmental Learning Materials
7440 Natchez Avenue
Niles, IL 60648

Developmental Vision Assn., Inc.
2950 Hearne Ave.
Shreveport, LA 71103

The Devereux Foundation
19 SW Waterloo Road
Devon, PA 19333

Dial, Inc.
Box 911
Highland Park, IL 60035

Didax, Inc.
3 Dearborn Road
Peabody, MA 01960

Dukane Corporation
2900 Dukane Drive
St. Charles, IL 60174

Ealing Corporation
Pleasant Street
South Natick, MA 01760

Earmark, Inc.
449 Putnam Avenue
Hamden, CT 06517

Eastman Kodak Company
343 State Street
Rochester, NY 14650

Eckstein Bros., Inc.
4807 West 118th Place
Hawthorne, CA 90250

The Economy Co.
P.O. Box 25308
Oklahoma City, OK 73125

The Edgemeade Centers
Rt. 1 Box 423
Roanoke, VA 24012

EDL/McGraw-Hill
1221 Avenue of the Americas
New York, NY 10020

Edmark Associates
13241 Northup Way
Bellevue, WA 98005

The Education Center
1042 East Lindsay
Greensboro, NC 27405

Educational Activities, Inc.
P.O. Box 392
Freeport, NY 11520

Educational Communication Services
P.O. Box 1147
Hattiesburg, MS 39401

Educational Consulting Associates
3311 S. Broadway
Englewood, CO 80110

Educational Design, Inc.
47 W. 13th Street
New York, NY 10011

Educational Dimensions
P.O. Box 126
Stamford, CT 06904

Educational Patterns, Inc.
62–83 Woodhaven Boulevard
Rego Park, NY 11374

Educational Performance Assoc.
600 Broad Ave.
Ridgefield, NJ 07657

Educational Progress
4900 S. Lewis
Tulsa, OK 74145

Educational Research, Inc.
2916 Independence Ave.
Shreveport, LA 71109

Educational Service, Inc.
P.O. Box 219
Stevensville, MI 49127

Educational Teaching Aids
159 W. Kinzie Street
Chicago, IL 60610

Educators Publishing Service, Inc.
75 Moulton Street
Cambridge, MA 02138

EMC Corporation
180 East Sixth Street
St. Paul, MN 55101

Encyclopaedia Britannica, Inc.
425 North Michigan Avenue
Chicago, IL 60611

Enrich, Inc.
760 Kifer Road
Sunnyvale, CA 94086

Enrichment Reading Corp. of
   America
Iron Ridge, WI 53035

Exceptional Play
Box 1015
Lawrence, KS 66044

Exceptional Press
Box 188
Glen Ridge, NJ 07028

Eyegate Media
146-01 Archer Avenue
Jamaica, NY 11435

Fearon Pitman Publishing Co.
6 Davis Drive
Belmont, CA 94002

*Films for the Deaf
Distribution Center
5034 Wisconsin Avenue NW
Washington, DC 20016

Flaghouse Inc.
18 West 18th Street
New York, NY 10011

Follett Publishing Co.
1010 W. Washington Boulevard
Chicago, IL 60607

Gallaudet College
Kendall Green
Washington, DC 20002

Gamco Industries, Inc.
P.O. Box 1911
Big Spring, TX 79720

Game Time, Inc.
900 Anderson Road
Litchfield, MI 49252

Ginn and Company
191 Spring Street
Lexington, MA 02173

Grolier Educational Corp.
845 Third Ave.
New York, NY 10022

Grosset & Dunlap, Inc.
51 Madison Avenue
New York, NY 10010

Grune & Stratton, Inc.
111 Fifth Avenue
New York, NY 10003

Guidance Associates
757 Third Avenue
New York, NY 10017

Hammatt & Sons
P.O. Box 2004
Anaheim, CA 92804

Haptic Perceptual Development
1111 Delaware
Marysville, MI 48040

Harcourt Brace Jovanovich, Inc.
757 Third Avenue
New York, NY 10017

*Harper & Row Publishers**
Department 61
10 East 53rd Street
New York, NY 10022

Harvest Educational Labs
Pelham Street
Newport, RI 02840

HC Electronics, Inc.
250 Camino Alto
Mill Valley, CA 94941

Herrick Success Centers
123 Broadway
DePere, WI 54115

Hester Evaluation System
120 S. Ashland
Chicago, IL 60607

H & H Enterprises, Inc.
P.O. Box 3342
Lawrence, KS 66044

Holt, Rinehart and Winston
College Division
383 Madison Avenue
New York, NY 10017

Hopewell Books, Inc.
730 Jefferson Drive
Pittsburgh, PA 15229

Horton Handicraft Co., Inc.
P.O. Box 330
Farmington, CT 06032

Houghton Mifflin Co.
1 Beacon Street
Boston, MA 02140

Howe Press/Perkins School for
the Blind
175 N. Beacon Street
Watertown, MA 02172

Hubbard Scientific Co.
1946 Raymond Drive
Northbrook, IL 60062

Human Development Training
Institute
7574 University Avenue
LaMesa, CA 92041

Humanics
881 Peachtree Street
Atlanta, GA 30309

ICT
10 Stepar Place
Huntington Station, NY 11746

IDEA
3901 W. 86th Street
Indianapolis, IN 46268

Ideal School Supply Co.
11000 South Lavergne Avenue
Oak Lawn, IL 60453

Imperial International Learning Corp.
Box 548
Kankakee, IL 60901

Incentive Publications, Inc.
2400 Crestmoor Road
Nashville, TN 27315

Independence Press
Drawer HH
Independence, MO 64055

Instant Buttons Machine Co.
18 Selden Street
Woodbridge, CT 06525

Instructional Fair, Inc.
3180 3 Mile Road
Grand Rapids, MI 49504

Instructional Industries
Executive Park
Ballston Lake, NY 12019

Instructo/McGraw-Hill
Cedar Hollow & Matthew Hill Roads
Paoli, PA 19301

Interpretive Education Co.
400 Bryant Street
Kalamazoo, MI 49001

January Productions, Inc.
13-00 Plaza Road
Fair Lawn, NJ 07410

Jayfro Corp.
P.O. Box 400
Waterford, CT 06385

The Judy Co.
250 James Street
Morristown, NJ 07960

*Keith Jennison Books/Franklin
Watts, Inc.**
845 Third Avenue
New York, NY 10022

Kiddie Kreations, Inc.
906 N. Woodward
Royal Oak, MI 48067

Kimbo Educational
P.O. Box 477
Long Branch, NJ 07740

*The Kurzweil Reading Machine
Kurzweil Computer Products
33 Cambridge Parkway
Cambridge, MA 02142

Lafayette Instrument
P.O. Box 57
Lafayette, IN 47902

Learn, Inc.
113 Gaither Drive
Mt. Laurel, NJ 08057

Learning Concepts
2501 N. Lamar
Austin, TX 78705

Learning Designs, Inc.
P.O. Box 310
Eureka Springs, AR 72632

Learning Ladder, Inc.
P.O. Box 247
Oak Park, IL 60303

Learning Products
11632 Fairgrove Industrial Road
St. Louis, MO 63042

Leary School, Inc.
7515 Lee Highway
Falls Church, VA 22042

LectroLearn, Inc.
Box 127
Berwyn, PA 19312

Lectro-Stik
3721 N. Broadway
Chicago, IL 60613

Leicestershire Learning Systems
Chestnut Street
Lewiston, ME 04240

Libin & Associates
3107 Wilshire Blvd.
Los Angeles, CA 90010

Library of Special Education
866 Third Avenue
New York, NY 10002

J.B. Lippincott Company
East Washington Square
Philadelphia, PA 19105

Little Kenny
1315 West Belmont Avenue
Chicago, IL 60657

Long Island Film Studios
P.O. Box 49403
Atlanta, GA 30359

Love Publishing Co.
6638 East Villanova Place
Denver, CO 80222

Mafex Associates, Inc.
90 Cherry St.
Johnstown, PA 15902

Magnus Craft Materials, Inc.
304 8 Cliff Lane
Cliffside Park, NJ 07010

Makit Products/Wescon Corp.
100 Powers Street
Milford, NH 03055

Manson Western Corp.
12031 Wilshire Boulevard
Los Angeles, CA 90025

Mast Development
2212 East 12th Street
Davenport, IA 52803

Charles Mayer Studio, Inc.
168 E. Market Street
Akron, OH 44308

McGraw-Hill Book Company
1221 Avenue of the Americas
New York, NY 10020

McGraw-Hill Films
1221 Avenue of the Americas
New York, NY 10020

David McKay Company, Inc.
750 3rd Avenue
New York, NY 10017

Media Materials, Inc.
2936 Remington Avenue
Baltimore, MD 21211

Melody House
819 NW 92nd Street
Oklahoma City, OK 73114

Melton Book Co., Inc.
111 Leslie Street
Dallas, TX 75207

Charles E. Merrill Publishing Co.
1300 Alum Creek Drive
Columbus, OH 43216

Michigan Products, Inc.
1200 Keystone Avenue
Lansing, MI 48909

Midwest Publications
P.O. Box 129
Trox, MI 48099

Milliken Publishing Co.
1100 Research Boulevard
St. Louis, MO 63132

Milton Bradley Company
Springfield, MA 01101

Mino, Inc.
1 King's Highway North
Westport, CT 06880

Miracle Recreation Equipment Co.
P.O. Box 275
Grinnell, IA 50112

Modern Curriculum Press Inc.
13900 Prospect Road
Cleveland, OH 44136

Modern Education Corp.
P.O. Box 721
Tulsa, OK 74102

Modern Talking Picture Service
2323 New Hyde Park Road
New Hyde Park, NY 11040

The C.V. Mosby Co.
11830 Westline Industrial Drive
St. Louis, MO 63141

Mosier Materials
P.O. Box 3036
San Bernardino, CA 92413

Motor Skills Research
712 Inverness Drive
Horsham, PA 19044

M&W Electronics, Inc.
330 South Zang
Dallas, TX 75208

NASCO
901 Janesville Avenue
Fort Atkinson, WI 53538

Nasco Science Materials
901 Janesville Avenue
Fort Atkinson, WI 53538

*National Association for the Visually
    Handicapped**
3201 Balboa Street
San Francisco, CA 94121

*National Braille Press, Inc.
88 Street/Stephen Street
Boston, MA 02115

*National Center for Audio Tapes °
University of Colorado
Stadium Building
Boulder, CO 80302

National Educational Laboratory
    Publishers, Inc.
813 Airport Blvd.
Austin, TX 78702

*National Library Service for the
    Blind & Physically Handicapped °
Library of Congress
1291 Taylor Street, NW
Washington, DC 20542

*National Listening Library
Headquarters
49 Great Cumberlane Place
London W.1

National Tutoring Institute, Inc.
P.O. Box 2112
Kansas City, MO 64142

NCS/Educational Systems Division
4401 W. 76th Street
Minneapolis, MN 55435

New Dimensions in Education, Inc.
83 Keeler Ave.
Norwalk, CT 06854

New Readers Press
P.O. Box 131
Syracuse, NY 13210

New York Institute for Child
Development
36 East 36th Street
New York, NY 10016

North American Recreation
P.O. Box 758
Bridgeport, CT 06601

Nystrom/Division of Carnation Co.
3333 Elston Avenue
Chicago, IL 60618

Open Court Publishing Co.
P.O. Box 599
LaSalle, IL 61301

Orion
P.O. Box 131
Terryville, CT 06786

Ortho-Kinetics, Inc./Child Care
Division
420 Frederick Street
Waukesha, WI 53186

The Orton Society, Inc.
8415 Bellona Lane
Towson, MD 21204

Pathescope Educational Media, Inc.
71 Weyman Avenue
New Rochelle, NY 10801

Pendulum Press, Inc.
Saw Mill Road
West Haven, CT 06516

Performing Arts for Exceptional
Citizens, Inc.
P.O. Box 14302
Gainesvile, FL 32604

Phonovisual Products, Inc.
12216 Parklawn Drive
Rockville, MD 20852

Photo Motion Corp.
Morrison Building
King of Prussia, PA 19406

Playco-Datasquare
Bartley Road
Chester, NJ 07939

Playworld Systems
315 Cherry Street
New Berlin, PA 17855

Prentice-Hall Developmental
Centers
P.O. Box 37
Orange, NJ 07050

Prentice-Hall Learning Systems, Inc.
P.O. Box 47X
Englewood Cliffs, NJ 07632

Prentice-Hall Media, Inc.
150 White Plains Road
Tarrytown, NY 10591

Prentke Romich Co.
Box 191
Shreve, OH 44676

Prep, Inc.
1575 Parkway Avenue
Trenton, NJ 08628

Pre-School Learning Centers
P.O. Box 6244
Overland Park, KS 66290

Pre-School Publications
P.O. Box 272
Commerce, TX 75428

J.A. Preston Corp.
71 Fifth Avenue
New York, NY 10003

P.S. Associates
4501 Warrington Drive
Flint, MI 48504

The Psychological Corp.
757 Third Avenue
New York, NY 10017

Psychotechnics, Inc.
1900 Pickwick Avenue
Glenview, IL 60025

RCA Records/Educational Department
1133 Avenue of the Americas
New York, NY 10036

Readers Digest Educational Service
Pleasantville, NY 10570

Reading Joy, Inc.
P.O. Box 404
Naperville, IL 60540

*Recordings for the Blind °
215 East 58th Street
New York, NY 10022

Research Press
2612 N. Mattis
Champaign, IL 61820

REX Sales Co., Inc.
2727 N W 10th Street
Oklahoma City, OK 73107

Rhythm Band, Inc.
P.O. Box 126
Fort Worth, TX 76101

Frank E. Richards Publishing Co.,Inc.
330 First Street
Liverpool, NY 13088

Sasso Special Education
   Materials, Inc.
2115 Main Street
Fort Myers, FL 33902

Frank Schaffer Publications
23770 Hawthorne Boulevard
Torrance, CA 90505

Scholastic Magazines, Inc.
50 West 44th Street
New York, NY 10036

Scholastic Testing Service, Inc.
480 Meyer Road
Bensenville, IL 60106

Schools, Inc.
2615 Mayfair Drive
Brookfield, WI 53005

Science Research Associates, Inc.
259 East Erie Street
Chicago, IL 60611

Shield Mfg., Inc.
68 St. Paul Street
Buffalo, NY 14209

Sico Inc.
7525 Cahill Road
Minneapolis, MN 55435

Singer Career Systems
80 Commerce Drive
Rochester, NY 14623

Skill Development Equipment Co.
1340 N. Jefferson
Anaheim, CA 92807

Society for Visual Education, Inc.
1345 Diversey Parkway
Chicago, IL 60614

Special Child Publications
4535 Union Bay Place NE
Seattle, WA 98105

Special Education/Early
  Childhood Department
George Washington University
2201 G Street
Washington, DC 20052

Special Education Materials, Inc.
484 South Broadway
Yonkers, NY 10785

Spellbinder, Inc.
33 Bradford Street
Concord, MA 01742

The Spice Company/Educational
  Service, Inc.
P.O. Box 219
Stevensville, MI 49127

Spoken Arts
310 North Avenue
New Rochelle, NY 10801

S&S Arts & Crafts
Colchester, CT 06415

Stanley Tools
600 Myrtle Street
New Britain, CT 06050

Stanwix House, Inc.
3020 Chartiers Avenue
Pittsburgh, PA 15204

Step, Inc.
South Complex-Paine Field
Everett, WA 98204

Syracuse University Press
1011 East Water Street
Syracuse, NY 13210

Tandy Leather Co.
3 Tandy Center
Ft. Worth, TX 76102

Teachers College Press
1234 Amsterdam Avenue
New York, NY 10027

Teaching Audial & Visuals, Inc.
250 West 57th Street
New York, NY 10019

Teaching Resources Corp.
100 Boylston Street
Boston, MA 02166

Teaching Resources Films
2 Kisco Plaza
Mt. Kisco, NY 10549

Telesensory Systems, Inc.
1889 Page Mill Road
Palo Alto, CA 94304

TheraPlay/Division of PCA
  Industries, Inc.
29-24 40th Avenue
Long Island City, NY 11101

3M Company
Commercial Tape Division
2501 Hudson Road
St. Paul, MN 55119

3M Company
Paper Products Division
2501 Hudson Road
St. Paul, MN 55119

TQ Publishers
3912 Ramsey
Corpus Christi, TX 78415

Trend Enterprises, Inc.
P.O. Box 3073
St. Paul, MN 55165

Triarco Arts & Crafts
110 W. Carpenter
Wheeling, IL 60090

Tutoring Works
2733 Sixth Avenue
Altoona, PA 16602

United Canvas & Sling Inc.
248 River Street
Hackensack, NJ 07601

United Learning
6633 West Howard Street
Niles, IL 60648

U.S. History Society
8154 Ridgeway
Skokie, IL 60076

University of Illinois Press
Urbana, IL 61801

The Viking Press
625 Madison Avenue
New York, NY 10022

Visualized Instructural Products
1200 Hargen Road
Oakbrook, IL 60521

Vocational Research Institute
1913 Walnut Street
Philadelphia, PA 19103

Vort Corporation
385 Sherman Avenue
Palo Alto, CA 94306

Walker Educational Book Corp.
720 Fifth Avenue
New York, NY 10019

Wayne Engineering
4120 Greenwood
Skokie, IL 60076

Webster/McGraw-Hill
1221 Avenue of the Americas
New York, NY 10020

Webster's International Tutoring
    Systems, Inc.
2416 Hillsboro Road
Nashville, TN 37212

West Georgia College
Carrollton, CA 30117

Western Manufacturing
Box 130
Marshalltown, IA 50158

Albert Whitman & Company
560 W. Lake Street
Chicago, IL 60606

John Wiley & Sons, Inc.
605 Third Avenue
New York, NY 10016

B.L. Winch & Associates
45 Hitching Post Drive
Rolling Hills Estates, CA 90274

The Woods Schools
Langhorne, PA 19047

World Research Co.
307 S. Beckham
Tyler, TX 75701

World Wide Games, Inc.
P.O. Box 450
Delaware, OH 43015

Xerox Education Publications
245 Long Hill Road
Middletown, CT 06457

Zweig/Foundation Valley
20800 Beach Boulevard
Huntington Beach, CA 92648

Zygo Industries, Inc.
Box 1008
Portland, OR 97207

Appendix III
Organizations/Publications
Related to the Handicapped

The following compilation includes addresses of organizations that serve the handicapped. Most have a publication which speaks to their ongoing research, services, and/or programing. Some of the publications also serve the non-handicapped population but include, on an irregular basis, articles about the handicapped. The reader might wish to write the specific organizations requesting information regarding their services and a sample of their publication to develop a vertical file of current materials for and about the handicapped.

ORGANIZATION	PUBLICATION
Accent on Information, Inc. P.O. Box 700 Bloomington, IL 61701	*Accent on Living*
Alexander Graham Bell Association for the Deaf Volta Bureau 3417 Volta Place, NW Washington, DC 20007	*The Volta Review* *Newsounds Newsletter*
American Alliance for Health, Physical Education, Recreation and Dance Unit on Programs for the Handicapped 1201 16th Street, NW Washington, DC 20036	*Journal of Health, Physical* *Education and Recreation* *Research Quarterly* *Practical Pointers*
American Association for the Education of the Severely/ Profoundly Handicapped 1600 W. Armory Way Seattle, WA 98195	*American Association for the* *Education of the Severely/* *Profoundly Handicapped Review*

ORGANIZATION	PUBLICATION
American Association of Workers for the Blind 1511 K Street, NW Washington, DC 20005	*Blindness*
American Association on Mental Deficiency 5101 Wisconsin Avenue, NW Washington, DC 20016	*American Journal of Mental Deficiency* *Mental Retardation*
American Cancer Society 219 E. 42nd Street New York, NY 10017	
American Coalition for Citizens with Disabilities 1346 Connecticut Avenue, NW Suite 1124 Washington, DC 20036	
American Council of the Blind 1211 Connecticut Avenue, NW Suite 506 Washington, DC 20036	*Braille Forum*
American Diabetes Association 600 Fifth Avenue New York, NY 10020	*Diabetes Forecast*
American Foundation for the Blind 15 West 16th Street New York, NY 10011	*Journal of Visual Impairment and Blindness* *New Outlook for the Blind*
American Library Association 50 East Huron Street Chicago, IL 60611	*Interface* *American Libraries* *School Media Quarterly* *Top of the News* *College and Research Libraries*

ORGANIZATION	PUBLICATION
American Occupational Therapy Association 6000 Executive Boulevard Rockville, MD 20852	*American Journal of Occupational Therapy*
American Physical Therapy Association 1156 15th Street, NW Washington, DC 20005	*Physical Therapy*
American Printing House for the Blind, Inc. 1839 Frankfort Avenue Louisville, KY 40206	
American Speech and Hearing Association 9030 Old Georgetown Road Washington, DC 20014	*ASHA* *Journal of Speech and Hearing Disorders* *Journal of Speech and Hearing Research*
Arthritis Foundation 3400 Peachtree Road, NE Atlanta, GA 30326	
Association for Childhood Education International 3615 Wisconsin Avenue, NW Washington, DC 20016	*Childhood Education*
Association for Children with Learning Disabilities 5225 Grace Street Pittsburgh, PA 15236	*Newsbriefs*
Association for Education of the Visually Handicapped 919 Walnut Street, 4th Floor Philadelphia, PA 19107	*Education of the Visually Handicapped*

ORGANIZATION	PUBLICATION
Boy Scouts of America Scouting for the Handicapped North Brunswick, NJ 08902	*Boy's Life*
Bureau of Education for the Handicapped Office of Education Department of Health, Education, and Welfare Washington, DC 20202	
Canadian National Institute for the Blind 1929 Bayview Avenue Toronto, Ontario M4G 3E8 Canada	*National News of the Blind*
Closer Look National Information Center for the Handicapped Box 1492 Washington, DC 20013	*Report from Closer Look*
Co-ordinating Council for Handicapped Children 407 S. Dearborn, Room 1075 Chicago, IL 60605	
Council for Exceptional Children 1920 Association Drive Reston, VA 22091	*Exceptional Children* *Teaching Exceptional Children* *Education and Training of the* *Mentally Retarded*
Dogs for the Deaf San Francisco SPCA 2500 16th Street San Francisco, CA 94116	
Epilepsy Foundation of America 1828 L. Street, NW Washington, DC 20036	

ORGANIZATION	PUBLICATION

Fight for Sight, Inc.
National Council to Combat Blindness, Inc.
41 West 57th Street
New York, NY 10019

Gallaudet College   *Gallaudet Today*
Seventh and Florida Avenue, NE
Washington, DC 20002

Girl Scouts of the U.S.A.
Scouting for the Handicapped
    Girls Program
830 Third Avenue
New York, NY 10022

Goodwill Industries
9200 Wisconsin Avenue
Washington, DC 20014

Hadley School for the Blind   *Student Information Bulletin*
700 Elm Street
Winnetka, IL 60093

Handy-Cap Horizons   *Handy-Cap Horizons*
3250 East Loretta Drive
Indianapolis, IN 46227

Indoor Sports Club   *National Hookup*
1145 Highland Street
Napoleon, OH 43545

Helen Keller International, Inc.   *HKI Report*
(formerly American Foundation for
    Overseas Blind, Inc.)
22 West 17th Street
New York, NY 10011

Helen Keller National Center for   *Nat-Cent News*
    Deaf-Blind Youths and Adults
111 Middle Neck Road
Sands Point, NY 11050

ORGANIZATION   PUBLICATION

Human Growth Foundation
28 Sylvia Lane
Plainview, NY 11803

Human Resources Center
Albertson, NY 11507

International Society for Rehabilitation
   of the Disabled
219 E. 44th Street
New York, NY 10017

Lions International   *Lion*
300 22nd Street
Oak Brook, IL 60521

Media Development Project for the
   Hearing Impaired
University of Nebraska—Lincoln
318 Barkley Memorial Center
Lincoln, NE 68583

Mental Health Association,
   National Headquarters
1800 North Kent Street
Arlington, VA 22209

Muscular Dystrophy Association   *Muscular Dystrophy Association*
810 Seventh Avenue   *News*
New York, NY 10019

Myasthenia Gravis Foundation   *MG Conquest*
230 Park Avenue
New York, NY 10017

National Accreditation Council for   *Standard Bearer*
   Agencies Serving the Blind and
   Visually Handicapped
79 Madison Avenue
New York, NY 10016

ORGANIZATION	PUBLICATION
National Association for Retarded Citizens 2709 Avenue E, East P.O. Box 6109 Arlington, TX 76011	*Mental Retardation News*
National Association for Visually Handicapped 305 East 24th Street New York, NY 10010	
National Association of the Deaf 814 Thayer Avenue Silver Spring, MD 20910	*The Deaf American*
National Audiovisual Center Special Education National Archives and Record Service General Services Administration Washington, DC 20409	
National Association of the Physically Handicapped 6473 Grandville Avenue Detroit, MI 49229	*NAPH National Newsletter*
National Braille Association 654A Godwin Avenue Midland Park, NJ 07432	*NBA Bulletin*
National Center for a Barrier Free Environment 8401 Connecticut Avenue Washington, DC 20015	*Report*
National Easter Seal Society for Crippled Children and Adults 2023 West Ogden Avenue Chicago, IL 60612	*Rehabilitation Literature*

ORGANIZATION   PUBLICATION

National Education Association   *Today's Education*
1201 16th Street, NW
Washington, DC 20036

National Eye Institute
National Institutes of Health
Bethesda, MD 20014

National Federation of the Blind   *Braille Monitor*
218 Randolph Hotel
Des Moines, IA 50309

National Foundation—March of Dimes   *NF News*
P.O. Box 2000   *Maternal/Newborn Advocate*
White Plains, NY 10601

National Information Center for   *Frankly Speaking;*
    Special Education Materials/NICSEM   *The Program Tree*
University of Southern California
University Park—RAN
Los Angeles, CA 90007

National Institute of Neurological
    and Communicative Disorders
    and Stroke
National Institutes of Health
Bethesda, MD 20014

National Handicapped Sports and
    Recreation Association
4105 East Florida Avenue
Denver, CO 80222

National Library Service for the Blind *Talking Book Topics*
    and Physically Handicapped   *Braille Book Review*
Library of Congress   *DBPH News*
1291 Taylor Street, NW   *Update*
Washington, DC 20542

ORGANIZATION	PUBLICATION

The National Media Materials Center
  for Severely Handicapped Persons
P.O. Box 318
George Peabody College
Nashville, TN 37203

National Multiple Sclerosis Society   *MS Messenger*
205 East 42nd Street   *MS Briefs*
New York, NY 10017   *MS Patient Service News*

National Paraplegia Foundation   *Paraplegia Life*
333 North Michigan Avenue
Chicago, IL 60601

National Rehabilitation Association   *Journal of Rehabilitation*
1522 K Street, NW
Washington, DC 20005

National Retinitis Pigmentosa
  Foundation
Rolling Park Building
8331 Mindale Circle
Baltimore, MD 21207

National Society for Autistic   *NSAC Newsletter*
  Children
169 Tampa Avenue
Albany, NY 12208

National Society for the Prevention   *The Sight Saving Review*
  of Blindness, Inc.
79 Madison Avenue
New York, NY 10016

National Therapeutic Recreation   *Therapeutic Recreation Journal*
  Society
1601 North Kent Street
Arlington, VA 22209

ORGANIZATION	PUBLICATION
National Wheelchair Athletic Association 40-24 62nd Street Woodside, NY 11377	*National Wheelchair Athletic Association Newsletter*
New Eyes for the Needy 549 Millburn Avenue Short Hills, NY 07078	
Office for Handicapped Individuals Department of Health, Education, and Welfare South Portal Building, Room 33 200 Independence Avenue, SW Washington, DC 20201	
Orton Society 8415 Bellona Lane Suite 115 Towson, MD 21204	*Bulletin of the Orton Society*
Paralyzed Veterans of America 4330 East West Highway Suite 300 Washington, DC 20014	*Paraplegia News*
Parkinson's Disease Foundation William Black Medical Research Building 620 West 168th Street New York, NY 10032	
Pi Lambda Theta National Honor and Professional Association in Education 4101 East Third Street Box A 850 Bloomington, IN 47401	*Educational Horizons*

ORGANIZATION	PUBLICATION
President's Committee on Employment of the Handicapped 7131 Dept. of Labor Building Washington, DC 20210	*Disabled USA*
President's Committee on Mental Retardation Washington, DC 20201	
Recording for the Blind 215 East 58th Street New York, NY 10022	*Recording for the Blind Newsletter*
Rehabilitation International U.S.A. (RIUSA) 20 West 40th Street New York, NY 10018	*Rehabilitation/World*
The Resource Center Metropolitan Cooperative Library System 285 East Walnut Pasadena, CA 91101	
Royal National Institute for the Blind 224 Great Portland Street London, WIN 6AA England	*The New Beacon*
Social and Rehabilitation Service Rehabilitation Services Administration Department of Health, Education, and Welfare Washington, DC 20201	*Social and Rehabilitation Record*
Social Security Administration 6401 Security Boulevard Baltimore, MD 21235	

ORGANIZATION   PUBLICATION

Telephone Pioneers of America   *Pioneer Progress*
195 Broadway
New York, NY 10007

Travel Information Center
Moss Rehabilitation Hospital
12th and Tabor Road
Philadelphia, PA 19141

United Cerebral Palsy Associations   *The Crusader*
66 East 34th Street
New York, NY 10016

Western Union
Two mail-delivery services serving
    the handicapped:
    1. Braillegrams: messages in
       braille
    2. Large-print: messages set in
       14 point type
[less than regular telegrams]

Publications Reporting Information Regarding Programing for Handicapped Students

Academic Therapy
1539 Fourth Street
San Rafael, CA 94901

American Annals of the Deaf
Conference of American Instructors
    of the Deaf
5034 Wisconsin Avenue, NW
Washington, DC 20016

American Education
US Department of Health, Education
    and Welfare
US Government Printing Office
Washington, DC 20402

Educational Technology
140 Sylvan Avenue
Englewood Cliffs, NJ 07632

The Exceptional Parent
Psy-Ed Corporation
264 Beacon Street
Boston, MA 02116

Focus on Exceptional Children
Love Publishing Company
6635 East Villanova Place
Denver, CO 80222

Instructional Innovator
Association for Educational Commu-
    nications and Technology
1126 16th Street, NW
Washington, DC 20036

The Instructor
Instructor Publications, Inc.
Instructor Park
Dansville, NY 14437

Journal of Learning Disabilities
101 East Ontario Street
Chicago, IL 60611

Journal of Special Education
111 Fifth Avenue
New York, NY 10003

Journal for Special Educators
P.O. Box 171
Cater Conway, NH 03813

Language Arts
National Council of Teachers
    of English
111 Kenyon Road
Urbana, IL 61801

Library Journal
R. R. Bowker Company
1180 Avenue of the Americas
New York, NY 10036

The Pointer
4000 Albemarle Street, NW
Washington, DC 20016

School Library Journal
R. R. Bowker Company
1180 Avenue of the Americas
New York, NY 10036

Teacher
Macmillan Professional Magazines,
    Inc.
22 West Putnam Avenue
Greenwich, CT 06830

Index

Compiled by Sanford Berman